NORTH SEA

DENMARK

The Sound

Copenhagen

Great Belt

HOLLAND

cheren

Antwerp

GERMAN STATES

# The Royal Dockyards
## during the Revolutionary and Napoleonic Wars

# The Royal Dockyards
## during the Revolutionary and Napoleonic Wars

Roger Morriss

Leicester University Press 1983

First published in 1983 by Leicester University Press

Copyright © Leicester University Press 1983

Designed by Arthur Lockwood
Phototypeset in Linotron 202 Sabon
Printed and bound in Great Britain by The Pitman Press, Bath

*British Library Cataloguing in Publication Data*

Morriss, Roger
    The Royal dockyards during the Revolutionary and Napoleonic wars.
    1. Navy-yards and naval stations –
    Great Britain – History
    I. Title
    623.8'3'0941   VA460.A1
    ISBN 0-7185-1215-4

# Contents

# Preface

Naval histories used to begin with a fleet already at sea. This book is an attempt to answer some of the questions about how fleets in the age of sail were actually put to sea. How were ships fitted? Who fitted them? How quickly were they prepared for sea? How were they maintained and what were the problems involved in their maintenance? Such questions about practice and procedure lead to others about resources and their mobilization, to questions about policies and, inevitably, the politics of administration. What follows, therefore, is not a study of naval affairs in general, but a study of the civil ingredients of naval power. In framework it is primarily administrative. Yet, concentrating as it does on the largest industrial organization in Britain at the end of the eighteenth century, it is equally concerned with the technological, economic and social aspects of the dockyards. The yards had problems with mechanization, contracting and labour supply similar to those of the private industrialist. But these were faced in a very different context: within the relatively protected world of a governmental establishment, geographically separated from the rising industrial Britain and with problems of communication inherent in control from London.

The book ranges across the whole length of the Revolutionary and Napoleonic Wars, each chapter focussing on a different aspect of the organization that took the strain of the prolonged conflict, broken only by the year's 'truce' of Amiens, which taxed national energies and resources to the full. Tracing developments at yard level has involved the neglect of contiguous and no less important areas of naval administration – the work, notably, of arming, manning, victualling and financing the navy – an understanding of which would of course give yard operations larger meaning. Nevertheless the object has been to examine the process of change in microcosm, to look at a single unit of the governmental machine and to detect how, under the pressures of waging war on an unprecedented scale, traditional practices and methods of management were reassessed and adapted to new ideas so that a modified and in some respects new organization emerged.

At this level there is a tendency to lose sight of the importance of such detailed changes to the efficiency of government and to the successful prosecution of war. Individually indeed the changes had but little consequence; but taken together they had major effects. In the Navy Office and the dockyards the changes made for greater reliability and economy of operation: control was improved, responsibilities emphasized and procedures improved. By the end of the wars, an already long-established and well-tried organization had become a smoothly humming instrument of war. If Britain amassed during the Napoleonic war the greatest fleet the world had ever seen, it also created probably the most efficient organization for keeping that fleet at sea.

Administrative improvements were of course closely connected with contemporary attitudes. The desire for governmental reforms had initially arisen from the disappointments of the American War of Independence but, once set in train, changes in the cause of efficiency and economy had a self-perpetuating action. In the dockyards, changes in the forms of payment and demands for greater probity and responsibility affected every employee, from the Navy Board commissioners down to the lowest artificer. The commissioners, officers and clerks were in turn imbued with a heightened sense of professionalism and desire for efficiency. The pressure for reform became institutionalized. The period of the Revolutionary and Napoleonic Wars in consequence saw not only the consolidation of the organization necessary to a fleet that could dominate the world, but the hardening of a common will to make that organization work.

In the dockyards we therefore see a silent revolution: a series of changes that comprehensively affected the whole of yard affairs. No other period of comparable duration in the eighteenth and nineteenth centuries saw change of such an extent. This is, however, hardly surprising. The wars demanded an efficient dockyard service. Some developments post-dated the great series of naval victories during the Revolutionary War, but many were contemporary with Trafalgar and all contributed to Britain's ability to dominate the seas thereafter. They thus had a direct bearing on the final victory of 1815 and established in the dockyards some of the conditions necessary for Britain's subsequent naval hegemony.

These ideas have emerged from a doctoral thesis on the royal dockyards during the period 1801 to 1805. The thesis was presented to the University of London in 1978, since when it has been completely rewritten, its scope being enlarged through further research. Many people have contributed to the appearance of this book and I would like to thank them all. I am particularly grateful to Professor I. R. Christie, without whose interest and careful guidance the initial thesis may never have been written. Dr A. H. Newman was very helpful in suggesting the alterations necessary to transform the thesis into a book and in reading the draft of my revision when it was completed. My debt to Professor J. S. Bromley is great: his thorough knowledge of writings on naval administration and his meticulous attention to detail permitted me to make innumerable improvements in both content and style. Dr R. J. B. Knight has been an unfailing source of advice and encouragement since I first took interest in the dockyards, and I am grateful to him, to Mr J. Coad, Miss P. Crimmin, Dr A. Hood, Mr P. Ince, Mr H. C. McMurray and Mr A. W. H. Pearsall for their kindness in reading chapters. My thanks go also to Mr A. Viner for checking the glossary and to Dr J. Breihan, Mr J. M. Collinge, Mr B. Lavery and Mr R. Stewart for providing me at various times with useful references. Mrs E. M. Simpson converted my longhand into typescript with her customary efficiency, while the staff of Leicester University Press was most helpful throughout the business of turning typescript into print. I am grateful to the staffs of the British Library, Devon Record Office, Institute of Historical Research, Public Record Office, Scottish Record Office and especially to the staff of the National Maritime Museum. As one of their number for the last three years, many of them have given me assistance or advice which has influenced the content of the book. I acknowledge with thanks the permission of the Trustees of the National Maritime Museum and of the National Portrait Gallery to reproduce paintings within their care, and am indebted for a grant, which facilitated retyping, to the Twenty-Seven Foundation of the University of London. A grant from the Isobel Thornley Bequest helped to meet the costs of publication. Above all, however, I thank my wife. By shouldering the main burden of running our home and raising two young children, she left my mind free to pursue this study. Her encouragement and support made the book possible.

R.M.
April 1982

# Illustrations

# Tables

# Introduction

By the end of the eighteenth century, some of the six royal dockyards had already been in existence for more than 300 years. Their sites were consequently the choice of a far earlier age, while their size and facilities were the marks of a maturity gained from a long succession of wars. As might be expected, early dockyard developments had largely coincided with periods of governmental growth. Three of the yards in existence in 1793 initially developed in the early sixteenth century, while two were laid out in the second half of the seventeenth century. To the first of these periods belongs the establishment of the core of that bureaucracy which still controlled the yards; the second saw that bureaucracy expand along lines still determining its shape in 1793. These phases of development were the product of growth in the size of the standing navy. Throughout the medieval period the size of the royal fleet had fluctuated according to the immediate needs of the State, most ships simply being bought and sold as required. From the mid-fifteenth century, however, the navy commenced a slow growth that was sustained under Henry VII.[1] And since a permanent fleet of course needed maintenance, the late fifteenth century also saw the small beginnings of shore establishments that were to be placed on a permanent footing by Henry VIII.

Deptford yard probably grew around a storehouse hired at Greenwich, possibly at Deptford Strand, then called West Greenwich, in 1486. Another storehouse was built there in 1513, and a basin, wharf and sheds in 1517.[2] The yard was to continue to grow and to become by the end of Henry VIII's reign the navy's principal yard. During the seventeenth century its relative importance was to decline but its situation always retained for it a number of advantages. It was close to London, the centre of naval administration and the principal market for naval stores, and at the heart of the most important ship building and repairing region in the country. As a result, even after the Thames silted too much for the draught of larger ships, Deptford retained some prestige and continued as a centre for the distribution of naval stores and victuals.[3]

Portsmouth was also a base before the end of the fifteenth century and has been regarded as the location of the first dock constructed for the navy. Yet it had long been an assembly point for expeditions and a storage and distribution point for naval equipments. Already of some size by the accession of Henry VIII, the establishment was enlarged during the first half of the sixteenth century, but after 1560 it was almost totally neglected until the time of the

1

Commonwealth when the series of wars against the Dutch made a western base necessary. However, it was to the wars against the French that Portsmouth owed its uninterrupted growth.[4] Following an extensive programme of construction from 1698 the yard was pre-eminent by 1739 and continued as such until the end of the century.[5]

Woolwich dockyard grew around the *Henry Grace à Dieu*, laid down in December 1512. Enlarged in 1518 and again in 1546, it was regularly used until the first half of the seventeenth century when, like Portsmouth, it was neglected and virtually abandoned. The first Dutch war gave rise to renewed use and new facilities but, though thereafter maintained, the yard always remained of secondary importance. With a confined site, distant from the sea, yet without Deptford's particular advantages, it was declining relative to the other yards throughout the eighteenth century.[6]

Chatham dockyard developed during the reign of Elizabeth, though a storehouse had been hired at Gillingham in 1547 and ships belonging to the Crown had wintered in the Medway at least from the time of Edward VI. Wharves and storehouses were built after 1567 but it remained without a dock until late in the reign of James I. Nevertheless its situation in relation to the North Sea was of particular advantage during the wars against the Dutch, and by the time of the Restoration it had become the kindom's most important yard. With a large proportion of the national facilities and room to expand, its growth continued. Nonetheless its relative importance declined as the principal theatre of naval operations shifted westward into the Channel, as the draught of ships became deeper, and as the Medway gradually became more silted.[7]

Sheerness yard was an extension from Chatham at the time when that yard was pre-eminent. In 1665 a graving place was formed on little more than a mud flat close to the sixteenth-century fort at the mouth of the Medway. Hulks were sunk on the foreshore as breakwaters and as accommodation for men who were initially drafted from Chatham. Officers too were assigned from there until 1673, when its own were appointed. One dock was built in 1688, another in 1720. Wharfage, storehouses and workshops were also added.[8] Nevertheless, the yard was unhealthy and merely maintained for its wartime convenience for ships at the Nore. Only limited improvements took place during the second half of the eighteenth century and in 1793 it retained the haphazard, makeshift appearance that it had had a century earlier.

Plymouth dockyard, the last of the six major yards to develop, grew like Portsmouth in response to demands for a western base. Plymouth Sound had served as an assembly point for expeditions since the sixteenth century and a temporary establishment existed there at the time of the Commonwealth. Permanent development dates from 1689. A basin and dock were begun in 1691, a second dock completed in 1727.[9] The yard was well positioned for the wars against France and, as these developed into wars on a global scale, for operations across and beyond the Atlantic. Growth thus continued throughout the eighteenth century and placed the yard second to Portsmouth in importance by the end of the American War of Independence.

The development of these six major dockyards during the sixteenth, seventeenth and eighteenth centuries was matched by that of the central

government departments responsible for naval maintenance. The department primarily responsible for the dockyards at the end of the eighteenth century was headed by the Navy Board. The board had evolved from a Council of the Marine, established in 1546, which originally controlled the whole of the civil business of the navy except that relating to Ordnance.[10] The Council had then consisted of a Clerk of the King's Ships, appointed from time to time since the reign of King John and later known as the Clerk of the Acts; a Surveyor, appointed for the first time in 1544; a Treasurer of Marine Causes; and a Lieutenant of the Admiralty. The powers of the latter soon lapsed, a Comptroller of the Navy being appointed later to head the board. The Treasurer acquired a department of his own and did not usually meet with the other commissioners from the time of the Restoration. In 1660, however, two extra commissioners were also appointed, thus making the board up to five.[11]

As the civil business of the navy grew after the Restoration some areas of business were transferred to new boards created for the purpose. A Victualling Board was formed in 1684 to control each stage in the provisioning of the navy, and a Transport Board existed to hire and equip ships for the transport of troops between 1690 and 1724, and once again from 1794. Commissioners were also appointed to care for sick and hurt seamen, the first being appointed in 1653, with a permanent board being retained in peace as well as war from 1740 until 1806.[12] Nevertheless, the Navy Board remained the principal naval board beneath the Admiralty, with control of the dockyards and of most areas of naval finance.

The enlargement of the Navy Board after the Restoration reflected this central role in the civil administration of the navy. To relieve the Comptroller of some duties three new board places were soon created. Comptrollers of Treasurer's Accounts and of Victualling Accounts were appointed from 1667 and a Comptroller of Storekeepers' Accounts from 1671. In addition, between 1706 and 1714 and from 1745, a second Surveyor was appointed. The greater volume of work represented by this increase in the number of commissioners also produced a growth in the clerical force serving the board. The wars between 1689 and 1783 each produced a growth in the various sections constituting the Navy Office. Between 1714 and 1740 the number of clerks was reduced, but the additions in wartime both before and after that period were never fully reversed during the succeeding intervals of peace.[13]

The enlargement of the Navy Office during the Revolutionary and Napoleonic Wars conformed to this general pattern of wartime growth. Between 1792 and 1813 the number of established clerks grew from 84 to 124, while the number of extra and temporary clerks increased from 10 to 80. The size of the Navy Office more than doubled.[14] The size of the six main dockyards grew to a lesser extent, rising from less than 9,000 men to over 15,000 in the same period;[15] but they were augmented by the enlargement in the number of minor refitting yards and stores depots around the coasts of the British Isles and scattered around the globe. Although of varying sizes and importance, these small naval establishments were extensions of the existing dockyard organization. New shore bases were often improvised by local commanders-in-chief who appointed a storekeeper from one of their ships, yet these officials were usually replaced by men appointed from one of the

dockyards in England. The artificers were also often volunteers from the dockyards, and the stores usually came either from the nearest major yard or directly from Deptford. They usually stocked victuals as well as materials for refitting, but as part of the dockyard organization they were managed on the whole as small-scale versions of their larger counterparts.

In 1793 seven small yards already existed, three in Britain and four abroad.[16] In the south of England a yard at Deal had served ships in the Downs since 1672; in the north there had been a depot for stores at Leith on the Firth of Forth during the War of Spanish Succession and another was formed there in 1781; and in southern Ireland, from 1690, stores were supplied from an establishment at Kinsale. All three yards continued to function during the Revolutionary and Napoleonic wars, although the establishment at Kinsale was transferred in 1811 to Hawlbowline Island. Abroad, Gibraltar served the Mediterranean briefly following its capture in 1704 and continuously from 1721. Likewise Port Royal, Jamaica, was regularly used for refitting after the capture of the island in 1655 and a storekeeper was stationed there permanently from 1721. A yard on Antigua in the Leeward islands served the eastern Caribbean from 1730 and another at Halifax, Nova Scotia, served the north-eastern seaboard of North America from an early stage in the Seven Years' War. In addition, the East India Company's yard at Bombay was usually available to meet the needs of squadrons in the east.[17]

These existing yards were supplemented after 1793 as supply points were required close to ships' stations and as hostilities spread to new areas of operation. Around the British coasts supply depots were maintained at Falmouth in 1795–6 and between 1805 and 1814, and at Yarmouth from 1803 until 1820. A small building yard was also maintained from 1800 at Milford Haven. In 1813 this yard's establishment was transferred to Pater, across the haven, and later became known as Pembroke Dock. Abroad, new yards were more numerous, their formation and abandonment reflecting by and large the local strength of the British navy.

The initial phase of British dominance in the Mediterranean saw the formation of a base for stores on Corsica. It was abandoned in 1796, however, following Spain's change of sides, the neutralization of the Two Sicilies on the penetration of the French to Leghorn in Italy, and the subsequent decision to withdraw the British navy from the Mediterranean. Yet three new bases were formed following the Battle of the Nile, which regained command at sea in the Mediterranean at a single stroke. Port Mahon, Minorca, which had seen earlier British use from 1708 until 1756 and from 1763 until 1782, was reoccupied in 1798 and used for the last four years of the Revolutionary War. Malta, which had been taken by the French on their way to Egypt in 1798, was retaken by the British in 1800 and thereafter employed as a base for supplies. Further east, another stores depot was formed at Alexandria in 1801. Primarily intended to meet the needs of the ships necessary to cover the operations on shore against the surviving French, it was maintained for another two years.

British dominance in the West Indies and Caribbean was reflected in the number and greater stability of shore establishments. Antigua and Port Royal were supplemented by a source of stores on Martinique for most of the

Revolutionary War; another on Bermuda from 1795 – the base surviving for a century and a half; one on Haiti in 1797–8; and one on Barbados – an island used previously in 1690 and during the America War of Independence – from 1805 until 1816. In addition, further south, a storekeeper was employed at Rio de Janeiro between 1812 and 1815.

In the east, bases for supplies and refitting were less numerous. Following the realignment of the Dutch with the French in 1795, the British occupied the Cape of Good Hope which thereafter became a British port of call. On the Indian sub-continent, Bombay was supplemented after 1796 by the availability of stores at Madras, the establishment there being maintained until the end of the Napoleonic War when it was run down in favour of the fine harbour at Trincomalee in Ceylon, captured from the Dutch in 1795. Between 1798 and 1816 a storekeeper was also stationed at Penang, an establishment from where operations could be mounted against the Dutch East Indies that were eventually overrun in 1811. The capture of Mauritius in 1810, which ended the French naval presence in the Indian Ocean, gave rise to a supply of stores for British ships for the next two years. And finally, possibly for the purpose of gathering naval stores for transportation to England, but probably also to meet the needs of naval and convict ships, there was a storekeeper stationed at Sydney, New South Wales, between 1812 and 1816.[18]

The number and distribution of these establishments, combined with the great size of the six major yards in England, perhaps best represents the scale of the organization managed by the Navy Board between 1793 and 1815. It was, however, in the solution of the innumerable detailed problems involved in running each single yard that the board was really tested. At each one of the yards, work had to flow smoothly for ships to be made ready for sea on time. This demanded that obstacles to the performance of each operation were removed, supply problems eased and labour disputes settled. It was not the case, moreover, that the Navy Board could concentrate purely on the dockyards, for the board was also responsible for the manning and payment of the fleet, and accounting for naval expenditure. With a fleet of nearly 1,000 vessels, it is not surprising that some administrative details were overlooked and some problems mishandled. Among contemporaries these failures were of course a source of scandal, and in criticizing the details, the greater organizational achievements were usually ignored.

That the Navy Board should have received more criticism than praise throughout this period was perhaps inevitable. It resulted in part from the nature of its work and of its administrative situation. Naval officers were invariably dissatisfied with the quality and speed of dockyard work; and politicians made capital from their discontent. The Board of Admiralty too was often dissatisfied with its principal subordinate board. Composed of permanent officials, its members could not be easily removed and they too frequently took professional pride in insisting on their own opinion against that held at the Admiralty. Against such criticism, the members of the Navy Board were ill-placed and ill-equipped to defend themselves. The naval members, though usually well-meaning and efficient men, were not the most outstanding men in their profession; and the others were simply senior civil servants. The Comptroller had a seat in the Commons but was not chosen for his political or speaking ability. Consequently the Navy Board did not easily answer its critics.

Looking back, the members of the Navy Board, and particularly the successive Comptrollers, can be compared to their disadvantage with the Comptroller in the 1780s, Sir Charles Middleton, later Lord Barham. He was on friendly terms with Pitt, had a family connection with Henry Dundas, a flair for administration, great determination and vital reforms to achieve. He thus spoke his mind with confidence and with reason. But during the late 1790s and early nineteenth century the Comptrollers, Sir Andrew Hamond and Sir Thomas Thompson, had less influential connections and were more preoccupied with making a reformed system of management work, rather than with attempting to obtain further change. Being the subjects – if not the victims – of reform, they were also on the whole on the defensive, for by their time at the Navy Board public opinion was decidedly in favour of greater efficiency and economy in government.

Reform was the oustanding feature of this episode in the history of the Navy Board and the dockyards. The traditional perquisities of office, the organization of board management and the very machinery of control, the standing orders for the civil departments of the navy, were all examined and altered to suit the changing standards of public administration. The process of reform had begun with the failures of the American War of Independence and were given impetus by the movement for economical reform.[19] The latter gave rise to a succession of commissions of enquiry into the workings of different departments of government and there was consequently a series of reports on organizational inadequacies. Between 1785 and 1808 the civil affairs of the navy were subject to three searching inquiries, the earliest of these providing the first public reports on administrative practice in the Navy Office and the dockyards for a hundred years.[20] Each of these three inquiries was prompted by varying and particular motives, and each accordingly had its own immediate objectives. Yet all three had as their general aim the check of wastage and extravagance in public expenditure and the maintenance of the traditional system of organization in effective working order.

This objective was not so readily achieved as the formation of the initial commissions and reports. The Commissioners of Enquiry into Fees, Perquisites, Gratuities and Emoluments produced a report on the Navy Office and another on the dockyards in 1788, many of the recommendations being derived from the energetic Charles Middleton. But, to Middleton's chagrin, the reports were shelved for four years and the recommendations not adopted in the Navy Office until 1796 and in the dockyards until 1801. The latter were rewritten by Samuel Bentham, Jeremy's brother, who was appointed Inspector General of Naval Works in 1796. Bentham wrote into them schemes of his own and the following years consequently saw changes in the management of timber and in the training of apprentices as well as in the nature of payment.

Bentham's appointment as Inspector General, a post created at the Admiralty, was particularly important for the dockyards. Although his influence at the Admiralty and in the yards was resented by the Navy Board, he did much to introduce into the yards both the latest technology and his strongly held belief in individual responsibility. There is reason to suppose that this idea influenced

St Vincent, First Lord between 1801 and 1804, and contributed to the virtual breakdown of relations between the Admiralty and Navy Board during his administration. But Bentham's work did more than this. By introducing new technological and administrative ideas, it brought into the highly traditional world of the yards ways of thinking that broke with the past and looked forward to the future.

St Vincent's support of Bentham in the face of Navy Board hostility was vital to the implementation of Bentham's schemes. Even though the Navy Board dominated dockyard administration, St Vincent was determined to impose reforms on the yards. As a naval officer, he knew that wastage and inefficiency in the yards both squandered public money and ultimately damaged the navy. After frauds were discovered in the performance of yard contracts and in the calculation of wages, he consequently obtained late in 1802 the Commission of Naval Enquiry. With instructions to investigate irregularities, frauds and abuses throughout the naval departments, these Commissioners produced detailed reports on omissions, oversights, malpractices and misconceptions that reflected poorly on officials in almost every department.

In the sense that evidence of failure far outweighed recommendations, the reports of the Commissioners of Naval Enquiry were more damaging than constructive. Their tenth report on the office of Treasurer of the Navy resulted in the impeachment in 1805 of Henry Dundas, first Viscount Melville, a proceeding that forced Melville to resign as First Lord. But the Commissioners' sixth report on the dockyards recommended the revision of the standing orders issued to the yard officers and it permitted Pitt to bring their inquiries to an end by appointing as successors the Commissioners for Revising and Digesting the Civil Affairs of the Navy. Led by Charles Middleton, who had become First Lord on Melville's resignation, the new Commissioners comprehensively examined and drew up new standing orders for all concerned in the civil administration of the navy.

In the dockyards some of the recommendations of the Commissioners of Revision were not carried out until 1812. Their eventually successful adoption owed much to the work of John Payne of the Navy Office. Together the work of the Commissioners and of John Payne had four effects. They produced a more precise system of control in areas of yard management like wage payment; they provided all yard officials with their first comprehensive set of regulations since the seventeenth century; they reduced most administrative procedure in the yards to a single pattern, so that each yard worked, as the Commissioners intended, like the parts of one great machine; and they gave the Navy Board a new grasp of yard business, a control which contributed to a significant growth in its administrative confidence.

The growth in confidence was not restricted to the Navy Board. At the Admiralty, officials had far more knowledge of the civil departments of the navy from the series of reports produced by the succession of Commissions. Their knowledge and confidence, moreover, was but part of the growing awareness throughout government of the methods employed and problems experienced in managing subordinate departments.[21] Combined with a greater appreciation of the value of accountancy as a tool of management, a new administrative standard was developing. Whereas the naval departments in the

1790s had revealed an apparent complacency over the costs of traditional perquisites and practices, by 1815 there was a conscious struggle after greater economy and efficiency.

In this new environment, large-scale structural reforms were not long delayed. In the dockyards in 1822 two principal yard officers' posts and numerous inferior officers' positions were simply cut from the traditional system of management.[22] The cuts performed the first structural alterations in the basic organization within the yards for at least a century and a half, marking the end of a period of administrative continuity stretching back to the Restoration. The traditional board system did not long survive either. This had been under erosion since the beginning of the century. Between 1794 and 1806, including the Ordnance Board, there had been five civil boards providing for the needs of the navy. In 1796, however, the care of prisoners of war, for which the Sick and Wounded Board had been responsible, was transferred to the Transport Board. Then in 1806 the former board was abolished, the Transport Board becoming responsible for the care of sick and wounded seamen as well. After the Napoleonic War the process of rationalization continued, undoubtedly reinforced by the pressure for economy. The Transport Board was itself abolished in 1817 and was followed 15 years later by the last two remaining civil boards beneath the Admiralty, the Navy and Victualling Boards. All the civil business of the navy was then transferred to five principal officers, each accountable to a member of the Board of Admiralty.[23]

In 1832, at the time of this last reorganization, the guiding administrative principle had become individual responsibility, the concept advocated by Samuel Bentham. Sir James Graham, then First Lord, founded his argument for reform on the belief that subordinate boards were inefficient and a bar to direct control from the Admiralty, ideas in which he felt confirmed from reading the reports of the Commissioners of Naval Enquiry.[24] Later developments in the management of the dockyards were accordingly based on concepts and judgments formed during the Revolutionary and Napoleonic Wars. That Graham's ideas dated back to this time was no coincidence, for it was a protracted period of crises and pressures when, as the process of governmental reform got under way, new ideas and experiments were made and conclusions drawn.

This book looks at the dockyards during this particularly formative period. Traditionally they have always been regarded as technologically backward compared with private industry, wasteful of public funds and ship-building resources, and a check, from their inefficiency, on the efforts of the fighting navy. In some respects these strictures were true, for there were great problems of scale, communication and organization. The size of the yards, the system of central board control and the strength of custom and practice were all resistant to change and improvement. Officials within this cumbrous organization must naturally have become accustomed to its inadequacies or, if aspiring to create a better one, have tended to despair of ever achieving their end. Contemporaries, and consequently historians, have blamed the Navy Board for not having done more to eradicate the inefficiency and wastage of resources. In so doing, however, they took a partial and limited view and ignored the difficulties of control under which the Board laboured.

The picture of yard affairs which emerges here is one that reflects creditably on the majority of yard and board officials alike. At a period of change in the standards and in the machinery of management, there was a need for flexibility and adaptation on the part of both. Especially during its conflict with St Vincent's Admiralty, the Navy Board was depicted as a shield of inefficiency and corruption. Yet over the whole period of wars, the board clearly appears as a relatively progressive institution, persistently pursuing improvements which it recognized as beneficial to the public service. Over the whole period, it consequently achieved much that made for greater efficiency in the construction, repair and refitting of ships and for greater economy in the expenditure of public funds and naval stores. Equally conspicuous is the dedication of most yard officials, who consistently performed their duties to a high standard. Again during St Vincent's administration, owing to the critical reports of the Commissioners of Naval Enquiry and to the discharge of several officers for negligence, the yard officials were generally depicted as lax and incompetent; but without their conscientious attention to detail the British navy could not have been equipped and maintained for the tasks it had to perform. Maintaining these ships was not just a matter of routine but presented problems that had to be solved with imagination and resourcefulness. The general impression that emerges is thus one of industry, enterprise and gradual improvement. It is an impression with which the traditional assumptions about the dockyards and their management do not coincide. It is nevertheless one that does justice to the Navy Board, the dockyards and the men who served in them.

The chapters that follow reconstruct yard affairs from the ground upwards. Yard operations – refitting, repairs and new construction – are examined first, followed by the facilities which to a large extent determined yard performance. The three basic elements necessary to operations – the materials, a workforce and officials – figure in turn. Procedures are mainly the subject of the chapter on the materials, their passage through the yards being traced from their acquisition to their use, wastage or loss through embezzlement. The problem of getting sufficient labour is the dominant theme running through that on the workforce, for it had a bearing on every aspect of managing the artificers: the provision of employment incentives, recruitment, the systems of apprenticeship and piecework, and the task of maintaining order in the yards. The officials are examined in reverse order of seniority: the clerks and inferior officers first, followed by the principal officers and commissioners. Their problems of management are the subject of Chapter 6: the officers' difficulties in complying with a burdensome check system; the deficiencies in the powers of the resident commissioner; the problems of control from the Navy Board and of communication with the Admiralty. Chapter 7 traces the course of the reform movement from the growth of public opinion in favour of greater efficiency and economy, through the effort of St Vincent and Barham (connected as these were to the Commissions of Naval Enquiry and Naval Revision) to the reforms performed on behalf of the Navy Board by John Payne of the Navy Office, and the ideas and influence of Samuel Bentham. Of course many aspects of yard affairs, though here discussed pages apart, were closely connected. The book therefore concludes by placing the many various developments in the dockyards and their management into a single pattern of change.

# 1

# Yard operations

The royal dockyards have generally been regarded by naval historians as inefficient, as the navy's Achilles' heel. This view, derived from the comments of sea officers, does the yards and the men who worked in them little justice. The sea officers received only a partial view of yard operations and, anxious to get to sea with ships in the best condition possible, they inevitably condemned the speed or the standard of work when it fell short of their often perfectionist requirements. Considering the scale of yard operations, it would be surprising indeed had they had no shortcomings. But there is on the other hand much evidence to show that within their limitations the yards performed a vast amount of work relatively efficiently. The great majority of ships were taken to sea without complaints from their officers; while the achievement of British naval supremacy itself partly reflected the yards' capabilities, for their performance was the principal factor determining both the number of ships commissioned and the time those ships could stay at sea. By contemporary industrial standards these vessels represented a work output of extraordinary proportions. It was remarkable, not that work was sometimes performed badly, but that the dockyards were capable of performing the amount of work they did.

Equally remarkable was the fact that the yards sustained their level of performance over 22 years. Traditional naval history has always laid emphasis on the great fleet victories of the wars: the Glorious First of June, St Vincent, Camperdown, Nile, Copenhagen and Trafalgar. It is thus sometimes forgotten that even Trafalgar did not reduce the necessity to maintain a huge British force at sea. After 1805 the demands made on, and made by, the navy in fact increased before they diminished. As in the Revolutionary War, so effective was the counterpoise of French land power to British sea power that the resources of the navy were almost constantly stretched. Defeat at sea, almost certainly a prelude to invasion, was a threat that could never be discounted. Indeed, following the treaty of Tilsit in 1807 French sea power gradually increased again. French ships of the line then totalled only 34, though with those of subject states they amounted to over 100. Bonaparte had, however, set a target of 150 and in 1813 had more than 80 completed, with another 35 still building.[1] The threat this posed was serious. Sir Thomas Byam Martin, later Comptroller of the Navy, observed:

Although we captured and destroyed in the course of the war 156 ships of the line, 382 large frigates, 662 corvettes, and altogether 2,506 armed ships and vessels, which might almost lead to a conclusion that the ocean had been swept of our enemies; yet in 1814 it was necessary to strain our efforts to the utmost to keep pace with the French in building; and, had the war continued, the French, then in possession of Holland and Antwerp, would in a short time have outnumbered us, so ample were the means and so determined was Bonaparte to try and master us on our own element.[2]

To counter this enemy, the dockyards were required to equip and maintain an unprecedented number of vessels. Ships were needed for various purposes. Convoys, colonies and the British coastline had all to be protected, while a blockade was maintained on every enemy port. At their height in 1809 these

Table 1. *The composition of the British Navy, 1793–1816*

| on 1 Jan | 1st rates 100–120 guns | 2nd rates 90–98 guns | 3rd rates 64–80 guns | 4th rates 50–60 guns | 5th rates 32–44 guns | 6th rates 20–28 guns | sloops and other vessels | total |
|---|---|---|---|---|---|---|---|---|
| 1793 | 5 | 19 | 114 | 22 | 90 | 41 | 99 | 390 |
| 1794 | 6 | 19 | 117 | 22 | 94 | 42 | 120 | 420 |
| 1795 | 6 | 20 | 120 | 20 | 112 | 41 | 164 | 483 |
| 1796 | 6 | 19 | 117 | 30 | 118 | 44 | 200 | 534 |
| 1797 | 7 | 19 | 120 | 25 | 130 | 47 | 239 | 587 |
| 1798 | 8 | 20 | 130 | 25 | 135 | 49 | 293 | 660 |
| 1799 | 8 | 21 | 137 | 23 | 132 | 51 | 322 | 694 |
| 1800 | 9 | 19 | 136 | 26 | 132 | 47 | 360 | 729 |
| 1801 | 8 | 19 | 139 | 26 | 134 | 47 | 362 | 735 |
| 1802 | 8 | 19 | 138 | 26 | 141 | 44 | 370 | 746 |
| 1803 | 7 | 15 | 126 | 20 | 124 | 33 | 283 | 608 |
| 1804 | 7 | 15 | 129 | 20 | 128 | 33 | 291 | 623 |
| 1805 | 8 | 14 | 131 | 23 | 142 | 34 | 374 | 726 |
| 1806 | 8 | 15 | 139 | 22 | 153 | 36 | 416 | 789 |
| 1807 | 8 | 15 | 145 | 20 | 166 | 41 | 470 | 865 |
| 1808 | 8 | 14 | 165 | 19 | 175 | 46 | 494 | 921 |
| 1809 | 8 | 15 | 170 | 18 | 179 | 40 | 549 | 979 |
| 1810 | 8 | 15 | 177 | 17 | 185 | 40 | 534 | 976 |
| 1811 | 9 | 17 | 177 | 15 | 181 | 38 | 523 | 960 |
| 1812 | 9 | 15 | 181 | 14 | 173 | 30 | 476 | 898 |
| 1813 | 9 | 16 | 188 | 13 | 165 | 31 | 477 | 899 |
| 1814 | 9 | 12 | 183 | 19 | 180 | 40 | 493 | 936 |
| 1815 | 10 | 12 | 169 | 17 | 167 | 47 | 419 | 841 |
| 1816 | 9 | 14 | 150 | 17 | 147 | 42 | 364 | 743 |

*Note:* Ships of the line throughout this period comprised vessels of 60 to 120 guns. 74-gun ships were the most common ships of the line. Their numbers remained relatively stable in the Revolutionary War: 70 in January 1793, 71 in 1797, 77 in 1802. But they rose markedly during the Napoleonic War from 81 in January 1803 to 113 in 1808 and 143 in 1813.

services required in commission at sea 113 ships of the line and 596 smaller vessels. There were in addition ships on harbour duty, which raised the totals in service to 141 and 632.[3] Blockade duty absorbed the greater part of these forces. In July 1794 70 of the 81 ships of the line available were allotted to blockading Brest and Toulon. By July 1809, including 25 in the Mediterranean and 22 in the Baltic, the ships of the line available for blockade duty numbered only 64.[4] But by then, with more ports in Europe to watch and interests to guard in every quarter of the globe, the navy was stretched to the limit. British naval resources were most sorely tried when, by thinning the squadrons at sea and commissioning old ships, additional forces were gathered for expeditions. That against the Danish fleet in 1807 eventually included 40 ships of the line, and the Walcheren expedition in 1809 included 37. Most transports for these expeditions were hired by the Transport Board under contracts which left the owners responsible for their maintenance; nevertheless they sometimes required fitting for particular purposes. The 1807 expedition took 377 transports, the Walcheren expedition about 500; in 1807 a dockyard officer at Ramsgate saw '150 go out in one tide'.[5]

The scale of these operations and the fact that ships were often required at sea for a particular time had a streamlining effect on the yards. The strategy which governed the conduct of the naval war was itself more systematic than in any previous war and the dockyards were directly influenced by it.[6] The blockade system was itself an exercise in logistics. Sir Charles Middleton, a member of the Board of Admiralty in 1794–5, worked from accounts showing the 'supposed force of the enemy' at their different ports and 'the British force required to oppose them effectually'. The forces within and those outside were weighed in terms of gunpower, ships of the line being distinguished from frigates, with the ideal blockading force set against the actual number of ships available, the number always to be kept outside and that which could be back refitting. In 1794 Middleton allowed for the absence of one in four ships from duty off Brest and one in three from Toulon. By 1812 only one ship in six above the enemy's strength was thought adequate for 'home stations' and one in four for the Mediterranean.[7] In a blockade lasting 12 months of the year regular refitting was essential: Sir Home Popham in July 1805 proposed the blockade's abandonment owing to the wear and tear culminating in 'calamities that increase in so great a ratio as to threaten the annihilation of the fleet in a few years'.[8] The 74-gun ship, backbone of the line, had to be re-equipped or repaired on average every two and a half years. Yet to permit such work, ships had to be prepared for sea as regularly as those on duty required relief. The yards were driven to an unprecedented extent to match their pace to the deterioration rate of ships at sea.

Although the blockade policy thus imposed a framework and pressure of its own, the system by which ships were maintained at the yards worked independently of the system at sea. Ships returned for attention as reliefs allowed. These came out as soon as work at the yards was completed. The process of service and relief was cyclic and was controlled from the Admiralty. In 1794–5 Middleton kept lists of the commissioned ships that had defects or had been two years without docking, from which he was able to anticipate those ships that should probably return to port first and the size of those that would be needed as replacement.[9] It was simply a matter of the dockyards working fast enough to get as many ships to sea as possible.

The workload imposed on the yards, however, was by no means evenly distributed. By the end of the eighteenth century the yards most accessible to ships blockading the French ports, Portsmouth and Plymouth, possessed over half the dry docks available. They therefore dealt with most of the ships and especially with those that had to be refitted or repaired in the minimum time. As their approaches were least affected by the problem of silting, which most seriously affected the inland eastern yards, these western yards also dealt with the great majority of ships of the line. This is evident from the number of ships of this size docked at each yard in 1794, still primarily a period of mobilization. Portsmouth docked 14, Plymouth 11, Chatham 9 and Woolwich 1.[10] An analysis of the yards at which the 74s received attention between 1801 and 1805 reveals a similar distribution: Portsmouth dealt with 74s on 50 occasions, Plymouth on 52, Chatham on 32 and Woolwich on 13. Sheerness dealt with only 3 and Deptford none at all.[11] Though handling fewer ships of the line, the eastern yards nevertheless performed functions which clearly complemented the operations of the two larger yards in the west. Sheerness refitted many frigates and other smaller vessels, while always having a dock available for ships requiring attention at the Nore. The less accessible – Chatham, Deptford and Woolwich – tended to perform more new construction and large repairs, the two Thames yards also serving as depots for stores required at the other yards, by the fleet at sea and at bases abroad.

The tendency to specialize reduced the inconveniences and delays involved for ships using the dockyards. It also enhanced the importance of the co-ordinating role performed by the Navy Board in advising the Admiralty to which yards ships should be sent and where particular operations could be most easily carried out. That the Board filled this role reasonably well is revealed in the trust with which it was treated by most Admiralty Boards. By the end of the Napoleonic War, indeed, dockyard performance was simply regarded at the Admiralty as a mass-production process with a predictable capacity and output.[12] Considering the great number of ships maintained and the problems overcome in the process, it was a view that was wholly justifiable.

The efficiency of all six yards was perhaps most fully tested during the mobilization periods which began both wars between 1793 and 1815. The navy was not unprepared for war at either time. While in January 1793 there were 26 ships of the line and 109 other vessels in service at sea, the comparable figures for early 1803 were 32 and 200. To gain control at sea, however, these ships had to be reinforced as rapidly as possible. By the end of 1795 the dockyards had thus prepared for sea another 79 of the line and 172 smaller vessels: a rate each month of about two ships of the line and five other vessels, with another of the line coming forward. A similar pace was achieved in the Napoleonic War, though slightly fewer ships of the line and more smaller vessels were fitted. War was not officially declared until mid-May 1803, but orders had gone to the yards to fit ships for sea 'without a moment's loss of time' by the night post of 10 March.[13] By the end of 1805 a further 72 ships of the line and 275 frigates and other vessels had been equipped. Including ships commissioned in the first two months of 1803, this was a rate of just over two of the line each month with about eight frigates, brigs and sloops. This did not quite accurately represent the work of the dockyards, for to counter Bonaparte's fleet of flat-bottomed invasion boats, merchant shipyards were used to fit gun-vessels, brigs, sloops and some ships of 64 guns.[14] The ships commissioned between 1803 and 1805 were also in worse condition than those in 1793–5 owing to the wear and tear of the Revolutionary War. The figures nevertheless bear some comparison.

In 1793 the navy and the yards had probably never been better prepared for war. Primarily owing to Pitt's interest and readiness to finance the work, 84 ships of the line were repaired between 1783 and 1793, 15 more were built in the dockyards and another 30 built by contract.[15] A series of minor 'armaments' – the Duch alarm in 1787, Spanish in 1790 and Russian in 1791 – also kept the yards in readiness. Charles Middleton presided at the Navy Board until 1790 and ensured that no lesson from these minor mobilizations was overlooked. 'I will advert to what you say', Commissioner Laforey replied to Middleton from Plymouth in November 1787, 'and recommend to the officers the consideration of a timely provision of all supplies necessary for accelerating a future armament from the instances they have now before them of what may be deficient in this . . .'[16] Middleton himself ordered the arrangement of the ships laid up in Ordinary into divisions, each with a superintending master to attend to their needs; he also ordered the collection of these ships' equipment and stores into individual storehouse berths, each of which was then applicable to a ship of the same class; and to expedite the commissioning of ships in good condition, he directed that their magazines and store-rooms be fitted in readiness for sea. Middleton later informed Lord Melville that when he left the Navy Board there were 'upwards of 90 sail of the line in good condition and every article of their stores provided and so arranged that when the fleet was armed soon after it was done with such rapidity as was never known before and which will never be done again without the same kind of forethought and preparation'.[17]

Middleton's preparations paid off. During the mobilizations of 1793 and 1803 stores and equipment lay ready. Initially ships of the line took precedence, those in the best condition being fitted first. Orders thus went to the yards in May 1803 to equip those that could be completed without docking and those in dock which could be repaired within a month. Others, even those under repair, were temporarily left. To permit the formation of priorities, the yard officers supplied the Navy Board with lists of the vessels in Ordinary in a condition for immediate service, specifying how long each would last without repair. At times the junior Surveyor or a committee of the Navy Board visited the yards to determine which ships should take priority. The Admiralty Board then simply sanctioned the list of ships proposed by the subordinate board or made its own choice of ships, ordering at the same time the quantity of stores to be put on board – enough for three, four, or six months or even 'as much . . . as she can stow'.

Owing to the concentration on vessels that did not require docking, during the first few weeks the rate at which ships came forward was high. Twenty-eight ships of the line were equipped during May 1803.[18] After a month or two, however, the rate slowed: ships brought forward required re-coppering or minor repair and docks were often needed for ships returning from service demanding urgent repair. As a result the Navy Board was no longer able to predict with precision when ships would be brought forward. The pace of work was nevertheless still sufficiently steady for the Admiralty to plan which ships should be commissioned in each month for up to eight months in advance. During the main course of the war, when refitting and repairs became the main concern, there were still times when ships from the Ordinary were fitted with the utmost urgency.[19] These were, however, minor 'heats' compared to the initial great effort.

The equipment of each ship was the product of close co-operation between the departments of the Master Shipwright, Master Attendant and Storekeeper. For, after the best ships had been commissioned, the others were usually docked, their bottoms cleaned, caulking checked and copper repaired or renewed. Only then could they be rigged and stored like the others. Apart from

Table 2. *Ships of the line in commission and in Ordinary, 1793–1817*

| on 1 Jan | for sea service in commission | for sea service in Ordinary | for harbour service in commission | for harbour service in Ordinary | % of total in commission |
|---|---|---|---|---|---|
| 1793 | 26  | 87 | 3  | 25 | 20 |
| 1794 | 85  | 32 | 6  | 22 | 63 |
| 1795 | 91  | 23 | 10 | 20 | 70 |
| 1796 | 105 | 11 | 10 | 20 | 79 |
| 1797 | 108 | 8  | 15 | 19 | 82 |
| 1798 | 104 | 16 | 21 | 21 | 77 |
| 1799 | 105 | 20 | 33 | 12 | 81 |
| 1800 | 100 | 24 | 30 | 14 | 77 |
| 1801 | 100 | 27 | 21 | 22 | 71 |
| 1802 | 104 | 22 | 17 | 26 | 72 |
| 1803 | 32  | 79 |    | 39 | 21 |
| 1804 | 75  | 40 | 9  | 29 | 55 |
| 1805 | 83  | 33 | 11 | 28 | 61 |
| 1806 | 104 | 16 | 17 | 27 | 74 |
| 1807 | 103 | 20 | 20 | 27 | 72 |
| 1808 | 113 | 13 | 19 | 44 | 70 |
| 1809 | 113 | 14 | 28 | 40 | 78 |
| 1810 | 108 | 16 | 35 | 42 | 72 |
| 1811 | 107 | 17 | 38 | 42 | 71 |
| 1812 | 102 | 18 | 40 | 46 | 70 |
| 1813 | 102 | 22 | 41 | 50 | 66 |
| 1814 | 99  | 19 | 39 | 47 | 68 |
| 1815 | 47  | 62 | 11 | 71 | 30 |
| 1816 | 30  | 70 | 3  | 70 | 19 |
| 1817 | 14  | 84 |    | 40 | 10 |

the shortage of docks, the main restriction on these operations was the shortage of labour. In 1803 the Master Shipwright's department at Sheerness was reinforced with three gangs of shipwrights from Deptford and Woolwich, while over 200 contract riggers were employed under the Masters Attendant at Chatham, Sheerness, Portsmouth and Plymouth. Riggers were permanently employed at the yards, but many of them were used to man lighters and other yard craft, along with the Masters Attendant's 'extra men', of whom there were also shortages. Hired men thus almost completely rigged most ships, leaving only that work for the crews that did not prevent them sailing.[20]

Quite often the rigging proceeded before the sea officers took up their appointments. Then the details of the work sometimes went unchecked and it was invariably rushed, for contract riggers were paid by the ship and allowed only 11–15 days for a first rate, 8–10 for a third rate and 6–8 for a frigate. Only when the captains of ships had read aloud their commissions, and thus formally announced their command, were they in a position to check rigging and to order the process of stowing and equipping. A captain was then

Table 3. *Frigates and other vessels in commission and in Ordinary, 1793–1817*

| on 1 Jan | for sea service in commission | in Ordinary | for harbour service in commission | in Ordinary | % of total in commission |
|---|---|---|---|---|---|
| 1793 | 109 | 82 | 11 | 47 | 48 |
| 1794 | 194 | 17 | 26 | 38 | 80 |
| 1795 | 235 | 14 | 59 | 31 | 78 |
| 1796 | 271 | 18 | 60 | 39 | 85 |
| 1797 | 293 | 26 | 65 | 53 | 82 |
| 1798 | 347 | 35 | 64 | 51 | 82 |
| 1799 | 364 | 28 | 82 | 50 | 85 |
| 1800 | 368 | 18 | 101 | 74 | 84 |
| 1801 | 372 | 12 | 113 | 68 | 86 |
| 1802 | 347 | 32 | 111 | 87 | 79 |
| 1803 | 200 | 131 | 10 | 117 | 46 |
| 1804 | 320 | 39 | 36 | 74 | 76 |
| 1805 | 425 | 36 | 34 | 76 | 80 |
| 1806 | 475 | 30 | 38 | 81 | 82 |
| 1807 | 533 | 34 | 38 | 90 | 82 |
| 1808 | 529 | 46 | 34 | 123 | 77 |
| 1809 | 596 | 32 | 36 | 120 | 81 |
| 1810 | 584 | 21 | 37 | 133 | 80 |
| 1811 | 551 | 21 | 31 | 153 | 77 |
| 1812 | 519 | 22 | 31 | 120 | 79 |
| 1813 | 511 | 18 | 31 | 124 | 79 |
| 1814 | 545 | 24 | 30 | 133 | 78 |
| 1815 | 438 | 53 | 24 | 135 | 71 |
| 1816 | 230 | 135 | 15 | 190 | 43 |
| 1817 | 110 | 197 | 7 | 164 | 24 |

handicapped by the number of men at his disposal, for the gunner, carpenter and boatswain had not only to draw their stores but prepare them for use.[21] Provisions, and sometimes guns too, had to be taken aboard and manhandled below, and work was often delayed in large ships as they increased their draught and had to move to deeper water to finish loading. Even when rigging went smoothly accidents to stores, insufficient yard lighters, inclement weather and unfavourable winds all created problems in getting away. Nevertheless the main obstacle at mobilization remained a shortage of seamen. Sufficient drafts of men, whether new-pressed or sent from ships returning from sea, were often not received until the later stages of fitting. Sometimes the failure to receive them prevented ships from sailing. In 1803 8,000 men were wanted, leaving 32 ships of the line short; in May 1805 there were still ships 'laying ready to receive men and none to put aboard'.[22] Thus, though rigging took one or two weeks, it was often a month or more before ships put to sea.

After ships sailed and before they were completely refitted, they usually made several brief visits to dockyards or naval stations to replenish stores and have minor defects corrected. Stores were supplied from the dockyards on the demand of the admiral of the fleet or squadron to which ships were attached and were taken on board by arrangement between the port admirals at the Nore, Spithead or Cawsand Bay and the respective commissioners at Sheerness, Portsmouth or Plymouth. At such lesser naval stations as those at Yarmouth, Deal, Falmouth and Torquay, stores were obtained by a simple request from a ship's commanding officer to the Storekeeper. At both yards and naval stations artificers were also taken on board to perform minor repairs: caulkers, carpenters and sailmakers were constantly at work at the Nore, Spithead, in Cawsand Bay and Plymouth Sound, while a gang of caulkers worked in the Downs and off Yarmouth. Although these operations were termed by sea officers 'refitting', they were of short duration. When in command of the western squadron St Vincent advised his captains and commanders that refitting in Plymouth Sound and Cawsand Bay 'never ought to exceed six days unless a mast is to be shifted and in that event not more than ten'; squadrons which came into Spithead and Plymouth Sound nevertheless sometimes stopped for 10 or 12 days.[23]

The work involved in a complete refit took much longer. Until ships were sheathed with copper, a practice established during the American War of Independence, they had been refitted in general every three years. Owing to the necessary regularity of the work, it had been known as 'triennial trimmings'. After 1793, however, ships were evidently kept at sea until their condition began to impede their performance and there were enough in commission to permit some to return for refitting. Although the average period between such visits for 74s was 30 months, some of these vessels remained at sea more than four years. By then their copper, caulking, rigging and fittings were not necessarily trustworthy.

At the dockyards refitting was divided between the ships' crews and the yards artificers. After a survey by the yard officers, each vessel was stripped of its rigging, guns, gunners', boatswains' and carpenters' stores, provisions, cables and ballast,[24] and pumped out ready for docking. This work, performed by each ship's crew, demanded particular order and care. Everything had to be listed and much of the rigging tallied to facilitate replacement. Many items were returned to store but some, like provisions and equipment still usable, went to a hulk. As the work neared completion the crew was drafted in batches either to a receiving ship or to a vessel ready to sail. Charge of the ship was then transferred to the Master Attendant. He arranged each docking as vacancies, tides and Admiralty priorities allowed. On completion the ship was launched, or rather hauled out of dock, and a crew restored. The work by which the ship had been stripped was reversed and the vessel made ready for service.[25]

From arrival to departure, the whole process took on average two months for a frigate and four for a 74. The work involving the ships' crews was performed relatively quickly. With the best use of time, space and labour, rigging and topmasts could be stripped in 'a few hours'.[26] Had yard lighters always been ready, a dock available, tides convenient and a minimum of work to be performed, ships could have been docked in a week, out again in a fortnight and departing four to five weeks after arrival. Yet refitting rarely went smoothly. At every stage there were delays.

Organization was not lacking. The docking of one ship was generally closely co-ordinated with the undocking of another; as one came out on the height of a tide the next to go in was usually ready. Yet there were far more ships awaiting docking than there were docks. Ships of the line were invariably given priority. Even so, 74s waited on average a month between the time of their arrival and the day when they were taken into dock. Smaller vessels no doubt waited longer. The latter were, however, less restricted by the state of the tides. Owing to the shallowness of even the deepest of docks, ships of the line had to

*Table 4. Ships refitted at each dockyard, 15 May–26 December 1805*

| | Deptford | Woolwich | Chatham | Sheerness | Portsmouth | Plymouth | totals |
|---|---|---|---|---|---|---|---|
| 1st rates (100–120 guns) | | | | | 1 | 1 | 2 |
| 2nd rates (90 or 98 guns) | | | | | 1 | 1 | 2 |
| 3rd rates (64 or 74 guns) | | | 4 | 1 | 7 | 6 | 18 |
| 4th rates (50 or 56 guns) | | | 1 | 2 | 3 | | 6 |
| 5th rates (32–44 guns) | | | 1 | 9 | 15 | 7 | 32 |
| 6th rates (20–28 guns) | | | | 5 | 4 | 1 | 10 |
| Sloops | | | | 15 | 10 | 6 | 31 |
| Schooners | | | | | | 1 | 1 |
| Bomb vessels | | | | 5 | 3 | | 8 |
| Cutters | | | | | 4 | 1 | 5 |
| Storeships | | 4 | | | | | 4 |
| Gunboats | | | | 25 | 3 | 1 | 29 |
| Yachts | 2 | | | | | | 2 |

be hauled in on spring tides and could not be removed until the next series of these tides a fortnight later. A few ships were launched again on the same day or that following docking, but they either required the minimum of attention or were found to have serious defects and were placed in Ordinary to await repair.

Once in dock there was a relative flurry of activity. The hull was inspected, some sheathing being stripped to expose the caulking; this, if necessary, was renewed; otherwise all worn copper sheets were replaced and minor defects made good. These activities were, however, sometimes protracted either by the discovery of more serious defects, which after reference to the Navy Board were immediately repaired, or by the necessity to renew the coppering completely. 74s required re-coppering after four or five years at sea. These operations inevitably extended the period in dock. Of those 74s which simply had worn sheets replaced, half were undocked in a fortnight, and the remainder in a month; but of those completely re-coppered, less than half were out in a month and the majority in six weeks. Other defects of course increased the period still longer.

However, once the hull was completed, they were launched as soon as possible. Further work on upper works, interior and fittings was often performed at moorings. Indeed the very act of launching invariably effected some damage which had to be made good. Seamen from receiving ships were then available to rig masts and stow ballast, guns, stores and equipment. Even so, with insufficient 'extra men' to man yard craft and never enough of these to ferry everything to ships, as during mobilizations, fitting for sea went slowly. Less than a third of all 74s sailed within a month after launching, the majority getting away two or three weeks later.

Perhaps the major cause of the delays at each stage in refitting was the shallowness of the docks. Although the business of unloading and reloading large ships was partly to reduce the strain on their frame when grounded, it was mainly to reduce their draught. This absorbed labour as well as time and did not obviate the necessity for ships of the line to dock and undock on spring tides. With deeper docks, more ships might have been maintained and thus more kept in commission. This was Samuel Bentham's aim when, as Inspector General of Naval Works, he directed the enlarging and deepening of the basin at Portsmouth and the construction of two deep docks leading from it. Completed about 1801, Bentham claimed in 1812 that as a result of these facilities

> ships-of-the-line at any draught of water . . . can, with all in, be fitted and
> equipped, even to the taking in of their sea stores of water, within the
> boundary of the dockyard; and by these means such a degree of dispatch has
> been there obtained as that ships that have come in from sea have been taken
> into dock even at neap tide, have undergone repairs and have sailed again
> for their station in as few days as the weeks that were requisite for the
> performance of the same business before these accommodations were
> provided . . .[27]

Yet such dispatch was attained less often than Bentham implied and then more commonly with frigates than with ships of the line. Between 1801 and 1805 only one 74 was returned to sea in days rather than in weeks: in August 1801 the *Saturn* was docked within three days of arriving at Portsmouth; her copper was repaired in one day and she sailed five days after being launched; she was at the dockyard a total of nine days. But this was exceptional. Otherwise the most rapid refitting at Portsmouth took at least seven weeks, a speed achieved there before 1796 and also common at Plymouth. Nevertheless a small proportion of frigates, less than 15 per cent, were docked and returned to sea two weeks after arriving at Spithead and occasionally within days of their arrival. In March 1801, for example, the *Loire* (40) was docked, had her copper repaired and sailed within six days of arrival; and again in July 1803 the *Mercury* (28) received similar attention and sailed after only two days in port.

On occasions, therefore, the dockyards were capable of rapid refitting. On the whole, however, fitting and refitting, especially of ships of the line, was a relatively drawn-out business. Had this meant that the work performed was of a high standard, the slow pace might have been of ultimate advantage. Yet the standard achieved was often a matter of contention. The dockyard officers had different, if not lower, standards from those of sea officers, to whose opinions they were often sharply opposed. Thus a mast described by a naval officer as possessing 'the appearance and almost the property of touchwood' was considered by a Master Mastmaker to bear no sign of defects; and timber which was regarded by a ship's carpenter as rotten to the core was viewed by a yard officer as only bruised.[28]

It was of course only natural that sea officers should be particular about the quality of equipment, stores or workmanship they permitted on board their ships; and the logical comparison for what they tolerated were the materials and workmanship available at dockyards. Disgust or scorn for the standards accepted in the yards was therefore expressed by most naval officers who recorded their views. Nelson was no exception. Following the mobilization of 1803 he informed St Vincent at the Admiralty:

> Every bit of twice-laid stuff belonging to the *Canopus* is condemned, and all the running-rigging in the fleet except the *Victory*'s. We fitted the *Excellent* with new main and mizzen rigging; it was shameful for the dockyard to send a ship to sea with such rigging.[29]

St Vincent on the other hand was able to encourage Nelson with the apparent truism that 'caulking and every other refitment which in England requires dockyard inspection your Lordship knows is much better performed by the artificers of the squadron'.[30]

There was certainly an element of truth in this. For the contempt poured on the dockyards was to some extent earned. A relative tolerance among yard officers of inadequacies in work performed or equipment supplied is not surprising. During periods of mobilization there were so many ships to prepare for sea that minor defects had regularly to be overlooked; and, even after the pace of work slackened, some still had to be fitted for temporary service though in need of general repair. The quantity of stores and equipment needed to maintain the fleet also dictated that vast amounts were repeatedly re-used. In 1803 many ships were thus fitted with an accumulation of used but 'serviceable' rigging. Even worn but undamaged hempen ropes were relaid. The yard officers were constantly making do. Their difficulties were crowned by their inability to supervise all work performed, especially that afloat, a problem acknowledged in October 1807 with the appointment of a Master Rigger at each yard. The contract riggers had a notorious reputation; they performed their work, according to Sir John Borlase Warren in 1791, 'in a slovenly and most indecent manner'.[31] But even they were not fully responsible for the behaviour of ropes fitted in wet weather which usually slackened on drying out.

Naval officers did not usually appreciate the shortages of reliable ships, equipment and labour which were often the real causes for their complaints. There was usually little understanding at the Admiralty either, and the complaints led to demands for explanation and inquiry by the Navy Board. Sometimes naval officers were also aggrieved at being refused alterations in the rig, equipment or internal fitting of ships. For, with the possibility of having to answer for their conduct, yard officers invariably kept to the letter of regulations governing ships' fittings. This had the advantage of avoiding exceptions which might form precedents for sea officers' future requests but it did little for immediate concord. Relations between yard and naval officers were accordingly often strained, with disagreements and disputes a regular feature. The poor opinion of the dockyards shared by sea officers was not therefore to be wholly trusted. Rather, the circumstances suggest that dockyard officers did well to achieve what they did in spite of numerous problems.

This view is reinforced when repair work is also considered. Thorough repairs were performed under much the same circumstances as refitting. Ships were wanted at sea but the time taken over the various stages of work was prolonged by insufficient docks and artificers. The quality of the work when completed was nevertheless usually sound and to a large extent vindicated the time spent upon it.

Without regular repair the life of a ship was short. Richard Pering, Clerk of the Cheque at Plymouth, claimed in a pamphlet printed in 1812 that first rates could run no longer than five or six years without repair and that the average life of the whole navy was no more than eight. This was contested by the *Quarterly Review* which claimed that the average life of the whole navy was $12\frac{1}{2}$ years.[32] Pering however was far closer to the truth. In the accounts the Navy Board provided for the information of the Admiralty only the very newest ships were estimated as being capable of running 'without repair' for eight years; an average for all the ships in commission was three to four years.[33] But approximations for the whole navy concealed much variation. Individual ships differed widely in their durability: some went years without repair while a few like the *Queen Charlotte* (100), launched in 1811, required almost immediate attention. Merchant-built ships were thought to have only two-thirds the life of dockyard ships; yet the timber shortage and increasing use of unseasoned and new materials made the durability of all, wherever they were built, a cause of growing concern.[34] It remained true, nevertheless, that regular, thorough repairs preserved ships from complete decay. It was significant, for example, that 12 of the ships of the line in commission in 1812 had been laid down before or during the American War of Independence.[35] Thanks to repeated repairs some of these ships had no doubt been almost completely rebuilt. But in this way, through repair in the dockyards, the navy was not only maintained but grew cumulatively.

The necessity for repairs stemmed from the nature of the ships that were built for the navy. Although damage was of course sustained in engagements or in grounding, their frames generally worked and their timbers were liable to be in a constant state of decay from 'dry rot'. Some defects were thus obvious to those who sailed in them; others were concealed and only uncovered during refitting; but most were discovered when the yard officers performed the survey which all ships received when they entered port in need of attention.

Until 1809 these surveys were relatively superficial. Certain timbers were bored to test their soundness, but the conclusions drawn were not always accurate enough to permit the Navy Board to advise the Admiralty of the amount of work involved and when it could be performed. The officers' reports simply described the scale of the defects, the time needed for their repair, whether docking was necessary and the probable costs in materials and workmanship. The scale of the defects was represented in terms of the estimated size of repair: either small, middling or large, these classes themselves being subdivided by such descriptions as 'very small', 'small to middling' or 'middling to large'. These descriptions were often seriously wrong: indeed 'so fallacious ... as to have occasioned ships to occupy a dock for a considerable time, the repair of which would not have been undertaken at all had their real state been known'.[36] As well as wasting dock capacity, the reports resulted in a gross waste of money. In 1806 the Commissioners of Naval Revision thus recommended that when boring suggested that repairs were necessary, planking should be stripped off and the amount of work properly examined with a new officer, the Master Measurer, accurately estimating the cost of the work on a detailed *pro forma*.[37] Nevertheless the amount of unplanking this involved was so considerable, with some ships having to be docked to be opened up, and the estimates proved so time-consuming to produce, that in 1811 there was a partial return to surveys which again relied to some extent on boring and the intuitive broad assessment of defects.[38]

When repairs were considered necessary the immediate fate of a ship depended on three factors: the relative extent of her defects; whether any other vessels at the yard needed docking more urgently; and whether a dock was available to take her. It was usually the policy that ships requiring the smallest repair had the preference. When defects in different ships were roughly comparable, ships of the line usually took preference. Even so the number of ships requiring repair always exceeded the number that could be taken in hand. At the height of both wars about 20 per cent of all ships of the line and 16 per cent of other vesels remained in Ordinary; between 1808 and 1812 ships of the line were being relegated to the Ordinary at the rate of 13 a year.[39]

The main problem was again the shortage of docks. Over half the 74s that were repaired between 1801 and 1805 were docked within two months of arriving in port; yet the average period for all of them was extended to five and a half months by some ships that were left in Ordinary more than a year.[40] The naval boards did what they could to reduce these periods. For example, in 1802 the occasional repair of private vessels was prohibited, unless specifically sanctioned; this had been a practice at Sheerness when private vessels had been damaged while under hire to the navy or by an accident involving naval vessels.[41] During particular emergencies repair work was also contracted out. In the first two years of the Revolutionary War nine frigates were repaired in this way; and in 1805 eight 64s and 12 frigates.[42] Yet these measures made little significant difference to the great number of ships repaired overall.

For, though there were considerable delays before work could begin, the longest stage in the repair process was the work itself. Even a 'small' repair for a 74 took about 10 weeks; a 'middling' one around 10 months; and a 'large' one approximately 16 months. 'Very large' repairs, which took anything up to two years, were condemned in 1792 on the grounds of their expense by Gabriel Snodgrass, Surveyor to the East India Company, who recommended that highly defective vessels should simply be replaced. He was echoed 20 years later by Richard Pering, who maintained that 'no ship ever received a thorough repair without costing more money than when she was built'.[43] The replacement of seriously defective ships by new ones, especially if these were built in merchant yards, would certainly have saved labour and made more docks available for refitting and minor repairs; but major repairs, extending so far as internal reconstruction, were never abandoned, for three reasons. The time they took was still usually much less than the time in which vessels of the same force could be built, even in the merchant yards. In general, they were performed on ships which, for their 'character', sailing qualities or a shortage of their class, the Admiralty wished to preserve. And during the Napoleonic War the increasing shortage of large oak timbers, especially those suitable for beams and knees, made the conservation of the largest ships easier than assembling the quantity of materials necessary for a new one.

Very large repairs were performed on only a minority of ships. But even small and middling repairs had their problems. After 1803 the timber shortage became so serious that shipwrights were sometimes forced to break off work on ships that required materials not then available and move on to other vessels. This reduced the earnings they were able to make by the piece, and thereby damaged morale.[44] Until 1803 'Job work', the system of piecework designed for repairs, was anyway of limited use as an incentive scheme, for until March 1803 a ceiling on earnings always restricted the amount men could make and thus the work they were prepared to perform in any one day. The removal of the ceiling, in the view of the yard officers, accordingly did much for the pace of repair work.[45]

The time taken over repairs was also reduced to a small extent by the introduction in 1800 of apparatus for gaining access to ships' keels. Previously when a keel, false keel or their adjacent timbers were inspected or repaired, the vessel had to be physically levered up on to blocks. When work was completed it had then to be gradually lowered. Great stresses were put on ships' frames and the whole business, raising and lowering, took three days for a 74. But in 1800 Robert Seppings, then assistant to the Master Shipwright at Plymouth, used with success a method of settling ships' keels onto iron wedges when they came into dock, shoring the ships up and removing the wedges one by one with a specifically designed battering ram until the necessary length of keel was exposed. When the inspection or repair was complete, the wedges were replaced and the shores removed. The Navy Board calculated that Seppings' apparatus saved seven-eighths of the expense of lifting ships by the old method, an economy in real terms of £11,000 over three years at Plymouth alone. But the saving achieved in time was even more valuable. The new apparatus permitted the whole length of a keel to be inspected within a day, and it therefore became possible to dock, inspect and launch a ship all while a spring or neap tide was near its height.[46] While ships requiring major repairs could be placed in Ordinary immediately, thereby permitting others to be docked, those that could be made good straight away could be repaired with relative ease and with less strain on their frames than formerly.

Nevertheless these innovations made little difference to the total length of time taken for thorough repairs. The patching of visible defects in ships wanted urgently for temporary service therefore continued throughout the wars. Indeed, even large repairs were done quickly on occasions when ships were desperately needed. Early in 1805 a considerable number of highly defective ships from the Ordinary had to be strengthened and made relatively water-tight. A method of strengthening was employed that had been used successfully on East India Company ships and had been proposed for the navy by Gabriel Snodgrass in 1795; it was recalled ten years later by Charles Patton and suggested to his brother Philip, then a Lord of the Admiralty. In February 1805 ships weak in the frame were thus ordered to be 'braced' and those rotten in their sides to be 'doubled' with three-inch plank from keel to gunwale. Minor defects were to be ignored, the yard officers being ordered 'not to strip the ships in search of defects or to mind decayed ceilings, riders or even a few timbers'.[47] Owing to the shortage of suitable frame timbers, iron knees, standards and diagonal braces were used. Between mid-March and the end of December 1805, 22 ships of the line, 11 frigates and a storeship were repaired in this way. According to the son of Charles Patton, over a dozen ships of the line were made ready for sea in six weeks, an achievement 'which would have required nine months by the old system'.[48]

Later Charles Middleton, Lord Barham, attributed some of the success of the squadrons at sea to the support of these rapidly repaired vessels. Yet those responsible for managing the repairs of ships, the Surveyors and Master Shipwrights, only approved of the method of repair as an expedient to be adopted in an emergency. When it was ordered, some yard officers feared that doubling would reduce the vessels' stability: 'an Indiaman and a man of war are ships of a very different description, the one carrying their weights below and the other aloft; of course their imperfections require to be remedied by different systems'.[49] A post mortem in July 1806 generally concluded that doubling simply fastened good wood to bad; that diagonal bracing provided the temporary transverse strength but could not prevent decayed timbers working; and that both methods of repair actually hastened a ship's disintegration.[50] Even so, in the spring of 1807, when ten ships of the line were wanted for service from the Ordinary, doubling was again thought necessary for two of them. Diagonal bracing was abandoned, however, horizontal shelfing and more iron fastenings being used to support deck beams and tie them to the sides.[51] Doubling nevertheless appears to have become a standard method of rapid repair. By 1813, when the Navy Board felt capable of speaking from experience, it approved of doubling because it saved time, workmanship and (as no English oak was used) materials. According to the Board, it had no serious effects on the sailing qualities of the ships.[52]

Relatively rapid repair, even of highly defective vessels, was not therefore out of the question. Yet, as ships aged, their suitability for service at sea naturally declined and there came a time when their condition did not justify repair. These vessels were eventually sold or taken to pieces. The simplest method of disposal was by sale, the purchasers of ships of the line or large frigates being bound by contract to break them up wherever there was a possibility of their being made good. This saved labour, for the dismantling of a frigate took a gang of shipwrights, another of scavelmen and two teams of horses more than a week; it saved public money, for the value of the timber obtained often failed to cover the cost of the labour; and it avoided the use of a dock. At the beginning of the Napoleonic War only about 20 ships were thus taken to pieces annually. During the Napoleonic War, however, the acute shortage of large beams, knees and other frame timbers gave those taken from old ships of the line a scarcity value. Often they were of little use 'on account of their varying so much from the form of the works in view and being so much bored in the course of ... several repairs and refittings'.[53] Even so, some timbers were occasionally useful and the possibility of obtaining others resulted in more ships being dismantled than formerly.[54] Thus of the 74s in the navy between 1801 and 1805, only 15 per cent were eventually sold and 68 per cent were taken to pieces.

During the Napoleonic War, apart from the need for timber, there was an added reason for dismantling old ships which otherwise had to be maintained in Ordinary. There was growing discontent at the cost of war and, to those unacquainted with the dockyards, the construction of new ships seemed more simple and more economical than the maintenance and repeated large repair of old ones. Facilities for new construction, moreover, were always available. After 1796 the building slips in all six yards had capacity to build simultaneously 11 first rates, 5 third rates, 8 frigates and 2 sloops. Yet it was a feature of the dockyards during wartime that this capacity was never fully used. Between 1793 and 1815 the royal yards launched only 41 ships of the line and 78 other vessels; and in many cases these ships took a considerable time to build. The *Temeraire* (98), launched in 1798, took five years; the *Centaur* (74), completed the year before, took more than six; the *Queen Charlotte* (100), completed in 1810, took five and a half years; the *Vindictive* (74), launched in 1813, only two months less.

The problem was relatively simple. With refitting and repairs taking priority there was never enough labour to devote to new construction, especially at the yards most accessible from the sea. In addition, during the Napoleonic War, the timber shortage caused serious difficulties. These problems were perhaps most fully examined by the Navy Board in August 1805, when Barham requested a complete report on the yards' building potential. The Board reported that at that time only 13 of the yards' 26 slips were actually in use and that over half of these were building ships smaller than those which they were capable of taking. But, the Board claimed, to have constructed ships of the largest size on each of the vacant slips and completed them in the shortest possible time would have absorbed the full-time labour of 40 men for a first rate, 30 for a third rate, 16 or 20 for a frigate (according to her size) and 12 men for a sloop. To have built the largest ship each slip would take in the shortest possible time would, therefore, have required the permanent employment on new construction of 150 shipwrights at Deptford, 140 at Woolwich, 192 at Chatham, 34 at Sheerness, 122 at Portsmouth and 130 at Plymouth. Yet skilled labour in such quantity was not available unless refitting and repairs were neglected. Similarly, the timber available would not meet the demand. At a time when its price was at a peak, the Board foresaw 'infinite difficulty in procuring . . . a sufficiency . . . to put the plan of laying down so many ships . . . into full activity'.[55]

The shortage of resources inevitably shaped the Navy Board's policy towards the acquisition of new vessels. When they were required, the Board generally depended on their availability for purchase or their construction by contract. Most vessels entering the navy were purchased, though only 250 over the whole period of the wars from private proprietors. The majority of these, moreover, were brigs and sloops, but including five 64-gun ships from the East India Company in 1797 and 1798. Most ships purchased were prizes, the Navy Board having first refusal from the agents of their captors. In all, 83 British ships of the line and 450 other vessels had this origin, making a large proportion of the navy foreign-built: over 25 per cent between 1797 and 1812 and as much as 35 per cent in 1801. Nevertheless, in that ships were built to specifications and to a completion date, construction by contract was a more reliable source. Sixty ships of the line, all 74s and 627 frigates, brigs and sloops were acquired in this way.

Together with ships purchased, construction by contract fully complemented the limited amount of building the dockyards performed. Indeed, apart from the year of peace, the navy grew steadily from 390 vessels in 1793 to 979 in January 1809, only then gradually falling away to 841 vessels in early 1815. Though ships of the line rose in number only slowly from 141 in 1793 to 215 in 1813, that of frigates and smaller vessels increased relatively rapidly at times, thereby permitting a fairly quick response to the demands of the war.

Nevertheless sea officers in particular believed that the quality of dockyard construction was superior to that achieved in merchant yards and that the failure to build to a greater extent in the dockyards left the navy heavily dependent on ships of dubious quality. It was a view which, as the length of the wars extended and the proportion of dockyard-built ships declined, had some justification. For there were a number of differences between dockyard and merchant operations. In the royal yards an Admiralty order required a stock of timber to be kept equal to three years' consumption, partly in order to allow the wood to season; but contractors had insufficient capital to do the same and purchased materials specifically for individual contracts, often with the aid of advances from the Navy Board. The duration of building provided more time for seasoning in the royal yards; but to maintain their profitability contractors had to complete their ships as quickly as possible, only allowing their frames to stand to season when this was specified in their contracts and, at the appropriate time, was authorized by the Admiralty. Workmanship was also thought to suffer on account of the speed of contract construction. Overseers were appointed from the nearest dockyard to check the quality of work but their supervision was not always effective. Thus the *Ajax* (74), launched in March 1798 at a cost to the public of £57,000, required 'defects made good' in December 1798 and a 'middling repair' in April 1802. Many of her knees had been 'grain cut' and broken. The two repairs cost an additional £44,000.[56]

Such instances of poor workmanship tended to confirm the contractors' general reputation. The latter believed it was a case of a few exceptions

Table 5. *A comparative account of naval tonnage launched in the Royal dockyards and in the merchant shipyards, 1793–1815*

| during course of year | Royal dockyards of line | under line | tonnage | merchant yards of line | under line | tonnage | total tonnage launched |
|---|---|---|---|---|---|---|---|
| 1793 | 2 | 2 | 4,606 | | 5 | 1,506 | 6,112 |
| 1794 | 2 | 5 | 6,350 | | 34 | 15,635 | 21,985 |
| 1795 | 1 | | 2,351 | | 20 | 10,410 | 12,761 |
| 1796 | | 9 | 6,845 | | 12 | 4,176 | 11,021 |
| 1797 | 2 | | 3,691 | | 46 | 16,220 | 19,911 |
| 1798 | 2 | 2 | 5,630 | 7 | 5 | 16,496 | 22,126 |
| 1799 | | 4 | 4,185 | | 1 | 956 | 5,141 |
| 1800 | 1 | 1 | 2,843 | 1 | 3 | 4,842 | 7,685 |
| 1801 | 2 | 2 | 4,258 | 1 | 22 | 7,451 | 11,709 |
| 1802 | | 2 | 2,221 | 1 | | 1,743 | 3,964 |
| 1803 | 1 | | 1,881 | 4 | 4 | 10,041 | 11,922 |
| 1804 | 1 | 6 | 6,518 | 2 | 78 | 22,156 | 28,674 |
| 1805 | 3 | 6 | 7,422 | | 66 | 18,466 | 25,888 |
| 1806 | | 2 | 1,653 | 2 | 71 | 26,266 | 27,919 |
| 1807 | 2 | 1 | 4,029 | 5 | 41 | 29,969 | 33,998 |
| 1808 | 4 | 4 | 10,478 | 3 | 69 | 26,884 | 37,362 |
| 1809 | 1 | 3 | 4,660 | 7 | 13 | 19,724 | 24,384 |
| 1810 | 3 | 4 | 10,614 | 8 | 14 | 22,215 | 32,829 |
| 1811 | 2 | 5 | 7,432 | 6 | 3 | 11,830 | 19,262 |
| 1812 | 1 | 7 | 8,575 | 11 | 32 | 31,751 | 40,326 |
| 1813 | 2 | 7 | 9,329 | 1 | 59 | 39,795 | 49,124 |
| 1814 | 4 | 3 | 11,506 | 1 | 23 | 13,380 | 24,886 |
| 1815 | 5 | 3 | 14,881 | | 6 | 2,860 | 17,741 |
| totals | | | | | | | |
| 1793–1815 | 41 | 78 | 141,958 | 60 | 627 | 354,772 | 496,730 |

proving the rule.[57] But the odds were against them. Of the 683 frigates and smaller vessels in the navy in June 1805 63 per cent were contract-built and only 13 per cent came from the dockyards. As contractors were restricted to ships no larger than 74s, the figures for ships of the line were more balanced; of 160 vessels, 36 per cent were merchant built and 39 per cent came from the dockyards.[58] Yet over all, even if contract-built ships were no more defective than dockyard-built ships, as they were more numerous in absolute terms there were always more needing repair. That they were not so poorly built is indicated by the life of the 74s in existence between 1801 and 1805: those from merchant yards had an average life of 40 years; those from the dockyards lasted only four years longer. Nevertheless at the time attention understandably focussed on the actual number of merchant-built ships needing repair.

There was accordingly a reaction to the heavy dependence on merchant building and efforts were made to increase dockyard construction. These efforts were first made, significantly, not by the Navy Board which was familiar with the merchant yards and relatively content with contracting, but by St Vincent when he was First Lord between 1801 and 1804. As a sea officer his indignation at the cost of replacing the knees in the *Ajax* knew no bounds and he instigated a prosecution of its builder. This only brought about a refusal of all the merchant builders to sign future contracts unless there was a clause 'to exonerate them from any responsibility [for their ships] after receiving the usual certificate for ... final payment'.[59] Yet St Vincent himself abstained from making contracts for ships of the line, initially on account of the return of peace in 1802 and later, when war resumed, due to the rising price per ton demanded by the builders, a price which reflected the scarcity and soaring price of large timber. St Vincent was convinced that the price of timber would stabilize and its availability would increase if merchant builders were not competing for it in the open market. He was led to believe that new construction in the dockyards could then be increased by shoaling or classing the shipwrights by ability. He was informed that, so organized, 46 shipwrights could build a 74 in one year and that in this way ten new ships of the line could be launched from the dockyards every year even during wartime when the whole fleet could still be kept in repair.[60]

St Vincent's scheme was nonetheless opposed by the dockyard artificers and by the Navy Board. The former were reluctant to have men of different abilities making significantly different earnings. The Board considered that, if deprived of the efforts of the most able, the artificers of middling and low ability would perform less work than when they had been grouped in gangs of mixed ability, and the total amount of work performed would drop. The Board was also deeply aware of the main advantage of contract building: that ships were built quickly, the time limits included in contracts being enforced by bond, thereby ensuring that 74s were regularly completed within three years. It was a method of construction which, in contrast to St Vincent's scheme, was tried and tested and, on this account, outweighed the disadvantage that ships so built might soon need repair.[61]

Melville and Barham, St Vincent's successors at the Admiralty, were both concerned to increase new construction in the dockyards. Ironically, St Vincent's refusal to contract for ships of the line left the navy in mid-1804 with few building and no immediate prospect of any being launched from private yards; the strength of the navy therefore depended on ships being laid down on every available slip without loss of time. Both Melville and Barham thus encouraged the Navy Board to make contracts with the merchant builders. Initially there were difficulties: St Vincent's policy had created considerable animosity. Some builders were unwilling to make agreements with the navy and the remainder only at an even higher price per ton than previously. Though it took eight months and the contract prices remained a record for the rest of the war, new contracts for an adequate supply of new 74s were made by January 1805. Yet these difficulties only drew attention to the need for a more reliable supply of new ships from the dockyards. Melville observed in September 1804:

> I had imagined that at any time we could derive substantial aid from the merchant yards and you know what blame was started against the late Board of Admiralty for not availing itself of that resource; but if it is a resource not to be depended upon when we are most in need of it we must turn all our minds to think how we can most effectually extend the means that now are or may be brought within our power . . .[62]

Aptly, in view of his great experience of yard management, it fell to Barham to take the steps necessary to improve the pace and output of dockyard construction. As First Lord, one of his first measures was to raise earnings by 'Task' – the system of piecework by which new building was performed – by 20 to 25 per cent.[63] As head of the Commission of Naval Revision, he was also responsible for recommending that the prices paid for articles of Task work be comprehensively overhauled and that Master Measurers departments be introduced. The new price schemes were introduced in 1811, when the new measuring departments were established. While the prices achieved a more equitable distribution of earnings than formerly, the measuring departments introduced a new independence and professionalism into the work of calculating wages.

There is some evidence to suggest that these measures had the desired effect. The tonnage of ships launched from the six royal yards in the nine years between 1805 and 1813 was almost double that launched over the same number of years between 1793 and 1801 – 73,337 tons as opposed to 41,498 tons.[64] And the average time taken to construct 74s diminished from almost four and a half years to less than three, though 10 were built in the later period and only six in the earlier one. By 1812 this increase in construction seems to have even influenced the attitude of the Navy Board. It intended in the following year to make no new contracts for ships of the line or frigates but to rely wholly on those completed in the dockyards.[65]

By this time, however, the Navy Board may have also been influenced by the enlargement of its sources of new ships. For ships were by then being built specifically for the navy at Milford in south Wales and at Bombay. Those built at Milford were few in number, the amount of labour and timber allowed the yard being relatively small to prevent the supply to the major yards being significantly reduced. The *Milford* (74) was launched there in 1809, having taken almost 11 years to build! New construction took place at Bombay from 1803, ships being built by the East India Company which drew bills on the Navy Board to meet the cost; since they were built of teak using company artificers, their construction made no drain on dockyard resources.[66] Attempts were also made to develop other new sources of new ships; Samuel Bentham, as Inspector General of Naval Works, was sent to Russia in 1805 in the hope that two 74s and two 36-gun frigates could be built there under his direction.

That venture was a failure. The construction of ships abroad was nevertheless regarded as desirable owing to the continuation of the timber shortage in England throughout the Napoleonic war. Though this reached crisis proportions early in 1804, when St Vincent attempted to do without timber contractors, and it often temporarily halted new construction during the remainder of the war, it never stopped building work at any yard for any significant time. This was principally because the shipwright officers in the yards quickly became accustomed to improvising, and the Navy Board to condoning departures from traditional practice. Knees and riders made from iron replaced those of wood and the scarphing or joining of timbers became usual.[67] In fact the timber shortage, while repeatedly providing cause for anxiety, created an environment in which innovation was encouraged and new building techniques were progressively developed. Coincident with attempts to evolve a greater body of theory and to instil a greater knowledge of these concepts into English shipwrightry, it is hardly surprising that important improvements were made. They were indeed long overdue.

During the eighteenth century warships had grown larger and heavier but their system of construction had remained largely unchanged; and, though the senior shipwright officers were usually literate and meticulous, construction had remained a craft proceeding primarily from practice and experience. After the keel was laid, stem-post, stern-post and deadwood were positioned and the futtocks, comprising the ribs or framing of the ship, were assembled and erected; deck-beams were secured to the frame timbers with knees and the whole was planked (to a large extent inside as well as out), caulked, launched and masted. The system had one particular weakness, however. The main framing was largely rectangular to the keel which was itself composed of several pieces. Under the stresses of service all ships worked and suffered from 'hogging', an arching of the keel whereby their stem and stern gradually settled lower in the water than the midships section. This process, by which the back of the ship was eventually broken, in fact began at launching; a ship of the line was then expected to 'break its sheer' by six or seven inches.[68]

Throughout the French wars improvements were made in both the design and the fittings of ships. But the Navy Board, and in particular the Surveyors, judged all proposals for improvements according to two main criteria, their dependability and their cost: 'However eligible plans which have from time to time been suggested, the result has not always answered the expectations formed from them.' The Board therefore considered it a duty 'to act with caution' and to point out to the Admiralty what was advisable 'previous to the adoption of any general plan which has not the authority of practice to prove the utility proposed by it, however plausible it may be in appearance'.[69] A similar caution governed its response to investments in experiments: it

# 1 Yard operations

*Shipping off Portsmouth Dockyard, 1790, by R. Dodd*

# 1 Yard operations

*Woolwich Dockyard, 1789, by R. Dodd*

'uniformly acted' according to the principle 'of not advancing money upon speculative improvements until some proofs have been had of their utility'.[70] Such caution was reinforced by a prejudice against any designs deviating from traditional patterns. Both Samuel Bentham and Robert Seppings, the two most innovative shipbuilders of the period, ran into it and their proposals for improvements suffered accordingly.[71]

Even so, improvements that were proved dependable relatively cheaply and conformed sufficiently with established ideas were adopted. Thus, for example, vertical air pipes were installed in ships between their lower decks and forecastles from February 1803; and an additional pintle was fitted to ships' rudders from March 1804. Such minor developments were preceded by few trials and little discussion. Yet even major changes were adopted relatively quickly as long as they conformed to the same criterion. Thus ships were constructed with high circular bows instead of the traditional beakhead after the improvement had been demonstrated in 1805 by Seppings when cutting down the *Namur* (90/74).[72] Even the traditional 'tumbling home' of ships' sides was moderated after wall-sided ships had been built by the East India Company.[73] Neither innovation was proved at a cost or risk to the navy.

Nevertheless the main course of shipbuilding practice remained conservative. In September 1806, for instance, Henry Peake, recently appointed a Surveyor at the Navy Board, took as the basis for his plan for a new 74 the draught of the *Courageux*, captured in 1762 and built at Brest before the Seven Years War. Ships like the *Leviathan* (74), built on her lines, he believed incapable of substantial improvement. Indeed, on account of the great similarity in the forms of ships, he could imagine 'little amendment . . . provided the principal dimensions are suitable to the required purpose of the ship and the plane of flotation such as to ensure stability'. He therefore solemnly assured the Board of Admiralty that he could propose no significant changes to what was continued long before his time, his alterations being 'more to ensure the qualities of the ship than to improve them'.[74]

Against such conservatism it required great confidence and persistence to carry projects for improvement even so far as a trial. Outstanding among those who did was Robert Seppings who, after rising in the yards to Master Shipwright at Chatham, became a Surveyor in 1813. While still a yard officer, from force of circumstances, he addressed himself to the two problems facing shipbuilding – the increasing shortage of large oak timbers and the structural weakness of large ships – and developed a new, comprehensive scheme of construction. His ideas possibly derived something from the repair of ships using diagonal bracing and shelf pieces in 1805 and 1806. For the main features of his scheme were the employment of diagonal trusses and riders to strengthen bottom and sides; the connection of beams to frame using shelf pieces and waterways instead of knees; the in-filling of the spaces between the bottom frame timbers to make a solid mass of timber; and the planking of decks diagonally to increase latitudinal strength.[75] Apart from resulting in more compact, tightly constructed ships, the scheme conserved timber, the diagonal trusses and in-filling consisting to a large extent of sound, previously used, timbers.

The whole scheme was not introduced at once. Rather, it was developed by stages, the parts being initially tried on ships under repair. In 1805 diagonal riders and trussing were proposed, and accepted, for the repair of the *Kent* (74).[76] In March 1810, however, on proposing the same method of repair along with in-filling for the repair of the *Tremendous* (74), the Navy Board failed to comply and directed Seppings 'to proceed with her in the usual manner'. It was only the intervention of the Admiralty, at this time led by Charles Yorke, that permitted Seppings to employ his method.[77] The *Tremendous* repair was a qualified success, diagonal decks being added later to strengthen her further. The repair of the *Ramillies* (74) and *Albion* (74) followed. The former was virtually rebuilt and her strength on completion was beyond doubt. Seppings requested that sights be placed on her decks prior to undocking and that, after she was afloat, her bowsprit, foremast and mizen-mast be put in but the main mast and all ballast left out so that great strain was put on her extremes without anything midships to counteract the pressure. Prior to undocking, supported under the bilge by the bare minimum of shores, the *Ramillies* altered her form one inch and an eighth, though remaining in that 'trying situation' 44 hours. Undocked and under stress for almost two days the plane of her decks again altered little more than one inch.[78] The report to the Navy Board was followed three weeks later by an order for all new ships then building and under large repair at Chatham to be fastened on Seppings' principle. Eight months later Seppings was made a Surveyor. At the Navy Board he was well placed to defend his system of construction and to extend it to all new ships building in the dockyards. The first of this new type was the *Howe* (120), completed in March 1815.

As the prime mover, Seppings himself must of course receive most of the credit for this great development in naval shipbuilding. But it should be noted that he was not working in isolation. Other officers, perhaps equally talented, were as prolific in their proposals.[79] Seppings also owed a great deal to Charles Yorke, a debt he formally acknowledged himself in August 1813.[80] Yorke was First Lord for barely 18 months but that brief period was of particular importance for naval shipbuilding. As a member of the Royal Society he had connections with men of science with whom he appears to have interested

---

*Table 6. The moorings for ships laid up, c. 1807*

|            | ships of the line | frigates | sloops | total |
|------------|-------------------|----------|--------|-------|
| Deptford   |                   | 32       | 5      | 37    |
| Woolwich   |                   | 14       | 16     | 30    |
| Sheerness  | 11                | 8        | 11     | 30    |
| Chatham    | 22                | 24       | 5      | 51    |
| Portsmouth | 48                | 31       | 5      | 84    |
| Plymouth   | 59                | 15       | 5      | 79    |
| totals     | 140               | 124      | 47     | 311   |

himself in the theory of floating bodies.[81] A practical consequence of the interest was the successful establishment of the school of naval architecture at Portsmouth in 1811. Recommended by the Commission of Naval Revision, the school was the first official attempt by government to bring about a fusion of the craft and embryonic theory of naval shipbuilding.

These developments nevertheless made little difference to the immediate concerns of the dockyards. In 1814–15, as in 1801–2, only the prospect and eventual arrival of peace altered the main pattern of operations. As priorities altered, refitting and repairs gradually gave way to a concerted effort to pay ships off and to reduce the expense of maintaining almost the whole fleet in commission. Pressure of work did not ease, for with ships entering port in a steady stream there was a vast quantity of equipment to receive, many thousands of men to pay, and the task of placing those vessels not sold or dismantled in Ordinary. A general plan of peace reduction was organized to some extent beforehand, the Admiralty being advised by the Navy Board of the yards to which ships should be sent, the distribution being primarily governed by the depth of water at available moorings. At the yards, after rigging, stores etc. had been returned and the ships checked by a superintending master and a clerk from the office of the Clerk of the Survey, the crews were paid off.

At this stage the superintending master who checked the ship took charge. 'Extra men' in the department of the Master Attendant stowed topmasts and yards between decks, and either dismantled the guns, placing them on the ballast in the hold, or, to reduce rust, secured them on their carriages as far from the gun ports as possible. To prevent hogging and to compensate for the loss in weight of men and equipment the ballast was increased so that the water-line remained within a foot of the ships' sailing draught.[82] The ships were then removed to their moorings, skeleton crews being appointed, consisting of petty officers and men responsible to the superintending master in charge of their division. By August 1803 the Chatham Ordinary consisted of 20 ships in Chatham Reach, 10 in Bridge Reach, 8 at Cockam Wood, 13 at West Gillingham and 4 in Long Reach, with 56 boatswains, 53 gunners, 58 carpenters and 145 seamen dispersed among them. These 55 vessels were organized in six divisions, each with a Superintending Master responsible to the Master Attendant. A similar Ordinary existed at the other yards.

The purpose of the 'shipkeepers' was to maintain the ships. They were expected to watch for fire, dragged moorings and pilferers, to maintain internal paintwork, but above all to ensure complete ventilation: for decay proceeded no less quickly in ships laid up than in those in service. The state of the Ordinary was accordingly described in 1812 as that 'in which a good sound ship may in the quietest manner possible become rotten in a given number of years without being of any use whatever in the meantime'.[83] To increase air circulation and reduce decay, shipkeepers were required to take up deck plants, open hatches and ports, and rig 'windsails' whenever possible to channel air below. Airing stoves were also used to dry out damp corners. As a protection against the extremities of the weather, awnings were rigged and lower masts 'housed', a protection that was increased after the Napoleonic War by the extension of roofing across some ships' upper works. Under these conditions, ships awaited their next commissioning.

# 2

# The facilities

Even to the undiscerning eye, the royal dockyards were impressive places at the end of the eighteenth century. Their very scale dwarfed the vast majority of other industrial establishments, even their component parts forming larger units of production than could be found elsewhere. Today their scale and appearance are still impressive, their past appearance being perhaps best appreciated from the remarkable bird's-eye views painted by Nicholas Pocock in the late 1790s (see pp. 62–71). These, used in conjunction with plans of the yards, show a similarity of arrangement between the larger yards – Portsmouth, Plymouth and Chatham – and the smaller ones – Deptford, Woolwich and Sheerness. Along the harbour or river frontage were wharves and jetties, mounting the occasional horse-powered crane. Breaking up the frontages were docks and building slips running back into the yard, and at Deptford, Portsmouth and Plymouth, the entrance to a basin from which radiated further docks and slips. Smaller channels also ran from the frontage to mast and boat ponds. Filling the remaining space were storehouses, mast and plank houses, seasoning sheds, saw pits, carpenters', joiners', smiths' and painters' shops, rigging houses, and at Chatham, Portsmouth and Plymouth ropewalks – that at Woolwich being a short distance from the yard. Open ground was invariably stacked with timber, while to the rear were officers' houses. A short distance from the frontage, in the river or harbour, was the sheer hulk, necessary for positioning ships' lower masts, and positioned at regular intervals up to several miles from the yards were ships in Ordinary, secured to chains moored to the sea or river bed.

If men, noise and activity were added to Pocock's scenes, it would be relatively easy to gain a sense of what the dockyards were actually like. Less easy to appreciate, however, would be the physical problems which limited the amount and the quality of dockyard work. According to the report of John Rennie in 1807 these were problems arising from the yards' age.

The several naval arsenals having been established at a period when her [Britain's] commerce was in its infancy and the arts of navigation but little understood, when her colonies were unimportant and the naval power necessary to protect her dominions was equally inconsiderable with that of the surrounding states, it was natural to choose situations adapted to the security, number and small dimensions of her ships of war and to lay out their establishments of docks, quays and storehouses upon a corresponding scale. But the vast increase that has taken place particularly of late years in the size and number of her vessels of war and the extent and frequency of repairs induced by the different system of naval warfare now pursued have rendered these arsenals . . . quite inadequate to the reception and renovation and equipment of her numerous fleets.[1]

The yards' accessibility, arising from their situations, was perhaps their principal problem. Plymouth was the yard best served by its harbour, which gave easy access to the sea. Even so, in 1806 St Vincent observed that in winter months Cawsand Bay was 'a very unsafe place for large ships to resort to, dangerous in the extreme and such a swell that five days out of seven nothing can lay alongside of them. Several have been put to the utmost hazard of knocking their bottoms out.' He believed Plymouth Sound had become 'shoaler' than it was and that if embankments forming above Catwater were not 'put an immediate stop to and the tide suffered to flow as formerly' the Sound as well as Catwater would be ruined as anchorages.[2] These comments reflected the geography of the area. The waters around Plymouth were almost all exposed to southerly gales: in a sudden storm of wind early one morning in January 1804 three yard lighters, two launches, a barge, a gun brig and the ships *Loire* (40), *Boadica* (38) and *Temeraire* (98) all received damage, though moored relatively close to the yard. Even during calm weather shoals still made the waters dangerous and were increasing in Catwater and Hamoaze, where the rivers Plym, Tamar and Tavy entered the Sound and deposited matter gathered from mine workings as well as natural erosion. During the first eight months of 1805 five ships took the ground coming in or going out of Hamoaze.[3]

Portsmouth harbour was more sheltered but there the silting was far more serious. The local bedrock was less resistant to erosion than the granite of the south-west; the rivers entering the harbour were smaller and more full of alluvial matter during floods; and the harbour itself was smaller and had been subject to man-made encroachments, which combined with the narrow harbour entrance to check the flow of the tide and river currents and reduce their power to carry alluvium out to sea. Silting most gravely affected the navy at the harbour mouth, where a bar had gradually reduced the depth at low water from (according to Rennie's information) 18 feet in 1693 to 16 feet in 1724 and 14 feet in 1784. The problem was exacerbated by a relatively moderate rise in the tide, spring tides adding 12 to 15 feet and extraordinary ones up to 16 feet. Ships with a 24-foot draught could get out of the harbour on a spring tide with a fresh breeze relatively easily;[4] but at the height of these tides, steerage was difficult, especially with the flow turning: an eddy ran across the channel on both sides of the harbour mouth and ships risked being driven ashore, particularly when a cross wind added to the force of the eddy. In 1804 the yard officers rejected the suggestion that ships could be warped or towed out on the grounds that even six-oared cutters were too weak to pull against the tide at its height. During neap tides the same problems occurred to a smaller degree, ships up to 23 ft draught being able to navigate the bar.[5] Ships of the line were consequently surveyed at Spithead; their lowerdeck guns were removed before they were brought into harbour; and their movements both in and out were timed to coincide with the ebb and flow of tides of the necessary height.

If the harbour at Portsmouth was too confined, at Sheerness it was too exposed. At the mouth of the Medway and close to the Little Nore, the waters off Sheerness were sometimes congested with ships, obstructing traffic to and from the yard. But this area was exposed to prevailing south-westerly winds and vessels laying alongside 'receiving ships' were often damaged by heavy seas. Serious damage was sustained by four ships during gales in 1803 when each broke its moorings and went aground or collided with another. Ships moored opposite the yard, across the Medway, were no more safe for there deep water alternated with foul ground and they could not easily beat back towards Sheerness or out to the Nore.[6]

The inadequacies of these harbours were, however, merely inconveniences compared with the navigational problems of reaching Deptford, Woolwich and Chatham. The meandering courses of the Thames and Medway made progress along any of the reaches dependent on favourable combinations of wind and tide. With Deptford about 50 miles from the Nore, Woolwich 42 and Chatham almost 20, combinations that were unfavourable inevitably resulted in delays. Even to begin these journeys all but the smaller frigates were detained by the necessity of reducing their draught.

For those progressing to Deptford or Woolwich, spring tides provided only 19 feet of water and neap tides 2 feet less.[7] Only frigates up to 38 guns were thus sent to Deptford and even they had their guns removed at Northfleet Hope or Gravesend. Larger ships going to Woolwich left guns and stores at Gravesend. Rennie believed that the natural silting of the Thames was aggravated by two further factors: the amount of matter deposited in the river in London and the reduction of the pace of tidal flow by the proliferation of wharves and jetties and by the partial damming of the river by London Bridge. During the Revolutionary War silting at Woolwich was also increased by the digging of foundations for a new river wall for the dockyard. Owing to a private wharf and hardshore upstream, the silt settled in front of the yard between the moorings for the Ordinary. This in turn resulted in the progressive movement of the main river channel towards the opposite shore. With even frigates going aground at lower water, the moorings for the Ordinary had also to be moved further from the yard.

The Medway below Chatham was less shallow than the Thames below Deptford, but deposition had nevertheless reduced the depth of the moorings in the river by an average of two and a half feet between 1724 and 1803. By the later date ships up to 64 guns could sail no higher than Gillingham Reach without removing their guns, and all larger vessels had to do so before leaving Pinup Reach. Those fitting had invariably to be taken as far as Blackstakes at the mouth of the Medway to receive guns, stores and provisions by lighter. As in the Thames, Rennie believed that the problem was aggravated by a reduction in the pace of tidal flow, resulting from the partial dam formed by the bridge at Rochester.

Rennie's report on these problems of access was unprecedented in its detail. But the problems he examined were clearly not new. A cause of growing inconvenience throughout the second half of the eighteenth century, they had

*Portsmouth Harbour in 1797*

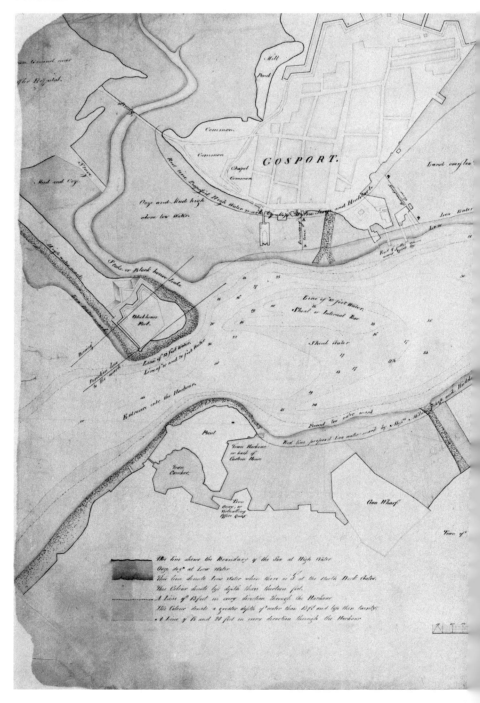

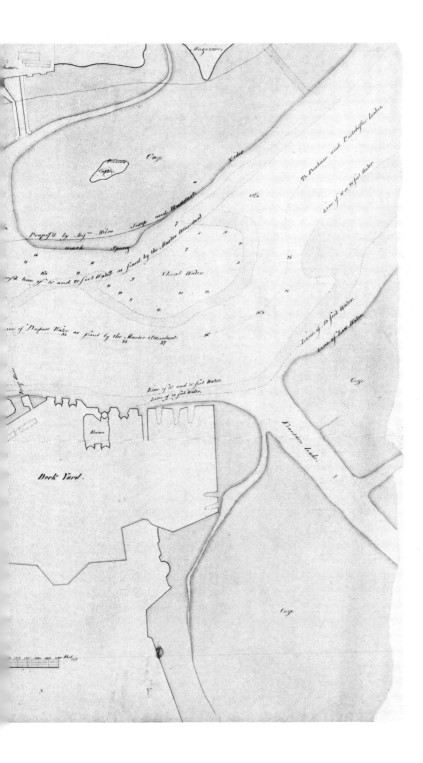

43

not however been considered sufficiently serious to warrant the adoption of any long-term solutions. The growing difficulties of reaching the eastern yards had, on the other hand, been reflected in the failure to build more docks in the east than had existed at the beginning of the Seven Years' War. Consequently by the end of the century – as the distribution of ships refitted in 1805 reveals – the relative inaccessibility of the inland eastern yards severely curtailed their contribution to the work of maintaining ships in commission. Their shortage of docks, moreover, meant that even had more ships been sent east, to reduce the queues at Portsmouth and Plymouth, they would have been dealt with no earlier. Indeed, their wait for a dock was likely to have been longer.

In general, the docks themselves did not meet the needs of the navy either. Until about 1800 the docks at all the yards were too shallow to receive large ships of the line without their draught being reduced and their being hauled in and out on spring tides – operations which inevitably damaged keels and coppering. Also they were not water-tight, water seeping in as tides rose and interfering with work in dock bottoms. It was noted that at Chatham, even at the end of the Napoleonic War, docks did not close with gates turning on hinges 'but with three great wooden panels, set at low water, and kept in their places by solid stanchions'.[8]

The number and size of the building slips available was less of a problem. The number of artificers that could be spared from the more urgent tasks of refitting and repairs meant that the amount of new construction performed even in the eastern yards was limited. Consequently there was rarely difficulty in finding a vacant slip whenever a ship was ordered to be laid down. Indeed in 1796 the yards lost a slip at Portsmouth, when more docks were built, without its loss being felt afterwards.

There were, however, a number of other inadequacies that were common to most of the yards. There was in particular a shortage of storage space. Sheerness required the use of the garrison buildings and the hulks on the

---

*Table 7. The number of docks in 1753–5 and 1793–1815*

(s = single   D = double)

|            | 1753–6 |     | 1793–6 |     | c.1801–15 |     |
|------------|--------|-----|--------|-----|-----------|-----|
| Deptford   | 1s     | 1D  | 1s     | 1D  | 1s        | 1D  |
| Woolwich   | 1s     | 1D  | 1s     | 1D  | 1s        | 1D  |
| Chatham    | 4s     |     | 4s     |     | 4s        |     |
| Sheerness  | 2s     |     | 2s     |     | 2s        |     |
| Portsmouth | 4s     |     | 4s     | 1D  | 8s        |     |
| Plymouth   | 1s     | 1D  | 3s     | 1D  | 3s        | 1D  |
| totals     | 13s    | 3D  | 15s    | 4D  | 19s       | 3D  |

foreshore for storage; at Portsmouth the only new land available was that which could be formed from 'the ooze'; space at Plymouth had to be blasted from the hill backing the yard; Deptford and Woolwich yards were simply confined until lands adjoining came up for sale. Overcrowding compounded a further problem, the often inconvenient siting of offices and storehouses; for until space was made or released reorganization was difficult. The problem affected not only the ease with which the officers could reach, and stores be transported to, the places where they were needed, but the related problems of control and embezzlement. Finally, three yards – Portsmouth, Plymouth and Sheerness – had no natural supplies of fresh water, having their respective requirements shipped from Southampton Water, Southdown and Chatham.[9] Not only was the water needed for work in the yards but for the supply of ships replenishing or fitting.

Table 8. *The building slips, showing the largest rate of ship each could accommodate*

| Deptford yard | Slip | 1 | 74-gun 3rd rate |
| | | 2 | 1st rate |
| | | 3 | 1st rate |
| | | 4 | 32-gun frigate |
| | | 5 | 32-gun frigate |
| Woolwich yard | Slip | 1 | 1st rate |
| | | 2 | 74-gun 3rd rate |
| | | 3 | 1st rate |
| | | 4 | 38-gun frigate |
| Chatham yard | Slip | 1 | 1st rate |
| | | 2 | 1st rate |
| | | 3 | 1st rate |
| | | 4 | 36-gun frigate |
| | | 5 | 74-gun 3rd rate |
| | | 6 | 33-gun frigate |
| Sheerness yard | Slip | 1 | 38-gun frigate |
| | | 2 | sloop |
| Portsmouth yard | Slip | 1 | 1st rate |
| | | 2 | 74-gun 3rd rate |
| | | 3 | 74-gun 3rd rate |
| | | 4 | 28-gun frigate |
| | | 5 | sloop |
| | | [6 | destroyed in 1796–7] |
| Plymouth yard | Slip | 1 | 1st rate |
| | | 2 | 1st rate |
| | | 3 | 1st rate |
| | | 4 | 28-gun frigate |

# 2 The facilities

These deficiencies were apparent to most officials in the yards and at the Navy Office. Yet in the late eighteenth century they were generally accepted. They were problems that had been inherited, had always caused difficulties so far as anyone could remember, and probably always would. Plans of improvement were carried out. Sums were earmarked for repairs, enlargements and new building in each year's naval estimates. Nevertheless the sums so obtained did not go far, while the prevalence of war for 15 of the last 25 years of the eighteenth century hindered major works being carried out. Thus Portsmouth yard in the 1790s was still being improved according to a scheme drawn up in the 1760s.[10] Moreover, these plans were from necessity governed by immediate needs and by existing yard structures rather than by the unforeseeable needs of the far greater navy of the future. The technology these schemes employed was also, by the 1790s, relatively outdated, for – except for a brief period during the American War of Independence, when an 'inspector' of civil building works had been employed – the execution of these works had been entrusted to yard officers who had no expertise in the developing sciences of civil and mechanical engineering. Early in the 1780s the use of steam power had been considered but not adopted, probably owing to a fear of fire, although various operations were adaptable to its use.[11] To those interested in the latest engineering developments, the level of technology employed in the dockyards was a fact of some note. The surveyor to the East India Company, Gabriel Snodgrass, observed in 1791 for example that the practice of heaving ships into dock with tackles was 'very absurd' and was surprised that it should have continued to that time,

> when by taking a view of the locks . . . on the various inland navigations in this country, they would at once point out a more rational and much easier method of docking . . . large ships . . . without the least difficulty by filling the docks with water to any height required by means of a reservoir sufficiently large for that purpose, which may be always supplied and kept full by a steam engine . . . at a very small expense and to the greatest advantage.[12]

The relative backwardness of the dockyards and the possibilities of the new technology were not allowed to escape the attention of the Admiralty during the 1790s. Even before the Revolutionary War, naval officers made known their belief that ships as well as yards required improvement. Pressure on the Admiralty mounted as plans to effect such improvements were proposed from outside the naval departments. In 1795 it was the 'very general wish and expectation' of the House of Commons 'that something should be done by Administration'; it was thought foreign nations were 'labouring and may be expected to labour more and more strenuously every day in pursuit of improvements' and it seemed 'neither becoming nor provident . . . to be left altogether behind in a pursuit so much our own'.[13] Charles Middleton, then at the Admiralty, responded with a proposal for an 'intermediate sea board . . . qualified to inspect and report on all plans of improvement which may be offered relative to naval matters'. But following communications with Samuel Bentham in June 1795 he altered his recommendation in favour of an arrangement proposed by Bentham for an individually responsible Surveyor General with an office staff attached to the Admiralty.[14]

Bentham was the great innovator in this period of dockyard development. Though from a cultured well-to-do family, brother to Jeremy and step-brother to Charles Abbot, later Lord Colchester, he had served a shipwright's apprenticeship in Woolwich and Chatham dockyards. But then, frustrated by the premium placed on practical experience and the need for seniority and influence to obtain rapid promotion, he had travelled abroad and entered the Russian service in which he had risen to the rank of Brigadier-General by 1791. At this time he had taken leave of absence to study the progress made in the introduction of machinery into manufacturing processes in England and had himself patented machinery for working in wood in 1791 and 1793.[15] He was no great scientist; Captain Thomas Hamilton's later opinion of him was probably near the mark: 'General Bentham is a clever knowing man; "amongst the blind the one-eyed are kings"; his mechanical science goes no further than what is common among ingenious artists'.[16] But he was enthusiastic, ambitious and not to be deterred by officials, whatever their status. In 1795 Middleton was impressed by him: 'undoubtedly a man of first-rate abilities and of great experience in practical mechanics'.[17] Bentham had, moreover, with Admiralty sanction, already inspected the dockyards and subsequently proposed alterations in the plan for improving Portsmouth yard which permitted the Admiralty 'for their present estimate to treble the capabilities of the yard'.[18] He had in addition, having proposed novel methods for constructing ships, been authorized to build according to his own specifications two sloops of war, four schooners and a water vessel at Redbridge, Hampshire. However, before any of these schemes could be practically tested, his office arrangement was accepted and he, as he had no doubt hoped, was nominated for the post (now altered in title) of Inspector General of Naval Works.

Bentham's office was officially established at the Admiralty by an order in council of 23 March 1796. He was instructed to consider all matters relating to 'the improvement of the building, fitting out and arming of . . . ships and vessels as well as what may conduce to the better navigating and victualling of them; the construction of docks, slips, basins, jetties and other works subservient to the construction of the ships and vessels; together with the choice, preservation and economical employment of the several stores and provisions made use of in the navy'. Besides a secretary and two clerks, he had to assist him an architect/engineer, a mechanist, a chemist and a draughtsman.[19]

Between 1796 and 1805, when he was sent to Russia, Bentham laboured to introduce the latest technology. Throughout his work, partly owing to his own ideas and personality and partly to a mutual interest in the dockyards, he was repeatedly in conflict with the Navy Board. Holding an advisory post and being uninvolved in the immediate business of waging war, he was able to form comprehensive plans for the redevelopment of the yards. The Navy Board, on the other hand, concerned to maintain for the present the highest level of dockyard performance, was unwilling to allow works which could have seriously handicapped a yard. On the whole, however, while he had the support of First Lords Spencer and St Vincent, Bentham gained more in the contest than did the Board.

Indeed, for a period of activity lasting less than a decade Bentham's achievements were considerable. Having referred to him by the Admiralty all business connected with physical improvements, he had repeated opportunities to propose innovations and reorganization. As they were in constant use, buildings often reached a state of serious dilapidation before they were referred to him; over six months in 1805 four were reported as falling down and dangerous. When complete reconstruction was necessary, Bentham attempted to reorganize the location of offices and workshops, bringing the offices of subordinates under the same roof as that of their principal officer, locating them close to the area of practical work with which they were concerned, and creating the optimum working space both inside the offices and outside.[20]

He also addressed himself to the problem of water supply. At Plymouth the Plymouth Dock Water Company had been empowered by an Act of 1793 to channel water from Dartmoor to supply local towns and naval establishments and by March 1797 had pipes laid to the dockyard gates. Disagreements between Bentham and the yard officers over the site of the reservoir then, however, delayed the provision of supplies within the yard until after 1804.[21] Another water company was prepared to supply water to Sheerness dockyard by 1800, but Bentham suggested the completion of a well in Mayor's Marsh near to the yard which had been begun early the previous century by the Navy Board. The recommendation was adopted, the well being ready to supply water by March 1801.[22] At Portsmouth Bentham also had a well dug by 1801. There he had cast iron pipes laid by 1805 to convey water to all parts of the yard where ships fitting, water vessels and artificers required their supplies.[23] By 1809 these pipes were, in addition, part of a ring-firemain connected to a water tower.

It was at Portsmouth that Bentham performed his most important work. Following his visit there in 1795 he proposed two schemes. By one, in spite of Navy Board opposition, the boat pond was converted into a basin for small vessels, and the channel leading to it into two docks for frigates, separated from the sea by a lock.[24] The other, his principal scheme, was intended to allow ships of the line to dock without the removal of their guns and stores. It entailed halving the length of the existing double dock, deepening and enlarging the basin, and increasing the number of docks leading from it to four by the construction of two new deep ones. Bentham argued that the scheme would result in several distinct benefits: the yard's dock capacity would be enlarged; a saving would be effected in the expense as well as in the delay involved in dismantling and later re-equipping vessels; four ships could be docked or undocked at any time regardless of the tide; and the turn-around time of ships in commission would be improved, so increasing the frequency with which the docks were used. There were additional parts to the plan, such as the erection of jetties into Portsmouth harbour to facilitate ships' refitting, but they met with solid and irrefutable objections from the yard officers and Navy Board.[25]

Both schemes were completed about 1801. The addition of the new docks at Portsmouth was important in itself. It is true that the deep docks and basin did not result in a noticeable improvement in the turn-around time of large ships at Portsmouth, possibly because (as the yard officers pointed out in 1795) four ships were rarely ready to go into dock together; work on them had to proceed by stages, most stores and ballast having to be removed to provide access for caulkers, who often uncovered timbers that had to be shifted; and the weight of fully loaded ships on shores would have been damaging to both the ships and the docks.[26] They were nevertheless a marked improvement on the original facilities. While ships could be put out of dock into the basin, others could be taken from the basin into dock, and to this extent the yards' operations became independent of the tides.

This small advance in efficiency depended to a large extent on the method by which the water levels in the docks and basin were regulated. To ensure that the basin and docks were water-tight, Bentham designed movable caissons or floating dams which were raised and lowered within grooves by being emptied and filled with water by means of a penstock and pump. The water with which ships came into the basin and docks was removed by natural drainage and pumping and retained in a reservoir; it could later be returned when a ship was ready again for undocking. A steam engine was employed for these pumping operations, a small 12-horse-power Sadler engine which Bentham had ordered for Redbridge in Hampshire being installed in 1798. This was soon succeeded by a Watt 30-horse-power engine, a second engine being installed by 1805 to prevent inconvenience when one broke down. In 1818 one engine was said, somewhat improbably, to drain a dock in 'a few minutes'.[27]

Apart from pumping, these engines were used for a number of other purposes. Soon after his appointment Bentham began planning a woodmill (containing machines that could side, slit, edge, plane, tongue and groove) to be driven, and to which timber could be drawn, by the power of an engine.[28] Though the mill was formed by September 1802, it was then extended over the next six years to include Marc Isambard Brunel's block-making machinery. Simultaneously a copper smelting and rolling mill was developed to recycle old copper sheathing for ships' hulls. In 1801, to facilitate pumping, driving and haulage operations at different places, Bentham even proposed a movable steam engine which came into operation in 1802.[29]

The success of these innovations stimulated a more widespread adoption of machinery during the closing years of the Napoleonic War. Yet Bentham's initial efforts to vindicate the advantages of mechanization were only achieved at a cost, for the developmental stages in the establishment of the mills, and of the block-making and copper recycling processes, were more of a nuisance to the Navy Board than of any advantage to the navy.

The Navy Board was not averse to innovation, especially where it improved the performance of manufacturing processes. This is evident from the history of one existing process, ropemaking. Proposed improvements were regularly given trial: for example, in 1792 a horse-powered engine of Benjamin Seymour's construction.[30] And some improvements were made: Watson Fenwick made five contributions to the manufacturing process between his appointment as Master Ropemaker at Chatham in December 1798 and December 1803. The improvers were, moreover, usually rewarded: Fenwick was recommended for a dockyard house in 1803 even though this 'convenience' was not usually attached to his post.[31] But the Board had other factors to consider besides the simple efficiency of a process. In 1805 it thus opposed Bentham's plan for a new steam-powered ropery at Woolwich, though the plan had been preparing for three years, with arguments that included the beliefs that the site chosen would leave insufficient space for landing, surveying and storing timber and other stores, and that in spite of its expense the ropery would not meet the full needs of the navy.[32] In 1808, however, when the navy's demand for cables and cordage necessitated an increase in supply, to avoid increasing the quantity obtained by contract, the Board itself proposed the partial use of steam power at Chatham, a proposal eventually adopted 30 years later.[33]

The Navy Board was above all concerned with the quantity and quality of supplies. It required, as far as was possible, absolute dependability. It accepted the need for steam power when it obviated the need to employ contractors, when manual labour to perform the work was not available in the yards, when the risk of fire was slight, and when the quality of the product could be assured. Only if these conditions were fulfilled was it prepared to abandon the convenience and security of existing arrangements. For the development of new or expansion of existing manufacturing departments entailed no less organization than that which faced a private industrialist. Once the finance was available, the workshops had to be found or built, equipment and machinery installed, supplies of raw materials or components arranged, workmen recruited and trained, and a wages scale and production process established. Even then there was the risk that the contractors on whom the Board had formerly relied would find new markets or cease production before yard output could meet demands.

The formation of both the block and the metal mills involved all these problems. Their development, moreover, was overlaid with the difficulties of Board relations with Bentham. It was his superior influence with the Admiralty that got the schemes adopted but it was the Navy Board which had the responsibility for supplying the navy and felt directly the risks of failure. In the case of the block mill, the Navy Board had in fact already rejected Brunel's proposed machines for mass-producing blocks. Bentham, however, argued for their installation using statistics drawn from Navy Board accounts of contracts for blockmakers' wares and of yard consumption of those supplies.

Bentham's arguments for developing both mills were that improvements in efficiency and economy would result. By enlarging the woodmill at Portsmouth and installing Brunel's machines, blocks would be 'made better as well as cheaper'.[34] By establishing the metal mill and re-processing old sheathing and manufacturing other copper articles, experiments could be conducted on different types of copper, including foreign metals, to determine specifications for the best quality product; with copper of increased resistance to wear, ships would require sheathing repairs less often; the public would also be saved the expense of the contractors' transport costs and profits, some of the losses from embezzlement, and the wasteful practice of burning off weeds from old sheathing.[35]

Bentham concentrated on the political task of retaining Admiralty support for the mills while delegating much of the practical organizational work at

Portsmouth to more competent men – the inventor of the machinery, M. I. Brunel, in the case of the block mill, and W. E. Sheffield, recruited from private industry, for the metal mill. Their skills were absolutely essential to the success of the projects. They experienced similar difficulties, though Brunel's, due to the novelty of the block mill, were less easily solved.

What seemed Brunel's most serious problem, the construction of the block-cutting machines, in fact proved the least intractable. Brunel communicated his plans to Henry Maudsley by the semi-secret Monge method of mechanical drawing.[36] Maudsley then appears to have produced the machines with such precision that his casting, forging and tooling rarely, if ever, had to be corrected. Machines to complete blocks from 7 to 10 inches long were completed in July 1803, from 4 to 7 inches in 1804, and from 10 to 18 inches in 1805.[37] As he installed these machines, Brunel himself occasionally required alterations to improve the production process. To achieve a steady flow of block parts through the mill, he also ordered more of some types of machine than of others.

Manning the production lines proved more difficult. Although the yards had each employed several blockmakers to repair blocks, insufficient skilled men were available, especially for finishing the machine-made blocks. Labourers and house carpenters had to be employed from the men already in the yards, using extra allowances for those who 'attained assiduity' to encourage them to acquire the necessary skills.[38]

Certain parts and materials were hard to get too, especially the lignum vitae for the sheaves which turned inside the blocks. Most of it was brought back to England as a private venture by the masters of merchant vessels delivering cargoes in the West Indies and its price was 'exorbitant'. The Navy Board was obliged to request Commissioner Stirling at the naval establishment in Jamaica to obtain a supply and to send it to England in returning transports.[39] It was planned that the iron pins and brass coaks or bearings upon which the sheaves rotated would be supplied by the metal mill – for which purpose Brunel in 1806 designed a particular machine. Until the metal mill was functioning, however, Brunel had to obtain his pins and coaks from Maudsley. Any other contractor, Brunel considered, would have been 'impracticable', for to achieve a mass production and assembly process the coaks had to be 'cast with sufficient nicety so as to fit' the block parts 'without the least trimming'. Brunel's confidence in Maudsley was well founded: by October 1804 the latter was ready 'to cast ten or twelve thousand of the sizes which are now wanted' and all at a few days' notice.[40]

Through Brunel and Maudsley's attention to detail, from 19 November 1803 the block mill began supplying the six dockyards with blocks of between 5 and 10 inches. Between that date and 30 April 1805 the mill produced parts for over 57,000 blocks.[41] As more machines were installed and men trained, the range of blocks produced and the total size of output gradually grew. By 1808 the mill had an annual output of 150,000 blocks.

But completion of the mill took far longer than expected, according to the Navy Board, on account of the many additions and alterations Brunel thought necessary. According to Brunel, however, it was due primarily to the continuing growth in the size of the navy and the necessity repeatedly to enlarge the output target. This had originally been based on the demands of the navy between 1797 and 1801; but after the mill was already far forward he 'found it necessary to give such a disposition to the building and machinery so as to enable it to supply a much greater proportion of work than was at first calculated'. The additions, alterations and improvements were, moreover, 'much more difficult to be carried into execution than the first erection'.[42]

For the Navy Board the delays in completion simply prolonged its uncertainty over its supply of blocks. The contractors too had no assurance for their future, though repeatedly requested to continue production for the navy. Between March 1803 and June 1805 the contract of Mr Taylor of Southampton, who supplied all the yards except Plymouth, was renewed four times. Both he and Mr Dunsterville, who supplied Plymouth, expected to have to sell their works. There was thus real foundation to Taylor's complaint in November 1804 that the board was 'really making . . . use of us for the present, leaving us to bear all the expense, trouble and loss in the future'.[43]

Independence of the block contractors drew one step closer in March 1805 when the metal mill began supplying some of the coaks for the blocks. For the Navy Board the principal problem in the development of this mill was again the uncertainty of supplies during the period before it was able to supplant the sheathing contractor in meeting the navy's requirements. The machinery and skilled labour necessary were more readily available than they were for the block mill, but there were delays and breakages in the delivery of the equipment. A furnace for melting the old copper was installed at Portsmouth by October 1803, but the second furnace for refining it and the rolling machinery were not ready to produce sheathing until September 1805. In addition, the furnaces necessary at the other yards to melt the old copper into pigs for shipment to Portsmouth were not ready for use until May 1804.[44] Yet by then, owing to the accumulation of old copper at Portsmouth from October 1801 and at the other yards from August 1802, the contractors had become short of the quantity of copper necessary to meet the navy's demands for sheathing. In August 1803, 470 tons of old copper were stored in the six yards.[45] As there was already a national shortage, the Navy Board was obliged thereafter on a succession of occasions to request the Admiralty to permit the contractors to purchase a quantity. Losses of ships belonging to the Mines Royal Company by capture and foundering in 1804, and the bad weather and frosts, resulting in the freezing of canals during the following winter, sustained the sheathing supply problem until the metal mill was completed.[46]

The principal technological innovations of the period were therefore not accomplished without significant difficulties. In view of the Navy Board's responsibility for supplying the navy, these difficulties perhaps explain why the Board was consistently chary of the advantages of improving the output of yard departments through greater mechanization. Bentham and his influence with the Admiralty was of course regarded as the primary cause of the difficulties associated with the block and metal mills. It was thus almost inevitable that while he was in Russia between 1805 and 1807 the Commissioners of Naval Revision, on the recommendation of the Navy Board, should propose that the office of the Inspector General of Naval Works be abolished and its principal personnel be moved to the Navy Office to form the department of the Civil Architect and Engineer. There, between 1808 and 1812, Bentham achieved little, his proposals being immediately subject to the will of the Board and his office being given supervision of building works in all naval establishments.[47] For views on major works, the Admiralty took more notice of outside specialists, in particular of John Rennie, who was making a reputation for himself. Bentham completely disappeared from naval works in 1812 when his office of Civil Architect and Engineer was abolished, only the assistant architect being retained as Surveyor of Buildings.

It was significant that during Bentham's period of influence at the Admiralty he proposed no major works at the Thames and Medway yards, merely providing plans for repairs that he pursued with little enthusiasm. At these yards decay proceeded apace: number one dock at Chatham was in need of serious repair in 1801 and still 'a disgrace to the arsenal' in 1805; the following year a dock at Deptford had to be repaired 'as in its present state it will not admit of a ship being repaired in it'.[48] In April 1800 Bentham, like Rennie in May 1807, gave as his official opinion that Deptford, Woolwich and Chatham yards would eventually have to be run down and a new yard formed.[49] Neither man saw any long-term reason to extend or improve the facilities at the eastern yards. Although Sheerness was accessible – Bentham thought its situation 'exceedingly well adapted for the supply and repairs of the fleets destined for service in the North seas' – the yard was small and the sandy nature of the subsoil meant that the excavation of deeper docking facilities and the construction of more buildings would be highly expensive.

Both Bentham and Rennie in fact concluded that a *new* eastern yard, fit to meet the long-term needs of a growing navy, was essential. Rennie observed that the existing yards were 'far from possessing such properties either in point of situation, of extent, of arrangement or of depth of water in the harbours as the large and growing power of this country demands'; he argued that by constructing a new yard 'a facility would be given to the building and fitting out of ships of war the political importance of which would far outweigh the probable expense'.[50] Both men had in mind the construction of a yard within which basins could accommodate ships equipped for sea as in the London, East India and West India docks then building. Both also proposed appropriate sites. In 1800 Bentham suggested one close to Colemouth Creek on the Isle of Grain, at the mouth of Medway, which St Vincent inspected while First Lord in September 1802. In 1807 Rennie proposed another at Northfleet which was recommended by the Commissioners of Naval Revision in a secret, unprinted fifteenth report.[51] Following an order in council of December 1808 land was actually purchased at Northfleet where by 1817 there were 543 acres in government hands.

However, though initially of considerable interest, support for the new yard gradually waned. To those with experience of the naval departments this was not unexpected. John Briggs, a member of the Commission of Naval Revision, wrote despondently to Lord Barham in October 1807:

The new dock yard may perhaps be allowed to linger on for a year or two more, but I have not the least hope of its being set about in downright earnest and put out of hand with all dispatch. It will most likely be transferred over to the Navy Board, and after 10 or 15 years have expired and a vast deal of money has been thrown away upon it in consequence of the delay which must attend the execution under them, we shall perhaps begin to think of building a ship or two there, Parliament will then perhaps call for an account of the expense incurred upon it, which will be found enormous, and the poor Board of Revision will be accused of folly and visionary speculations.[52]

Yet the idea of a new yard was discarded more quickly than Briggs anticipated. Bentham himself in fact contributed to its abandonment. For by 1803 he had successfully developed the first bucket-ladder steam dredger. Proposed in 1800, with an estimated capability of raising 1,000 tons of soil every 12 hours, it received the support of the Navy Board as well as the Admiralty and was completed at Portsmouth by October 1802. The effectiveness with which it cleared shoals in Portsmouth harbour led to the construction of a second, built at Deptford, for use in the Thames at Woolwich. This one was completed in October 1807.[53] Hand-operated Trinity House dredgers and yard scavelmen had until then merely performed a holding operation on some shoals near the yards, only being capable of work at relatively shallow depths and thus being particularly affected by tides. But the Portsmouth dredger proved capable of raising shingle from 14 ft at a rate of 80 tons an hour; the Deptford vessel, of working at 21 ft and raising 60 tons of shingle, or 90 tons of mud, every hour. Being able to reach these depths, they were capable of remaining active far longer each tide. The Portsmouth officers noticed in 1805 that whereas scavelmen would have taken five months to clear the yard camber of mud, the steam dredger could perform the task in $16\frac{1}{2}$ days.[54] This vessel remained in service in Portsmouth harbour until at least 1816. The Deptford dredger was used in the Medway as well as the Thames and remained in service until after 1823, another vessel that could dredge depths up to 28 ft being hired for use at Woolwich from 1809.

The capabilities of these vessels must have influenced the attitude of the Navy Board in particular. For the Board was almost certainly in favour of maintaining the accessibility of the existing facilities as an alternative to a new yard. It was especially conscious of the problems that would arise in supplying the existing yards with labour and materials were a new yard to be formed. Such awareness in fact governed its policy towards the early growth of what became Pembroke dockyard. This yard had been forced on the Board. In 1797 the Admiralty had arranged with the owner of a site at Milford Haven for ships to be built there for the navy by a private builder. The latter had, however, quickly gone bankrupt and the Board had been forced to take control in 1800. An order in council of 1809 authorized a formal establishment for the yard, which was then transferred to a more spacious site in Crown possession across the haven at Pater Church in 1813. Throughout these developments, the Navy Board consistently adhered to the policy of restricting the scale of operations ordered for the new establishment in order to prevent the major yards being deprived of either shipwrights or timber.[55] Undoubtedly a similar caution affected its support for the Northfleet scheme.

Without question, a third consideration also influenced thinking about the proposed new yard: its cost. The Commissioners of Revision were thinking in terms of basins to hold 300 ships; Rennie thought one might hold 70 ships of the line.[56] The cost of the works would have been extraordinary. It was not only simpler and more expedient to maintain the accessibility of the existing yards, it was cheaper. All these factors ensured that about 1810 the Northfleet scheme was shelved. However, this coincided with, and probably hastened, the decision to maintain and extend the eastern yards. Earlier, though every effort had been made to arrest silting and ensure accessibility, while the plan for a new yard was considered facilities in the east had been generally allowed to deteriorate. Yet from about 1810, when the idea of a new yard began to lose favour, there was an apparent increase in investment in all the existing yards, except Deptford.

At Woolwich investment was sparing. Dredging there begain in 1807 and continued until 1811, when it was discontinued on account of the expense. Eighteen months later it had to be resumed again. But by 1815 mud was preventing yard craft from approaching the wharf until the tide was two-thirds full, craft heavily loaded being unable to reach it until the top of high water.[57] The Admiralty ordered the removal from the frontage of the ships in Ordinary and, from upstream, a private wharf projecting into the river. According to Rennie, the projection of the southerly end of the yard wharf 100 ft into the river had still to be reduced.[58] Perhaps as a result, though every other measure was taken, the degree of accessibility still did not warrant significant internal expansion. Land was puchased in 1809 which permitted a seven-acre extension, but between 1810 and 1815 the only new building constructed was a steam-powered smithery.

Dredging was also necessary at Chatham, where a 'military bridge' below the yard and the projection of a yard jetty directed the current of the Medway towards the opposite shore. But the Medway to Chatham was more easily navigable than the Thames to Woolwich, especially after 1800 when transporting buoys and moorings were laid down between Gillingham and the upper end of Long Reach. These permitted the movement of ships to and from Chatham 'in the course of a few tides at all seasons and in all weathers' by allowing them to haul themselves up and down the river.[59] Consequently expansion and improvements were more marked. Between 1810 and 1815 two areas of adjacent land were annexed, new offices, a chapel and a smithery were completed, a hemp house and a saw mill were built, and cast-iron water pipes were laid around the yard. In 1815 a plan for an additional dock, which incorporated an improved line of frontage, was also approved.[60]

It was, however, at Sheerness, previously the most ramshackle of the yards, that the greatest improvements were made. As a later parliamentary committee observed, these were regarded as the main alternative to a new yard:

The project of Northfleet being, if not abandoned, at least indefinitely suspended, the rapidly increasing decay of Sheerness, the vast extent of the works which were making by the enemy in the Scheldt, and the gradual shoaling of water opposite the dock yards at Chatham, Woolwich and Deptford which rendered those yards unsafe places of refit for large vessels, imposed upon the naval administration the necessity of coming to a determination with regard to Sheerness.[61]

The initial factor that led to a decision was the serious state of the yard by 1808. In January of that year an unusually high tide, accompanied by a northerly gale, undermined the wharves and washed the land from behind them, cracking the foundations and threatening to bring down nearby buildings. An estimate for repairing the damage produced by Rennie and Joseph Whidby, the Master Attendant at Woolwich, was so high that the Admiralty then called for plans for further improving the yard. While a part of the river wall was repaired, in which all the submitted plans agreed, the other proposals were considered by a committee of Navy Board Commissioners and three engineers which returned its recommendations to the Admiralty in July 1812. Most of these being approved, Rennie was commissioned to prepare the final sections and specifications and work began in 1813.

Through an exchange of land with the Ordnance Board and the absorption of houses in Blue Town and the greater part of Mayor's Marsh, the yard was enlarged from 23 to 56 acres. Owing to the softness of the ground, the sea repeatedly undermined the foundations of the river wall which consequently had to be built within cofferdams and in the nature of a double, hollow wall set upon inverted arches and many thousand piles that spread the weight. A 'great basin', three docks and a mast pond were formed within the new ground, where store-, mast- and boat-houses were also built. The docks, originally designed for 74s, were eventually made large enough for ships of 120 guns. The new facilities were not all completed until 1823, when work began on renovating the old yard. This was completed about 1827.[62]

Expansion was necessary too at Portsmouth during the last half of the Napoleonic War. Ground reclaimed from the 'ooze' supplied space for 44 new saw pits and another building slip. A hawser-house, a millwrights' shop and a new iron and brass foundry were also built. But the silting of the harbour remained a problem. The rights of 'encroachers' were tried and set aside in 1803, though their wharves, jetties and buildings were allowed to remain, probably from the inadequacy of the powers to enforce their removal.[63] The harbour was found dangerously overcrowded too, when moorings were all taken but more ships were allowed to anchor, a situation simply aggravated by the anchoring of private vessels. It was probably to reduce these problems in particular that an Act of Parliament was obtained in 1814 (54 Geo. III, c.159) providing for the regulation of the harbours at Portsmouth, Plymouth, Chatham and Sheerness.[64]

By contrast Plymouth was now generally acknowledged as possessing the finest harbour of all six yards. Nevertheless the problem remained of the exposure of the Sound and Cawsand Bay to southerly winds. A breakwater had been suggested by the Master Attendant at Plymouth in 1788. Interest in constructing one revived in 1806 when St Vincent made known his conviction to the Whigs, then in office, that the only 'chance of resisting the insatiable ambition of the ruler of France' lay in 'making Plymouth Sound a secure mole at any expense'.[65] Rennie and Whidby surveyed the Sound, Cawsand Bay, Catwater and Hamoaze in March 1806 and supported the idea, believing 'a work may be formed in the bay capable of protecting a fleet of 50 sail of the line at anchor'.[66] Their report recommended a breakwater in two parts: a detached stone construction a mile in length along the line of the Shovel and St Carlos Rocks, with a pier of half the length extending from Andurn Point towards it. Although the report lay dormant until 1810, when other plans were also considered, Rennie and Whidby's scheme was adopted by the Admiralty in January 1811 and authorized by an order in council the following June.[67]

With Whidby as superintendent, work actually began early in 1812, the detached central breakwater taking priority. Separate contractors were employed to quarry the stone and to ship it to the Sound where it was thrown 'promiscuously' into the sea along the line of the mole. In water between eight and ten fathoms deep, the base had to be 70 yards across, the top 10 yards wide at a level of 10 feet above the low water of ordinary spring tides. To hold their place, the stones had to weigh between $\frac{1}{2}$ and 2 tons with some up to 10 tons. Local red sandstone, granite and limestone were all used, the latter coming from a quarry just over a mile up the Plym. It was brought in horse-drawn rail trucks to a quay where a fleet of 45 vessels, each capable of taking 45 to 50 tons, took the smaller stones and ten other vessels fitted with rails, windlasses and tilting platforms took the trucks loaded with larger stones. By the end of 1812 43,789 tons were sunk, the average daily tonnage rising to a remarkable 1,030 tons in 1816. By 11 August 1815, when 1,100 yards were showing above sea level, 615,057 tons had been unloaded.[68]

While these operations were going on, numerous improvements were also being made in the yard at Plymouth. There more space was made by blasting and digging away rock and levelling Whitehouse Hill. New buildings included a storehouse, foundry, pitch house, topping house, painters' shop, chapel and offices. Several other buildings were repaired, a boat pond was formed and water pipes were laid with stopcocks at regular intervals. Together with the breakwater, these improvements represented a scale of investment unequalled at any of the other yards except Sheerness. Plymouth was clearly regarded as potentially, if not already, the principal western yard.

These works at the six dockyards during the last half of the Napoleonic Wars had two major effects. Most obviously, they contributed to the gradually altering appearance of the dockyards. Writing in 1817, a Frenchman, C. Dupin, noticed an 'immense change effected within these few years'. For, in common with the great dock basins for merchant vessels along the Thames, the quays, docks and basins at the dockyards were being built or repaired in stone rather than timber.[69] Timber was also being replaced in the construction of buildings on land. Cast iron was of particular use for columns and beams, Samuel Bentham claiming credit for the design of the first completely fire-proof building. In addition between 1813 and 1815 great sheds appeared along the frontages of most of the yards. In an attempt to check the spread of dry rot in ships building and repairing, docks and building slips were being roofed.[70]

But it was not just appearances that were changing. During the last five years of the Napoleonic War, the technology which had previously been confined to Portsmouth was extended to all the yards. An early 'spin-off' from the Portsmouth wood mill were turning lathes for shaping pillars, coaks and

*Plymouth Sound showing the breakwater, 1831, by G. L. Taylor*

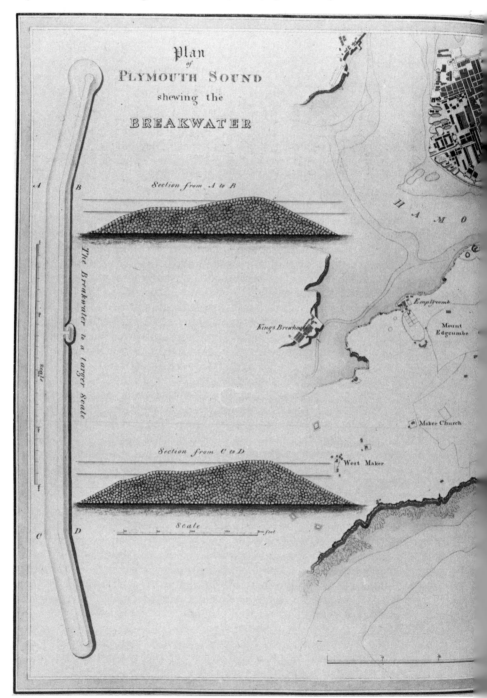

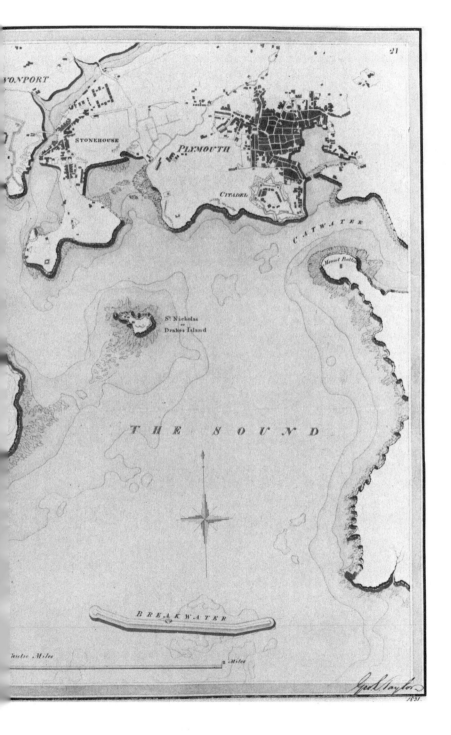

treenails. Made by Maudsley, they were supplied to all the yards in 1806.[71] More substantial machinery followed. The saw mill established at Chatham was formed by Brunel following the completion of the Portsmouth block mill. It contained eight saw-frames and two circular saws apart from windlasses and capstans to supply the mill with timber; each frame would be fitted with between one and 30 saws and could cut at a rate of 80 strokes a minute; two of the frames were allotted to deal-slitting and could produce 34,000 feet of timber in 43½ hours.[72] The smithery at Woolwich, designed by Rennie, contained lifting and tilt hammers adapted to the production of the largest anchors.[73] These new installations were all powered by steam engines that were also used for various pumping operations.

With this new machinery, the dockyards by 1815 were able to perform numerous operations with unprecedented ease and effect. However, the machinery represented an advance in efficiency on a relatively limited front; for with their sites unchanged the dockyards were no more accessible than before, and with no more docks than at the beginning of the Napoleonic War they remained as limited in the number of ships with which they could deal at any one time. The new installations nevertheless represented a rise in the general level of technology employed in the yards and reflected the fact that mechanization was by 1815 fully accepted as a means of improving efficiency.

This was an advance of far greater significance for future developments than the progress of actual innovation. It was important because dockyard management, being dependent on men who had been brought up in the yards and the navy, was dominated until about 1810 by thinking which accepted traditional problems and seemed blind to the means available to solve them. But Samuel Bentham's work as Inspector General, Brunel's inventions, the Commission of Revision's recommendation for a new yard, the availability of Rennie and Maudsley's expertise, all contributed to a greater awareness of the problems and the solutions available. As in the development of ship-building, the administration of Charles Yorke, First Lord between 1810 and 1812, was a turning-point, when the works of a grand scale, the expansion of Sheerness and the construction of Plymouth breakwater, were both set in train. The saw mill at Chatham also owed its origin to Yorke's Board of Admiralty, arising from a letter to the Navy Board calling its 'immediate attention' to the 'propriety of erecting steam engines in the Dock yards for sawing timber and using circular saws . . . with a view of saving manual labour, ensuring greater dispatch and allowing time for the plank to season'.[74] The Admiralty Board continued until the end of the war to provide the pressure to use the new technology. Preoccupied with the day-to-day problems of maintaining the navy, the Navy Board failed to install in other yards machinery whose value had already been proved in one. It was thus, for example, the Admiralty Board that suggested during its visitation of 1815 that a small steam engine be employed instead of horse-teams to pump water from the docks at Plymouth, although the machinery necessary had been in use for almost two decades at Portsmouth.[75]

By 1815 the Navy Board had nevertheless adapted itself to the sophistication of the technology and the scale of the works it had to supervise and had developed three procedures to deal with the problems involved. It had as a priority learned early that it could no longer expect non-specialist board or yard staff to direct complicated engineering operations. In 1797, when Bentham's ideas for the new docks and the basin at Portsmouth were sent to the yard officers, it had received the reply: 'having no plans or sections for carrying the said propositions into execution and it being a work of so great moment and we believe beyond any thing of the kind ever carried on in this country, we do not think ourselves sufficiently responsible to give our further directions to so great an undertaking until we have proper recited directions with plans etc.'.[76] By 1815 it had become standard practice to contract out all such works and to employ engineers to direct them. At the Board, even before the abolition of the office of the Civil Architect and Engineer in 1812, it had also become standard practice to consult professional engineers. The board was, for example, assisted in considering the plans for Sheerness by James Watt, Joseph Huddart and William Jessop. So aware had the Board become of its own technical ignorance that it unsuccessfully opposed the abolition of the post of Mechanist under the Civil Architect and Engineer, claiming it would need his opinion and advice 'to assist our judgement in the consideration of mechanical subjects . . . and in the application of machinery whenever it may be thought expedient'.[77] Simon Goodrich, who filled the post, had performed the managerial work connected with the maintenance of the block and metal mills. But in 1814 a third practice was extended to the mills and to the number of millwrights necessary at Portsmouth: that of forming them into new yard departments each with their own master craftsmen to direct operations. Goodrich was appointed almost at the same time as the supervising engineer and mechanist at Portsmouth. By 1815 the Navy Board had thus developed appropriate administrative responses to the variety of problems associated with the use of new machinery, the work of making physical improvements and the management of new or enlarged facilities. The conditions were accordingly established for further innovation and technological advance.

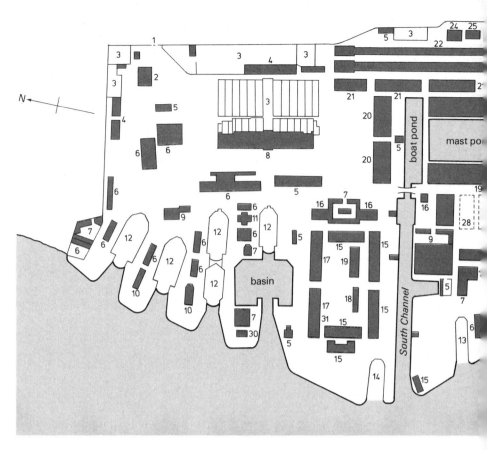

permitted a reduction in the interest on unpaid bills. In 1797 this rate was stabilized at $3\frac{1}{2}$ per cent and in December 1802 reduced to 3 per cent.[20]

These arrangements for the payment of contractors appear to have functioned effectively throughout the Napoleonic War. A measure of their success was that there were usually suppliers willing to undertake dockyard contracts. The only period when this was not the case was in 1803–4, when the timber contractors were prevented from doing business by a number of problems, mainly arising from St Vincent's attitude towards them. The timber supply crisis thus precipitated is worth examining, for it indicates that, even for this commodity, had the Navy Board been permitted to pay the prices demanded by the contractors – prices which in fact reflected the timber scarcity – there would have been no crisis.

The episode, which to contemporaries was part of an ever-present timber supply problem, has been described before. It was presented by R. G. Albion, writing in the mid 1920s, as the climax to his book on the timber problem and the navy between 1652 and 1862:

> That long-dreaded failure [of England's oak groves], more complete than on any previous occasion, materialized just at the time when Napoleon was threatening England with invasion. The native woodlands, exhausted by the decade of naval war with Revolutionary France, could supply scarcely half of the timber needed by the navy, and even that amount was withheld for some time by the action of a powerful timber monopoly. As a result, shipwrights at Portsmouth and Plymouth clamoured for oak which they could not obtain, while admirals on blockade duty were handicapped by battered ships which could not be repaired or replaced because of that same lack of oak. Unusual efforts to secure timber finally enabled the Navy to patch up enough ships to bring about the triumph at Trafalgar ...[21]

Albion's book placed the dockyards' problems in their context. But, writing at a time when monopolistic trading companies had recently been a subject of concern in the United States, Albion overestimated the power and organization of the timber merchants whom he bound together and termed the Timber Trust. In the 1920s, too, eighteenth-century public administration was considered more corrupt than it now appears and Albion attached more emphasis than now seems necessary to the contractors' reaction to the abolition of fees and the subsequent strictness of the Timber Masters. Conversely, he understated the ability of the Navy Board and yard officers to cope with the supply problem and ignored the steadiness and resourcefulness with which they overcame their difficulties.

In 1803 timber in the yards was at a low level. Admiralty orders required a stock of oak timber to be kept equal to three years' consumption. But the amount in store at the resumption of hostilities had fallen to 34,562 loads – about 1,500 loads short of the navy's needs in 1801. Best quality materials – English and foreign oak, beech and elm – were all needed on different occasions at Portsmouth and Plymouth to complete ships repairing. English oak, which had until then constituted 95 per cent of the wood employed in tended to become family concerns, they resulted in more economical sources of supply being ignored and mistakes or unfavourable terms in contracts sometimes going unchecked for many years.[15]

On occasion, when contractors were unwilling to supply stores on terms considered reasonable, or when the international market was closed to ordinary contractors, resort was had to the employment of merchants on commission, with brokerage and expenses. This was the case in 1804 when St Vincent was unwilling to pay the prices required by domestic timber contractors and several merchants were employed as agents on a commission basis abroad. Others appear to have been employed to obtain stores – timber in particular – with the decline in the Baltic trade after 1807. But their employment had two major disadvantages. They were regarded unfavourably by ordinary contractors who believed that they increased the competition for naval stores, reduced the quantity available for purchase and thereby increased the prices for which they themselves could offer to supply the yards. In addition, so far as the Navy Board was concerned, after accepting an agent's sample his whole purchase had to be received even though it might contain materials of an 'objectionable quality'.[16] As a result standard contracts containing both prices and specifications were generally preferred.

During the eighteenth century merchants who met the navy's wartime needs had at times been discouraged in their business by failures in naval credit. After 1797, however, improvements in naval finance gave business with the navy a stability which can only have added to the advantages of dealing with it. The problem prior to 1797 was a shortage of cash. This meant that when merchants presented certificates for the due performance of their contracts at the Navy Office, they were usually given 'In Course' navy bills which could only be encashed at the office of the Treasurer of the Navy in the order that they were made out. 'Ready Money' bills were occasionally issued, payable immediately on presentation, but these were reserved for payments demanded with urgency. The 'In Course' bills formed a naval debt which, before 1797, tended to grow during wartime, forcing holders of bills to sell them at a discount varying according to the size of the debt and the time the purchasers would have to wait for payment. Late in 1783 the naval debt reached nearly £13 million, giving rise to a discount rate in the market for navy bills of 21 per cent.[17] The contractors, who could foresee the gradual growth of the discount rate, naturally increased the prices they charged for undertaking naval contracts. Nonetheless, increases in discount rate could result in losses for contractors, which could only be redeemed by charging even higher prices to the navy.

In 1797 the situation was transformed by an increase in the funds available to the navy. The rate at which Parliament granted the navy its financial supplies was increased from the seventeenth-century rate of £4 a man per lunar month to £7 a man per month.[18] The larger sums of money granted to the navy tended to keep its debt in check. In 1800 it was over £8½ million, in 1801 £7, in 1805 down to under £6 millions.[19] With greater funds, the holders of navy bills could be paid earlier. In 1797 'In Course' bills were accordingly made uniformly payable 90 days after issue. In addition, the state of naval credit than others, the smallest agreeing to supply 300 tons and the largest 2,200 tons. The ships they employed carried between 150 and 200 tons so that the smallest contractor required the disposal of only two ships, the largest 11 to 15 ships. One of the largest contractors for hemp in 1812 had the services of 34 ships when he undertook his hemp contract in 1808.[11] These merchants, even the largest, had to be sure of their profits. Their caution over the costs involved in shipping from different regions, and their established connections, combined with the preferences of the dockyard officers, all militated against the development of new sources of supply.

According to well-tried practice, merchants were engaged to provide the major stores by 'public' or 'open' contracts, arranged annually. Advertisements were placed in newspapers inviting tenders for particular commodities and a day and time were set for the attendance of interested merchants at the Navy Office. There a Board commissioner explained the terms of the contracts available and the merchants were called on one by one to enter offers for the supply of part or whole of the quantities required.[12] The practice of having merchants attend the Navy Office to make their offers was open to criticism. It was obvious that when the terms of contracts were not to their liking they had the opportunity to combine; and there was a possibility that the necessity to attend the office resulted in the loss of offers from merchants distant from London.

However, the system worked effectively. Board advertisements had a wide circulation. In 1803 an advertisement appearing on 9 October had replies from as far afield as Falmouth within four days. Attendance at the Navy Office was also justified by the necessity to conclude the variety of detailed arrangements at a single meeting. The Navy Board vindicated the procedure in 1804 by pointing out that different merchants undertook contracts of differing sizes for which they were paid related prices. For example, the merchants who supplied the larger quantities of hemp wanted higher prices per ton than those who supplied the smaller amounts. The quantities and prices for all six dockyards had therefore to be agreed through careful negotiation. Agreements were sometimes based on samples or patterns and discussion of these added to the value of the meeting. Thus a commissioner always inspected samples of the wares of merchants interested in contracts for the supply of tallow, glass, pitch, rosin, candles and kersey. Likewise, contractors wishing to supply marine clothing, copper sheeting, ironmongers' wares, line, twine and cordage had always to see the patterns and specimens in the Navy Office.[13]

Not all contracts were 'public' or 'open'. Many standing contracts were made by the yard commissioners with local merchants for the supply of materials of minor importance. Those for the supply of Portsmouth and Plymouth yards included contracts for tar brushes, ballast baskets, water scoops, lanterns, pieces of ironwork, sand, plasterers' wares and paving stones.[14] Such standing contracts cut down the work involved in regularly making new arrangements; they avoided the risk of making new contracts with small tradesmen of limited means who could fail to perform their undertakings; and they tended to stabilize contract prices for several years. However, as the Commissioners of Naval Enquiry pointed out after their investigation of contracts for blocks and teams of horses, standing contracts unreliable. The Admiralty consequently encouraged the importation of samples or greater quantities of stores from other sources, notably the colonies. The relative importance of the Baltic region therefore declined. In the dockyards, stores from north-eastern Europe were still generally preferred, but the traditional unquestioning dependence on that area was dispelled. The *Quarterly Review* of 1812 reflected this change of attitude. It pointed out that having 'been so long in the habit of drawing almost every material of which the navy is constituted, with the exception of oak and iron, from foreign powers', there was a tendency 'to consider every temporary interruption of the usual channels of supply as an irremediable calamity'; but after a time of 'lamentation and despondency' the discovery had been made of 'ample resources within our own reach', colonial resources with which it was unnecessary 'to place a precarious dependence on foreign powers'.

The *Quarterly Review* was complacent in 1812. It could observe with satisfaction that the Treaty of Tilsit had simply led to a greater import of American spars, to the encouragement of the cultivation of hemp in Bengal and along the Malabar coast, and to the manufacture of canvas at Calcutta; that there were also potential substitutes for pitch and tar in Trinidad and India, and immense forests abounding in oak and pine in Canada, Nova Scotia and New Brunswick.[8] The uncertainty of supplies from the Baltic after 1807 was, however, accompanied by a search for alternative supplies of timber and hemp that was obviously urgent. The import of American mast timber had been quickly cut short by the United States Embargo Act of 1807 and Non-Intercourse Act of 1808. Masts, as well as oak and fir, had then been imported in greater quantities from Canada, a trade encouraged in 1809 and 1810 by the imposition of duties on imports from the Baltic (49 Geo. III c. 98; 50 Geo. III, c. 77).[9] The supply of hemp caused perhaps greater concern. Between 1801 and 1809 samples of different varieties were received from Ireland, Spain, New South Wales and Canada as well as India. But the procurement of large quantities of the right quality was a different matter. Although, for example, in 1808 20,000 tons of Sunne hemp were ordered from the East India Company for delivery in 1808, 1809 and 1810, the first shipments were not received until almost two years later and then, the hemp not being of 'adequate quality', 'an immediate end' was put to its further supply. Canvas produced at Bombay proved more satisfactory and was ordered for the supply of naval vessels in the east in 1809.[10] But the natural asphaltum available in Trinidad was not used, possibly, as the *Quarterly Review* observed, because there was a 'prejudice' against it, but more probably because the Baltic supplies of pitch and tar never completely gave out.

A problem in developing new sources of supply was the difficulty in encouraging merchants to tap them. In 1808 the East India Company was prepared to procure and transport hemp to England on a profit-free basis. But merchants operating in open competition could not afford such generosity. The merchants with whom the Navy Board contracted were not all large operators. In 1812, when 12,250 tons of Riga and Petersburg hemp were ordered, the board formed agreements with 12 contractors who required between them only 61 licences. Although on average each contractor thus had to charter an interest in only five ships, some merchants contracted for less were safeguarded to some extent by law. After war was declared, stores within the British Isles were prohibited from export by order in council, a prohibition that was periodically extended; and, even when the prohibition was not in force, merchants wishing to export stores had first to tender them to the board for pre-emption or refusal and, if refused, to obtain a certificate to that effect.[5] Neutral and captured cargoes were similarly available for pre-emption by the board. However, the greater part of the stores purchased in Britain were simply obtained through contracts at war-inflated, competitive prices.

The stores imported from abroad were similarly purchased by contract. In 1801, as throughout the eighteenth century, the navy was clearly still heavily dependent on materials imported from the Baltic. But the Napoleonic War was to see the development of other major sources throughout the world. Following the Treaty of Tilsit in 1807, the implementation of Napoleon's continental system and the closure of the Russian and north German ports to English ships, the flow of stores from the Baltic fluctuated alarmingly. In 1805, 11,000 ships passed the Sound; two years later the number had dropped to 6,000. Whereas the value of Britain's hemp imports was £639,507 in 1807, in 1808 it fell to £218,947. Trade revived in 1809, Britain importing double the amount of naval stores from the Baltic as in 1808, and the following year it flourished. In 1810 British exports to northern Europe reached figures that were slightly higher than those for the comparatively 'normal' year of 1806. But in 1811 Napoleon's successful enforcement of the continental system reduced this export trade from almost £14 million to £3½ million.[6]

Britain's measures to protect her Baltic trade reflected its apparent importance to her survival as a maritime power. The seizure of the Danish fleet in 1807, at the same time as the bombardment of Copenhagen, deprived Denmark of the means to close the Sound and Great Belt. Between the spring and autumn each subsequent year until 1812, Admiral Saumarez' Baltic squadrons policed the trade to the north-eastern ports, convoying great fleets of merchant vessels through the Sound until 1809 and thereafter through the Great Belt. Within the Russian and north German ports, the interest to continue trade was stronger than the political forces that worked for its abolition. The agents and correspondents of British contractors formed an organization which defied Napoleon's authority. Cargoes were therefore shipped from minor ports under little scrutiny and in vessels that were, or purported to be, neutral. The masters of these ships often carried false papers and certificates claiming their vessels to be owned in, and their trade between, places in amity with France. To facilitate British control of this trade, masters sailing on the account of British contractors were also furnished with a licence, usually obtained in London, conferring immunity from detention by ships of the Royal Navy 'notwithstanding all the documents which accompany the ship and cargo may represent the same to be destined to any other neutral or hostile port'. In 1807, 2,606 such licences were issued; in 1808, 4,910; in 1809, 15,226, and in 1810 – the greatest number – 18,356.[7]

The continuance of the Baltic trade, combined with the stockpiling in good years of stores in the dockyards, prevented the navy from being starved of materials. Nevertheless between 1807 and 1812 the flow of stores from the Baltic was irregular, the costs high and the Russian and German sources

# 3

# The materials

The business of maintaining an adequate supply of timber and other stores in the dockyards was fundamental to the navy's existence. Charles Middleton commented in 1788: 'When the variety of services that are to be provided . . . is considered, and how much the exertion of the fleet depends on punctual and proper supplies of stores, it must be allowed that no branch of the service is of more importance than this to the public'.[1] By the time of the Revolutionary and Napoleonic Wars the business had assumed massive proportions, involving innumerable contracts and requiring its own particular system of administrative control. Some conception of its scale can be obtained from the quantities of the main stores required for the navy in 1801. The Navy Board estimated that its annual consumption was then over 36,000 loads of timber (two such cartloads providing a little over one ton of shipping), 13,000 tons of hemp (the quantity necessary for the manufacture of about 15,260 tons of cordage), over 1,400 tons of iron, 949 tons of copper sheeting and 200 tons of copper bolt staves, over 95,500 bolts of canvas, at least 900 masts greater than 21 inches diameter, 18,800 barrels of tar, 5,500 barrels of pitch, 371,000 deals and 111,000 blocks.[2] These quantities made the Navy Board the largest 'consumer' of naval stores in the country. Its consumption, moreover, continued to grow. In 1812, for example, the amount of oak expended in the dockyards was double the number of loads consumed in 1801.

Such quantities inevitably posed procurement problems. The resources of the British Isles supplied only a few of the main stores and in most cases only a proportion even of these. By the end of the Revolutionary War the domestic supply of oak timber had become critical, while imported (mainly German) oak was still distrusted. Hemp could be derived from a variety of sources; but Russia (which supplied England and Scotland generally with over 37,000 tons in 1801[3]) had the preference. Iron was available in England but Swedish was favoured for its quality. Copper was obtained from north and south Wales and canvas mainly from Scotland. Of the masts, over half (500 in 1801) were expected to be Riga masts, the remainder American. The tar and pitch too came from the Baltic and the deals from Norway. Most blocks were manufactured until 1804 by contractors and thereafter in Portsmouth dockyard. In 1801 the cost of 'home'-produced stores totalled £1,433,000, while those purchased abroad cost £1,514,500.[4]

The Navy Board arranged for the supply of these materials by entering the domestic and international markets in naval stores. Its domestic purchases

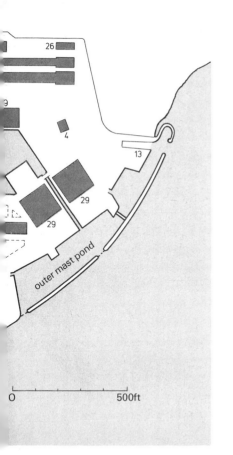

## Plymouth yard in 1808

| | | | |
|---|---|---|---|
| 1 | Gate | 18 | Junk shed |
| 2 | Chapel | 19 | Plank house |
| 3 | Garden | 20 | Boat house |
| 4 | Stables | 21 | Hemp house |
| 5 | Offices | 22 | Spinning house |
| 6 | Workshops | 23 | Laying house |
| 7 | Store cabins | 24 | Yarn house |
| 8 | Officers' houses | 25 | Tarring house |
| 9 | Smiths' shop | 26 | Topping house |
| 10 | Pump house | 27 | Seasoning sheds |
| 11 | Kilns | 28 | Timber storage area |
| 12 | Dock | 29 | Mast houses |
| 13 | Building slip | 30 | Pitch house |
| 14 | Graving dock | 31 | Sail loft |
| 15 | Storehouse | | Water areas |
| 16 | Saw pits | | |
| 17 | Rigging house | | Buildings |

*Plymouth Dockyard, 1798, by N. Pocock*

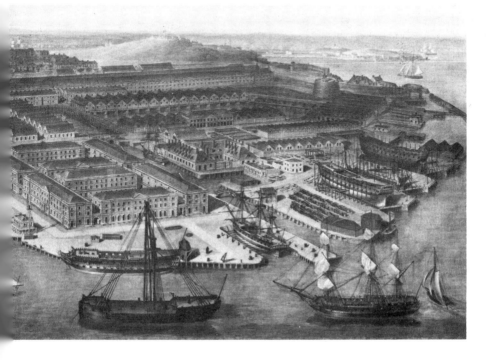

Portsmouth yard in 1810

1 Gate
2 Mast house
3 Saw pits
4 Offices
5 Naval Academy
6 Commissioner's house
7 Gardens
8 Lot yard
9 Rigging house
10 Sail loft and store
11 Storehouse
12 Hemp house
13 Topping house
14 Double rope house
15 Hatchelling house
16 Tarring house
17 Deal yard
18 Convertors' pound
19 Canvas painting shed
20 Dock
21 Building slip
22 Officers' houses
23 Workshops
24 Smiths' shop
25 Metal mills
26 Millwrights' shop
27 Boathouse
28 Block mills
29 Hawser house
30 Pitch house
31 Pumps
32 Mortar and engine house
33 Mould loft
34 Kiln
35 Store cabins
36 Stable
37 Timber storage area
38 Seasoning shed
39 Chapel

⬜ Water areas

⬛ Buildings

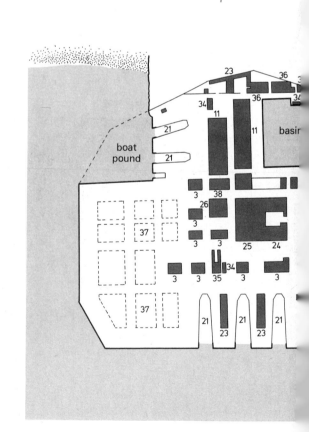

warships, was precisely the material most scarce, with 'compass' timbers and other large pieces of oak for knees, riders and beams most in demand. However, Plymouth had a stock of fir and other timber from ships broken up and other yards appear to have had a similar reserve. The situation was therefore not immediately critical: the yard officers were not free to choose the quality of timber they used, but they were not yet desperate for materials either.

The situation was nevertheless one in which the Navy Board had to use all the means at its disposal to prevent a crisis developing. As an immediate expedient, the board encouraged the yard officers to substitute 'inferior' quality timber for English oak; and, as the shortage continued, the quality of the materials it sanctioned sank progressively lower. In February 1803 the Board was only prepared to have the *Warrior* (74) repaired with foreign oak because 'if properly selected' the timber would 'last as long as the other parts of the ship or until she may stand in want of a more general repair'. But in April 1804 the Board was willing to use fir in the repair of ships for temporary service and by June it had sunk to the use of unseasoned timber. By March 1805 the necessity of repairing ships by doubling the sides of their hulls induced the Board to order the use of elm and beech in combination with fir and oak, a mixture that would formerly have been considered anathema.[22] Inferior quality timbers could not be used for knees and riders but in their case iron was used instead. New ships to be built from oak were temporarily out of the question, but in 1804 five frigates were ordered to be built from fir and another from American pitch pine.

Meanwhile every conceivable source of timber was explored. In 1802 'private gentlemen' were sent copies of new contracts and in 1803 requested

Table 9. *The quantity of oak timber used in the construction of ships of the stated classes, c. 1780*

| rate | guns | quantity of plank, knees and thickstuff (loads) |
|------|------|------|
| 1st | 100 | 5,560 |
| 2nd | 90 | 4,035 |
| 3rd | 74 | 3,212 |
| 3rd | 64 | 2,601 |
| 4th | 50 | 1,931 |
| 5th | 44 | 1,582 |
| 5th | 36 | 1,237 |
| 5th | 32 | 1,152 |
| 6th | 28 | 980 |
| sloops | | 480 |

through an advertisement to sell their timber directly to the navy. Little was obtained in this way. More was secured from Crown estates and even more from the royal forests. Between 1801 and 1811 these two sources supplied about 7 per cent of the navy's annual requirements, in 1803 3,546 loads.

These supplies from the royal forests were in many ways unsatisfactory. During the eighteenth century the forests had been allowed to decay: tree planting and tending had been neglected. Following the 1792 Commission on the Land Revenues of the Crown the forests were more closely supervised.[23] But the Surveyor General of Woods, who managed the forests under the authority of the Treasury Board, then pursued a policy of stringent conservation. To ensure that trees had reached their full growth, and thus their greatest value, he restricted felling to trees in an 'unimproving state' and, to provide the Crown with a regular annual income, permitted only a proportion of these deteriorating trees to be cut each year. Being at full maturity, and the Navy Board's purveyors having a part in their selection, these trees contained many timbers potentially suitable for large beams and knees. But because they were in a state of decay many were found more rotten than expected; and, because the Navy Board became responsible for their lopping, squaring and transportation as soon as they were felled, they were often the target for 'depredations'. There was consequently a long-standing disagreement with the Treasury over a 'ruinous' felling policy, the price which the forest timber was worth per load, and the necessity for the Surveyor General's officers to retain some interest in protecting the timber (through the withholding of full payment for it) until it was received at a dockyard.[24]

The yards were therefore dependent for at least 90 per cent of their timber on contractors. However, in 1803–4, as throughout the period of growing scarcity, they responded to the pressure of demand by raising their prices to the

*Table 10. The quantities of oak timber in the dockyards, 1793–1807*

|  | English straight, compass, thickstuff and knees (loads) | English 3–4″ plank (loads) | foreign straight, compass, thickstuff and knees (loads) | foreign 3–4″ plank (loads) | totals (loads) |
|---|---|---|---|---|---|
| 1 Jan. 1793 | 51,395 | 4,289 |  | 2,314 | 57,998 |
| 1 Jan. 1794 | 48,647 | 2,915 |  |  | 51,562 |
| 18 Feb. 1801 | 39,007 | 890 |  | 2,217 | 42,114 |
| 8 Mar. 1803 | 32,951 | 921 |  | 690 | 34,562 |
| 15 May 1804 | 33,539 | 1,004 |  | 2,027 | 36,570 |
| 1 Jan. 1805 | 37,164 | 1,070 | 1,150 | 2,542 | 41,926 |
| 1 Jan. 1806 | 58,175 | 1,997 | 2,596 | 4,079 | 66,847 |
| 1 Jan. 1807 | 64,737 | 2,341 | 5,993 | 7,589 | 80,660 |

Table 11. The quantities of oak timber received from the royal forests, 1801–11

| | New Forest (loads) | Dean Forest (loads) | Bere Forest (loads) | Which-wood (loads) | Salcey (loads) | Sher-wood (loads) | Alice Holt (loads) | Hainault (loads) | Whittle-wood (loads) | Crown lands (loads) | Annual totals (loads) |
|---|---|---|---|---|---|---|---|---|---|---|---|
| 1801 | 983 | 541 | | | | | 286 | 214 | 326 | | 2,350 |
| 1802 | 1,064 | 358 | | | 288 | | 846 | 362 | 235 | 135 | 3,288 |
| 1803 | 958 | 1,746 | | | 163 | | 302 | 126 | 251 | | 3,546 |
| 1804 | 946 | 2,496 | | | 65 | 240 | 365 | | 232 | 8 | 4,352 |
| 1805 | 1,912 | 1,772 | | | 303 | 412 | 514 | 245 | 533 | 417 | 6,108 |
| 1806 | 1,672 | 3,260 | | | 51 | | 158 | | 222 | 143 | 5,506 |
| 1807 | 899 | 1,001 | 168 | | 24 | | 138 | 419 | 399 | 137 | 3,185 |
| 1808 | 1,202 | 774 | 85 | 97 | | 158 | 148 | | 147 | 62 | 2,673 |
| 1809 | 1,760 | 807 | | | | 195 | 466 | 216 | 308 | | 3,752 |
| 1810 | 1,254 | 1,306 | 69 | 306 | 135 | 183 | 439 | | 262 | | 3,954 |
| 1811* | 1,295 | 1,753 | | 152 | 32 | 99 | 697 | | 467 | | 4,495 |
| Average annual supply | 1,268 | 1,438 | 29 | 50 | 96 | 117 | 396 | 144 | 307 | 82 | 3,928 |

* To 31 October 1811

levels which purchasers were prepared to pay. Timber, even oak, remained available, but the contractors obtained higher prices than those the Navy Board paid from merchant shipbuilders and, in the north, from the builders of mills, canals and houses.[25] One contractor told the yard officers at Portsmouth in 1804 that 'he could get a much greater price for his timber [were he] to send to the North by the colliers capital timber fit for the keelson pieces and other principal conversions in particular'.[26] The fact was, to make their profits and cover their costs, timber merchants were even prepared to convert the larger timbers into smaller pieces, which of course destroyed the timbers most needed in the dockyards.[27]

For the Navy Board, the main problem was the rate at which the price of English oak timber rose. The price rose slowly over the last two decades of the eighteenth century but then sharply following the turn of the century to stabilize temporarily in 1805. In March 1802 the Navy Board was forced to inform the Admiralty that the annual consumption of English oak in both the private shipyards and the dockyards was 'much beyond the ability of the kingdom to supply to the same extent', and that the timber obtained by contract had 'for some time past' fallen short of dockyard demands. For a while, the Admiralty permitted the Navy Board to make its timber contractors a series of concessions. Contract prices were increased; new contracts were prepared containing fewer specifications relating to the sizes of the timbers to be supplied; and the Timber Masters, who had been rejecting some timbers and accepting others at reduced prices, were directed 'not to throw vexatious difficulties in the way of the merchants'.[28] To reduce the competition among contractors for timber of large dimensions, the Navy Board was also permitted to negotiate an agreement with the Surveyor of the East India Company for a reduction in the dimensions of the company's ships.[29] Yet the price of oak timber continued to rise. Between 1801 and early 1804 the prices allowed the contractors were increased three times; and eventually the patience of the Admiralty Board gave out. In March 1804, when St Vincent was requested to sanction the fourth price rise since his appointment, he angrily refused any further 'concessions' and rejected altogether the Navy Board practice of contracting for timber supplies.

St Vincent's reaction against the contractors, born of a suspicion that they were profiteering at naval expense, must be seen in the context of his campaign for economies and of his low opinion of the civil administration of the navy. His lack of trust was crucial to the breakdown of supplies. Some merchants had made contracts in 1802 but had been unable to fulfil them, owing to rising purchasing prices. St Vincent maintained that they should all the same be forced to make their deliveries and to accept payment according to their engagements, even though he had also sanctioned new contracts at higher prices for other merchants. The Navy Board, on the other hand, repeatedly proposed that the 1802 contracts be cancelled and that all the merchants be free to make new ones. In March 1804, however, St Vincent rounded on the Navy Board, declaring that it was itself responsible for the difficulties with the contractors, having permitted them to become accustomed to laxity in the receipt of timber prior to the appointment of the Timber Masters in 1801. He ordered that the merchants be compelled to 'complete their agreements with the public' and directed the junior Surveyor of the Navy, Sir William Rule, to tour the country and purchase every quantity of suitable timber that came to his notice.[30]

Fortunately the dockyards depended on St Vincent's decision for only two months. His insistence on the completion of the 1802 contracts lost the navy the goodwill of the contractors, while the despatch of Rule into the country did further harm by advertising the dockyards' needs and driving up prices still further. One purveyor acting for Rule reported that merchants at an auction at Bewdley combined against him in the bidding, with the explanation afterwards that they were 'determined to have the timber' as Rule's mission 'had done the buyers very material injury at their sales'. Rule returned to London having made offers for less than 3,000 loads.[31] However, in May 1804 St Vincent was forced to resign. Melville, his successor, immediately cancelled the 1802 contracts and raised the prices that were permitted once more.

The dockyards' timber crisis was thus terminated. The shortage of timber, it is true, persisted for the remainder of the Napoleonic War, the price of English oak continuing to rise until 1815. But the Navy Board and dockyard officers ably effected measures that prevented the shortage becoming critical. The necessity to use green timber and to mix various types of wood certainly gave rise to more rapid decay; but the joining or scarphing of beams and use of small timbers where possible taught new techniques, including a new system of ship construction. These efforts and these problems were accompanied by a more urgent and more persistent search of the world for supplies than was necessary for any of the other naval stores; while in England, as a result of a

Table 12. *The quantities of English and foreign oak timber expended, 1803–12*

|  | rough timber and knees (English) (loads) | rough timber and knees (foreign) (loads) | thickstuff (English and foreign) (loads) | plank (English and foreign) (loads) | total expended (loads) |
|---|---|---|---|---|---|
| 1803 | 21,427 | 5,937 | 5,275 | 7,395 | 40,034 |
| 1804 | 30,728 | 2,709 | 6,572 | 11,385 | 51,394 |
| 1805 | 25,556 | 1,295 | 3,350 | 11,305 | 41,506 |
| 1806 | 37,813 | 4,202 | 6,127 | 11,090 | 59,232 |
| 1807 | 23,903 | 5,365 | 6,520 | 10,042 | 45,830 |
| 1808 | 26,674 | 16,355 | 5,077 | 12,780 | 60,886 |
| 1809 | 32,694 | 13,157 | 6,257 | 12,367 | 64,475 |
| 1810 | 27,014 | 7,517 | 4,155 | 9,107 | 47,793 |
| 1811 | 25,522 | 13,013 | 2,302 | 7,342 | 48,179 |
| 1812 | 34,403 | 25,633 | 5,815 | 8,495 | 74,346 |
| average annual expenditure | 28,573 | 9,518 | 5,145 | 10,131 | 53,367 |

secret unprinted report of the Commissioners of Naval Revision, nurseries of young oaks, specifically designated for the navy, were established in most royal forests between 1810 and 1815.[32]

Breakdowns in relations with contractors were rare. Even so the business of meeting dockyard requirements was never a smooth affair. For the contractors, there was a series of aggravating delays in actually delivering their cargoes to the dockyards. At the outbreak of war, owing to failures to issue 'protections' from the press before the declaration of hostilities, contractors' vessels were often stripped of their men, and even after their issue there continued to be cases of seizure. Delays occurred at the convoy rendezvous for contractors' vessels sailing to and from the western yards. And at the yards there were delays due to the number of cargoes constantly being delivered and the inadequacy of the workforce unloading them. The timber contractors were particularly affected after 1801, their cargoes also being subject to the inspection of the Timber Masters. At Plymouth in 1805 one ship could wait up to eight days to be unloaded, while in the Thames, given the time taken to unload, barge owners were unwilling to hire their vessels to timber merchants. Even after unloading, there were invariably delays while the Clerk of the Cheque traced the board orders for the deliveries and made out certificates for the due performance of contracts – the certificates permitting merchants to obtain their Navy Bills at the Navy Office.[33]

Distribution of materials to one or more of the dockyards was an integral part of contracting with the Navy Board. At the Navy Office the distribution was decided in the office for examining storekeepers' accounts, which determined the quantities required at each yard, and in the contract office, established in February 1803, where the contracts were prepared for the merchants to sign. The decisions taken in these two offices depended on the demands regularly sent to the Navy Office by the yard Storekeepers. These were of two types: occasional demands, despatched whenever stores became unexpectedly short and there was some risk of running out; and periodic demands – daily, weekly, fortnightly, monthly, quarterly, half-yearly and annual returns – despatched with the regularity ordered by the Navy Board. Each type of material was ordered on a separate demand and the regularity of the demands relating to a particular material varied with the rate at which it was expended.

The most important returns were the quarterly and annual demands. They provided the information from which periodic contracts were made for regular deliveries. Before completing these demands the Storekeepers were ordered to confer with the technical officers over the completion of a 'probable expenditure' column. The Master Shipwright and Master Attendant were then themselves required to examine their own accounts of the consumption of materials, being ordered not to rely on the Storekeeper's 'knowledge of the growing services, which ... would be very often sufficient ... though not always, particularly after a recent change of times by which the expenditure [of stores] must be greatly affected'.[34]

Because of the variety of headings under which the London offices required information, many demands were complicated documents. The demand for blocks included 36 types of block and for each the Storekeeper had to specify the number in store and due on order, the expected total, the yard establishment, the number required to complete the establishment or the number to spare. Clearly, however, the value of the demands declined if they were not easily read, if they were completed in an unorthodox manner, or if they were despatched to the Navy Office late. Accordingly the Navy Board waged a continuous campaign to maintain and improve the system. The number of printed pro-formas was increased to standardize the presentation of demands and their interpretation at the Navy Office, while failures to despatch them on time were repeatedly admonished.

The main problem was to enforce uniformity of procedure in completing the demands at all the yards. The Plymouth officers were told in November 1803 that, although local methods had prevailed 'more or less at every yard', they would not be 'admitted as an argument merely on that account for their being continued in practice of however long standing they may be'.[35] Yet local practices were difficult to stamp out. Before and throughout the American War of Independence the system of demands had been in disorder; the knowledge of each yard's requirements had depended on the experience of the Storekeeper and his clerks. In 1784 Charles Middleton had required a formal establishment for stores to be fixed for each yard and had had a new set of returns introduced.[36] But these innovations imposed only superficial uniformity on local methods of calculation that were maintained and reinforced by local circumstances.

The figures for the demands were derived primarily from the books of the Storekeeper. His principal ledger contained a simple abstract of receipts and issues. It was balanced quarterly and provided a statement of the materials remaining in the storehouses as a charge upon the Storekeeper. Within the ledger the balance was carried forward at the end of each quarter and the receipts of the following quarter were added to it. The totals thus formed for each of the different types of material provided the debit side of the account. The stores issued formed the credit side, the Storekeeper no longer being responsible for them.[37]

This system of book-keeping had developed at Portsmouth. Different methods had been in use at the different yards until at least 1786, when the Commissioners on Fees recommended that the Portsmouth system be adopted everywhere as the most logical. This had been done by 1798 but minor differences in practice still existed. Consequently, in March 1804, 'in order to render the Storekeeper's accounts more uniform than the former method . . . would admit', each yard was sent a new book of regulations for 'improving the method of forming, keeping and checking the store accounts'.[38] Nevertheless in 1812 the Navy Board was still prepared to acknowledge that 'the system of accounts is well known to be complicated and extremely defective', and it had John Payne, a chief clerk in the Navy Office, examine it with a view to effecting improvements.[39] Only in July 1815 was the Board confident that it was 'likely at length to arrive at a correct mode of accounting for the receipt and expenditure of stores', for the simplicity of a new plan that was proposed 'must evidently tend to produce correct results'.[40]

It was not only to achieve reliable demands that the Board was concerned to

# 3 The materials

improve the accuracy of these accounts. The accounts were the only instrument upon which the Board could rely to ascertain exactly what stores were located in each yard. The accounts were usually based upon initial figures derived from a survey, but surveys were too time-consuming to be performed regularly during wartime; a survey at Chatham in 1797 took three months. Consequently, prior to 1801 they were taken only on the death or retirement of a Storekeeper and the appointment of his successor. An order in council of 21 May 1801 stipulated that surveys were to be performed annually and the first were carried out in all six yards in 1802. However, with the resumption of war and consequent increase in pressure on time the surveys again became infrequent.

In the absence of surveys, the Storekeeper's accounts were also the only means of determining the materials for which he was responsible to the public. Although he delegated the responsibility for certain articles within the storehouses to artificers under his orders and relied for the compilation of his accounts on clerks who attended the receipt and issue of all stores, he remained answerable for everything listed on the debit side of his ledger. In contemporary terms the responsibility was enormous. The value of the unappropriated stores at each yard in early 1802 was as follows:

| Plymouth | £611,819 |
| Woolwich | £600,656 |
| Portsmouth | £567,243 |
| Chatham | £423,697 |
| Deptford | £308,093 |
| Sheerness | £99,400[41] |

These figures roughly equalled annual turnover. At Portsmouth in 1796, for example, stores received and stores issued were worth about £560,000.[42] But some yards had a higher turnover than others: thus, although Deptford and Woolwich were both used as stores depots for other yards, the fleet at sea and yards abroad, Deptford tended to ship slightly more than Woolwich. Between April and September 1804 the tonnage of materials that left Woolwich was

Table 13. The quantities of naval stores in stock, 1793–1805

| | Riga masts (over 21") | American masts (over 21") | hemp (tons) | iron (tons) | canvas (bolts) | copper sheets (no.) |
| --- | --- | --- | --- | --- | --- | --- |
| 1 Jan. 1793 | 1,325 | | 5,357 | | 11,815 | 52,192 |
| 18 Feb. 1801 | 1,186 | 198 | 7,097 | 1,820 | 48,081 | 97,363 |
| 8 Mar. 1803 | 728 | 501 | 15,964 | 2,532 | 45,082 | 57,282 |
| 15 May 1804 | 482 | 378 | 10,932 | 2,259 | 18,146 | 39,437 |
| 30 Apr. 1805 | 797 | 361 | 15,197 | 1,812 | 42,791 | 49,720 |

5,731 tons, that from Deptford 7,764 tons.[43] The total value of the stores passing through all six yards annually represented about 30 per cent of the whole cost of maintaining the navy.

Considering the amount of materials for which they were responsible, it was natural that the Storekeeper at each yard should feel some anxiety about the performance of his custodial duties. Under St Vincent the Storekeepers at Plymouth and Chatham were both discharged for failures to detect and prevent frauds. There was less cause to fear a similar fate under other First Lords. Yet the pressure of duties borne by the Storekeeper and the inadequacy of his staff were common complaints. Stores sent on board ships had to be accompanied by clerks with bills of lading and receipts for the ships' officers to sign and, owing to the 'immense quantity of stores' supplied and 'the great extent of His Majesty's fleet', these services often left the Storekeeper short of clerks. The Storekeeper at Plymouth complained in 1802 that 'for many days' together there was 'scarce a clerk' in his office to carry on the current business 'such as entering bills, letters, contracts, receipts to boatswains and carpenters for returned stores, answering the board's orders and other little matters . . .'[44]

The duties of the Storekeeper basically consisted of receiving, storing and issuing materials. He received them from other yards, from ships returning from service, from the manufacturing departments within his yard and from contractors. The last two were the principal sources of new stores. Yard manufacturing departments supplied flags (known as colours), cables, cordage, sails, anchors and other ironwork. In addition, after 1805 the metal mill at Portsmouth recycled copper sheathing and after 1808 the Portsmouth block mill manufactured all sizes of blocks. The yards were not self-sufficient in all these articles. The ropeyards, for example, at Woolwich, Chatham, Portsmouth and Plymouth produced only a little over half the quantity of cables and cordage necessary, the remainder being obtained by contract.

Table 14. *The quantity of cables and cordage received into store from the ropeyards and from contractors, 1804–6*

|  | Manufactured in ropeyards at | | | | received from 4 ropeyards (tons) | supplied by contract (tons) | Total received (tons) |
|  | Woolwich (tons) | Chatham (tons) | Portsmouth (tons) | Plymouth (tons) |  |  |  |
|---|---|---|---|---|---|---|---|
| 1804 | 924 | 1,895 | 1,546 | 2,359 | 6,724 | 8,787 | 15,511 |
| 1805 | 1,190 | 1,938 | 1,633 | 2,120 | 6,881 | 7,696 | 14,577 |
| 1806 | 1,428 | 2,394 | 1,533 | 2,387 | 7,742 | 3,989 | 11,731 |
| average each year | 1,180 | 2,075 | 1,570 | 2,288 | 7,115 | 6,824 | 13,939 |

# 3 The materials

At receipts from contractors, the Storekeeper was expected to co-operate with the other two clerical officers and the Master Shipwright or Master Attendant, according to the nature of the materials. While the 'operative' officer inspected the quality of the materials and was checked by the Clerk of the Survey, the Storekeeper examined the quantity and was checked by the Clerk of the Cheque. By 1797 pressure of work prevented some officers from attending deliveries and the Navy Board permitted a clerk to deputize for one of the officers inspecting quality and another for one inspecting quantity. The officers and clerks in attendance then had to sign their receipt books to show which materials they had inspected. However, the frequency of the Board's reminders to attend, together with the reports on frauds effected by contractors, indicate that even clerks sometimes failed to attend and, even when they did, they co-operated in the completion of their books rather than checking one another in their particular roles.

Failures to attend receipts occurred when the officers and clerks were particularly busy. Other factors, similarly beyond the officials' control, affected the thoroughness with which receipts were checked. Procedures were established by order, usually after agreement with the contractors. Quantities of casks or packages were sampled, in some cases half the sample being selected by the yard officers and the other half by the merchants. Weighbridges were erected at all the yards in 1797 and heavy materials like iron or cables were weighed. Bar iron was cut up to expose the grain of the metal and the ends of some bars were heated, beaten and bent to test their strength. Pieces of canvas were subjected to the strain of weights hung around their edges. Timber was measured, gouged and cut up. Nevertheless the detection of flaws and weaknesses in some commodities – line, twine and forge gear, for example – required a more specialized knowledge than that possessed by even the operative officers who used them; and the attitude taken to flaws tended to vary according to the extent to which the materials were required in the yards. Canvas was rarely in short supply, so that in 1800 as much as 37 per cent of the total annual consignment for one yard could be rejected on delivery.[45] Timber on the other hand appears to have been received with relative tolerance until the appointment of the Timber Masters in 1801, and that tolerance was quite clearly restored in 1804 after the resignation of St Vincent.

The Timber Masters were Samuel Bentham's idea and were introduced to reduce the wastage of timber from the time of its receipt to the time of its use in the construction or repair of ships. Their appointment was recommended to the Select Committee on Finance in 1798 and their positions established by order in council of 21 May 1801. Although they were expected to work with the Storekeeper, their instructions made them individually responsible for the preservation of timber. They were accordingly directed to 'reject every piece' not 'strictly conformable in all respects to the terms of the contract'. Whatever the customary method of measurement at their yard, they were not to trust to their eyes 'but to apply the straight edge of a batten or rule to ascertain the flatness, and to cause any inaccuracy to be corrected before the measurement be made'.[46]

The Timber Masters' orders resulted in much timber being rejected or paid for at a reduced price. Yet, as the Navy Board warned the yard officers in

October 1801, this was ultimately damaging for the navy: 'if the merchants be not paid the value of their timber according to their contracts it will be impossible for them to fulfil their engagements or make new ones'. The officers were accordingly directed for their future receipts of timber 'to fix the qualifications of it with such exact propriety . . . that justice may be done to the merchants as well as the public'.[47] After deliveries continued to be rejected, in August 1802 the merchants were instructed to send agents with their timber to act on their behalf. But this too had little effect. In May 1804 the contractors were still complaining, claiming that their difficulties had their source in the 'heavy responsibility' which attached 'to the sole judgment of the Timber Master' and influenced him 'to look on one side of the question':

> The root of the evil lies in the mind of the Timber Masters and it extends to the Master Shipwright to whom appeals may be made: they consider themselves responsible even to the loss of their situations for the receipts of any timber which might be found to have defects at a future distant period in the opinion of another person.

According to the contractors, the Timber Masters admitted that 'their places and bread' were at stake so that they had to 'take care of themselves'. The officers themselves denied saying this and claimed that 'they considered the apparent scarcity and impractibility of procuring perfectly sound timber and received timber with visible defects after making a reasonable deduction'.[48] Nevertheless there was probably some truth in the contractors' allegations. The complaints against the Timber Masters became less common after St Vincent's resignation in May 1804, no doubt because the officers then felt better able to comply with the order to allow the merchants 'every reasonable accommodation'. Earlier on, there was always the possibility that they would become the target of St Vincent's Commission of Naval Enquiry.

Another officer with whom the Storekeepers had to work was the Inspector of Canvas. He was appointed early in 1804 to assist the Navy Board in forming contracts, in determining the prices to be allowed, in inspecting the manufacturers' mills, and in supervising the receipt of canvas, mainly at Deptford and Woolwich yards. In proposing his appointment the Navy Board informed the Admiralty that though capable in most other respects, the yard officers were 'not competent' to ascertain the quality of canvas at its receipt. For the quality could not be determined either 'by its colour, by its texture, by its gravity or by the weight the weft [would] sustain'. In consequence the only person competent to receive it was someone who had been 'in the constant habit of attending to the several stages of the process in cleansing the yarn and manufacturing it into canvas'.[49] The Board recommended Charles Turner of Limehouse, who had already proved helpful to the navy in purchasing canvas on commission during a combination of manufacturers. Following his appointment, Turner continued to aggravate these same manufacturers by refusing to sanction dealings with those who failed to produce canvas according to the process he stipulated and by rigorously inspecting the canvas on its receipt. Turner resigned in 1809 but was replaced by Samuel Hood, who also had professional experience in canvas manufacture.[50]

Following their receipt, new materials were marked with the king's broad

# 3 The materials

arrow and placed in store. Timber was stamped and piled in pounds, masts were placed in mast-ponds and spars submerged in underwater locks. Some storehouses were used for particular materials. Others were subdivided into berths within which the equipment for each ship in Ordinary was kept separate. Middleton had introduced these berths in 1784 to facilitate mobilization, to reduce the pressure on market supplies, and to cut the cost of equipping the fleet at the outbreak of war. The equipment in each berth was marked with the name of the ship to which it belonged and it was issued to ships of the same class.[51] Stores and equipment that were worn out and for which there were no suitable 'second-hand' replacements were replaced with new materials. These arrangements simplified the business of accounting (the stores in each berth could readily be checked against a list), imposed an order on storage, and contributed to the speed and ease with which ships could be made ready for sea.

One major complication in the organization of storage was the variation in equipment required for ships of different classes within the same rate. These had arisen from the alterations made in the construction or rigging of ships, mainly to improve sailing qualities. Greater standardization would have been productive of great economies. Thus in April 1798 Samuel Bentham propounded 'a principle of interconvertibility', claiming that, if it was kept in view at the time ships were designed, it would 'not only enable ships at sea to possess within themselves a much more efficient supply [of stores] but may enable a much less expensive stock to suffice for our storehouses at home'.[52] Barham had the same idea in mind when the Navy Board was directed in July 1805 'to have regard in future to the advantage of the same masts, yards and sails being made to answer for a great number of ships, much inconvenience having arisen from the difference of the dimensions of such stores required for ships of nearly the same force'.[53] Barham had the Commissioners of Naval Revision recommend that a committee of naval officers be appointed to select the ships which could serve as models for future construction and rigging. Nevertheless continuing modifications in ship design appear to have prevented any advance towards greater standardization.

In the dockyards 'interconvertible' stores would have had the advantage of reducing the necessary storage space. This was always short, particularly at times of demobilization. Anchors, masts and yards were left on board ships when they were stripped for the Ordinary. So also were some guns, but these were the responsibility of the Ordnance Board. All other fittings were removed for their security. At Plymouth, sheds had to be erected for the 'mooring chains, swivels, shakles, rings' and other metal articles; at Sheerness, the stores of line-of-battle ships were taken along to Chatham while those of smaller ships were stowed aboard a storeship moored to a wharf. Receiving the equipment of fewer ships of the line, the inland yards were less affected by the influx of stores at demobilization. But storage problems still existed, especially at Deptford and Woolwich, where great quantities of materials awaited reshipment elsewhere. In 1801 and 1802 warehouses had to be hired in London to store hemp for which there was no space at the yards.

The issue of stores by the Storekeeper was controlled through a check system similar to that which operated at the time of their receipt. Materials were issued for one of three purposes: for work in the yard or on ships afloat, for the equipment of ships being brought forward for commissioning, or to complete the reserve stores issued to ships' boatswains and carpenters.

Materials required for work in the yard or afloat were ordered by the Master Shipwright or Master Attendant, their demand notes being checked by the Clerk of the Survey and the materials being issued by the Storekeeper in return for a signature in his issue book. The Storekeeper's immediate responsibility for the stores then ceased, but they still remained on his books until he received notice from a senior 'operative' officer that they had been used for a particular purpose. This was because a large proportion of materials was temporarily lodged with cabin keepers who issued them as they were wanted, their books being balanced monthly, with surveys of remaining stock every quarter. Also, after 1801, timber which required conversion was first issued to the Timber Master who returned it in a converted state with an account of its various parts; these were then issued individually as required.

The equipment necessary to fit ships for particular services was issued on the submission of a warrant from the Clerk of the Survey. The stores so issued would vary according to the nature of the services intended for a ship, ranging from harbour service to three, four or six months at sea.

The materials not consumed in fitting ships for sea were passed on to their respective boatswains and carpenters as the basis of their stock of reserve stores. The materials necessary to complete these stocks were ordered by the ships' captains. Their demands were examined by the Master Attendant or Master Shipwright, according to their nature, and, if approved, passed to the Clerk of the Survey who made out an issue warrant to the Storekeeper. While the materials were later being received on board, a ship's officer and one of the Storekeeper's clerks checked them off against a list that was signed and lodged in the office of the Clerk of the Survey. On the return of a ship to a yard and the return of stores not expended to the Storekeeper, a second list was made out for comparison with the first. Copies of both were sent to the Navy Office where, in the office for stores and slops (divided into two offices in July 1803), boatswains' and carpenters' accounts were cleared.

The system of accounting for materials transferred to the charge of the sea officers functioned quite effectively. Boatswains and carpenters did not easily escape responsibility for their stores, while their pay depended on the clarity with which they justified their stores' expenditure. On the other hand, materials issued for work in the yards or on ships afloat quickly passed out of the control of inferior officers in charge of cabins or gangs and into the hands of artificers who had every reason to consider that they possessed inexhaustible abundance. At their level, wastage and theft were perpetual problems. A check did exist on the use to which materials were put, the Storekeeper not being permitted to 'discharge' himself of materials issued until he had received notes from the senior 'operative' officers stating the services to which they had been applied. Most of these notes, moreover, were initially made out by cabin keepers. But these notes were insufficiently detailed to show the exact appropriation of every article taken from the cabins, and the senior officers had neither the time themselves nor the clerical staff to investigate the details.

It was time and staff shortage which resisted the implementation of better checks on store expenditure. Proposals for improvements were made, of course. Samuel Bentham proposed that a monthly statement be sent to the Admiralty Board of the cost in materials of each piece of work undertaken in every yard: 'some indication at least of the propriety of the appropriation of stores would thus be brought to view'.[54] And in 1803 Commissioner Coffin at Sheerness suggested that quartermen and cabin keepers should submit to their principal departmental officers monthly lists of all stores they had withdrawn from the storehouses; by comparing these lists with the Storekeeper's accounts, the officers could then check the materials for which their subordinates were responsible. Limited schemes were adopted. In May 1805 Commissioner Hope at Chatham could observe that 'not an article can be expended in the rigging house without the knowledge of the Master Attendant'.[55] And Bentham introduced, in his instructions to the Timber Masters in 1802, a system by which notes were made out, accounts kept, and copies sent to the Navy Office, for every single piece of timber issued and received by the Storekeeper. The objection to Bentham's system, as for the other check schemes that were proposed, was that it entailed a heavy additional workload. The timber system alone involved so much documentation that in 1804 the Plymouth Storekeeper complained that 'at present every inch of timber issued is thrice copied and twice abstracted'; that the 'intricacy and laborious process' of abstracting into one account all the timber used for a particular ship or service delayed the completion of his midsummer store accounts; and that the 'new timber regulations . . . cannot be transacted . . . as the system is at present conducted . . . without additional and professional assistance'. Bentham obtained copying presses to save clerks having to reproduce all the documentation by hand. But the pressed copies were dismissed by the Plymouth Storekeeper as frequently so 'unintelligible' and 'on such very thin paper' that he was unable to regard them as 'authentic . . . records of office'. The timber accounting system was accordingly later modified.[56]

The absence of an adequate check on store expenditure was compounded by the inappropriate or extravagant issue of materials. The Storekeeper's clerks could be discharged for irresponsibility in the issue of stores. But they were too often under pressure for materials of which they had little specialist knowledge and for which they had insufficient time to measure out. In 1802 the Navy Board noted that 'frequently canvas that might have been converted to more useful purposes has been issued as decayed and worn without any officer of sufficient ability passing judgement upon it'. It was the same for rope. Because there was no one in the Master Shipwright's department 'competent to pass an opinion on rope', new was 'often called for when half-worn would answer'. Consequently the board ordered that all applications for canvas or rope were to be referred to the Master Attendant.[57] Yet this did not prevent larger quantities than necessary being issued. Indeed this was often the outcome of the necessary speed of work, a speed that could not be sacrificed. In 1805 the Master Attendant at Portsmouth thus opposed the 'mode of weighing spun yarn by the pound or measuring old rope by the fathom for every particular purpose', claiming that it 'would be attended with delays in carrying on the service . . . particularly in cases where exertions and despatch were necessary'.[58]

Some wastage of materials was accordingly regarded as unavoidable. Nevertheless during the eighteenth century a fatalistic attitude seems to have prevailed more generally, especially where the materials in question were either plentiful or of little further use. Timber, for example, was then clearly wasted, about three-fifths of every log of rough wood being reduced to offal on conversion. Before 1801 and the appointment of the Timber Masters, moreover, artificers had simply selected their requirements from the top of timber piles without respect to the suitability or degree of seasoning of their choice. It became in consequence the principal task of the Timber Masters to ensure that conversions were performed as economically as possible. Each Timber Master had to keep a 'description book', containing an account or sketch of every piece of wood received by the Storekeeper, so that he could select the pieces best suited to the purposes for which they were required; he also had to keep a register to account for the use to which each separate off-cut from a conversion was put.

With so much wastage in timber conversion, it was natural prior to the order in council of 21 May 1801 that artificers should have regarded the offal, or 'chips', as a harmless perquisite. The practice of taking chips out of the yard had, however, developed into a notorious abuse, with 'entire articles of wood, particularly ... spars, deals and planks' being cut up and more valuable items being stolen under their cover. In 1783 an attempt had been made to stop the practice but it had continued unabated. It only ceased in July 1801 with the introduction of 'chip money', a daily allowance added to the artificers' pay, ranging from 3d for labourers to 6d for shipwrights. Although this cost in all approximately £50,000 a year, half the sum was raised by fortnightly sales of offal, chips and sawdust, and it did help to reduce embezzlement.

Even so, a large quantity of stores was still wasted. It was 'a very common thing to find amongst the saw dust' taken out of yards 'iron nails, rings and such like articles', one sifter of rubbish finding 'in the course of two or three months upwards of half a hundredweight amongst the rubbish' she sifted.[59] At Sheerness, in a personal effort to make both officers and men more waste-conscious, Commissioner Coffin made a practice of picking up nails wherever he went and 'immediately stuffing them in the pockets of the first Master workmen or foremen' he met.[60] Possibly in consequence of Coffin's influence with St Vincent, patrolling warders were appointed in 1803 at all the yards to collect up 'the variety of small articles' scattered about and 'holding an inducement to peculation'.[61]

Embezzlement in fact accounted for perhaps the greatest amount of wastage in the yards.[62] To those unfamiliar with the everyday problem, the quantity of stores lost in this way was alarming. In 1801 the Attorney General estimated that depredations in the six yards cost the public no less than £500,000 a year.[63] He was probably wide of the mark, but, owing to the lack of detailed accounts of materials actually used, a more exact figure was difficult to obtain and was never, as far as is known, attempted by the Navy Board. Wild exaggerations consequently obtained credence. Thus Sheridan was able to claim without contradiction in 1802 'that peculations committed in the naval departments for the last ten years amounted to three millions a year'.[64] And Patrick Colquhoun, the well-known London magistrate, wrote in 1796 that

# 3 The materials

frauds occurred in Plymouth and Portsmouth yards to the value of no less than £1 million annually.[65] This last statement was refuted in a letter to the Admiralty in 1801 by George Nunns, chief clerk to the Clerk of the Cheque at Portsmouth, who pointed out that in 1796, 'one of the most expensive years', the value of all the stores passing through his yard was only about £560,000. As Nunns observed, however, exaggerated estimates 'from so eminent authority' as Colquhoun must make 'impressions of the most fatal tendency . . . on the minds of Members of Parliament and other gentlemen in the elevated ranks of society'.[66]

Exaggerated estimates of losses from embezzlement, if based on the constant reports of losses, were nevertheless understandable. For peculation was obviously the customary resort of artificers who wished to supplement their earned income. It involved not just individuals, but groups of men working together, their families and, by implication, the greater part of the dockyard communities. This seems clear from the methods employed to smuggle materials out of the yards and the market that was evidently available for them.

Men who had to pass the yard gates under the inspection of officers and warders carried materials 'in very uncommon pockets' and beneath overalls or coats. Greatcoats and capacious trousers were regularly banned by the Navy Board. During the press of men through the gates, friends shielded others and occasionally large groups organized a rush past the officers. At Portsmouth in December 1803 'fifty or sixty of the ropemakers made a more than ordinary effort to push through the gates with the rest of the people'. The officers reported that 'about half of them were stopped and searched . . . the other half effected their escape'; among the latter, they suspected, 'were several of them enveloped with hemp like those detected'.[67] Even the breakfast and dinner baskets removed from the yards by wives and children sometimes contained stores. Hemp and cordage were the materials most commonly detected, but all types of stores were stolen. The opportunities available to carry away articles by boat made the ships under repair and ships in Ordinary particularly vulnerable. In the dark, and with assistance from men on board, the most bulky items were removed. For example, during 1802 100 fathoms of stream cable, $14\frac{1}{2}$ inches thick, disappeared from the *Holstein* (64); 17 panes of glass from the *Glenmore* (36); and men were detected removing a coil of rope from the *Magnanime* (44) and the iron ballast from a cutter.

Precautions against such thefts were taken. Naval stores wherever possible were marked with the King's broad arrow. Cordage was marked by coloured twine within each strand and the twin was folded back one fathom (6 feet) at each end to form a loop that would be destroyed if cut. During working hours the artificers were watched by warders, especially when they were employed with costly materials like copper; and at night the whole yard was posted with warders and patrolled. Those discovered in the attempt to remove materials were punished severely. Persons convicted were guilty of a felony and liable to transportation; the sentence was often obtained and then publicized as a warning to others. Such precautions and punishment nevertheless had little effect.

During the late 1790s the pressure for governmental economy, undoubtedly intensified by the great estimates of losses from the dockyards, led to further legislation to reduce the problem. During the session of 1799–1800 an Act 'for better preventing embezzlement' was passed (39/40 Geo. III, c. 89). Instead of being aimed, like earlier legislation, at the actual embezzlers, this Act strengthened the law against persons convicted of receiving or concealing materials. They were made liable to transportation for up to 14 years, to a fine of up to £200, to committal to a local house of correction or county gaol, or to be stood in a public pillory or to be publicly whipped.[68] The Act's particular features were the provisions for public punishment: the whole dockyard community was to be taught the retribution for connivance in thefts of naval stores.

The Act was put to immediate use. It was found, however, to have a major disadvantage. The identification of public property and prosecution of its receivers heavily involved the Storekeeper. In 1802 the Storekeeper at Plymouth reported that he was sometimes occupied in searching premises for stolen stores for two or three days a week. In addition, when stores were found, he had to arrange their conveyance to the dockyard, list the articles found, attend the magistrate to assist in drawing up depositions, and later attend the local sessions or county assizes to give evidence as required.[69] The Act consequently had the effect of reducing the attention the Storekeeper could devote to his proper duties within the yard.

The Act's deterrent value was also questionable. Men who embezzled naval stores did not necessarily suffer humiliation through public punishment. On the contrary, the punishment itself could inflate their local standing. In 1803 one man who was placed in the pillory at Chatham 'was cheered by the populace and two blue flags carried before him when he was taken away'.[70]

Local opinion in fact ran contrary to every effort to safeguard dockyard stores. To those concerned in preserving them, the attitude of the local community was a constant frustration. Even the attitude of local magistrates tended to be ambivalent: faced by the choice of committing men for trial at the county assizes or retaining them on bail for trial in the local town sessions, magistrates gave way in some cases to community pressure and chose the latter course. The magistrates at Portsmouth were particularly weak in this respect. In December 1803 they hesitated two weeks before committing three ropemakers for trial. While Commissioner Saxton pressed for them to be sent to Winchester – 'the only thing they dread' – the ropemakers used the time to obtain advice and support for a trial at the borough sessions. Of this, Saxton considered, they had good reason to be 'fearless', for they could be tried at the town sessions for no more than petty larceny and there were 'so many interested and influenced people' in the borough that there could be little doubt that a local jury would be sympathetic.[71]

In the face of an un-co-operative if not overtly hostile local community, the only persons upon whom dependence could be placed for the protection of public property were the dockyard officials themselves. Most yard commissioners were empowered to act as magistrates and they consistently committed men suspected of peculation to the county assizes. Inspectors were also employed outside the yards to search boats, watch those suspected of dealing in stolen stores and collect evidence to secure their conviction. One was employed at Portsmouth from December 1797 and two more were appointed to work in Maidstone and Rochester in August 1804. They were not paid a salary but received half the fines allotted to informers on summary convictions. Yet, working against local feeling, the efforts of these officials, supported though they were by yard officers, warders and night watchmen, were of little avail.

Although there is no quantifiable evidence, the reports of great losses of stores from embezzlement were clearly well founded. Rising prices during the 1790s gave artificers good reason to interest themselves to a greater extent in embezzlement and even in the theft of stores after hours. In April 1801, when food prices and discontent at the level of earnings in the yards were both at a height, the Navy Board informed the Admiralty that 'depredations' on stores, especially at night, were 'much more frequent than they used to be'.[72] Political as well as economic motives could be attributed to those who attempted to gain access to the yards at night, if only to pilfer stores, and the Admiralty acted promptly. The forces protecting the yards at night were immediately strengthened. Until 1801 the yards were mainly defended after working hours by watchmen who were not only usually elderly but drawn from the local population and so ready to avoid rather than to challenge intruders. A small marine guard was also stationed at the three largest yards – Chatham, Portsmouth and Plymouth – but the force, a total of 110 men, only provided about ten guards for duty at a time. Steps were therefore taken to increase this force, the quarters available being enlarged, so that in 1803 they could accommodate 954 men. This was sufficient to provide one armed guard for every night watchman. The landward defences of the yard were accordingly doubled. Along the water frontages defences were also increased. In 1801 the port admiral at each of the three main yards was ordered to provide guard-boats to patrol throughout each night. And in 1805 these patrols were strengthened with the extension of the operations of the Thames river police to Deptford and Woolwich, Chatham and Sheerness yards.[73]

Whether these defences reduced the rate of nightly thefts is open to question. Probably they did. During the course of the Napoleonic war embezzlement during the day probably also declined to some extent. It certainly subsided as a subject of public concern during the early years of the war, when the frauds publicized by the Commissioners of Naval Enquiry attracted greater attention. But improvements in the system of wage payments may also have contributed to an actual reduction in the amount of stores stolen; and late in the war, the work of John Payne on the Storekeepers' books seems to have resulted in an improved system of cabin keepers' accounts and a more effective check on materials issued. Payne's widow claimed in 1813 that as a result, 'the embezzlement of stores by the cabin-keeper and workmen is rendered extremely difficult – the monthly expenditure is completely controlled and this is effected by a system of accounts so well considered yet so simple that the application of them to the subject has been attended with much advantage'.[74] There is plenty of evidence to show that embezzlement was not completely stopped. Nevertheless, like the amount of wastage, it appears to have been checked.

# 4

# The workforce

The workforce at each of the dockyards was composed for the most part of men who had been born in the local towns, apprenticed and brought up in the yards. Sons followed fathers, the yards often containing at any one time several generations of the same family. These men with deep roots and strong connections in their communities formed the nuclei of the workforce, their number corresponding roughly with the peace establishment. On their fringe there was always some turnover, men joining and leaving the yards as their inclinations or necessities determined; some seeking higher wages in the merchant yards, others seeking the compensations of employment under government.[1] But it was the settled, permanent number who were the strength of each yard. Once war broke out, it was their concentrated efforts that saw to the initial mobilization of a fleet, their skills and experience which ensured that refitting and repairs were completed properly as ships came in from the sea.

With an established local labour supply, there was no question that the dockyards could equip and maintain a naval force of limited size. But the marked growth of the navy in both the Revolutionary and Napoleonic Wars demanded, perforce, that the dockyard labour force be enlarged. Even in 1792 the men available to the yards seemed insufficient to Gabriel Snodgrass, surveyor to the East India Company, who warned that government should 'attend to the shipwrights' in the royal yards,

> for at present they are much too low in estimation and too few in numbers and if there is not a greater number brought up and kept in the King's yards it is probable the navy and of course the nation will receive a severe check whenever there may be a necessity of fitting out a fleet in an emergency.[2]

Although in 1793–4 Snodgrass's prediction proved wrong, in March 1804 the opposition in Parliament was disposed to regard the shortage of artificers in the mobilization of 1803–4 as a threat to the safety of the nation and called for a statement of the number of shipwrights in the country. A return to the House of Commons in April revealed that at that time the dockyards employed over a third of all the shipwrights available. With 3,300 already in the royal yards, there remained only 5,100 shipwrights throughout the rest of the British Isles and these, moreover, apart from a considerable concentration along the Thames, were dispersed in small numbers round the coasts.[3] Throughout the wars, the recruitment of more skilled men to the dockyards was consequently considered a particularly troublesome problem.

One reason why it was so regarded was because earnings in the merchant shipyards were generally far higher than in the dockyards. The Navy Board, for example, attributed the slow pace of government ship construction to the inability to compete for labour with the private yards. It informed the Admiralty in August 1805 that, possibly on account of its distance from the capital, Plymouth was the only yard capable of keeping up its complement of shipwrights,

> while Portsmouth, Chatham, Sheerness and the river yards are very considerably short of the numbers they had in the last war; and whilst the merchant builders continue to give such high wages to their workmen . . ., without further encouragement being held out in the King's yards, no great increase of numbers can be expected[4]

The problem was the greater because earnings in the merchant yards were not simply a little higher than those in the dockyards but sometimes as much as two to three times as great. In 1805 shipwright earnings in merchant yards along the Medway were double those of their counterparts in Chatham yard and in 1812 it remained the same. An examination of daily earnings in private trade at this time revealed that shipwrights and caulkers could make up to 9s. by the day and 20s. by the piece elsewhere, but only about 5s. by the day and 8s. by the piece in the dockyards. Similar differentials prevailed right down to the earnings of common labourers; in 1812 they could make up to 4s in the dockyards but up to 10s digging canals.[5]

It was of course generally recognized, both by the Navy Board and by artificers, that in spite of a lack of comparability in earnings employment in the royal yards had some compensations. In the merchant yards, hours were generally longer, efforts more intensive, and employment usually terminated with the completion of particular jobs. Under government, however, work was performed with long- rather than short-term objectives. Hours were less exhausting; basic yard hours differed with the seasons but generally totalled $11\frac{1}{2}$–12, and included 1–2 hours (according to season) for dinner and a customary half an hour for breakfast. Mobilizations and 'heats' certainly extended these hours with overtime but the greatest amount of this permitted was five hours. In addition, dockings and launchings were sometimes performed on Sundays but as a rule these days were officially reserved for rest and religious worship. In 1795 the Admiralty Board observed that 'it must not only be injurious to the men's health to work seven days in the week but a means of corrupting their morals and which ought carefully to be avoided but particularly in the present moment'.[6]

A more conspicuous advantage of dockyard employment was its relative security. The need for labour ensured that the minimum term of employment was the duration of hostilities; and even when the yards were reduced from a war to a peace establishment most men had a large chance of being retained, for discharges were normally limited to the old, the infirm and the refractory. The value attached to such security by artificers is perhaps best indicated by the treatment afforded a party of Admiralty officials who visited Deptford following an unusually large peace reduction in 1802. This involved the discharge of numerous able-bodied men and the officials 'experienced much abuse from the enraged families of the workmen' and only 'with some difficulty escaped from worse treatment'.[7]

With the need to retain a large proportion of the wartime workforce during peace, as well as to improve the attractions of government employment during war, by 1793 provisions had long since been made to reinforce the security of the workforce. Men injured at work were allowed sick pay; there was also a surgery at every yard, with a surgeon and an assistant who were required to visit artificers' homes when necessary. Sick pay consisted of six weeks' basic day pay followed by a small weekly allowance of 2½–4s. until the recipient returned to work or received his discharge. This not only retained men who were temporarily indisposed, but provided temporary relief to the more seriously injured, of whom there was always a number. For, owing to the heavy and sometimes physically hazardous nature of dockyard work, injuries were common. In 1800 and 1801, 4 per cent of the workforce at Chatham was discharged injured each year, nearly 1 per cent with hernias.[8]

Another mutually beneficial provision was that of superannuation. Pensions were introduced for shipwrights and caulkers by an order in council of 1764; they were extended to all the other trades except ropemakers and sawyers in 1771; and the two remaining trades were eventually provided for in October 1802. Pensions were provided both to men injured in the yards and rendered incapable of earning a living and to men who had done 30 years' dockyard service. Had it been effective, the scheme would have benefited the yards by removing the elderly and infirm. But only one pension was provided for every 40 men borne on the yard books, and the service qualification excluded some who, though having spent the greater part of their lives in the yards, were still short of the requisite number of years. In consequence old and infirm men continued to accumulate, the yard officers being reluctant to discharge them simply on account of their age.[9]

These official provisions were supplemented by an element of paternalism on the part of the Navy Board and yard officers, and by the advantages of the fraternity formed among large numbers of men in the same trade and circumstances. This was remarkably evident in the care taken of the aged. Younger men in their 'company' or gang often did more than a fair share of labour to ensure that earnings were relatively equal. St Vincent in 1802 was scandalized to learn that old and young men thus received similar amounts of pay. He was told, however, that

> it was well known to those who are acquainted with dock yards that the young and able men preferred making the sacrifice of what their vigour enabled them to earn in favour of their aged relations and friends, expecting in turn to receive the same indulgence when the decline of their strength should require it; and upon this principle the earning of the old men appear higher in proportion to the actual labour.[10]

Yet welfare provisions, both official and unofficial, did not completely compensate for lower earnings, especially in a period when prices, particularly those of food, made life expensive. At times in the 1790s and early 1800s the yards therefore lost as many men as they recruited. Had the Navy Board had its way, earnings would have been considerably improved. The basic daily rates had been established in the 1690s and not been altered since. Moreover, as a handbill posted outside Chatham yard gates in April 1801 pointed out, the cost of keeping a family of two adults and six children in bare necessities almost doubled in the 20 years before 1795 and tripled in the six years after that.[11] However, being almost as old as the system of yard management itself, the traditional daily rates had become institutionalized and fundamental changes in payment were postponed until reform became absolutely necessary and the whole system of payment was revised.

The situation in the dockyards in relation to wage rates was comparable to that of the seamen before 1797. Only their mutinies had brought about significant change. It took time, however, for even this improvement to be passed on to the seamen connected with the dockyards. These were the men employed as ship-keepers on board ships in Ordinary. As good seamen either sought higher wages in the merchant service or were taken as ships were commissioned into active naval service, the men in the Ordinary were not the most able. In 1802 they were 'for the most part aged and infirm'.[12] They obtained 'petty warrant provisions' and a place to live, yet their weekly earnings were less than some shipwrights earned in a day; and for this they lived apart from their families and were on call night and day. Between 1797 and 1803 the Navy Board accordingly requested four times that the pay of the Ordinary be made the same as in the navy. But only in January 1804 was the request conceded and seamen in the Ordinary placed on the same footing as able seamen in the fleet.[13]

One practical objection to changes in the artificers' traditional rates of day pay was that the rates formed the basis for the calculation of earnings for overtime and piecework. About a quarter of the daily rate was obtained for one and a half hours' overtime, known as a 'tide', and a single day's pay for five extra hours, known as a 'night'. The prices set upon work performed by the piece were also related to the daily rate, the ceiling for these earnings being usually two or three times that rate. From 1794, because trades working by the piece were so often given the ceiling of 'two for one', that is, two days' pay for piecework during the normal working hours of the yard, two days' pay became standardized as the usual amount of their pay, overtime also being added.[14]

Potentially, piecework offered a means of permitting men far greater earnings than their basic rates, while at the same time giving them incentive to perform greater amounts of work. Yet at the beginning of the Revolutionary War the system was still relatively new. Although incentive schemes had been suggested as early as 1694, the proposal had only been revived in 1794, introduced into a few trades in 1758 and into others in 1772. The shipwrights at Deptford, Woolwich and Sheerness eventually accepted a scheme in 1775 but those at the other three yards resisted with a five-week strike. The shipwrights at Chatham and Portsmouth were only induced to accept it on the termination of hostilities in 1783, when overtime was cut and men at yards working by the piece were found to earn more than those still paid by the day. Yet it took another five years before it was accepted at Plymouth.[15]

Table 15. Rates of pay in the dockyards, 1690–1812

| | basic daily rate s. d. | overtime | | when rate established | lodging money per week d. | chip money per day from 1 Jun. 1801 d. |
|---|---|---|---|---|---|---|
| | | per 'night' of 5 hrs s. d. | per 'tide' of 1½ hrs d. | | | |
| Shipwrights | 2 1 | 2 1 | 7½ | Dec. 1690 | 2½ | 6 |
| Caulkers | 2 1 | 2 1 | 7½ | Jan. 1693/4 | 2½ | 4 |
| Joiners | 2 0 | 2 0 | 7½ | Jan. 1693/4 | 2½ | 4 |
| House carpenters | 1 10 | 1 10 | 6 | Jan. 1696/7 | 2½ | 4 |
| Masons | 2 6 | 2 6 | 7½ | July 1717 | 2½ | |
| Bricklayers | 1 8 | 1 8 | 5 | Jan. 1696/7 | 2½ | |
| Smiths | 2 6 | | | Oct. 1726 | 2½ | |
| Scavelman | 1 6 | 1 6 | 4 | 1696/7 | | 3 |
| Labourers | 1 2 | 1 2 | 4 | 1690 | | 3 |
| Sailmakers | 1 10 | | | Jan. 1693/4 | 2½ | |
| Riggers | 1 6 | 1 6 | 4 | 1693/4 | | 3 |
| Ropemakers | 1 8 | | | 1699 | 2½ | |
| Locksmiths | 2 6 | 2 6 | 7½ | 1715/16 | | |
| Plumbers | 2 6 | 2 6 | 7½ | 1704/5 | | |
| Braziers | 2 6 | 2 6 | 7½ | 1704/5 | | |
| Blocksmiths | 2 1 | 2 1 | 7½ | 1693/4 | | 6 |
| Coopers | 2 0 | 2 0 | 7½ | 1787 | | 4 |

Throughout the Revolutionary War, the employment of shipwrights on piecework was thus very much at the experimental stage, especially at the three major outports. It consequently contained numerous operating faults: in particular, the imposition of relatively low earnings ceilings of only two or three times a traditional basic day's pay; the existence of areas in its management where frauds permitted men to claim the highest rates of pay without their having performed the amount of work needed to earn those rates; and the failure to distinguish work and earnings by the piece during the day and work performed in overtime. Piecework therefore increased earnings, but these increases were limited and the means by which they were achieved were not always legitimate. However, in attempts to improve the scheme, from March 1803 men working by the Job (that is, doing repair work) were permitted to receive as much pay as they could make, the earnings' ceiling being lifted completely; in 1805 shipwrights working by Task (doing new construction work) had the articles of their work increased in value by 20 to 25 per cent; and in 1811, following a recommendation of the Commissioners of Naval Revision, a committee of master shipwrights produced new price schemes for both Task and Job work.[16]

The fundamental change in basic daily rates only occurred in March 1812. In line with the recommendations of the Commissioners of Revision the 'two for one' earned by many artificers since 1794 was adopted as the basic daily rate, though with a slight addition, and variations in the rate were established for summer and winter in war and peace.[17] The new rates represented a realistic attempt to compete for labour wih the merchant yards, where wages reached their highest wartime level in 1811–12. In proposing them the Commissioners of Revision observed that 'workmen in general do not put a fair value on the remote advantages' of sick pay and superannuation and that the new rates should not therefore 'be so much lower than the current wages in private works of a similar nature as government might perhaps fairly expect'.[18]

The increase in wage rates was long overdue. It did not, though, do as much to increase the amount of money actually available to artificers to spend as the improvement in the system of payment that shortly followed it. Partly owing to a cumbersome system of wage calculation, and partly to the shortage of ready money available to the Treasurer of the navy before 1797, earnings in the dockyards were traditionally paid at least three months late. As a result artificers were obliged to live on credit, most resorting to money lenders who exacted an 'exorbitant interest' of 10 or 15 per cent and sometimes insisted on other 'vexatious conditions' as well. In addition, to obtain their loans, prior to the prohibition on unofficial payments in 1801, they had to pay a clerk in the office of the Clerk of the Cheque a fee for a note confirming that they would be receiving wages.[19] Their situation was improved in 1805 with the introduction of 'subsistence money'. In April of that year the Navy Board was obliged to pay a number of men at Chatham yard one-third of their earnings weekly owing to the failure of the Chatham Bank and of the moneylenders with it. This was noted by the Commissioners of Revision who promptly recommended that all the artificers be paid three-quarters of their usual earnings weekly, a practice which was introduced that September. Each man was

Table 16. *The earnings of a shipwright, caulker, rigger and labourer in Portsmouth Dockyard, 1791–1817*

For 1812–1817 the "by the day" figures are given as summer / winter.

| | shipwright | | caulker | | rigger | | labourer | |
|---|---|---|---|---|---|---|---|---|
| | by the day s. d. | by Task work s. d. | by the day s. d. | by Task work s. d. | by the day s. d. | by Task work s. d. | by the day s. d. | by Task work s. d. |
| 1791 | 3 4 | 4 3 | 3 11 | | 2 2 | | 1 8 | |
| 1792 | 3 4 | 4 2 | 3 4 | | 2 2 | | 1 10 | |
| 1793 | 4 2 | 5 6 | 4 2 | | 3 0 | | 2 2 | |
| 1794 | 5 3 | 5 10 | 5 3 | | 3 0 | | 2 2 | |
| 1795 | 4 9 | 4 9 | 4 9 | | 3 0 | | 2 5 | |
| 1796 | 4 9 | 5 5 | 4 9 | | 3 0 | | 2 5 | |
| 1797 | 4 9 | 5 5 | 4 9 | | 3 0 | | 2 5 | |
| 1798 | 4 9 | 5 5 | 4 9 | | 3 0 | | 2 5 | |
| 1799 | 5 5 | 5 5 | 5 5 | | 3 0 | | 2 5 | |
| 1800 | 5 5 | 6 0 | 5 5 | | 3 0 | | 2 5 | |
| 1801 | 6 3 | 6 1 | 5 5 | | 3 0 | | 2 11 | |
| 1802 | 4 2 | 5 2 | 6 3 | | 3 0 | | 2 5 | |
| 1803 | 5 5 | 6 6 | 4 2 | | 3 0 | | 2 5 | |
| 1804 | 5 5 | 6 5 | 5 5 | | 3 0 | | 2 5 | |
| 1805 | 5 5 | 6 9 | 5 5 | | 3 9 | | 2 5 | 2 4 |
| 1806 | 4 9 | 6 10 | 5 5 | | 3 9 | | 2 5 | 3 0 |
| 1807 | 4 9 | 6 5 | 6 3 | | 3 0 | | 2 5 | 3 8 |
| 1808 | 4 9 | 6 8 | 6 3 | | 3 0 | | 2 5 | 3 9 |
| 1809 | 4 9 | 7 1 | 6 3 | | 3 4 | | 2 5 | 3 3 |
| 1810 | 4 9 | 6 9 | 6 3 | | 3 4 | | 2 5 | 3 7 |
| 1811 | 4 2 | 6 4 | 4 2 | 6 2 | 3 4 | | 2 2 | 3 2 |
| 1812 | 5 0 / 4 0 | 7 7 | 5 0 / 4 0 | 8 4 | 3 4 / 2 8 | | 2 7 / 2 1 | 3 7 |
| 1813 | 5 0 / 4 0 | 7 3 | 5 0 / 4 0 | 8 8 | 3 4 / 2 8 | | 2 7 / 2 1 | 3 5 |
| 1814 | 5 0 / 4 0 | 7 2 | 5 0 / 4 0 | 7 5 | 3 4 / 2 8 | | 2 7 / 2 1 | 3 10 |
| 1815 | 5 0 / 4 0 | 6 6 | 5 0 / 4 0 | 8 7 | 3 4 / 2 8 | | 2 7 / 2 1 | 3 4 |
| 1816 | 3 6 / 2 9 | 4 2 | 3 6 / 2 9 | 4 0 | 2 6 / 2 0 | | 1 10 / 1 6 | 2 3 |
| 1817 | 3 6 / 2 9 | 3 10 | 3 6 / 2 9 | 4 5 | 2 6 / 2 0 | | 1 10 / 1 6 | 2 0 |

Labourers were not employed by Task until 1805, caulkers not until 1811, and riggers not at all.

thereafter paid between 12s. and 25s. weekly according to his trade, the payments being received with 'universal satisfaction'.[20]

Nevertheless artificers continued to slip into debt. John Payne of the Navy Office found in 1812 that although the artificers were relieved from complete dependence on money lenders:

> But still while any part of the wages of the men is withheld from them a great many will have recourse to dealers to supply their wants. And it is to be regretted that in many instances industrious workmen with large families are driven to such persons. . . . Another obvious evil attends the workmen being kept in ignorance of the amount of their wages until nearly three months after the quarter has expired in which the wages were earned. The men regulate their expenditure *according to what they have earned* and are apt to be too sanguine in this calculation and not a little suspicious and dissatisfied when they are disappointed. In numerous instances the balance received has not been sufficient to cover the assessment on account of the property tax and in some instances, after the allowance of subsistence money has been deducted, the balance has been against the workmen who are thrown upon the mercy of their creditors.

Payne, who was sent to the yards to improve the system by which wages were calculated, reported that as Master Measurers' departments had recently been established, complete weekly earnings could be paid as easily as 'subsistence money'; moreover, as quarterly pay-day holidays would then be unnecessary, more work would be performed and greater earnings made.[21] Weekly payment was consequently introduced in July 1813.

The Napoleonic War thus saw several improvements in both the scale and the punctuality of artificers' pay. It would be wrong, however, to suppose that artificers were very much better off at the end of the war than they had been during the Revolutionary War. For from 1801, when the recommendations of the Commissioners on Fees were implemented, the artificers were deprived of certain extra perquisites and emoluments that must formerly have added considerably to their income.

In view of the payment until 1805 of all earnings at least three months late, the loss in 1801 of 'chips' was particularly important. This was a payment in kind to which most trades were entitled – the timber-working trades being allowed to remove bundles of surplus pieces of wood and the smiths, for example, being allowed their moulds. The bundles provided a significant daily income: some bundles were reported to have been sold at the yard gates in 1793 for 1s. and in 1801, when the artificers were approached about the amount for which they would forego the perquisite, they were valued by them at 8d. a bundle. However, this is not surprising, for the privilege had become an abuse, men spending the last half-hour of each day finding wood to remove, some cutting up good timber and the bundles sometimes providing cover for embezzlement of more valuable materials. By the order in council of 21 May 1801 they were consequently commuted to daily allowances, paid quarterly, of 3 to 6d. according to trade.[22]

Another considerable loss at this time was the earnings of artificers' apprentices. The allowance of an apprentice was used in the yards both as a reward for conscientious attention to duty and as a means of relieving men with large families. Although sons were often apprenticed to fathers, this was not always the case and, unless allowances for the boys' upkeep were specified in indentures, the artificers were entitled to pocket their earnings. However, in a belief that the amounts passed on for the boys' maintenance were inconsiderable and with the intention of introducing greater theoretical content into their education, in December 1802 all apprentices were rebound to the principal officer in their department. Their former masters were renamed 'instructors' and the apprentices were limited to a single day's pay even when working piecework or overtime, these earnings being officially divided between the instructors (two-thirds) and parents or guardians (one-third). Earlier an apprentice had added about £70 a year to an artificer's wages. In 1802, however, the value of each boy was reduced to about £16.[23] As this severely reduced both the number of boys entering the yards and the quality of their instruction, the earnings of older boys in particular were later enlarged. Even so, apprentices never again acquired the value they had possessed before 1802.

Certain other allowances continued to supplement earnings. A traditional lodging allowance of two and a half pence a week was continued until 1812. Each smith received a dozen pints of table beer and three of strong beer each day on account of the heat of their work; while from 1813 scavelmen, who cleared mud from docks and channels, obtained £2 a year for boots. Yet these allowances were of little account compared to the value of chips and the earnings of apprentices. The regulation of these two supplements to wages in 1801 and 1802 marked a decline in the extra attractions of dockyard employment which was only repaired with the introduction of subsistence money in 1805 and of weekly payment in 1812. The period 1802 to 1805 was consequently one in which dockyard employment had least to recommend it, a period in which there was more than usual reason for recruitment to be poor.

Recruitment was a major problem between 1803 and 1805, not only on account of the falling attractions of dockyard employment. Throughout the wars regulations governed the entry of artificers: they had to have served a regular apprenticeship of seven years, be certified by the surgeon as being in good health and sound in body, and be under an age specified by the Admiralty. But St Vincent, First Lord between 1801 and 1804, applied the age regulation with particular rigidity. Having found during his visitation of the yards in 1802 that men of 'advanced ages' had been entered during the Revolutionary War, he stipulated that thereafter new entrants should be under 28. In March 1803, Deptford, Woolwich, Chatham and Portsmouth each being short of their peace establishments by about 100 shipwrights – a shortage 'principally to be attributed to the limitation of the age of men to be entered' – the Navy Board was permitted to raise the age limit to 35. By October recruitment had still not picked up and the subordinate Board proposed lifting the age limit completely, but this time St Vincent refused. Recruitment consequently remained poor until June 1804 when Melville agreed to raise the age limit to 45. Yet even this was inadequate. The age limit had to be lifted completely in August 1805, when Barham also saw fit to recommend 'advertising in the public newspapers' the inclination of the Admiralty 'to re-enter in H.M. dockyards at home such artificers as have left them during the last four or five years'.[24]

St Vincent was consistent with Admiralty policy in attempting to enforce a relatively low age limit between 1802 and 1804. In 1806 the limit was restored to 35 and remained there until 1813. During this period a relatively low age limit was acknowledged as necessary. The Navy Board observed in 1813 that the employment of shipwrights 'almost entirely' by the piece gave 'the greatest stimulus to their exertions' but had 'at the same time the effect of shortening the period during which they remain at full vigour'. Some flexibility was nevertheless imperative. In 1813, although the Navy Board requested a limit of 45, the Admiralty compromised at 40, an age which in the circumstances

Table 17. *The total number of artificers and labourers, and total number of ship-wrights, 1793–1815*

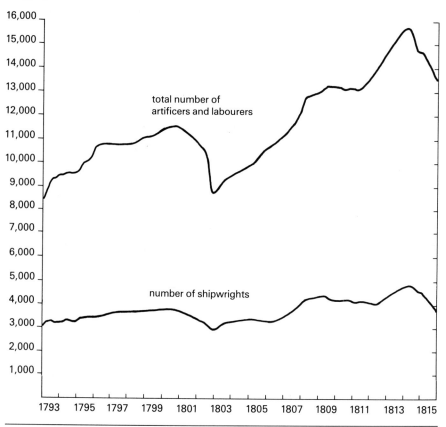

appears to have been adequate. Whereas between 1803 and 1804, with the reintroduction of wartime pay rates in the merchant yards, the shipwrights in some dockyards actually declined in number, in 1812–13, with the help of the new system of weekly payment, the numbers grew markedly.[25]

Recruitment during the mobilization of 1803–4 was also handicapped by the refusal of St Vincent to re-enter men he had already had discharged for disciplinary reasons. These discharges accounted for almost 450 skilled men in 1801 and 1802 – a number which, on top of a peace reduction of over 1,100 in 1802, deprived the dockyards of labour they could ill afford to lose. With the loss of more men in 1803 as merchant yard wages again rose to war levels, the dockyards were left in a desperate position. After St Vincent's resignation the Navy Board was divided as to whether to permit the re-entry of men who had left the dockyards for higher wages; but by 1805 even men discharged for disciplinary purposes had to be accepted – the proviso being that they otherwise had good characters.[26]

Recruitment seems to have been more difficult in 1803–4 than at any other time. Nevertheless, even though there were periods when more men left the yards than were entered, the long-term tendency was gradually to enlarge the workforce. Recruitment practices ensured that at times of emergency the whole country was scoured. In 1813 notices were printed for distribution in the north and at Liverpool advertising the availability of work in the yards. In 1803 men applying for entry were either sent protections from impressment or brought south in naval tenders carrying pressed men. They were allowed day pay from the time of their discharge from their previous employers and given advances on their wages on arrival. Emigration on the part of artificers had been forbidden by Acts of 1718 and 1750 (5 Geo. I, c.27 and 23 Geo. II, c.13) and attempts, when discovered, were immediately prevented. In 1807, the abolition of the slave trade having thrown many artificers at Liverpool out of work, measures were promptly ordered for those attempting to emigrate to be impressed.[27] Artificers faced by the choice of applying for employment in the dockyards or impressment must understandably have chosen the yards.

Shipwrights were most in demand throughout the wars but labourers, 'extra men' and riggers were also needed, especially in the difficult mobilization period of 1803–4. Then, as well as new construction being stopped, repairs had also to be abandoned: thus at Sheerness in 1803 a ship requiring six weeks' repair was simply put aside because there were 'so few shipwrights belonging to the yard'. Most vacancies for labourers were in the Thames yards, but at Chatham in 1804 the Master Shipwright was unable to stow away masts, spars and other stores landed at the wharf and the yard was 'in such a lumbered state' that he was 'unable to carry on the works thereof'. The shortage of 'extra men' held up the movement of yard craft conveying materials to artificers working afloat; in March 1803 over 90 such men were required at Sheerness and nearly 160 at Plymouth. Nearly three years later over 200 'extra men' were still wanted at Plymouth and the yard officers complained that after filling up lighters' and boats' crews they had a working party of only 20 men. Where 'extra men' were too few even to fill up boats' crews or had insufficient experience of local waters to move ships in Ordinary, riggers and riggers' labourers were used in their place. But riggers were also in short supply; at Chatham in June 1803 ships were 'standing fast' for want of them.[28] The periods of demobilization, when ships were entering port in a steady stream, similarly overwhelmed the labour available. In 1802 it was simply acknowledged by the Navy Board that 'the very great and pressing demands for people on account of dismantling the fleet . . . put it out of the power of the Master Attendant's department[s] to keep pace with the whole of the work'.[29]

Under such pressure the Navy Board and yard officers made use of every source of additional labour, concentrating their skilled men at the yards and on tasks where they were most needed. In 1797 gangs of shipwrights and caulkers were sent from Deptford and Woolwich to Portsmouth; in 1803, they went to Sheerness, where gangs were also sent from Chatham. At times ships' carpenters from ships in Ordinary worked alongside yard artificers, while seamen were employed both to rig and equip ships for service and to strip them for Ordinary. Contract riggers were employed during mobilization periods and in 1803 merchant yard caulkers who had offered their services to government were permitted to enter either a Thames yard or Chatham. At the eastern yards Greenwich pensioners were paid as labourers for receiving and shipping off stores and for ballasting, transporting and clearing ships in Ordinary. Local

*Table 18. The workforce on 26 March 1814*
(Account includes inferior officers, cabinkeepers and apprentices.)

|  | Deptford | Woolwich | Chatham | Sheerness | Portsmouth | Plymouth | total |
|---|---|---|---|---|---|---|---|
| Blockmakers | 4 | 3 | 4 | 4 | 7 | 6 | 28 |
| Braziers | 1 |  | 2 |  | 2 |  | 5 |
| Bricklayers | 12 | 23 | 38 | 13 | 38 | 57 | 182 |
| Bricklayers' labourers | 10 | 20 | 27 | 9 | 42 | 22 | 130 |
| Carvers | 2 |  | 1 |  |  |  | 3 |
| Caulkers | 29 | 43 | 67 | 49 | 129 | 116 | 433 |
| Coopers |  | 1 | 1 |  | 1 | 2 | 5 |
| Engine repairers |  | 2 |  |  |  |  | 2 |
| Founders |  |  |  |  | 2 |  | 2 |
| Glaziers | 1 | 1 | 1 |  |  |  | 3 |
| Hair bed manufacturers | 18 | 10 |  |  |  |  | 28 |
| House carpenters | 89 | 21 | 110 | 78 | 245 | 245 | 888 |
| Joiners | 47 | 38 | 76 | 39 | 158 | 107 | 465 |
| Locksmiths | 1 | 2 | 2 | 1 | 2 | 4 | 12 |
| Masons | 2 | 3 | 5 | 2 | 21 | 29 | 62 |
| Messengers | 9 | 10 | 10 | 10 | 16 | 11 | 66 |
| Oakum boys | 13 | 13 | 21 | 17 | 44 | 45 | 153 |
| Oarmakers | 1 | 1 | 1 | 1 |  | 1 | 5 |
| Painters | 13 | 15 | 15 | 10 | 47 | 29 | 129 |
| Painters' labourers |  | 12 |  | 5 | 14 |  | 31 |
| Paviers | 2 | 1 |  |  |  |  | 3 |
| Pitch heaters | 1 | 1 | 1 | 1 | 2 | 2 | 8 |
| Plumbers | 2 | 2 | 4 | 3 | 7 | 5 | 23 |
| Riggers | 75 | 58 | 108 | 33 | 181 | 141 | 596 |
| Sailmakers | 47 | 29 | 52 | 26 | 77 | 68 | 299 |
| Sawyers | 140 | 135 | 167 | 44 | 240 | 208 | 934 |
| Scavelmen | 40 | 40 | 90 | 40 | 120 | 170 | 500 |
| Shipwrights | 553 | 584 | 783 | 267 | 1,433 | 1,316 | 4,936 |

militia regiments supplied labourers and hemp dressers at Deptford and Chatham, and regular troops stationed near yards were made available for fitting ships in 1805. Prisoners of war were used for this purpose at Chatham during the 'heat' of 1801; while convicts were employed loading yard craft at Portsmouth, ballasting ships, landing stores and stowing timber at Woolwich, and performing some skilled tasks at Plymouth. Although there were attempts to enter women for spinning twine at Portsmouh and Plymouth, women were only used on a regular basis for sewing 'colours'.[30]

These expedients more or less permitted the difficulties arising from the shortages of labour to be overcome. During periods of pressure, however, the yards appeared to operate only through a perilous combination of expedients. Long-term solutions to the problems were considered. The Navy Board, for example, was fully aware of the labour-saving advantages of mechanization; in 1802, when labourers were needed to sort junk in Portsmouth yard, it simply assumed that 'as the moveable steam engine has been found to answer so well we trust there will be no difficulty in sparing the labourers necessary for this service'.[31] And in October 1802 Samuel Bentham's idea that apprentices should be trained in more than one trade was adopted when orders were given

Table 18. *The workforce on 26 March 1814 (contd.)*
(Account includes inferior officers, cabinkeepers and apprentices.)

| | Deptford | Woolwich | Chatham | Sheerness | Portsmouth | Plymouth | total |
|---|---|---|---|---|---|---|---|
| Smiths | 99 | 86 | 120 | 49 | 182 | 234 | 770 |
| Teams | 19 | 21 | 22 | 9 | 40 | 31 | 142 |
| Tinmen | | 1 | | | 1 | 1 | 3 |
| Trenail mooters | | 2 | | | | | 2 |
| Warders | 12 | 13 | 20 | 23 | 36 | 26 | 130 |
| Waterman | 1 | | | | | | 1 |
| Wheelwrights | 2 | 2 | 2 | 2 | 3 | 3 | 14 |
| Yard labourers | 640 | 486 | 520 | 153 | 556 | 606 | 2,961 |
| Persons employed at the: | | | | | | | |
| Wood mills | | | | | 94 | | 94 |
| Metal mills | | | | | 66 | | 66 |
| Millwrights' shop | | | | | 72 | | 72 |
| **Rope yards** | | | | | | | |
| Boys | | 24 | 48 | | 42 | 42 | 156 |
| Cordage remanufacturers | | 19 | | | | | 19 |
| Foremen | | 3 | 4 | | 3 | 5 | 15 |
| Hemp dressers | | 6 | 13 | | 16 | 14 | 49 |
| Labourers | | 52 | 84 | | 85 | 82 | 303 |
| Layers | | 4 | 4 | | 5 | 4 | 17 |
| Line and twine spinners | | 3 | 6 | | 5 | 16 | 30 |
| Messengers | | 1 | 1 | | | 1 | 3 |
| Overseers | | 1 | | | | | 1 |
| Porters | | 2 | | | | | 2 |
| Spinners | | 124 | 210 | | 183 | 189 | 705 |
| Wheelboys | | 7 | 13 | | 10 | 18 | 48 |
| Yarn knotters | | 1 | 19 | | 30 | 13 | 63 |
| total | 1,886 | 2,026 | 2,672 | 888 | 4,257 | 3,869 | 15,598 |

for shipwright apprentices to be instructed in the work of a caulker in the last year of their training.[32] But such minor innovations could make little impression on operations of the scale performed in the yards. In reality the only long-term solution to the dockyards' labour shortages was a large increase in the number of artificers available for employment. Yet, though the dockyards themselves were regarded as the main training grounds for national supplies of skilled men in the shipbuilding trades, there was little systematic planning behind the numbers of boys apprenticed in the yards. These numbers were primarily governed by immediate demands: the number of 'deserving' men needing 'encouragement' and the proportion of boys to men the artificers would tolerate in their gangs. There is little evidence that the Navy Board ever attempted to plan for the long-term growth of the navy and the dockyards even in the Napoleonic War.

The relationship between the number of apprentices and the skilled men available to the yards was nevertheless appreciated. During the eighteenth century the dockyard smiths, ropemakers, joiners and house carpenters were prevented from having apprentices because 'as many workmen of these descriptions as were wanted . . . could always be procured at short notice'; the allowance of apprentices in these trades in 1802 was accordingly an acknowledgment that those trained elsewhere no longer sufficed to meet the yards' growing needs.[33] However, by the end of the Revolutionary War it was also acknowledged that apprentices were only trained at a cost. Attention focussed in particular on the pocketing by boys' masters of some, if not all, of their earnings and the purely practical nature of their instruction. From the public's point of view, both aspects of dockyard apprenticeship left much to be desired. Although large amounts were paid out in apprentices' earnings, the artificers that were produced were no more than basic craftsmen. Reform seemed highly necessary. From 1801, when St Vincent introduced Samuel Bentham's revision of the recommendations of the Commissioners on Fees, the system of apprenticeship was consequently subject to a series of 'improvements', the changes only being completed in 1811. The initial changes, however, had unforeseen effects both on the standard of instruction and on the number of boys entering the yards. The reforms in fact reduced rather than increased the number of skilled men raised in the yards. They enhanced rather than diminished the long-term likelihood of recruitment problems.

The ideas behind the reforms were Bentham's. He hoped to develop a system of instruction for shipwright apprentices which included tuition in the theory as well as in the practice of shipbuilding. The driving force behind them was St Vincent. On his visitation of the yards in 1802 he was struck by the 'most flagrant abuses' that had been practised by officers who had apprentices prior to 1801; at Sheerness, for example, shipwright officers' servants had 'been borne out with the full extra of the yard upon a variety of work which it is impossible they could have been employed upon during the course of the day'.[34] St Vincent intended that a system should be created in which neither officers nor men had a vested interest in frauds that increased the cost of training apprentices.

Bentham prepared the way for more far-reaching changes in his revision of the Fees report implemented in May 1801. Yard officers were deprived of their apprentices, who were distributed among deserving artificers. Then in November 1802 he provided St Vincent with a scheme of further changes. It clearly appealed to St Vincent, for Bentham claimed that parents or guardians of boys in the yards received only a quarter of the wages paid to boys' masters and that the public could safely be saved large amounts in wages.[35] If rebound to the principal officer in their department, the masters could be renamed 'instructors' and the pay they received on account of the apprentices could be limited to a single day's pay, this being officially divided between instructor and parents. The apprentices could then be removed when necessary from their instructors and given theoretical tuition in schools. The apprentices would thereby receive a better education and the artificers would receive a reward for their instruction that was fair to the public. St Vincent gave the Navy Board no time to consider the scheme. Six days after Bentham had submitted it to the Admiralty, on 28 November 1802, St Vincent ordered it carried into effect.[36]

The system of apprenticeship was accordingly transformed, new regulations defining a relationship that had once been a matter of private arrangement between masters, parents and 'servant'. But the failure to allow the Navy Board time to receive comments on the scheme from yard officers quickly became apparent. Bentham had not been accurate in his assessment of the sums that masters had previously allowed boys' parents. Whereas from November 1802, for their one-third share of an apprentice's day pay, parents received about £8 a year, some had previously received amounts ranging between £10 and £30 a year.[37] And inevitably parents immediately found that the new amounts were inadequate for upkeep. Boys were accordingly required to leave the dockyards to make higher earnings elsewhere: and these included some who, prior to the order in council of May 1801, had been apprenticed to officers. Although the 1801 regulations provided that they should be continued any allowance from their masters that had been stipulated in their indentures, some were not covered by such clauses. With boys leaving the yards and a decline in the number entering, the complement of apprentices dropped. In 1800 there were 770 shipwright apprentices in the yards; in 1803 only 605. Deptford yard received applications for entry from boys in poor circumstances but many were refused entry on account of their small stature and by February 1804 the yard was 36 shipwright apprentices short of its complement.[38]

At this stage measures were attempted to keep boys in the yards and attract back those that had left. In February 1804 boys previously apprenticed to officers, but not covered by a clause in their indentures entitling them to a particular allowance, were given an extra 1s. a day as long as they had already served half their time and could take a man's place; and from April 1804 all apprentices who had served half their time were allowed the whole of their earnings by Task or Job. Both parents and instructors of older boys consequently received more for their respective one-third and two-thirds shares. Nevertheless, with younger boys still restricted to their day pay whatever their employment, all except 'the most indigent classes' continued to have reason for apprenticing their boys elsewhere.[39]

Perhaps the most damaging aspect of this decline was the failure to recruit boys who had sufficiently affluent backgrounds to have been given some basic education before entering the yards. These boys' parents were not affected by the decline in apprentices' earnings. But by the order in council of May 1801, when the receipt of unofficial payments was prohibited, parents wishing to assure their sons of every career advantage had been prevented from binding them to yard officers for the payment for an appropriately large premium.[40] The Commissioners of Revision found that not one apprentice who was entered between May 1801 and the end of 1805 was allowed to work in the mould-lofts 'where the plans of ships are drawn and where consequently some knowledge might be gained', and the explanation given by the yard officers was that 'none could be found of such education as to be fit for it'. The Commissioners observed that this was a shortage that was likely to result in a deficiency of able officers and consequently could have given rise to 'much danger to the country'.[41]

Had Bentham obtained schools for the theoretical education of shipwright apprentices, this failure to recruit educated boys might not have occurred, for such boys would have been precisely those who would have most benefited from the schools. Distinguishing themselves in this way, they would have had less need of connections with rising yard officers to smooth their way in their careers. There were semi-official schools established in the yards: a school-master was employed in Plymouth yard, unbeknown to the Navy Board until 1804; and reading, writing and the common rules of arithmetic were taught in a school instituted by the commissioner and yard officers at Chatham in 1802. However, nothing was organized on a formal basis in all the yards. Bentham had a system of theoretical education ready. Indeed he had presented this plan for the information of the Admiralty Board in 1795, claiming that he had drawn it up in 1779 and that it was based on the ideas of Sir William Petty.[42] But owing to the resumption of war in 1803, St Vincent's commitment to economy and Bentham's relative lack of favour with St Vincent's successors, the schools Bentham had planned were not immediately established.

Ironically, a further effect of the reorganization of apprenticeship was the evident deterioration in instruction of the traditional practical form given to boys in the yards. On account of the small amount of their pay during the first three and a half years of their servitude, young apprentices were regarded by their instructors as more of a liability than an asset. Indeed, because the deserving men who were rewarded with apprentices were generally found in Task or Job gangs, these gangs tended to contain more apprentices than usual. Consequently, instead of earning more than average because they were working by the piece, these artificers earned less because young apprentices could neither perform the work of men nor earn more than their day pay. In 1804 and 1805 the shipwrights at both Chatham and Plymouth complained of this situation and received the support of their officers. In April 1804 two gangs of shipwrights at Plymouth contained 15 apprentices, most of whom were 'very young'. According to the Master Shipwright, for every boy in each gang the artificers lost a guinea a week from their collective earnings.[43] This situation did not encourage men to waste time in instructing apprentices. Instead it gave them a strong incentive to neglect them in order to increase their earnings by performing more work themselves.

The Commissioners of Revision justly noted in 1806 that Bentham's and St Vincent's reorganization of apprenticeship revealed 'a want of foresight and due consideration'. They ignored the less obvious achievements: the dissolution of a traditional system more productive of useful connections and profit than of educated shipwrights; the preparation of artificers for the introduction of schooling and of promotion according to theoretical as well as practical ability; and the demonstration of the need for a consciously planned pay and career structure for all apprentices. These were, however, achievements that permitted the Commissioners of Revision to propose a new and more effective system that was adopted by order in council in 1809 and brought into operation in 1811.[44]

Within this system apprentices were divided into two classes, the first consisting of boys qualified for instruction in the duties of yard officers, and the second of boys capable of performing the work of ordinary shipwrights. To be considered for the first class, applicants had to be at least 16 years of age, to understand 'the rules of vulgar and decimal arithmetic and to be so far advanced in mathematics as to understand the first six books of Euclid's Elements'; also, in order to obtain instruction from publications in French, they had to be able to read that language with ease. After having passed the examination of a Navy Board committee, these boys were bound to the yard commissioner at Portsmouth, where they spent their first six years working half of each day with shipwrights in the yard and the other half receiving instruction in the School of Naval Architecture, established in 1811 on the premises of the Royal Naval College and transferred about 1817 to its own purpose-built building. The School provided a comprehensive course in the skills and knowledge then considered necessary for an educated shipwright officer and included tuition in mathematics, the drawing of draughts and 'laying off', actual building, French and painting. In December 1813 James Inman, the School's professor, reported for the information of the Admiralty that, having been there three years, the most advanced of the 'superior class of apprentices' had

read in Mathematics an introduction to Algebra, Euclid plane and Spherical Trigonometry, a short chapter on Curve Lines, Mechanicks, Hydrostatics, Emerson on the pressure of Beams and the strength and stress of timber, and Atwoods' paper in the Philosophical Transactions on the stability of ships. They are at present engaged in making the necessary calculations for stability at different angles of inclination for the ships of war of which we have the draughts. They will afterwards read Chapman's Treatise on the construction of ships, of which I hope to finish a translation for them this vacation, and selections from the best French writers on Naval Architecture. This will take up probably another year. They will then, it is to be hoped, be properly prepared for designing plans for ships of different kinds themselves, in which they must be well exercised. In all the detail of executing a Draught from given dimensions, Laying off on the mold loft, and actual Building, I have reason to expect both from my own observation and from Mr. Fincham's reports that in the course of another year the most advanced and best among them will not have much to learn. Steps will possibly be then taken to give them a thorough insight into the conversion of timber, mast making, fitting of ships etc.[45]

It was intended that the last year of the course should be spent at sea observing the operation of ships in motion, and at least some of the boys actually had this experience. Eventually they were employed as inferior dockyard officers or as overseers for ships building in the merchant yards until established officers' places became available for them.

Apprentices of the second class were to be at least 14 years of age at entry and to be able to read, write and understand basic arithmetic. Preference was to be given to the sons or orphans of yard officers, shipwrights, caulkers, naval officers, superannuated officers and other workmen in that order. Higher basic daily rates of pay were established than those laid down in 1802, of which half went to parents or guardians. These apprentices could enter the first class by passing an examination, to help with the study for which suitable persons were selected by the yard commissioners and rewarded with an official allowance. By 1811 at least one schoolroom was established for this purpose.[46]

This two-tier system of apprenticeship seems to have had some success. The young men who obtained membership of the first class were deterred from leaving the dockyards within ten years of completing their training by being required to give a bond and provide two sureties of £800 to be forfeited if they left. By 1832 the dockyards had consequently benefited from the services of 41 specifically trained officers. However, this relatively small number of trainees was counterbalanced by the far greater number of apprentices of the second class who continued to receive a purely practical education as before. Although provision was made for aspiring boys to join the first class, they were in practice deterred from leaving their day-to-day work for purposes of study by a regulation that required them to compensate their instructors for the loss of earnings the latter would otherwise have received on their account. There was consequently little movement from the second to the first class and, one can assume, few attempts at it. There appears indeed to have been no more incentive than there ever had been for ordinary apprentices to take an interest in the theory of ship construction. It was, possibly, partly for this reason that the School of Naval Architecture was closed in the rationalization of 1832 and replaced by schools in all the major dockyards 12 years later. These schools extended the theory of naval architecture to all apprentices of whom the best were then selected for instruction as officers.[47]

The unforeseen consequences of the changes in apprenticeship gave a long-term dimension to the shortages of labour in the dockyards. But reforms affecting the workforce did not all have an adverse effect on the problem of recruitment. Indeed reforms during the Napoleonic War in employment by the piece did much to make the best possible use of all the labour available. Again, the improvements were initiated by St Vincent but they were carried through primarily on account of the desire for economy and efficiency affecting the whole of government bureaucracy. As in the case of the system of apprenticeship, St Vincent's attention was caught by apparent frauds being committed in the accounts of work performed by the piece. Partly as a result of fabrications, the wages bill for the six dockyards rose progressively each year between 1793 and 1800, and in 1801 the bill for Plymouth yard was almost double the amount it had been in 1780.[48] St Vincent particularly disapproved of the system of Job work (under which repairs were performed) because, each job varying in detail one from another, standard sums could not easily be fixed even for similar jobs. The Navy Board, on the other hand, believed that work was performed more quickly when paid for by the piece rather than by the day, yet had no evidence to support the view. It admitted in 1803 that, although regular accounts were kept of the repair of every ship, 'from the uncertainty of what work would have been actually performed by the same number of men in the same time if they had been paid by the day no exact calculation can be made to prove the actual advantage of employing the artificers by Job'.[49]

Following his visitation of the dockyards in 1802, St Vincent obtained the Commission of Naval Enquiry to investigate the range of apparent managerial failings in the naval departments, but in particular the management of piecework at Plymouth. Before this investigation actually occurred, the Navy Board made some progress with the piecework problems. The future of Job work nevertheless remained in doubt. In October 1803 the Comptroller, Sir Andrew Hamond, wrote to the leading Commissioner of Enquiry, Sir Charles Morice Pole, requesting him and his colleagues 'not to come to any decision upon its merits' until they had had an opportunity of making inquiries into its operation at all the yards:

> The Admiralty Board conceived so much prejudice against it during their stay at Plymouth at the late visitation that they were determined to get rid of it, but when they had been at the other yards and heard what the Navy Board had to say in favour of the principle, they gave orders for its continuance. It certainly had been liable to abuses at Plymouth from the negligence of the officers, but I hope the new cheques and regulations have done all that away and I confess I know of no mode so likely to ensure an equal proportion of work for the same expence. When I look back to the time when the artificers of the yards worked by the day, I perfectly remember the observations of all us sea officers on the shameful manner in which they wasted their time. In short the dockyard men in general are a description of people who are always upon the watch to get as much money as they can and to do as little for it as possible; nor are the quartermen even to be depended upon sufficiently to enforce a proper degree of labour from the men unless specific quantities of work are required for certain forms of money.[50]

The Commissioners of Enquiry nevertheless devoted almost the whole of their sixth report to the operation of piecework at Plymouth, clearly basing their recommendation for a return to payment by the day for the performance of most repairs on their observations there.

The completion of their report, however, coincided with St Vincent's resignation and was followed early in 1805 by the appointment of the Commissioners of Revision led by Charles Middleton, who as Comptroller had been responsible for extending piecework to the six yards. Middleton naturally remained strongly in favour of the system; he believed it was 'of such importance towards hurrying up the fleet as cannot be given up without ruin attending it' and that 'by working Task and Job the public receive at least one half more of the labour of the artificers'.[51] He did, however, recognize that the reforms necessary posed formidable problems. He wrote in December 1804 to his friend, J. D. Thompson:

> The Task work will be a Task indeed and will require much information and consideration, but I am doubtful whether more can be done in war than cheque the existing abuses and forming a new establishment to be carried into execution when a peace is concluded. So great an alteration as must take place should be done with caution. The work as carried on at present is contrary to every principle by which the common labour of the country is executed and by that means involved in extricacies and difficulties than can only be mended by simplifying the whole and bringing it as near as the nature of the work will admit to common practice.[52]

The commitment of these Commissioners to retaining piecework ensured that both Task and Job work were continued in operation, the form of work of which they disapproved – employment by Job afloat – also eventually being retained. Yard officers were appointed in committees to consider all schemes of piecework, both those in operation and those considered possible. Consequently, in spite of the fears that innovations would have to wait until war was concluded, between 1808 and 1811 piecework in the dockyards was overhauled and extended, further improvements being added by John Payne of the Navy Office.[53]

Throughout this long period of revision and reform, changes were found necessary in four areas. Priority was given to the separation of piecework from the more traditional system of payment by time. At Plymouth confusion had arisen from the use of multiples of the traditional rates of day pay as ceilings for earnings by piecework. As payments for overtime were also expressed in these multiples, earnings made for piecework during the day had become dependent upon making those rates in the evening for overtime. Men working 'three for one' by the piece thus had to stay five hours' overtime to make their three days' pay, even though they might have performed sufficient work in the day to qualify them for the money. The combination of piecework with overtime payments could be justified as a means of preventing men rushing their work. But, as Commissioner Coffin observed in 1800, men would not and could not work all hours: 'the great Extra people of every description are set down for does not produce the intended effect . . . in other words artificers and labourers cannot be trusted to work in the dark, nor can it be expected that men worn out . . . with a hard day's work can earn what they receive'.[54] Although a ceiling was retained on earnings by Task, the Navy Board's order of March 1803 for shipwrights working by Job to receive as much pay as they could make broke the link between piecework and overtime.

The new earnings policy initially made the management of artificers more difficult, for they developed a new attitude to their work. This was evident in the failure of the Chatham shipwrights to return to the yard one wet afternoon in May 1805, even though work was usually provided for them under cover in such weather. Commissioner Hope reported that this had 'never happened when they received their extra pay by time and not by measurement of their work'. Yet, 'since the mode has been established of paying the men for what they earn, they have formed the idea that their time is their own because if not making earnings they are no expense to Government'.[55] Nevertheless the order of March 1803 was a logical improvement. Even the Commissioners of Naval Enquiry approved. They saw 'no good reason why any restriction should have been laid upon the amount of their earnings' provided the prices set for the articles of work performed were 'fair and equitable'.[56]

The adjustment of these prices was next in priority. The schemes of prices used by the various trades in the yards were systematically revised. The Job prices set for shipwrights and caulkers were standardized in January 1802; new price schemes were issued for Task work by sawyers and ropemakers in 1803 and 1804; and a new scheme of Task prices for shipwright and caulkers' work was produced in February 1804. Nevertheless the adjustment of prices so as to ensure comparability between earnings made by men on different works was a long, drawn-out process of trial and error. In July 1804 the Plymouth officers complained that the new prices made it 'utterly impossible . . . to make their wages come out alike'; and, to prevent discontent, it was necessary to 'put those gangs which have fallen short on such works as may pay them better and shift all the men at the dock side so circumstanced at the end of the month'. The officers were, though, of opinion that to shift men from one ship or work to another would mean the loss of working time and thus be 'of detriment to the service and the men in general'.[57]

In fact the Commissioners of Revision found that both Task and Job prices contained many anomalies, men employed on some articles making less than half the earnings that could be made on others. Task prices were particularly disparate: those fixed for the construction of small vessels were dispro-portionately lower than those fixed for larger ones; and the amount of wages paid for all new construction was generally lower than the market value of the vessels. As recommended by the Commissioners, a committee of Master Shipwrights again revised the shipwrights' Task and Job prices, and new schemes were issued in 1811. Thereafter, in consequence of the work in the yards of John Payne, monthly reports were made to the Surveyors' assistants of works upon which earnings exceeded or fell under the prices set for them and every two or three months these prices were revised.[58]

The adjustment system established by Payne gave the Navy Board greater control over earnings from piecework, and thus over the total wages bill, than had ever been possible before. But this system itself owed much to develop-ments in the process by which accounts were formed of the amount of work performed by artificers. Until the end of the Revolutionary War, a loosely regulated system of accounting, combined with the vested interest of principal and inferior officers in artificers' earnings, facilitated fabrications in accounts. Statements of Job or repair work were most easy to fabricate as the prices paid for common jobs were not standardized throughout all six yards until January 1802. Until then propositions for jobs were sent to the Navy Office, but the Navy Board was unable to check the prices proposed exactly, no repair being quite the same as any other. As the accuracy of the prices had to be left to the yard officers, they in time came to regard them as formalities. In some instances, according to the Commissioners of Enquiry, 'the men were paid previous to the propositions having received the sanction of the Navy Board or previous even to their having been transmitted to them for that purpose'. In these cases it was a simple matter to make out the propositions for the number of men and the amount of work that obtained the full rates of pay allowed. The accounts of work completed were then made out to agree with the propositions. These accounts also defied comparison at the Navy Office for their form varied from yard to yard and some made no distinction between the jobs on which separate gangs were employed.[59]

The immediate response of the Navy Board to the exposure of these defects by the Commissioners of Enquiry was to standardize and simplify the job notes at each yard. These were made out by the inferior officers in charge of gangs and recorded the amount of work each gang performed. From March 1804 the notes were 'plain and clear' and permitted an exact calculation of individual gangs' earnings. The inferior officers were also required to give bond that they would supply the Job office with accurate statements of work performed. This initially caused difficulty. At Plymouth in April 1804, 29 shipwright quarter-men were discharged for refusing to sign a memorandum book signifying their willingness to conform to the new regulations. However, 28 were later re-entered and most of them then signed the book.[60]

It remained to ensure that the men taking account of work performed were sufficiently disinterested in the amounts of earnings made to maintain their accuracy. It has already been noticed that until 1801 the principal yard officers themselves had apprentices and thus a vested interest in ensuring that the gangs in which their boys worked claimed the maximum earnings permitted. But, following the principal officers' loss in 1801 of their apprentices, in 1804 the inferior officers who supervised gangs also lost theirs. Moreover, by the end of 1804 these inferior officers were also given salaries, instead of wages affected by the rates of 'extra' allowed the artificers for overtime and piecework. The vested interest of the responsible yard employees in the size of the wages bill was thus gradually cut down. Inferior officers continued to measure the work performed by their gangs. But in 1810 the Job offices in each yard were re-established as Master Measurers' offices; and in 1811 John Payne recommended that these establishments be enlarged with sub-measurers and clerks so as to take over the inferior officers' accounting business. In Payne's view the measurement of the work performed by the inferior officers gave rise to those officers being unreasonably harassed, the men neglected, the accounts imperfect, and business impeded in the Master Measurer's office. The accounting business was accordingly transferred to the Master Measurers' department by 1813. The possibility of deception and fraud in earnings' accounts was consequently reduced to a minimum.[61]

A final touch to these four main developments in payment by the piece was the introduction by the end of 1812 of tables intended to simplify and expedite the calculations by which work performed was translated into earnings made. Their introduction was a further result of the employment of John Payne to supervise the adoption of the recommendations of the Commissioners of

Revision and perhaps best represented his personal achievement. The tables transformed the business of calculating wages: 'when the number of separate works done by upwards of twelve thousand artificers in the course of a day is considered, the greatest part of which are to be paid for at certain fixed rates but uncertain quantities, as it respects measure, weight or number, the importance of such tables may in some degree be estimated, the result sought for being ascertained by these tables immediately on inspection'. So rapid did the calculation of earnings become that it led in 1813, in accordance with another of Payne's proposals, to the payment of all earnings weekly.[62]

By the end of the Napoleonic War most variations in the employment and payment of artificers in the different dockyards had been ironed out. Nevertheless, until the very end of the war, minor differences in practice still made each yard unique. This was evident in the differences in the division of earnings that existed until 1811. At Plymouth and Sheerness gangs were paid separately; at Deptford, Woolwich and Chatham all gangs on the same ship were paid the same; and at Portsmouth all the men employed by Job had their total earnings by Job divided between them. From 1811 the practice at Plymouth was adopted universally.[63]

Differences in opinion existed, too, over the manner in which men were 'shoaled' – grouped into gangs. Customarily this was done on a voluntary basis, industrious and poor workmen being chosen by the foremen and quartermen in a periodic 'picking of teams'. This practice, of course, did not facilitate the division of earnings on an individual basis. In November 1803 the Plymouth officers therefore proposed that shipwrights working by the piece be shoaled according to ability, the good being separated from the middling and poor workmen. They argued that a mixture of abilities was 'discouraging to the good and able . . . as the earnings of the worst men in the company are equal to theirs [and] as the good men must in many instances wait and cannot proceed till the middling man has brought his work forward'. On the other hand, by shoaling men by ability their earnings 'will be equal to their exertions, more work will be done and the ablest men [will be] encouraged by receiving wages in proportion to their merits and the whole be employed to advantage'.[64] St Vincent, First Lord at the time, was attracted by the idea and ordered two fir frigates to be built at Plymouth with gangs shoaled as proposed.

However, neither the Navy Board nor the artificers regarded the innovation with enthusiasm. The opinion of the Board's Surveyors was diametrically opposed to that of the Plymouth officers:

if the men were shoaled as . . . recommended more work would not be performed by the whole body of the workmen altho' the best workmen if selected would individually perform more than they at present appear to do. But it is to be considered how much less would be done by the indifferent workmen when deprived of the abilities and exertions of those men who are proposed to be taken from among them, whose example cannot fail of acting as a stimulus to the others of inferior abilities. And it has been proved by experience (the best proof which can be obtained) that when too great a number of Task companies have been formed the Day companies, by being deprived of their leading men, have been thereby rendered very inefficient.[65]

The Plymouth shipwrights appealed against the shoaling order, describing the new method as 'injurious and dangerous':

> although nature has not formed every man with equal talents yet in every department on a stage of work every man has a proportionable part so that every man strives to be equal with his sidemate; but this new mode will tend to make every company enemies to each other when we consider the great differences it may make in our wages, as some jobs are more lucrative than others.[66]

The Plymouth officers dismissed this petition, claiming that it was only the idle who opposed shoaling by ability and 'who unfortunately have generally a volubility of speech and take the lead on such occasions'.[67] The shoaling issue was consequently debated by the naval boards throughout the early months of 1804, the Admiralty requiring the subordinate Board to vindicate its support for the traditional method, while condemning it as having 'been attended with various ill consequences' and being 'defective in its principle and therefore not capable under any regulations of being rendered beneficial to the public'.[68] Yet in the end it was the Navy Board that won, St Vincent being forced to resign in May 1804 and his successors having no strong feelings on the subject. Barham cautiously deferred any decision until the Commissioners of Revision had fully considered the matter. They favoured shoaling by ability but believed it required a full trial and, in view of the shipwrights' opposition, recommended that this be postponed till there was less pressure of work in the yards. The shipwrights maintained their opposition and shoaling thus continued on traditional lines until the end of the war.[69]

The changes in the administration of piecework gave the Navy Board every reason to expect a greater work output daily than had ever been achieved in the Revolutionary War. Even by the end of 1804 the changes in Job work answered the Plymouth officers' 'utmost wishes', for, as they reported to the Board, 'the people greatly exert themselves in hopes of obtaining so much money as their opposites which we judge to be for the benefit of the service and of advantage to the men'.[70] The work was also performed at a smaller cost in frauds and fabrications, thus making not only for greater economy but for a more stable basis in labour relations: in so far as the artificers knew more exactly how much work they had to perform to make different levels of earnings, expectations were more settled and disappointments over earnings less common. The improvements in the management of piecework consequently made their contribution to peace in the yards. Order, however, was the reflection of more factors than simply the efficiency with which work was converted into pay. It owed as much to the personalities and attitudes of board and yard officials, to the aspirations of the artificers themselves, and to the economic and legal framework of labour relations.

At a purely economic level, labour relations in the yards can be related to the bargaining power the artificers exercised in wartime. During peace they had little power as recalcitrant men could simply be discharged; the naval boards thus had the upper hand. But during war the necessity to keep as many men as possible made the naval boards more willing to negotiate and make concessions. Contemporaries concerned with dockyard efficiency acknowledged the artificers' wartime power. It was indeed clear enough in the late eighteenth century, with the relatively rapid alternation of war and peace, and was regarded at the beginning of the Revolutionary War as a major threat to dockyard operations. A bill drafted in 1794–5 'for the better government of His Majesty's Dock Yards' observed that 'on several occasions . . . when the energies of the state were most called for' the artificers had 'manifested . . . dispositions to take the advantages of the times . . . to combine together for the purpose of extorting from the Government an increase of wages or for the purpose of opposing some order or regulation issued by the Commissioners of the Admiralty or the Navy Board and intended to expedite the equipment of His Majesty's navy'.

Stiffened by the fear of Jacobinism, the 1794–5 bill made the men who 'excited' combinations to strike guilty of treason, and those 'aiding or abetting . . . or affording them support by voluntary contributions' guilty of sedition. It was envisaged that the law might also extend to workmen employed by merchants who undertook naval contracts, either for the construction of ships or for the supply of ropes, sails, anchors, cables and other equipment.[71] St Vincent may have had something similar in mind when he proposed in July 1797 'a law to regulate all the artificers employed in shipbuilding, caulking, sailmaking and anchor work'. He observed in his letter to Spencer, then First Lord, that it would be necessary to go to Parliament with the approbation of all the principal persons engaged in the trades and of all the great shipowners throughout the kingdom.[72] Probably the Thames shipbuilders would have approved. They had their labour problems too and obtained in September 1795 an agreement from the Admiralty not to employ in any naval establishment any man inserted on a 'black list' signed by any seven shipbuilders.[73]

Nevertheless neither of the bills proposed was actually brought forward. The eighteenth century had seen a distinct elevation in the status of the shipwright. Early in the century shipwrights had been liable to impressment for dockyard service; the ultimate threat remained, but by the 1790s artificers in the shipbuilding trades claimed, and were generally if not infallibly acknowledged to possess, freedom from coercion by the State. It was probably considered that a combination law would have aggravated relations in the yards even though the number of strikes might have been reduced. After all, the quality of work in the yards depended to a large extent on harmonious working relations. It was thus only in 1799–1800, with the enactment of more general prohibitions, that strikes in the dockyards became subject to combination laws. And these were neither applied to, nor noticeably affected, the conduct of artificers in the yards.

Although to the Admiralty it appeared that the workforce was repeatedly attempting to impose its will on government, an examination of the issues which gave rise to strikes reveals that on the whole the artificers were extremely conservative. Their claims contained little of novelty, but defended primarily their status as free citizens and skilled craftsmen, with the privileges

# 4 The workforce

and standard of living that went with it. Their insistence on the right to treatment as free citizens was a natural defence against threats of impressment and of subjection to naval discipline while working on board ships in harbour. Whenever a shipwright, caulker or ropemaker was impressed the whole of his respective department struck until it had the assurance of his release. In January 1797 all the shipwrights and caulkers in the Thames struck work, even those in the merchant yards, until one of their number had been freed; and in January 1800 the whole of the workforce in one dockyard petitioned the Admiralty for protection after a gang of artificers had been threatened and insulted while working on a ship afloat – 'if not under martial law yet not far therefrom removed'.[74]

Threats to the value of their skills were similarly opposed. Their 'art' in their eyes had a particular national importance.[75] They accordingly 'horsed' and ejected from the yards men with flaws in their indentures, and they refused to allow other trades access to work of which they had the traditional monopoly. Refusals on the part of the shipwrights in 1795–6 to allow the employment of house carpenters on shipwright work led in January 1796 to a threat of discharge for the whole of that trade from Deptford. Other tradesmen were just as particular: house carpenters and joiners refused to allow carvers to work in their 'shops' and the ropemakers objected to the use of steam-powered machinery in operations they performed manually.[76]

The artificers were no less determined to defend their standard of living and terms of employment. Combinations sometimes developed, linking one or more trades in all the yards or all the trades in a single yard. Organization on the largest scale occurred in 1801 when all the trades in every yard petitioned for increases in their basic rates of pay – perhaps the most radical of their demands between 1793 and 1815. At this time petitions were even delivered to Pitt and the House of Commons and, though there was no general withdrawal of labour, riots occurred at Plymouth and Sheerness.

The manner in which the artificers conducted themselves was, of course, affected by the personality and experience of the yard commissioners. By legislation of 1715 (1 Geo. I, 2 c.25) these commissioners were empowered to act as magistrates and deal with problems of disorder – and these occurred frequently. Apprentices created a perpetual undercurrent of youthful noise and occasional turmoil; while drunkenness was common, a problem increased by the presence of a Tap at each yard. Artificers' relatives brought men their meals and 'too frequently' remained straggling about the yards. Authority was sometimes flouted, when minor punishments such as the mulcting or stopping of pay often followed. Where a nunber of men were concerned, the ringleaders were sometimes discharged, and their followers suspended until such time as they showed contrition; discharge was reinforced by the circulation of descriptions of men dismissed to the Clerks of the Cheque of the other yards and the entry of their names, age, height, complexion, yard and trade in a 'black book' at the Navy Office. Yet, faced by whole departments of men over details of work routine or organization, working hours or earnings, the commissioners required tact, consideration and knowledge as well as presence of mind, firmness and determination. Negotiations took the form of conversations with leading spokesmen in or outside the commissioner's office. Sometimes an angry, rowdy crowd surrounded the office to watch.[77] Occasionally petitions were submitted for the Admiralty; and on almost all these occasions reference had to be made both to the Navy Board and yard officers. Throughout these proceedings much depended on the local commissioner's patience and self-control.

Without question the most serious breakdown of order resulted from the crisis in relations in the spring of 1801.[78] Although food prices had been rising steadily, petitions to the Admiralty for relief and new rates of pay were ignored until late in March; by then the offer made of an extra temporary 'ration' proportionate to the size of artificers' families was too late. At Plymouth on 31 March the artificers became involved in food riots by rescuing a yard sawyer arrested by the local magistrates. Their intention of rescuing him was evidently known beforehand, for by the time they left the dockyard the magistrates had prepared to meet them. According to Jonathan Elford, an observer, the magistrates awaited them

> supported by a troop of the Queen's Bays, the Piquets of the Wilts and East Devon and the Artillery with four field pieces loaded with grape and canister . . . at the upper end of Fore Street near the main guard house where the prisoners were. The dockyard men came out of the yard in a body, whooping and huzzaing and came to the spot where the magistrates were. Upon which the Dock Volunteer cavalry and infantry formed in their rear. The committee, as they are pleased to term about a dozen whom they had selected, approached the magistrates and demanded the release of the prisoners. This was refused and they were told that the hour was elapsed and that if they did not disperse they would be fired on. The threat, however, had not the desired effect. But instead of acting with energy the magistrates, to their eternal disgrace, ordered the prisoners to be released. The rioters then demanded the release of all the other prisoners which was also conceded to them. They then took the men on their shoulders and carried them through the town huzzaing and making shouts. All this passed in the face of the insulted soldiery who were ready and willing to act if called upon. . . .[79]

The prisoners were hidden in the dockyard and on 16 April the rescue was repeated. This time a rioter was released by breaking down the front gates of the yard in front of the court house 'by means of large pieces of wood' used as battering rams and then breaking through the front door and windows.[80]

Although these riots were primarily a response to local difficulties, they were linked in minds at the Admiralty with the disturbances that occurred at Sheerness. There, in the interests of yard order and security, Commissioner Coffin had imposed a vigorous reorganization that had created considerable discontent. He himself appears to have had little regard for the artificers' interests. On 12 April he had a drunken yard man named Bennett impressed for insolence and disobedience. The response from the artificers was immediate. He reported the next day:

> this morning between six and seven, walking on the Rampart Battery, to my surprise and astonishment the greatest part of the artificers, riggers and labourers sallied out of the yard in a most tumultuous and riotous manner,

advanced towards me with great rapidity, forced me violently against the wall, one and all shouting "throw him over, kill him". When I asked the cause of this unreasonable conduct, which was scarcely allowed me to do, after being severely jostled and violently pushed against the wall, I was told the only means I had to avoid instant destruction was to promise Bennett should be given up. In this dilemma, with loss of life staring me in the face and no possible assistance near, I was induced to comply. . . . Still they kept me in this unpleasant predicament near an hour using very opprobrious language until the Lieutenant-Governor, Sir James Malcolm, came to my aid when they allowed me to retire.[81]

After several days of uncertainty, order was eventually restored at Sheerness. Yet the coincidence of riots at two yards with the combination for higher pay rates made the worst possible impression in London. St Vincent thought the artificers at Plymouth were 'governed by the very worst spirit and intention', and even the Navy Board was forced to the conclusion that the riots were 'instigated by the insinuations of evil disposing and designing men'.[82]

In the political environment of the time, it was perhaps inevitable that the men who organized the combination or took the lead in the riots should be regarded as republicans. They were highly organized: each yard had its own committee with members drawn from each department, its own money collectors, and each financed its own delegates to travel from yard to yard and to stay in London. The leaders also maintained an appearance of democracy. An informant at Portsmouth described how the workmen voted to accept the offer of the extra ration 'by upwards of two thousand to two hundred and seventy-four'; but delegates from the eastern yards persuaded the committee to reject the offer so as to conform with the decisions of the committees at the other five yards.[83] Rumour, moreover, tended to suggest a revolutionary intent. At Plymouth it was feared that the artificers intended seizing the arms of the watchmen; and during the second of the disturbances men from the yard were seen to signal to two ships in the harbour with the intention, it was supposed, 'to incite the crews' to join them.[84] It can only have been expected therefore that the combination leaders would be discharged. In May 1801, on the orders of the Admiralty, a committee of the Navy Board toured the six yards and discharged 340 men. Four men were later prosecuted at Canterbury for assault while others were prosecuted at Exeter for riot.[85]

The scale of these discharges reflected fears for the fleet, and perhaps for social stability, rather than any real evidence that the artificers intended anything more from their combination than higher pay. Actual evidence of the leaders' motives in fact suggests strictly limited and moderate intentions. One letter intercepted by the Post Office later in April 1801 asserted that their object was simply 'to ameliorate the distress of our brother workmen in common with ourselves' and that there was no other 'sordid or improper' motive. Another, written to committee men who had just been discharged, wished

> that our suffering friends will bear themselves with that decent and manly spirit which becomes them and [that] those remaining [in the yard] will be

liberal toward them . . . in whose honest cause they may have drawn on themselves the judgement of power. We have no violent measures to recommend but hope our Plymouth friends will still correspond with us, which innocent and lawful privilege we would persevere in maintaining. . . . We cannot conceive that any criminality can justly attach to you.[86]

Even so, as the letters suggest, the artificers' leaders were conscious politically; in the political environment of the time this was scarcely to be avoided. It was possibly their influence that held back the artificers from going on strike. Certainly they themselves escaped prosecution under the recent Combination Laws because, as the Attorney and Solicitor General observed, their petitions avoided 'any particular expression of intimidation or any intimation of an intention to strike work'.[87] They also avoided the danger of arrest and imprisonment without trial, clearly heeding Commissioner Coffin's advice to the Sheerness leaders 'to beware of the effects the suspension of Habeas Corpus might . . . have on them . . . as far as regards their corresponding with any set of men plotting against the interests of His Majesty's Government'.[88]

From the Admiralty's point of view, the scale of the discharges therefore had the advantage of clearing from the dockyards men who were potentially dangerous, even though only those who had participated in the riots had to that time done anything illegal. It was possibly this clearance that accounts for the failure of any combination to develop on a similar scale during the Napoleonic War. It did not, however, deter the remaining artificers from defending the interests of their particular trades. Indeed, if anything, they appear to have done so with greater determination. In 1802 over 100 caulkers were discharged for refusing to go to the merchant yards in the Thames to refit East India company ships stranded there by a strike. And after the resumption of war, the trades containing the greatest numbers of men – the shipwrights, smiths and ropemakers – exploited their bargaining power to the full. Between 1803 and 1805 the shipwrights at Chatham, Portsmouth and Plymouth, who had more bargaining power than any of the other departments in the six yards, made seven complaints about their terms of employment – three about their pay, three concerning their dinner time, and one about the length of their working day – and on six of these occasions they received concessions.[89]

In spite of the Combination Laws and the discharge of the 1801 leaders, some artificers thus continued to possess considerable power. In 1806 the Commissioners of Revision could only point out that the retention at the peace reduction of 'rather more' shipwrights than might seem to be absolutely necessary would 'tend both to economy and good order': 'there should be so many that the officers can discharge any troublesome man without inconvenience and that his discharge should be felt as a punishment'.[90] Nevertheless during the second half of the Napoleonic War labour relations appear to have gradually attained more stability. Reports of discontent, demands for changes in working conditions and strikes occur less frequently. This may be related to the expansion in the size of the workforce during the Napoleonic War, the improvements in the frequency and the calculation of payment; and the continuity of work procedure resulting from the sustained and seemingly interminable demands placed on the dockyards. It can also be set against the gains made by the workforce itself in the wars: the artificers' repeated use of their bargaining power ensured that conditions of work in the yards did not on the whole deteriorate. From the artificers' point of view, in terms of their pay and conditions, the dockyards were more satisfactory places of employment by the end of the Napoleonic War than they had been 20 years earlier.

# 5

# The officials

The traditional image of the dockyard official is not a respectable one. Because until the end of the eighteenth century many officials took informal payments in addition to their salaries they have generally been regarded as corrupt, even by their contemporaries. Middleton himself, for example, argued that they profited at the navy's expense. 'Under the name of fees', he informed Pitt in 1784, the officers and clerks who received new stores and sold old ones took 'presents to the great injury of the public, both in respect of the quality and quantity of the articles supplied and sold'.[1] Reinforced by the occasional case of glaring dishonesty, sometimes advertised and exploited for a political purpose, this corrupt image provided a convenient explanation for failures of supply, inadequacies in materials and even financial problems.

If the navy did suffer on occasion from the cupidity of individuals, the corrupt image was not generally applicable to the whole of yard officialdom. For it was more a caricature created by politicians needing scapegoats and reformers seeking change than an accurate representation. Until the end of the eighteenth century unofficial emoluments were conventionally taken and condoned in transactions in most government departments. Dockyard officials to that extent simply conformed in their business morality to contemporary practice. On the other hand, the majority had real reason to regard flagrant profiteering at the navy's expense as objectionable. Their duties were in many cases highly responsible, demanding integrity as well as competence, and were performed with a sense of professionalism.

To the modern mind it appears paradoxical that men with a sense of professional integrity should be found within a system in which unofficial payments were regarded as legitimate. But, owing to the lack of formal provision for all needs, government service in the late eighteenth century contained a variety of payments and practices of an unofficial nature. Such payments were condoned in the first place to compensate for inadequacy in the provision of official salaries and pensions. Thus fees were taken partly because the size of official salaries had often not been increased since the seventeenth century, and partly because the levying of fees on routine tasks related the amount of work performed to the remuneration. Premiums were also paid on the entry to office of new or promoted staff partly because there was either no system of superannuation or merely a selective one, and partly because men who had themselves paid to gain their places, and therefore considered them their property, had to be paid to give them up. In their spare time officers and clerks in the Navy Office and dockyards acted on commission as agents for naval officers and contractors, a business which worked to their mutual advantage. And in the field of appointments, in the absence of an official system of selection, unofficial connections, influence and patronage were as important as the recommendations of those who, from their official situations, had knowledge of the ability of candidates for places and of the roles they had to perform.

For the period of the Revolutionary and Napoleonic Wars the image of the corrupt official is even less appropriate than it is for the earlier eighteenth century. By then most principal officers no longer received fees and gratuities. During the Revolutionary War, moreover, the pressure of public opinion for more economical and efficient government reached the level at which the Admiralty was obliged to adopt general changes in the terms of government service. It was accordingly a time when new principles of payment were applied and when the highest standards of business conduct were occasionally enforced. The changes were aimed generally at replacing the officials' private interest in the conduct of business, derived from private payments, by an enhanced sense of public interest based on salaries and pensions supplied entirely from the public purse. Recommendations made by the Commissioners on Fees were implemented first, in the Navy Office by the order in council of 8 June 1796 and later in the dockyards by the order in council of 21 May 1801. These changes were than followed between 1806 and 1809 by many of the recommendations made by the Commissioners for Revising and Digesting the Civil Affairs of the Navy.

There were therefore two periods of change during the wars. The first saw the abolition of unofficial emoluments, the withdrawal or limitation of some allowances, the compensating enlargement of most salaries and the introduction of superannuation schemes. The second saw the removal of anomalies, the elaboration of principles governing payment, and the introduction of revised salary scales. Between these two periods, terms of service differed. Before 1796 in the Navy Office and 1801 in the dockyards, they remained largely the same as had been accepted since the seventeenth century; then, following a relatively piecemeal regulation of the form that earnings could take, there existed various inequalities and discrepancies in salaries and allowances; but after about 1808 terms of service were further modified to conform more closely to the requests of the officials themselves.

The new code of business conduct underlying these changes was enforced by oath. With the abolition of unofficial earnings, each clerk and officer had to enter into a bond to an amount three times his salary and subscribe to an oath of fidelity not to receive any unofficial payment, act as an agent or have an interest in any ship, vessel or stores used by the navy; and every time he rose in office he had to give fresh bonds.[2] The new code was thus made financially as well as morally binding.

These reforms were imposed on the naval departments as part of the general transformation affecting the whole of government. The imposition of the changes was not, however, unaccommodating to the interests of the officials they affected. There was a strong element of paternalism in the consideration given to them by the Commissioners of Naval Revision; and an examination of the terms of service experienced by Navy Office and dockyard staff throughout the wars in fact suggests that most grievances repeatedly brought to Admiralty notice were eventually settled. Nevertheless the transformation in the terms of government service was not achieved smoothly. Difficulties abounded. Following the abolition of informal emoluments, in particular, discontent was almost universal among the more poorly paid officials; and during St Vincent's administration, when there was a new censorious attitude at the Admiralty, even the principal yard officers and board commissioners suffered on account of pressure to purge the yards of vices. At these times morale and motivation unquestionably deteriorated.

The experiences of the clerks were particularly discouraging. Of all the officials they had most to endure. The more senior had responsibilities of some weight, yet their routine work attracted little attention and their skills, having a low value in society at large, were little appreciated. Although they already received a salary, this was inconsiderable, and in 1793 they were expected to supplement it with informal earnings. In May 1793, 53 junior clerks in the Navy Office all received a £30 salary increase, the first increase in their salaries since 1690.[3] Yet the general level of income of most clerks remained low, especially following the regulations of 1796 and 1801.

*Table 19. The clerical establishment of the Navy Office in 1792 and 1813*

|  | 1792 | | 1813 | |
| --- | --- | --- | --- | --- |
|  | established clerks | extra and temporary | established clerks | extra and temporary |
| Secretary's office | 13 | 2 | 20 | 13 |
| Contract office (estab. 1803) |  |  | 2 |  |
| Bills and accounts | 15 |  | 15 | 5 |
| Foreign accounts (estab. 1807) |  |  | 7 | 3 |
| Surveyor's office | 5 |  | 5 | 1 |
| Office for stores (estab. 1796) |  |  | 6 | 11 |
| Seamen's wages | 11 | 2 | 15 | 4 |
| Slop office | 5 |  | 6 | 4 |
| Ticket office | 18 | 2 | 20 | 21 |
| Allotment office (estab. 1797) |  |  | 10 | 11 |
| For examining Storekeepers' accounts | 8 |  | 9 | 6 |
| For examining victualling accounts (abolished 1796) | 3 |  |  |  |
| For examining Treasurer's accounts | 5 |  | 8 |  |
| Fee office (estab. 1796) |  |  |  | 1 |
| Petition office | 1 |  | 1 |  |
| To extra commissioners |  | 4 |  |  |
| Total number of clerks in the Navy Office | 84 | 10 | 124 | 80 |

The principal unofficial emolument lost by the Navy Office and dockyard clerks at these times was fees. These were earned by the performance of routine duties such as the passing of accounts and petitions, the making out of bills, certificates, notes, warrants and orders, and the writing of contracts, charter parties or bills of sale.[4] Their loss was particularly regretted as they were regarded as a genuine reward for conscientious attention to duties which had little intrinsic interest and which otherwise would almost certainly have fallen into arrears. The total income they provided is known with accuracy only for the year 1784, a year of peace when the number of fees received would have been lower than in wartime. On average the clerks probably obtained two to three-fifths of their income from them.[5] These fees continued to be paid at the Navy Office after 1796 but were received into a fee fund that was used to offset the cost of increasing the clerks' official salaries.

Another unofficial emolument lost was derived from 'agency business'. This had been performed by clerks in the Navy Office in particular and had consisted of settling the accounts at the office of seamen, naval officers or contractors. Yet the business had come to be regarded as harmful to the interests of the public, especially when a clerk became concerned through his work for a contractor with stores or ships supplied for the navy. It was also performed at a cost to Navy Office stationery and postage. In 1796 the Admiralty thus ruled that the business should be given up on the return of peace and it was accordingly prohibited in March 1802.[6]

The clerks in the Navy Office and the dockyards were concerned about these losses for a variety of reasons. There was discontent above all because the increases they obtained in their official salaries were insufficient compensation, especially for a time when the cost of living was rising. By June 1800 the Navy

---

*Table 20. The clerical establishment of the dockyards in 1815*

| Office of the: | Dept-ford | Wool-wich | Chat-ham | Sheer-ness | Ports-mouth | Ply-mouth |
|---|---|---|---|---|---|---|
| Commissioner | 2 | 2 | 3 | 3 | 3 | 3 |
| Master Shipwright | 2 | 3 | 3 | 3 | 3 | 3 |
| Master Attendant | 1 | 1 | 1 | 2 | 1 | 1 |
| Clerk of the Cheque | 6 | 10 | 7 | 8 | 8 | 7 |
| Storekeeper | 7 | 11 | 6 | 7 | 12 | 12 |
| Clerk of the Survey | 6 | 9 | 4 | 5 | 8 | 8 |
| Timber Master | 4 | 5 | 4 | 3 | 7 | 7 |
| Master Measurer | 4 | 5 | 4 | 5 | 10 | 11 |
| Clerk of the Ropeyard | | 3 | 1 | | 1 | 2 |
| Total number of established clerks at each yard | 32 | 49 | 33 | 36 | 53 | 54 |

Board found that discontent was seriously affecting work in the Navy Office. It informed the Admiralty Board that

> The difficulties we labour under so far as relates to the new Establishment are to be solely attributed to the *abolition of all fees and emoluments* and to the salaries given to the clerks in lieu thereof not being in many cases nearly equal to their former income, which evidently occasions the business to go on with less spirit and facility than when the clerks had greater incitements to industry.[7]

By 1807 the situation was, if anything, worse. Samuel Gambier, a member of the Navy Board, despairing of the clerks being 'rescued from that state of discouragement and poverty . . . in which they have so long laboured', wrote himself to the Admiralty describing what the level of their salaries meant for each:

> When acquired, it [their salary] is the ultimatum of all their prospects in the service; that upon which they are to live and maintain a family and out of which they are to lay by what they can as a provision for that family when they are dead, and what that saving may be those best can tell who upon such small incomes have to maintain a family and support a gentlemanly appearance in these times when money is scarcely half the value it was when those salaries were proposed.[8]

After 1801 the yard clerks were similarly reduced in circumstances. Sir Andrew Hamond, the Comptroller, observed in August 1804 that they 'were much to be pitied . . . more than half their income was taken away by the late dockyard regulations and that at the very moment when every article of living was increased double'.[9] In 1807 these clerks themselves complained that while their labour and responsibilities had increased the pecuniary advantages of their posts bore no comparison with those they enjoyed before 1801, and that they therefore experienced 'great difficulties' in maintaining their families in 'a creditable manner'.[10]

Discontent was enhanced by the fact that both the dockyard clerks and those in the Navy Office could point to other offices where salary scales were more remunerative than their own. The Navy Office compared the amounts by which the total cost of the salaries in each of the different naval departments had been allowed to exceed the salary bills recommended for those departments by the Commissioners on Fees. The Navy Office in 1803 had an establishment of 103 clerks but its salary bill exceeded the Commissioners' recommendation by only £920; in contrast, the Victualling Office had only 51 clerks but exceeded the recommended bill by nearly £2,500; and the Admiralty Office, with only 17 clerks, exceeded the Commissioners' bill by £5,500![11] In the dockyards there was a lack of parity between the salary scales of the different yard offices. The salaries of the senior clerks to the Clerk of the Cheque in each yard were higher than those of their counterparts in the office of the Storekeeper, which were in turn higher than the salaries of clerks in the office of the Clerk of the Survey. In 1801 the chief clerk to the Clerk of the

Table 21. The earnings of established clerks in the Secretary's office

| | basic salary to 1796 £ | extra fees and gratuities in 1784 £ | net earnings with allowances, other emoluments and deductions in 1784 £ | salary from 1 Jul. 1796 £ | salary from 1 Nov. 1807 £ |
|---|---|---|---|---|---|
| 1st chief clerk | 100 | 649 | 826 | 700 | 700 |
| 2nd chief clerk | | | | | 600 |
| 2nd clerk | 70 | 63 | 193 | 300 | 450 |
| 3rd clerk | 60 | 114 | 174 | 200 | 350 |
| 4th clerk | 50 | 125 | 185 | 150 | 300 |
| 5th clerk | 50 | 101 | 168 | 150 | 250 |
| 6th clerk | 50 | 75 | 135 | 120 | 200 |
| 7th clerk | 50 | 55 | 115 | 120 | 180 |
| 8th clerk | 50 | 80 | 140 | 100 | 180 |
| 9th clerk | 50 | 42 | 98 | 100 | 170 |
| 10th clerk | 50 | 0 | 50 | 80 | 160 |
| 11th clerk | 50 | 0 | 50 | 80 | 150 |
| 12th clerk | 50 | 1 | 51 | 80 | 140 |
| 13th clerk | 50 | 1 | 51 | 80 | 130 |
| 14th clerk | 50 | 1 | 51 | 80 | 120 |
| 15th clerk | 52 | 0 | 52 | 80 | 120 |
| 16th clerk | | | | | 110 |
| 17th clerk | | | | | 100 |
| 18th clerk | | | | | 90 |
| 19th clerk | | | | | 80 |
| Reading clerk | | | | | 50 |

Figures are rounded to the nearest pound. It should be noted that 1784 was a year of peace and the fees received would have been less than in wartime.

*Table 22. The earnings of established clerks in the principal offices, Chatham yard*

| | basic salary to 1801 £ | extra fees and gratuities in 1784 £ | net earnings with allowances, other emoluments and deductions in 1784 £ | salary from 1 Jul. 1801 £ | salary from 1 Oct. 1808 £ |
|---|---|---|---|---|---|
| 1st clerk to commissioner | 50 | 56 | 179 | 300 | 400 |
| 2nd clerk | 50 | 0 | 114 | 180 | 250 |
| 3rd clerk | 40 | 0 | 40 | 120 | 120 |
| 1st clerk to Master Shipwright | 45 | 51 | 122 | 240 | 300 |
| 2nd clerk | 40 | 1 | 41 | 180 | 200 |
| 3rd clerk | 30 | | | 120 | 120 |
| Clerk to Master Attendant | 40 | 12 | 108 | 120 | 200 |
| 1st clerk to Clerk of the Cheque | 45 | 140 | 185 | 300 | 400 |
| 2nd clerk | 40 | 102 | 204 | 180 | 300 |
| 3rd clerk | 40 | 99 | 147 | 120 | 250 |
| 4th clerk | 35 | 69 | 134 | 120 | 200 |
| 5th clerk | 46 | 16 | 80 | 90 | 150 |
| 6th clerk | 30 | 10 | 40 | 80 | 100 |
| 7th clerk | 30 | 4 | 34 | 80 | 80 |
| 1st clerk to Storekeeper | 55 | 116 | 188 | 240 | 400 |
| 2nd clerk | 50 | 80 | 148 | 180 | 300 |
| 3rd clerk | 50 | 25 | 75 | 180 | 250 |
| 4th clerk | 45 | 20 | 65 | 120 | 200 |
| 5th clerk | 40 | 5 | 45 | 120 | 150 |
| 6th clerk | 40 | 5 | 45 | 90 | 100 |
| 1st clerk to Clerk of the Survey | 45 | 84 | 147 | 180 | 400 |
| 2nd clerk | 40 | 41 | 81 | 120 | 250 |
| 3rd clerk | 30 | 32 | 62 | 120 | 150 |
| 4th clerk | 30 | 5 | 35 | 90 | 90 |
| Clerk to Clerk of the Ropeyard | 40 | 25 | 71 | 120 | 200 |

See note to table 21.

# 5 The officials

Survey at Chatham pointed out that he had spent the best part of his life reaching his position, only to be deprived of half his income and given the same salary as the third clerk to the Clerk of the Cheque and fifth clerk to the Storekeeper.[12] Other clerks represented that in spite of their experience and responsibilities they had the mortification of seeing youths in another office receive the same salary though without knowledge of yard business and doing little else but copying.[13] In July 1804 the Clerk of the Cheque at Chatham also lamanted that, in spite of his office performing the same work as other cheque offices, his third and fifth clerks received 'considerably less' salary than their counterparts at Deptford, Portsmouth and Plymouth.[14]

The older clerks probably felt these disparities most, for they saw the effort and investment they had put into reaching the more senior positions going to waste. These posts had been the summit of their ambitions since they had carried the more lucrative, if not the most responsible, fee-earning tasks. Having spent 30 to 40 years achieving these posts, they regarded their unofficial emoluments as justly earned. They remembered having paid a Navy Board commissioner, if they had entered the Navy Office, or the officer in charge of their department in the dockyards, between 150 and 250 guineas for their first places. Some, who had been unable to raise such sums, had paid their principal in office £20 or more from their salaries for periods up to five years, though their salaries were themselves only £30 a year and the payments had made them completely dependent on the support of family or friends. They remembered no less clearly that each step up the promotion ladder had then cost them amounts ranging from £150 to 500 guineas.[15]

Some of these older men included chief clerks in the Navy Office who resented the reorganization of payment for less personal reasons. They felt that the abolition of unofficial emoluments and introduction of new salary rates, in reducing the difference between their earnings and those of their subordinates, had reduced their standing, 'more especially as to those immediately under us, the raising of whose emoluments so much nearer to ours than heretofore tends to do away that difference in rank, respect and profit which it has ever been thought advisable should exist between the junior and senior instruments in offices where so much depends upon the principal as it does in ours'.[16] The absence of adequate differentials was a grievance among the more junior clerks too. In two departments in the Navy Office, the secretary's office and the office for bills and accounts, it was necessary for clerks to obtain seven successive promotions from the most junior posts before they could obtain a higher salary and 10 or 11 rises to earn £100 a year. The prospect of promotion consequently provided little incentive to industry. Because the offices were smaller, the problem did not occur on the same scale in the dockyards. Even so, in an office like that of the Storekeeper's at Portsmouth, a junior clerk had to obtain three successive rises before he could obtain more than the minimum salary.

The grievances gave rise in the Navy Office to a general go-slow. During the office hours of ten until four, work was deliberately allowed to stand so that overtime was necessary. By June 1800 work had fallen so far in arrears that the Navy Board requested that the extra allowance for overtime be abolished and the clerks' attendance be regulated not according to office hours but by the amount of business to be performed. The Board also recommended a general increase in salaries, a recommendation it continued to make for another seven years. It also unhesitatingly forwarded the clerks' petitions – four between 1800 and 1805. The Board was particularly concerned to improve the clerks' earnings because alternative employment was readily available in London even for relatively inexperienced men. In 1801 'some of the best clerks' had already resigned and others were 'on the point of doing so'; in 1806 another left in response to an offer of £240 a year, an amount three times the sum he had received at the Navy Office.[17] Resignations from the dockyards themselves seem to have been less numerous, possibly because alternative posts were less plentiful. Nevertheless there were resignations and widespread discontent.[18] In March 1801, shortly before the abolition of unofficial emoluments, the Admiralty received over 25 petitions from different groups of yard clerks, who in May 1808 were still petitioning for relief from 'difficulties and inconvenience that have rendered their situations extremely embarrassing'.[19]

In spite of this manifest restlessness, the succession of Admiralty boards at the beginning of the century were inclined to ignore the appeals of the Navy Board and of the clerks themselves. Between 1801 and 1804 St Vincent was concerned above all with economy, while from 1805 the existence of Commissioners of Naval Revision permitted the postponement of relief until these Commissioners had made their recommendations. Even so, in May 1805, the clerks to the Clerk of the Cheque at Chatham were given the same salaries as their colleagues at the other three principal yards.[20]

More extensive alterations in salary scales followed the adoption of the proposals of the Commissioners of Revision for the Navy Office and dockyards, by orders in council of October 1807 and September 1808. These not only enlarged some clerks' salaries but increased the number of gradations in pay from the most junior to the most senior posts and established greater parity in earnings between clerks at similar levels in different offices. Junior clerks nevertheless still earned relatively poor salaries and in September 1811, in an effort to keep 'young men of abilities' in the Navy Office, minimum salaries were introduced, these increasing every two years from £90 after two years' service to £200 after twelve.[21] A month later the junior clerks in the dockyards appealed for similar minimum earnings but, though the Navy Board supported the application, the scheme entailed an additional expense which the Admiralty Board was not prepared to sanction.[22]

The petitions of the Navy Office and dockyard clerks were thus, in part, eventually answered. Nonetheless it appears that the incentive to industry for most of them remained remote. This was acknowledged in July 1815 when the Admiralty itself initiated the division in 1816 of the Navy Office clerks into three classes to which salary scales with regular annual increments of £10 were attached.[23] As the salary of a clerk in the lowest class could rise to a maximum of £300, it was hoped that promotion by seniority need no longer provide the only immediate prospect of higher remuneration. Indeed it was laid down that promotion from one class to another was to 'be the reward of qualification for the duties of the higher class, without any reference whatsoever to the seniority the person may hold in the lower class'.[24] The introduction of increments and official institution of promotion by merit filled a void which, in the minds of the clerks, could previously have been filled only by promotion by seniority, the regular succession from one place to the next above.

Throughout the wars this system of promotion was undoubtedly a source of frustration for able and ambitious young men. After 1796 in the Navy Office, and 1801 in the dockyards, the prohibition on the payment of premiums meant that promotion no longer cost money. Advancement by seniority from a junior position, in which the work was little more than copying, to a senior post carrying responsibility nevertheless remained a long-term, if not a life-long, process. Ability was necessary, but the lack of it seems to have been more important in checking promotion than outstanding qualities were in hastening it. The principal of each office being responsible for the work and conduct of his 'instruments', those who lacked talent in some respect were prevented from rising in their turn and juniors of 'superior ability' were promoted over their heads. Thus in April 1802 the second clerk to the Master Shipwright at Woolwich was not allowed to succeed to the place of the chief clerk because he was unable to arrange and state certain accounts without the aid of an elderly superannuated clerk employed on a temporary basis.[25] Similarly, in the Secretary's department of the Navy Office, late in 1812 the second clerk was not allowed to succeed to the chief clerk's position, the post being taken by a man with four years' less experience.[26] Yet such cases of men being held back while their juniors rose around them were uncommon. Usually a vacancy at a senior level led to all the clerks rising one post and an extra clerk being brought onto the establishment at the lowest level.[27] It is nevertheless noticeable that when such cases did occur the men in question were often near the top of their office promotion-ladders, a fact suggesting that men of mediocre or even of poor qualities could rise relatively high. But it also suggests that men of more obvious talent had to rise in turn, having little chance of overtaking their less able seniors until, on the verge of succession to the highest places, the disabilities of their seniors were acknowledged and their progress checked.

Under these circumstances it is not surprising that able and ambitious young men without ties took opportunities that offered to leave their posts in the Navy Office and dockyards. Experienced clerks became at different times ships' pursers, storekeepers of storeships and clerical officers at minor naval establishments in Britain or abroad. In 1812 one clerk from the Navy Office and three others from the dockyards were selected to fill the places in the pay office connected with the construction of the Plymouth Breakwater.[28] Those that remained in the Navy Office could hope to become a chief clerk or even Secretary to the Navy Board; those that remained in the yards could aspire to become one of the three principal clerical officers in each yard – a Clerk of the Cheque, a Clerk of the Survey, or a Storekeeper. But they could hope to climb no further. Until shortly before the American War of Independence, clerks who had served in the Navy Office and yards had sometimes been appointed one of the clerical commissioners at the Navy Board. Thereafter, however, no such appointments were made.[29]

After the abolition of fees, the clerks in the Navy Office and yards consequently had little to inspire their efforts. Many of them probably felt themselves to be simply time-servers, an attitude perhaps enhanced by the provision, following the abolition of premiums, of pensions related in amount to the size of their salaries at retirement and their number of years' service.[30] A regulated system of superannuation was a significant advance on the provision of annuities by order in council, the amount of which appeared to depend on rank and favour. Nevertheless, as an incentive to industry, the provision of pensions was a poor substitute for more stimulating systems of payment and promotion.

In the absence of other immediate work incentives, it was inevitable that the clerks should be kept to their duties with rules and regulations. The Navy Board regularly received complaints from yard officers of the misconduct and insubordination of clerks, and in August 1802 the Admiralty Board laid down that the latter were only to be paid after the production of certificates from their principals of their integrity, diligence and good conduct. Individual yard officers also laid down their own regulations: in 1805, for example, the Plymouth Storekeeper ruled that 'no liquor was to be drank' in his department, that 'barbers were not to shave and dress hair', and that 'the reading of newspapers was likewise prohibited during the hours of public business'.[31]

That such were the practices in many yard offices, and possibly in the Navy Office, seems likely. The hours of attendance during the wars were long. At the Navy Office they were 10 a.m. till 4 p.m., six days a week, though some started at 9 a.m., finished at 7 or 8 p.m. and worked Sundays when necessary. But in the yards hours were certainly longer: Samuel Bentham thought them 'perhaps double . . . what they are at the Navy Office', while the clerks themselves believed they were 'more than in any other department under Government'.[32] At Plymouth in 1803 the clerks in the Storekeeper's office worked from 6 or 7.30 a.m. until 6 p.m.; four then worked in rotation until 8 p.m. and six attended on Sundays. Yard clerks usually had one hour off for breakfast and another for dinner, but these breaks were sacrificed at times of pressure. In the Plymouth Master Shipwright's office in 1803, when they were working 'till eight or nine o'clock at night, and sometimes later besides Sundays', the clerks were 'obliged to send for their dinner and eat it in the office'.[33]

Confined to their offices and poorly rewarded, the clerks had perhaps the least glamorous and most tedious work involved in maintaining the navy. Though safe by the standards of those who went to sea, and physically undemanding by comparison with the work performed in the yards, the labours of paperwork nevertheless made their demands. Clerks with responsibilities suffered stress – like that of the 48-year old Navy Office chief clerk who was forced into premature retirement because his 'anxiety overcame his strength' – and almost all suffered the strain of overwork. To avoid setting precedents, only under the repeated and most plaintive requests would the Navy Board sanction the employment of extra or temporary clerks to supplement the number of established clerks. As a result, especially in the yards at times of mobilization (when the clerical force was still on a peace establishment) and during periods of illness, there was always more work than could easily be managed. Samuel Bentham's introduction in 1802 of copying machines made possible the reduction in the drudgery of some junior clerks.

But the main problem, the failure to adjust quickly enough the number of clerks in each office as their share of work grew, was one of communication and practice.

The working life of the clerks in the Navy Office and the yards was not therefore one of ease. They had posts certainly more comfortable than many others, a fact accounting for the unfailing supply of men and boys willing to enter an office. They also had security of tenure and safety from poverty even in old age. On the other hand they endured the frustrations and tedium of unremitting paperwork, unaccompanied by any prospect of relief, rapid promotion or substantial reward.

The experiences of the inferior officers in the dockyards during the wars had much in common with that of the clerks. They too were deprived of emoluments which had supplemented their official earnings and were left with reduced incomes. The opportunities of the great majority for rising further in

Table 23. *The establishment of inferior officers in 1810*

|  | Dept-ford | Wool-wich | Chat-ham | Sheer-ness | Ports-mouth | Ply-mouth |
|---|---|---|---|---|---|---|
| Boatswain of the Yard | 1 | 1 | 1 | 1 | 1 | 1 |
| Shipwrights |  |  |  |  |  |  |
| Foremen | 3 | 3 | 3 | 2 | 3 | 3 |
| Quartermen | 35 | 26 | 38 | 14 | 54 | 54 |
| Caulkers |  |  |  |  |  |  |
| Foremen |  | 1 |  |  | 1 | 1 |
| Quartermen | 2 | 3 | 5 | 4 | 9 | 5 |
| Boatbuilders Foremen | 1 | 1 | 1 | 1 | 1 | 1 |
| Mastermakers Foremen | 1 | 1 | 1 | 1 | 1 | 1 |
| House Carpenters |  |  |  |  |  |  |
| Foremen | 1 | 1 | 1 | 1 | 1 | 1 |
| Leading men | 2 | 4 | 2 | 4 | 1 |  |
| Joiners |  |  |  |  |  |  |
| Foremen | 1 | 1 | 1 | 1 | 1 | 1 |
| Leading men | 2 | 1 | 2 | 2 | 6 | 3 |
| Sailmakers Leading men | 3 | 2 | 2 | 1 | 3 | 3 |
| Riggers Leading men | 3 | 2 | 4 | 1 | 4 | 6 |
| Ropemakers Foremen |  | 3 | 4 |  | 3 | 5 |
| Smiths |  |  |  |  |  |  |
| Foremen | 1 | 1 | 1 | 1 | 1 | 2 |
| Firemen | 17 | 14 | 17 | 6 | 21 | 40 |
| Bricklayers Foremen | 1 | 1 | 1 | 1 | 1 | 1 |
| Scavelmen Leading men | 2 | 1 | 3 | 1 | 3 | 6 |
| Storehouse labourers |  |  |  |  |  |  |
| Leading men | 6 | 4 | 2 | 2 | 3 | 4 |
| Yard labourers Leading men | 24 | 17 | 7 | 3 | 17 | 20 |

government service were also limited. Yet they performed basic and essential duties for which they received little acknowledgement.

Their primary task was the supervision of artificers. This involved responsibility for the performance of specific work and the necessity to work with, as well as direct, their gangs. It also involved keeping accounts of the work performed and materials consumed. Some shipwright officers acted as overseers for ships building by contract in the merchant yards, but their numbers were few compared to those who remained in the dockyards.

Within the ranks of the inferior officers there was a hierarchy related to the size of the workforce each commanded. The Boatswain had charge of all the labourers, scavelmen and horse teams, and was consequently on equal terms with the three foremen of the shipwrights, known as the Foreman of the Yard, Foreman Afloat and Foreman of the New Work. Lower in status than these four were the foremen of the other craft departments; and beneath all the foremen were the quartermen. They were also subdivided, some being termed sub- and pro-quartermen. They had actual charge of the gangs which performed yard operations and were sometimes called 'leading men'. Naval officers called all these officials 'petty officers'. Nevertheless, though indeed only one step removed from the artificers at their lower end, the Boatswain and shipwright foremen were as important, and made earnings as high, as some of the principal officers.

The chief duty of the inferior officers was not an easy one. Samuel Bentham observed about 1800 that a quarterman or foreman

> being very little raised above the artificers themselves, either in point of emolument or rank, living amongst them and thence being continually liable to feel the momentary effect of their ill will, it cannot be expected that he should be very ready to stand forward in enforcing regulations which in many instances must bring upon him the resentment of hundreds of those whose interests he thwarts.[34]

In 1797 a quarterman named George Boddy had to be removed from Portsmouth yard after an 'altercation' with a shipwright whom he had previously described as 'impossible . . . as an officer to carry on duty with'. The shipwrights found Boddy, escorted him to the Master Shipwright's office, then insisted on taking him and turning him out of the yard. The Admiralty appointed Boddy carpenter of a ship then being laid down at Milford Haven, ordering at the same time that any difference in wages be made up to him.[35] Boddy was perhaps more conscientious than most. However, he was unusual. Other inferior officers survived without serious altercations and clearly learned to comply in some degree with the interests of their men. It was indeed conspicuous at different times that inferior officers were of little assistance during riots, provided but mild influence in combating embezzlement, and were instrumental, at least until 1801, in ensuring that the artificers obtained the highest earnings possible.

That the inferior officers should have been subject to the will of those whose conduct they were meant to govern was generally accepted in the yards. During the period considered here little was done *directly* to alter the situation.

The changes in the nature of payment in fact had the effect of lowering their incomes and thereby reducing their local standing; but the changes nevertheless reduced both the means through which they were open to influence and their own vested interest in the amount of their subordinates' earnings. They consequently increased the inferior officers' independence, thereby indirectly improving their ability to manage their men.

The emoluments these officers lost between 1801 and 1804 included a daily allowance traditionally obtained for lodgings, the premiums paid by parents for boys taken as apprentices and the earnings of their apprentices. Of these losses the latter were the most important. Each of the inferior officers was entitled until 1804 to one or two apprentices and to receive their pay, of which they were expected to pocket a proportion. These extra wages were considerable, amounting to at least £60 a year. During the first quarter of 1801 a foreman whose personal pay was £36 obtained over £72 with the pay of two apprentices; and a quarterman whose own pay was £28 obtained over £50 with the earnings of one apprentice.[36] However, it was realized that the pay of these apprentices gave the officers a vested interest in the amount of earnings made by the gangs in which these boys worked; that they therefore had an ulterior motive in obtaining grants of piecework and overtime; and that to obtain the full rates of 'extra' (for piecework or overtime) for their apprentices many were prepared to fabricate the figures for the amount of work performed by their gangs.[37]

The attempt to break down these officers' vested interest in the amount of the artificers' pay complicated and extended the process by which the nature of their earnings was altered. By the order in council of 21 May 1801 they were deprived of the 'extra' earned by the apprentices, leaving them only the boys' basic day pay. For shipwright apprentices this ranged between 14d. and 22d. a day, according to the year of their training, and for other trades between 12d. and 20d. In December 1802, however, after St Vincent's discovery of frauds in the calculation of 'extra' earnings, the Admiralty Board ordered that all apprentices be rebound to their principal departmental officers and that the inferior officers were to act simply as those boys' instructors, for which they were to have only two-thirds of their basic day pay, the other third being for their parents or guardians for their upkeep. As compensation, though, those officers who had formerly had only one apprentice were allowed two.[38]

Yet two years later, following the printing of the sixth report of the Commissioners of Naval Enquiry, the quartermen of the shipwrights and the foremen and quartermen of the caulkers who supervised gangs alike lost their apprentices and were given fixed salaries.[39] It was revealed by the Commissioners that these officers had continued to have an interest in the multiples of the basic daily wage that were set as a ceiling for earnings by piecework or overtime; for the ceiling to the amount of their own daily wages remained the same as that for the artificers at their tools. Accordingly, when the artificers obtained grants of overtime or piecework, these officers too obtained up to two or three days' pay for one day's work. The introduction of salaries therefore dissolved all common interest between the inferior officers and the artificers.

The more senior of the inferior officers, the Boatswain and foremen of the shipwrights, appear to have come out of these changes relatively well. In 1801 they were given salaries of £240, as much as officers at the head of the smaller yard departments. But the quartermen who supervised gangs apparently lost considerably. Including wages made by apprentices, they had been accustomed to receiving at least £180 a year during war and £130 during peace; but in December 1804, when their salaries were introduced, they were limited to £160.[40] There was accordingly some discontent. In February 1805 the quartermen at Woolwich and Sheerness felt they had been degraded in the eyes of their subordinates. They were particularly concerned at the loss of their apprentices which, according to them, meant the loss of their 'servants'' earnings to their dependants, should they die, and to themselves should they be obliged to retire. They claimed, moreover, that their new salaried earnings were reduced if they were sick and unable to work whereas their apprentices' earnings had previously provided a steady income.[41] This complaint led in April 1805 to the allowance of full salary to men whose absence was certified by a yard surgeon to have been caused by an injury at work and the allowance of 5s. a day to those whose indisposition was certified as arising from another cause.[42]

Nevertheless the inadequacy of the salary continued a grievance. The principal officers at Plymouth reported in October that at the last payment of their yard many of the artificers' wages had exceeded the quartermen's salary, some of them so considerably that they were 'fearful' that the quartermen would feel discouraged.[43] Their fears were fully justified. In March 1808 the quartermen from all six yards petitioned the Admiralty in the hope that they too might benefit during the spate of changes consequent on the recommendations of the Commissioners of Naval Revision.[44] In October of that year a few did, some quartermen being given salaries of £180. Nevertheless many continued to earn less than the artificers they supervised.

That many of these men did suffer financial difficulties seems clear. The Woolwich petition early in 1808 spoke of house rent and taxes taking nearly a third of their income; the Plymouth petition, of some of them having to share houses with workmen; and few can have expected to have been promoted out of these difficulties. The numbers of inferior officers required in the yards was growing: in 1780 there had been only 260; by 1800 there were over 400, and by 1810 there were 560.[45] The growth in numbers after 1801, moreover, was facilitated by the absence of any financial obstacle; previously premiums of between £100 and £126 were paid for quartermen's places, some of the sums going to retiring officers.[46] Yet these increased numbers simply enlarged the pool from which the principal yard officers were chosen; they would also seem to have increased the importance of 'connection' in determining who were selected to join the favoured few.

All the same, connection was not the only factor determining further advancement. Practical ability had always been essential and inferior officers continued to be recommended on the grounds that they were able, honest, diligent, sober, and had clear records of service. Where the claims to promotion of sub- and pro-quartermen were similar, seniority was given its due. But literacy, numeracy and physical vigour were no less important. Thus, for example, in 1802 the Admiralty Board criticized the employment of a shipwright in the 'cabin' of a foreman in Chatham yard because he performed the writing and calculations which the foreman should have done had he been 'properly qualified for his duty'; and in 1803 the principal officers at Portsmouth proposed that the fourth quarterman of the house carpenters should succeed to the place of the first as he had 'superior claims to those preceding him, not only from his knowledge of drawing, scholarship and officer-like method in conducting business . . . but from his age, he being only forty-three . . .' and the others between 58 and 66.[47]

For those who, perhaps from age, were incapable of advancing further, even within the ranks of the inferior officers, the dockyards had one major compensation: like the clerks, there was the prospect of eventual superannuation. Yet the provision of pensions for these officers was sparing. Foremen with 30 or more years of unblemished service could be recommended by the Navy Board for annuities which were sometimes as high as £100; but quartermen were grouped with the ordinary artificers in a superannuation scheme established by orders in council of 1764 and 1771. This provided pensions of £28 for 1 in 40 of all the men borne on the yard books. The aged consequently had to wait for their pension until a place fell vacant on the list of men receiving superannuation; and, as men injured in a yard were usually given priority, their wait was usually lengthy. In May 1802, for instance, 103 quartermen and artificers of the shipwrights were receiving pensions, there were no vacancies on the superannuation list, but there were 95 men awaiting a pension and the opportunity to retire.[48]

This situation resulted in many elderly 'petty officers' around the yards. The least active were given the more sedentary posts, such as the charge of the 'cabins' where small stocks of materials were kept for current work. These were perhaps the men whom Commissioner Coffin described at Sheerness in 1801 as 'drones that might be better employed'. But the leadership and supervision of the artificers then became the task of younger and more vigorous men appointed from the gangs. Thus the Admiralty Board noted in 1802 that 'the number of leading men who do not work as the others and receive some additional pay' was 'very great in proportion to the strength of the gangs'; it directed that the number of gangs be reduced, their strength increased, and the acting quartermen return to their tools as soon as the men for whom they were acting returned to their posts.[49]

Such orders had no lasting effect. To perform efficiently, the artificers' gangs required more active leadership than elderly men could supply. The relegation of aged quartermen to undemanding jobs and the dependence for the direction of gangs on younger men continued until 1809. Then a superannuation scheme was introduced for all salaried inferior officers. Initially, pensions varied in amount with the number of years' service as an officer: one-fifth the annual salary for 15 years' service rising to one-half after 35 years. From 1813 the term of service as an artificer was included and the pensions were made payable to widows.[50] For 'petty officers' who had spent all of their working lives in the yards, who had experienced the loss of apprentices and the period of inadequate salaries, these benefits made loyal service worthwhile. They helped form, moreover, a generally younger and more vigorous corps of inferior officers.

The more able and fortunate foremen and quartermen of the shipwrights who rose higher in the dockyards, few as they were, passed, often at a relatively rapid rate, through a succession of posts which formed a distinct hierarchy. The most junior were the Master Caulkers', Joiners', Mastmakers' and Boatbuilders' positions; after 1801 there were also Timber Masters' positions, and after 1810 those of the Master Measurers. Then came the places of the assistants to the Master Shipwright and ultimately those of the Master Shipwrights. It was not usual for an officer to rise vertically within a single yard for, as well as the order of posts within each yard, there was a hierarchy of yards. At the highest level in this hierarchy were Portsmouth, Plymouth and Deptford, the first two on account of their size and the latter on account of its proximity to the London Boards, to which yard officers were sometimes called for consultation. Prior to 1801 the greater amounts of unofficial emoluments received at the larger yards reinforced this ranking, yet their abolition made no difference to it. Chatham, Woolwich and Sheerness followed next in the hierarchy, Sheerness coming lowest due to its size and damp, unhealthy situation.

In consequence of this order of yards, the men working their way through the lower shipwright officers' places had to change yards frequently. The career of Nicholas Diddams was typical. He served as Master Caulker at Sheerness from March until May 1797, as second assistant to the Master Shipwright at Chatham until August 1798, in the same position at Portsmouth until October 1799, as first assistant at Portsmouth until July 1801, when he obtained the Master Shipwright's post at Sheerness. Having entered the lower level of officers' places at Sheerness, Diddams had to return to that yard for his first appointment as a Master Shipwright. Only after having served there until March 1803 was he able to return to Portsmouth and take a higher Master Shipwright's post. Out of the 15 Master Shipwrights appointed between 1793 and 1815 seven received their first appointment at this level at Sheerness, while eight were promoted to Portsmouth, Plymouth or Deptford as a final appointment.[51]

The men who filled the places of the principal clerical officers' posts did not have such itinerant careers. There was a hierarchy to their places; the highest position, that of Clerk of the Cheque, was often filled by men who had been in turn a Storekeeper, Clerk of the Survey and Clerk of a Ropeyard. Close adherence to the pattern of succession was here unnecessary, all four places being open to men who had held responsibility in the Navy Office or another naval department. Robinson Kittoe, for example, who rose to become Clerk of the Cheque at Woolwich in 1807, had entered the yard officers' ranks after being the Chatham agent for prisoners of war under the Transport Board;[52] and Benjamin Tucker, Clerk of the Cheque at Plymouth for four months in 1801, had been private secretary and prize agent to St Vincent while he commanded the Channel fleet.

A few of the other principal officers' places were also filled by men from outside the yards. The Masters Attendant had usually been ships' masters. The yard surgeons too had probably served at sea. But the masters of the ropemakers, smiths, joiners, sailmakers and bricklayers had usually risen in their departments and simply been appointed to succeed their previous principal. Once so appointed, like the Masters Attendant, these officers usually remained in their posts till retirement.

To reach these heights, connection was an asset. In the shipwright line, in which the numbers to select from were high, it was almost essential. The most useful connection was formed young, through the apprenticeship of a boy to an officer who was rising in the yards. Although, before 1801, such connections were only purchased with high premiums, a boy was thereby assured a privileged training, including employment in the mould loft, drawing out the patterns for ships' timbers, and work at an officer's side. The completion of training was soon followed by an appointment to quarterman, from where the pace of progress usually depended on that of the patron. At the quarterman's level appointments were made by the Navy Board on the recommendations of the yard officers, but more senior officers were appointed by the Admiralty Board. Influence there was accordingly crucial. One factor, for example, that favoured Seppings's appointment in 1803 as Master Shipwright at Chatham was his early tutelage and lasting connection with Sir John Henslow, Surveyor at the Navy Board between 1784 and 1806.

Seppings's achievements vindicated his appointment. Indeed it demonstrates that even appointments made under influence were discriminating. After the turn of the century, attention to the characters and abilities of candidates for appointments in fact seems to have been increasing. Charles Middleton, Lord Barham, First Lord in 1805–6, had occasion to complain to Pitt in 1786 that 'almost every efficient appointment in the yards being in the admiralty and frequently made an object of interest, officers feel less anxious for their conduct and particularly when they know that a proper vote would cover a corrupt practice'.[53] Twenty years later the pressures to appoint on account of interest or influence still existed. Yet men like St Vincent and Barham made ability their first consideration. 'It is my fixed determination', St Vincent wrote to Thomas Parlby in March 1801, 'to fill all vacant offices with the most efficient men I can find and to pay no regard to the recommendations of any person whatever where the qualification will not bear me out in the appointment.' St Vincent would thus neither oblige the Duke of Clarence, who recommended a man without 'precision or energy' for a Clerk of the Cheque's post, nor promote the son of the Clerk of the Cheque at Plymouth who was insufficiently experienced.[54] Barham too made clear his priorities. He observed in 1804 that 'men of knowledge in the business must be employed in every department of the service and neither rank in life, nor birth, nor country should stand in the way when integrity and ability are to be found'.[55]

Aware of the network of connections that brought officers to their notice, both St Vincent and Barham were cautious of recommendations from the yard officers. Barham had pointed out to Pitt in 1786 that the officers had 'so many relations and dependants . . . in the dockyards . . . that they never lose an opportunity of supporting them when in their power and on this account ought to have as small a voice as possible in creating them'.[56] For this reason, in March 1801, St Vincent applied to Commissioner Coffin for 'the merits' of all persons who fell sufficiently under his 'eye and cognisance' to justify him describing their characters. He also applied to Commissioner Saxton in July 1801 for an opinion as to the respective abilities of two officers who had served in Portsmouth yard. 'Pretensions' had been 'set up' in favour of the senior of the two on account of his seniority, but St Vincent was only prepared to promote him if 'his merits' were of 'a superior kind'. He indicated that he was ready to advance the junior of the two in preference to the other, but that he was 'well aware' how difficult it was to obtain 'precise knowledge of the real abilities and fitness of men . . . from those under whom they have been educated'.[57]

To avoid dependence on recommendations, often from interested parties, in 1788 when he had been Comptroller, Barham had had drawn up a comprehensive 'account of the several officers, their supposed respective ages, their names and employs . . ., their respective abilities in their different stations, how far they are such as fear God and hate covetousness, their moral character, actions, dispositions [and] whether married or single'.[58] Under Sandwich, he had experienced difficulties with the Admiralty in having his recommendations accepted.[59] By 1811, however, attitudes at the Admiralty had altered, for a similar account specifying the characters, abilities, and ages of shipwright officers was then drawn up for the Navy Board on the orders of the Admiralty.[60] Although this account possibly arose through the influence of John Deas Thompson, Barham's friend, who was then at the Navy Board, it also reflected the more enlightened attitude to dockyard affairs of Charles Yorke, then First Lord.

Throughout these wars, the Navy Board was a consistent influence in ensuring that officer appointments were seen to be fair. This was perhaps most evident in 1809 when the Board objected to the appointment of Jean Louis Barrallier, second assistant to the Surveyors of the navy between 1796 and 1815, to the Master Shipwright's post at Milford; also, to the appointment of Barrallier's son, Lewis Charles, since 1801 his clerk, to the post of Master Shipwright's assistant. Barrallier senior had been an engineer in the French arsenal at Toulon and had been employed to finish a line-of-battleship, a frigate and a sloop laid down according to his draughts at Milford. But in 1809, when a formal establishment was authorized for the yard, the Navy Board recalled that Barrallier's appointment as second assistant 13 years before had excited so 'much jealousy' among the inferior officers that he had had to be sent to Milford 'because there were some difficulties in his doing the duties of the assistant Surveyor in relation to the dockyards'. The board also recalled that Lewis Charles Barrallier had never served a proper shipwright's apprenticeship. Under these circumstances the board feared

> that the appointment of these two persons respectively to the offices of
> Master Shipwright and assistant to the Master Shipwright in the Royal Dock
> Yard at Milford would occasion very great dissatisfaction among the
> assistants and inferior officers of our several dock yards, who have devoted
> their whole lives to the duties of their profession, have from the hope of
> promotion undergone the drudgery incident to that profession, and many of
> whom have qualified themselves for the situations to which they naturally
> aspire.

To supplement their objection the Board pointed out that an order in council of July 1805 banned all foreigners from the dockyards and that, as Catholics, even naturalization would not put the Barralliers into a situation 'to hold offices of such great trust under His Majesty's Government'. So confident of its ground was the Board that, pending the Admiralty's answer, it withheld the delivery of the Admiralty warrants of appointment. The warrants were in fact immediately cancelled.[61]

As the Navy Board made clear, the yard officers themselves could make known their dissatisfaction with appointments that appeared unfair. Equally clear was the Board's belief that, for the benefit of the officers, it was essential that justice was seen to be done. Indeed, as the men on whom the practical business of yard operations depended, their encouragement was a prerequisite to yard efficiency. The Master Shipwrights themselves pointed out in a petition in 1808 that it was their ability, industry and zeal which stimulated to exertion all the subordinate officers and men under their command. But they also emphasized that the responsibilities of their posts were exhausting: 'the life of the Master Shipwright who zealously discharges his duties is such a continued scene of labour and anxiety, more particularly since the great increase of the navy, that it is not possible for any constitution, however robust, to sustain it for many years'.[62] At this level a system of promotion which provided the prospect of just rewards for such labour was fundamental to the vigour with which yard operations were directed.

The importance of this factor was enhanced after 1801, when other forms of reward were proscribed, in providing an element of stability in terms of service. For this period was no less unsettling for the senior officers than for their subordinates and clerks, although as a group they suffered less in a financial sense than the latter, since their unofficial perquisites and emoluments were a smaller proportion of their total incomes.

According to the accounts of perquisites taken in 1784, fees, for example, were not taken by any of the five principal officers at each yard except the Clerks of the Ropeyards at Woolwich and Portsmouth and the Masters Attendant at Plymouth. The three clerical officers – the Clerks of the Cheque, Clerks of the Survey and Storekeepers – took no unofficial emoluments except premiums from their clerks; but these were considerable, clerks paying up to £300 for entry into a yard office immediately prior to 1801. The masters of trades in the yards also took premiums from clerks and inferior officers, the latter paying up to £126 for their appointments. However, their main unofficial emoluments before 1801 were the earnings of apprentices, a Master Shipwright being allowed five, a Master Attendant two – often in the sailmakers' department – and the other master craftsmen two or three according to status.

A number of other perquisites and allowances were also abolished in 1801 or shortly before, but they had been taken by only a scattering of officers. In 1798, being considered too open to the influence of the recipients of prize money to be fit persons to value prizes and 'say what they please, whether fit for Government or not', officers were forbidden from acting as prize agents. In 1801 the Master Shipwright at Sheerness was required to give up the business of acting as coal merchant for artificers with quarters in the yard as coals could be purchased from outside.[63] In 1801, too, the Master Shipwright and Master Attendant at Chatham, who managed the Chest providing relief to seamen

*Table 24. The earnings of officers at Chatham yard*

| | Basic salary to 1801 £ | Extra fees and gratuities in 1784 £ | Net earnings with allowances, other emoluments and deductions in 1784 £ | Salaries from 1 July 1801 £ | Salaries from 1 Oct. 1808 £ |
|---|---|---|---|---|---|
| Master Shipwright | 200 | 0 | 509 | 720 | 720 |
| 1st Master Attendant | 200 | 0 | 265 | 480 | 650 |
| 2nd Master Attendant | 200 | 0 | 183 | 480 | 500 |
| Clerk of the Cheque | 200 | 0 | 303 | 600 | 600 |
| Storekeeper | 200 | 0 | 285 | 480 | 600 |
| Clerk of the Survey | 200 | 0 | 191 | 420 | 500 |
| Clerk of the Ropeyard | 100 | 0 | 97 | 300 | 350 |
| Assistants to Master Shipwright | 100 | 0 | 196 | 360 | 400 |
| Master Smith | 100 | | 185 | 240 | 260 |
| Master Ropemaker | 100 | 0 | | 250 | 250 |
| Master Joiner | 100 | | | 240 | 250 |
| Master House Carpenter | 100 | | | 240 | 250 |
| Master Boatbuilder | 100 | | | 240 | 250 |
| Master Mastmaker | 100 | | | 240 | 250 |
| Master Sailmaker | 100 | | | 240 | 250 |
| Master Bricklayer | 100 | | | 240 | 250 |
| Surgeon | 100 | 0 | 232 | 360 | 500 |

Figures for other emoluments before 1801 include the pay of apprentices. There were two assistants to the Master Shipwright at Chatham in 1784 and an average of their extra emoluments is given here. Their individual earnings were actually close to this average. The report for 1784 does not give the other emoluments, the deductions and allowances for the Master craftsmen of the smaller yard departments. See also note to table 21.

hurt or maimed in service at sea, were deprived of their remuneration for the work, the Chest shortly afterwards becoming part of the system of out-relief provided by Greenwich Hospital.[64]

All these emoluments were given up as a matter of course. This was not the case, however, with the loss to the Master Shipwright in 1801 of a 'piece of plate' worth £100 at the launching of each new ship. In April 1805 all six Master Shipwrights petitioned for its restoration claiming that the plate was esteemed by them far above its intrinsic value on account of 'that laudable pride which every man feels who has been the principal in conducting the executive part [in the construction] of the great machine, a ship'. Their appeal was then rejected, but in 1814 the Admiralty restored the plate, though reducing its value to £50 for three-deckers and £40 for two-deckers.[65]

That the other unofficial earnings or allowances were given up without appeal can be partly attributed to the fact that the compensating increases in salaries given to the officers in 1801 covered most losses. Some jealousy arose from the fact that the new salaries of the Masters Attendant were significantly lower than those of the Master Shipwrights, though the former believed they had 'always been considered as having the first charge in the naval departments under the [yard] Commissioner in time of peace as well as in war'. The Master Shipwrights' assistants and the Master Boatbuilders were aggrieved to find that their salaries, like those of the inferior yard officers, were sometimes exceeded by the earnings of artificers; these officers also complained that, unlike their seniors who had houses in the yards or an allowance for house rent, they had to pay rent as well as property and parochial taxes, expenditure that took a quarter of their income.[66] Subsequently, in October 1808, all the officers except for the Master Shipwrights, Clerks of the Cheque and Master Ropemakers received further increases in salary and, slight though these were for junior officers, they appear to have settled the discontent.

The introduction in 1801 of a superannuation scheme possibly also helped reconcile them to their losses. As for the clerks, pensions before 1801 had only been provided by orders in council and seem to have been a matter of favour. The scheme introduced in 1801 entitled officers to amounts ranging from one-third of their salary after 10 to 15 years' service to three-quarters after more than 35 years' service. The scheme was generous: immediately following its introduction, during the first half of July 1801, eight yard officers applied for their pensions.[67]

On balance the senior yard officers therefore lost little in the way of income between 1801 and 1808. For them, the problems of the period took another form. As the instruments through whom an alteration in business conduct had to be enforced in the yards, they were subject to the pressures and tensions associated with this profound change, intensified as these were by the presence of St Vincent at the Admiralty between 1801 and 1804. Accustomed to the rigour of naval discipline, indeed a notable exponent of it, St Vincent was uncompromising, even ruthless, in his treatment of officials. The receipt of payments from parties other than government he regarded as 'disgraceful transactions'. Though all had been prohibited 18 months earlier, in November 1802, he required all senior officers to declare on oath the amount of any such earnings they had made from their places. Explanations for failures to comply with yard regulations he regarded as excuses 'made upon false principles', to which every discouragement was necessary.[68] Accordingly those who broke regulations were punished as examples to the rest. After seven yard officers had been summarily discharged, the others clearly feared for themselves, especially after the confiscation of some of their papers and the appointment of the Commission of Naval Enquiry late in 1802. An anonymous writer informed St Vincent's successor at the Admiralty in 1804:

> For some time past it has been notorious that a system of terror has prevailed in the Dockyards. Spys have been set everywhere, informers have been encouraged and appointed to the places of those they accused so that no officer had any confidence in those that were acting with them. Their books and papers have been locked up and their minds agitated with some charge being laid against them before the Commissioners of Naval Enquiry.[69]

The examples made of the seven yard officers, the Commission of Naval Enquiry and the 'system of terror', imaginary though this may have been, were all part of the process of transition in naval administration and in government in general. At the Admiralty, St Vincent was undoubtedly aware of the effect the measures had. Having come to the Admiralty intending reform, he obviously intended that the naval departments should function, civil establishments though they were, with the precision of a ship at sea. Other naval officers, like Commissioner Coffin at Sheerness, had a similar desire. Coffin, for example, was surprised to find yard officers generally slack about time-keeping, arriving in the yard at 8 or 9 o'clock, often after himself. St Vincent's régime, merciless though it was, accordingly had its supporters. In reminding yard officers that the standards as well as the rewards of service were changing, its influence was long to outlast him.

At other times, under the paternal control of the Navy Board, the pressure on yard officers was less intense. Occasionally there were acrimonious sea officers, difficult artificers, and censures from the Admiralty for permitting poor workmanship. But the Navy Board itself was a relatively easy taskmaster. Governed in its response to yard affairs by its long-established members, it rarely roused itself to administer strong reprimands. The officers' minor breaches of regulation, such as the keeping of private boats in the yards, though the thin end of a wedge to St Vincent, were dismissed by the Navy Board as 'trivial'.[70] Suspensions or dismissals at officer level were thus uncommon. Indeed, having achieved the rank of yard officer there was (except during St Vincent's administration) almost absolute security of tenure. With 14 days' annual leave, with salaries continued through sickness (even through 'an infirmity commonly called hard drinking') and, for the principal officers, the advantage of a house in their yard, the officers enjoyed all the compensations, if also the heavier responsibilities, of Crown service.

Like the yard officers, the board and yard commissioners enjoyed many of the benefits of government service. On account of their more senior positions in the hierarchy of management, however, their experiences reflected to a greater extent the changing attitudes to office-holding at the Admiralty and in central government as a whole. As a result, while the role and responsibilities of the yard officers remained basically unchanged throughout the period, those of the commissioners developed far more. Some of the board places, from being virtual sinecures at the beginning of the Revolutionary War, were transformed into efficient offices. This was a transformation in which St Vincent's administration played a significant part. Even the restriction of the commissioners' incomes to amounts that bore little relation to their responsibilities also appears to have played its part. Indeed it was as though, through their own self-discipline and restraint, they were expected to set examples for those beneath them.

The transformation in the role performed at the Board by some commissioners was remarkable. As Comptroller in the 1780s, Middleton had found their attendance more of a nuisance than a help. He informed Francis Baring in 1787:

> Those commissioners who, contented with an easy official attendance, came and went as inclination had them . . . were satisfied with an arrangement which, when they had avocations, gave them convenient leisure to pursue them, and when they pleased to meddle, left them all the importance of office. Indeed I should do them injustice if I did not also acknowledge that their manner of leaving whatever required dispatch to my management showed a confidence in me that was not only necessary but pleasing.[71]

In accordance with recommendations made by Middleton, in 1796 the members of the Navy Board were organized into committees; and in 1803, under St Vincent, detailed definitions of individuals' duties were submitted to the Admiralty. Not only were the commissioners thus forced to take a full part in office business: each was made individually responsible for the performance of a part.

St Vincent ensured that the commissioners felt the real weight of these responsibilities. Indeed, as he held the Navy Board accountable for all the frauds and inefficiency uncovered in the dockyards, his primary object was to replace those Board members whom he regarded as negligent with his own nominees. He was, however, frustrated in this object because, though the First Lord could nominate new commissioners, they were appointed by letters patent under the Great Seal. The existing membership of the Navy Board was thus able to defy the First Lord to bring about their removal. It was later said, for example, that St Vincent 'would almost have given his two ears to dismiss Sir Andrew Hamond [the Comptroller] but he did not dare because Sir A. sat by the King's patent'.[72] Yet St Vincent's frustration in this matter drove him to great lengths to rid himself of the existing Navy Board. Shortly after the appointment of the Commissioners of Naval Enquiry, William Marsden, Second Secretary at the Admiralty, commented:

> Like most other boards and public offices they have left many things undone; but the Visitation [of the dockyards by the Admiralty Board] did not bring home to them any act of corruption or malversation. It was then

tried to drive them out by the most abusive letters that ever were written from one board to another but they were too prudent to gratify our gentlemen in this way. And now this extra-ordinary commission is resorted to in the hope of its operating some way (they cannot very well say how) to the end desired. I know it was their first idea to arm their friends, the new Commissioners, with the power of punishing but now it is only intended they should inquire and report.[73]

Marsden makes clear the unenviable situation of the Navy Board Commissioners between 1801 and 1804. St Vincent's administration was relatively short. It was nevertheless significant in reasserting the complete responsibility of the Navy Board for dockyard affairs.

The commissioners' sense of mistreatment during the St Vincent period was undoubtedly reinforced by their earlier financial losses. The Board commissioners in 1796 and yard commissioners in 1801 all received increased salaries, yet these did not completely cover their losses. These included their premiums, taken in rotation by the Board commissioners from clerks entering or rising in the Navy Office, and by the yard commissioners from clerks in their own offices. Of more importance was the loss of numerous official allowances. The six most senior Board members and their colleagues in the yards, all of whom had rent-free houses either in Somerset House or their yards, were deprived of a rent allowance and an allowance for coals and candles. Former sea officers also lost the allowance of their half-pay on top of their civilian salaries.

Certain allowances still remained. Board members were allowed newspapers. The Portsmouth commissioner continued to be granted £100 for acting as principal to the naval academy within the yard; while those who travelled on business had a guinea a day for subsistence and 1s. 6d. a mile for transport. Unlike their subordinates in the Navy Office and the yards they were provided with no regulated scheme of superannuation, but on retirement they continued to be granted pensions by order in council which were generally three-quarters the amount of their salaries.[74]

Nevertheless, after the erosion of the value of their salaries and surviving allowances by the wartime inflation, most commissioners appear to have considered their material circumstances to have deteriorated. The Commissioners of Naval Revision recommended them for a moderate salary increase but this recommendation was ignored. Consequently, in September 1810, when the Admiralty ordered the allowance of newspapers, calendars and pocket books to Board members to cease, the Board commissioners could contain their 'dissatisfaction and vexation' no longer. They complained bitterly that the newspapers were 'a privilege' which had been 'enjoyed from time immemorial' and then proceeded to point out that, because their salaries had remained static since 1801, their incomes had declined while the amount of their work had doubled. Their salaries were therefore 'comparatively inadequate to the national importance of their duties'.

We mean to state that at a period when the pressure of the times has been felt by all ranks of persons and when, in order to merit the pressure, an increase has been allowed in the salaries of most of the public boards, the

*Table 25. The earnings of Navy Board and yard commissioners*

| | Basic salary to 1794 £ | Salary from 1 Oct. 1794 £ | Average of extra fees and gratuities in 1795 £ | Net earnings with allowances in 1795 £ | Salaries from 1 July 1796 £ | Salaries from 1 June 1801 £ |
|---|---|---|---|---|---|---|
| Comptroller | 500 | 1,000 | 300 | 1,764 | 1,500 | 2,000 |
| Deputy Comptroller | 500 | 800 | | 1,060 | 1,200 | 1,200 |
| Surveyors of the navy | 500 | 800 | 80 | 1,140 | 1,000 | 1,000 |
| Other Board commissioners | 500 | 800 | 139 | 1,074 | 1,000 | 1,000 |
| Yard commissioners | 500 | 500 | | 993 | 800 | 1,000 |

Figures rounded to the nearest pound

Navy Board has not even been permitted to remain upon the same footing upon which it stood when that pressure began to be seriously felt, but has been obliged to submit to so material a deduction of emolument that the income of a Commissioner of the Navy is at the moment actually smaller by near £200 per annum than it was in the year 1796. In the mean time the business of the Navy Board, we must repeat, is at least double what it was when the present scale of salaries was fixed. . . .

They believed their attention was 'necessarily more close' and their labours 'more incessant' than those of any of the other permanent boards, the members of some of which had salaries of £1,200, 'a sum which was declared (without contradiction) by a minister in parliament to be the smallest for which a gentleman could be expected to give his time and talents to the public service'.

The Admiralty Board dismissed the commissioners' appeal. It observed that the withdrawal of a privilege to which other naval boards were not entitled was no occasion for 'general complaint and remonstrance'.[75] Nevertheless the commissioners had a case. They were subject to 'the pressure of the times' and the changes of the Revolutionary War had paved the way for regular office hours and application. In 1807 the Secretary to the Navy Board commented that his work with the Board required him to reach the Navy Office by 10 a.m. and stay till the Board broke up at 5 or 5.30 p.m. Ten years later Sir Thomas Byam Martin, then Comptroller, reported that he generally started at 9 a.m., remained till 6 p.m. and, after dinner, frequently worked till 1 a.m.[76] The yard commissioners were perhaps more flexible in their time-keeping but they were on call 24 hours of the day, every day of the week. Some commissioners received two weeks' leave of absence, a period to which they seemed entitled. Yet under the increasing weight of administrative duties, occasional holidays were undoubtedly essential.

Of all the commissioners, those perhaps who had most reason to feel aggrieved in 1810 were former sea officers. They were usually appointed to the posts of Comptroller and Deputy Comptroller, to one or more of the other Board commissioners' places and to the posts at each of the yards. Not only did they lose their half-pay as sea officers in 1801 but, having accepted a civil position in the naval departments, they had usually foregone the opportunity of promotion to flag-rank. Occasionally some commissioners obtained their flags: Isaac Coffin was transferred back on to the list of sea officers and obtained his in 1804; Sir Thomas Boulden Thompson obtained his in 1809; and Sir George Grey was offered his as an alternative to a baronetcy in 1812. But these cases were exceptions and denoted particular favour. Coffin was still only 45, obviously capable of vigorous work, and had done much to assist St Vincent in his campaign for reform; Thompson was Comptroller and had had a particularly notable naval career; and Grey, having been a commissioner at Sheerness before being transferred to Portsmouth, was well known to the king. Even though they might be near the top of the list of captains, most commissioners were simply passed over when promotions took place and removed from the list of the navy. In August 1810 Isaac Schomburg and Sir Robert Barlow, commissioners respectively at the Board and at Chatham, appealed against their being removed from the list and requested to be included as superannuated rear-admirals. The Admiralty simply directed they be listed as superannuated captains, but were not to receive pensions or half pay while retaining their civil positions.[77]

Although the practice of leaving commissioners at the rank of captain was probably based on sound reasoning – at the Navy Board they were thus usually subordinate in rank to admirals at the Admiralty, while at the yards they remained inferior to the port admirals – the practice emphasized the difference in status between the military and civil departments of the navy. The fact that commissioners' posts were still resting places for injured or aged sea officers underlined the difference. Thompson was made Comptroller after having lost a leg; and neither Sir Charles Saxton nor Charles Hope, the Portsmouth and Chatham commissioners who both died in 1808, saw any necessity to retire on account of infirmities that made their duties a strain. In 1805 Hope was confined for several weeks with gout, while Saxton admitted that at the 'advanced period of life' of 73 he was no longer physically active, though in 'pretty good health and spirits' for his age.[78]

Commissioners' posts did not therefore attract able and ambitious sea officers. Rather they attracted men who, through age, injuries or family ties, desired a shore position and were low on the list of senior captains. The Comptroller's post was slightly different for it carried more prestige and greater remuneration. It had onerous political as well as administrative burdens. Sir Thomas Byam Martin stated in 1817 that it was 'impossible for any person to discharge his duties faithfully in that office without ruining his constitution'.[79] The Comptroller had in particular to deal with the First Lord in informal meetings and unofficial correspondence, a difficult task with some First Lords. The Comptroller was also expected to sit in the House of Commons, which added to calls on his attention. Though rarely obliged to speak, there were invariably constituents to deal with. Representing a naval town or port, he was expected by them to use his authority and influence on their behalf. Middleton, for example, like Thompson later, sat for Rochester, but found the representation of the city disagreeable:

> not only from its vicinity and the additional labour occasioned thereby, but from the great number of freemen and their connections belonging to the dockyards of Deptford, Woolwich, Chatham and Sheerness. It is difficult to say from which of these circumstances I have suffered most; but in a public point of view, it must at all times be improper for a comptroller of the navy to represent so many dockyards, as he must either sacrifice the service to the will of his constituents or be at constant war with them and his own feelings.[80]

The Surveyors too had reason to complain of their salaries in 1810. They had incomes only 30 per cent higher than those of the Master Shipwrights, a differential inconsistent with their positions. For, although for sea officers a commissioner's post implied the loss of status, the reverse was true for the Surveyors. Having been raised through the yards, the Navy Board was a pinnacle of achievement. In 1813 the number of Surveyors was raised to three. Even then, the opportunities for Master Shipwrights to obtain one of these coveted places were infrequent; Sir John Henslow and Sir William Rule remained in office for more than 20 years, Henry Peake for 16. A Surveyor's position had a scarcity value.

Between 1793 and 1815, in fact, only four appointments were made. All four men had characters or careers marked by some distinction. William Rule, appointed second Surveyor under Sir John Henslow in 1793, was reported five years earlier as of 'good abilities in his profession, of very quick parts and sound judgement', though 'hasty in disposition'. Henry Peake, made second to Rule in 1806, was simply 'of good abilities' and 'diligent' in 1788; but he came from a family of shipwright officers and was released from his yard in the late 1790s to work with Samuel Bentham.[81] Joseph Tucker, who replaced Rule in 1813, though having trained in the dockyards and served in Woolwich yard for four years, had entered the service of the East India Company in 1784 where he was employed as an overseer for ships building and repairing and then as an assistant surveyor; St Vincent made him assistant to the 'builder' at Plymouth in 1801 and, eight months later, Master Shipwright.[82] Robert Seppings, who was made the third Surveyor in 1813, had of course developed the diagonally braced ship's frame by that time. Nevertheless all four men who reached the highest rank in their profession had more than these marks of distinction in common: they were all at the time of their appointments between 46 and 48 years old. Indeed, this common factor is so noticeable that it appears to have formed a qualification.

The commissioners who had perhaps least to complain about in 1810 were 'men of business', appointed for their administrative ability and experience. In background and aspirations they can best be termed civil servants, since they had had experience either in other areas of the naval service or in other branches of government, and tended to remain at the Board for a considerable time. The Hon. Henry Legge, for example, was appointed to the board by St Vincent in 1804 and John Deas Thompson by Barham in 1805. Although Legge appears to have had little previous 'naval' experience, he remained at the Navy Board until 1829. Thompson was the navy agent at Leith until 1804, was employed in the Navy Office on work subsequently transferred to the Commissioners of Revision, and then remained at the Navy Board until 1829 too.

In 1810 the membership of the Navy Board differed from what it had been during the early years of the Napoleonic War in not containing men of obvious political connections. The appointment of such men in fact appears to have been declining as some Board members, particularly the 'civil servant' type, remained longer in office. However, during St Vincent's administration, partly because the period was so highly charged politically, two appointments to the Board had strong political overtones. Benjamin Tucker, having been St Vincent's secretary in the Mediterranean, then Clerk of the Cheque for only four months at Plymouth, was appointed to the Navy Board in 1801 and subsequently made Second Secretary at the Admiralty early in 1804. His debt to St Vincent was demonstrated in the fact that on St Vincent's resignation in May 1804, Tucker too resigned his secretaryship. Osborne Markham, younger brother of John Markham who represented St Vincent's Admiralty Board in the Commons, was appointed in July 1803. However, after a dispute over the

# 5 The officials

keeping of a memorandum book of proceedings at the Board, he was regarded by most of the other commissioners as a spy in their midst. In January 1805 Melville, St Vincent's successor, suspended him from sitting at the Board and in July Barham arranged that he exchange places with Edward Bouverie of the Transport Board.

These last commissioners owed their places more than anything to patronage. Yet an investigation of the associations of all the commissioners would probably indicate that each one had some connection that worked in his favour. With different backgrounds, patrons and interests, the members of the Navy Board were not always of one mind. Indeed, under a relatively weak Comptroller, divisions clearly rent the Board, especially where the First Lord supported the views of a particular commissioner in preference to those of the Comptroller. This was the case in 1804 when St Vincent privately supported Osborne Markham against the other commissioners, claiming later in the House of Lords that he was the only Board member who did his public duty or was competent to his office.[83] Under most circumstances the Board nevertheless presented a united front. Junior members on the whole 'could not help giving credit' to their seniors' greater experience and clichés were sometimes used to cover a multitude of views. Welding the Board together, moreover, was the general belief that internal conflict was not in the public interest. Even in November 1802, when the Board was confronted with evidence of 'improper transactions' in the dockyards, the commissioners were all capable of putting their signatures to the belief that their common intention had always been to acquit themselves 'to the benefit of the state'.[84]

This declaration, produced in the commissioners' own defence, sums up the spirit emanating from much of the correspondence between the board and yard officials. Although they were all clearly concerned about their material rewards, throughout the wars they remained aware that they were first and foremost public servants. This awareness is perhaps best reflected in the fact that all the officials were restrained, and for the most part remarkably patient, in their agitation for better conditions of service.

Yet the public service ethic was itself developing, reinforced by the changes in terms of service during the wars. These changes can be properly seen as preparing the way for the great developments in the civil service in the mid-nineteenth century. Through the abolition of fees, premiums and gratuities, the improvement of salaries and extension of superannuation schemes, officials were made to a large extent independent of pecuniary influence from those with whom they dealt – whether contractors or subordinates – and completely dependent on the 'one certain salary' and pension paid by government. The changes accordingly rendered officials less susceptible to corruption, while also forming them into a more homogeneous service and removing from their number men fit for retirement. Accompanied by the repeatedly declared intention to ensure that appointments advanced the most able, the changes undoubtedly resulted in a more respectable and more vigorous service.

By the end of the Revolutionary and Napoleonic Wars, government service for dockyard officials had accordingly been transformed. At the beginning of the wars many were already professional in attitude; by the end, their conduct and terms of service had much in common with those of the modern civil servant. In view of the reforms that occurred and the adjustments in attitude they involved, it is not surprising that there was at times discontent. Of greater national importance, however, was the revival of moral among officials after about 1808 when the main anomalies and inadequacies in their terms of service had been removed. It was important because, at a time when public support for the war was waning, there was in the naval departments, so far as can be assumed from the decline in complaints, a probable increase in application and industry.

*Table 26. The principal officers, 1793–1815*

**Deptford yard**

| | |
|---|---|
| Master Shipwright | M. Ware (1787–95); T. Pollard (1795–9); E. Tippett (1799–1803); H. Peake (1803–6); R. Nelson (1806–13); W. Stone (1813–30). |
| Master Attendant | J. Gilbert (1791–1803); C. Robb (1803–23). |
| Clerk of the Cheque | R. Rosewell (1783–1807); G. Gainer (1807–21). |
| Storekeeper | R. Paine (1790–95); C. H. Harris (1795–1803); R. Kittoe (1803–7); J. W. Nelson (1807–8); J. Hodgskin (1809–27). |
| Clerk of the Survey | P. Butt (1771–1800); T. Grant (1800); J. Aubin (1800–2); J. W. Nelson (1802–6); J. W. Lloyd (1806–8); T. Netherton (1808–20). |
| 1st Assistant to Master Shipwright and, from 1801, Timber Master (new post) | J. Dann (1788–95); J. Frankland (1795–8); R. J. Nelson (1798–1803); W. Stone (1803–8); J. Welstead (1808–23). |
| 2nd Assistant and Master Caulker (latter post lapsing in 1801) | J. Frankland (1785–95); P. Hellyer. (1795); R. Rundle (1795–6); J. Bastard (1796–7); J. Hooker (1797–1812); J. Pinhorn (1812–1816). |
| 3rd Assistant (new post) | J. Bastard (1801–9); J. Hillman (1809–28). |
| Master Boatbuilder | H. Rogers (1779–1802); B. Slade (1802–5); J. Best (1805–22). |
| Master Mastmaker | W. White (1790–1804); J. Jenner (1804–22). |

**Deptford Yard** (*contd*)

| | |
|---|---|
| Master House Carpenter | J. Thompson (1787–94); J. R. Pitts (1794–7); I. Thomas (1797–8); W. Miller (1798–1807); J. Soles (1807–22). |
| Master Joiner | T. Burroughes (1792–1806); J. Clarke (1806–10); R. Bowley (1810–19). |
| Master Sailmaker | J. Day (1791–98); J. Evans (1798–1826). |
| Master Smith | C. Fleming (1790–1821). |
| Master Bricklayer | J. Baggett (1784–95); J. Stotesbury (1795–1823). |
| Master Painter (new post) | G. Lake (1804–11); W. Streek (1811–30). |
| Master Rigger (new post) | E. Burr (1807–12); J. Grayson (1812–22). |
| Master Measurer (new post) | R. Bingle (1810–27). |
| Surgeon | R. Bellas (1791–1800); J. Thompson (1801–1819). |

**Woolwich yard**

| | |
|---|---|
| Master Shipwright | J. Tovery (1793–1801); E. Sison (1801–16). |
| Master Attendant | R. Prowse (1785–1804); J. Whidby (1804–11); C. Halliday (1811–12); T. Brown (1812–32). |
| Clerk of the Cheque | D. Tassell (1793–4); J. Jeffery (1794–1807); G. Gainer (1807); R. Kittoe (1807–14); J. Williams (1814–30). |
| Storekeeper | C. H. Harris (1791–5); R. Pering (1795–1801); G. Gainer (1801–2); T. Burnett (1802–21). |
| Clerk of the Survey | J. Jeffery (1793–4); G. Gainer (1794–1801); T. Burnett (1801–2); J. Tyson (1802–8); T. Netherton (1808); J. Lloyd (1808–16). |
| 1st Assistant to Master Shipwright and, from 1801, Timber Master (new post) | H. Peake (1792–3); J. Trefry (1793–1801); J. Jagoe (1801–3); J. Knowles (1803–14); G. Boddy (1814–29). |
| 2nd Assistant and Master Caulker (latter post lapsing in 1801) | P. Hellyer (1793–5); J. Bastard (1793–6); J. Hooker (1796–7); J. Knowles (1797–1803); E. Churchill (1803); W. Sture (1803–19). |
| 3rd Assistant (new post) | T. Roberts (1801–6); J. Hillman (1806–9); G. Boddy (1809–14); W. Hookey (1814–21). |

| | |
|---|---|
| Extra Assistant to Master Shipwright | J. Pinhorn (1807–9). |
| Master Boatbuilder | S. Tadd (1790–4); G. Parkin (1794–1801); B. Slade (1801–2); R. Shipster (1802–8); J. Bridger (1808); W. Hookey (1808–14); J. Cow (1814–22). |
| Master Mastmaker | S. Spaulding (1787–94); S. Tadd (1794–1809); J. Davis (1809–16). |
| Master House Carpenter | S. Smith (1787–1807); W. Miller (1807–15). |
| Master Joiner | W. Maunderson (1791–1822). |
| Master Sailmaker | Josiah Evans (1793–8); John Evans (1798–1822). |
| Master Smith | T. James (1779–1823) |
| Master Bricklayer | J. Cox (1783–1822). |
| Master Painter (new post) | R. Crispin (1805–20). |
| Master Rigger (new post) | A. Moody (1807–31). |
| Master Measurer (new post) | W. Helland (1810–26). |
| Surgeon | J. Fidge (1793–5); J. Thompson (1795–9); W. Murray (1799–1803); T. Fitzmaurice (1803–10); R. Dunn (1810–32). |

**Chatham yard**

| | |
|---|---|
| Master Shipwright | T. Pollard (1793–5); E. Sison (1795–1801); D. Polhill (1801–3); R. Seppings (1803–13); G. Parkin (1813–30). |
| Master Attendant | 1st W. Nicholson (1783–99): S. Hemmans (1799–1816). <br> 2nd J. Madgshon (1786–1809): C. Duncan (1809–26). |
| Clerk of the Cheque | G. Thomas (1791–6); G. Palliser (1796–1821). |
| Storekeeper | J. Weatherall (1772–95); E. P. Henslow (1795–1802); J. Aubin (1802–8); W. S. Cooper (1808–16). |
| Clerk of the Survey | J. Hamilton (1770–98); J. Burton (1798–1806); J. Mobbs (1806–19). |

**Chatham yard** (*contd*)

| | |
|---|---|
| 1st Assistant to Master Shipwright | T. Mitchell (1790–5); A. Manley (1795–7); P. Hellyer (1797–1822). |
| 2nd Assistant | A. Manley (1790–5); P. Hellyer (1795–7); N. Diddams (1797–8); W. Hunt (1798–1812); J. Nolloth (1812–13); J. Weeks (1813–22). |
| 3rd Assistant and Master Caulker (latter post lapsing in 1801); and, from 1801, Timber Master (new post) | T. Coleman (1793–1801); W. Plucknett (1801–8); W. Stone (1808–1810); S. Jones (1810–24). |
| Master Boatbuilder | H. Boyce (1792–4); R. Moore (1794–1803); R. Hughes (1803–16). |
| Master Mastmaker | J. Knowles (1793–6); R. Hughes (1796–1803); R. Moore (1803–4); D. Cowley (1804–21). |
| Master House Carpenter | W. Bower (1793–8); J. Bower (1798–1806); T. Scott (1806–23). |
| Master Joiner | J. Thompson (1785–1814); J. Burgiss (1814–23). |
| Master Sailmaker | T. Moulden (1768–1803); W. Beare (1803–18). |
| Master Ropemaker | W. Fenwick (1798–1822). |
| Master Smith | J. Kincaid (1763–98); R. Edwards (1798–1809); J. Cheshire (1809–23). |
| Master Bricklayer | J. Vinall jr (1786–1829). |
| Master Painter (new post) | J. Stuart (1802–11); E. Maples (1811–22). |
| Master Rigger (new post) | J. Cressy (1807–11); M. Jones (1811–18). |
| Master Measurer (new post) | W. Manclerk (1810–1820). |
| Surgeon | To the Ordinary: E. Dyne (1767–94); C. and T. Blackston (1794–1802). To the Extra: H. Macleraith (1774–1803); J. White (1803–20). |

**Sheerness yard**

| | |
|---|---|
| Master Shipwright | J. Marshal (1793–5); T. Mitchell (1795–1801); N. Diddans (1801–3); R. J. Nelson (1803–6); G. Parkin (1806–13); W. Stone (1813); H. Canham (1813–16). |

| | |
|---|---|
| Master Attendant | S. Blyth (1791–4); J. Fraser (1795–99); J. Whidby (1799–1803); J. Douglas (1803–4); C. Duncan (1804–9); J. Douglas (1809–23). |
| Clerk of the Cheque | H. Luson (1791–1802); G. Gainer (1802–7); J. Williams (1807–14); J. Kennedy (1814–19). |
| Storekeeper | R. Pering (1791–5); E. P. Henslow (1795); G. Smith (1795–6); T. Grant (1796–1800); J. Hodgskin (1800–1808); W. Goddard (1809–11); E. Jessep (1811–21). |
| Clerk of the Survey | G. Gainer (1792–4); E. P. Henslow (1794–5); E. Shrubsole (1795–1814); B. Willmott (1814–16). |
| 1st Assistant to Master Shipwright and Master Caulker (latter post lapsing in 1801) | R. Rundle (1793–5); J. Bastard (1795); J. Hooker (1795–6); J. Knowles (1796–7); N. Diddams (1797); W. Hunt (1979–8); T. Roberts (1798–1801); G. Parkin (1801–6); S. Jones (1806–7); W. Ward (1808–11); J. Nolloth (1811–12); J. Peake (1812–13); S. Dadd (1813–15). |
| 2nd Assistant and, from 1801, Timber Master (new post) | W. Maddock (1801–11); W. Ward (1811–27). |
| Master Boatbuilder | J. Hooker (1791–5); W. Hunt (1795–7); W. Plucknett (1797–1801); W. McCreight (1801–14); J. Helby (1814–22). |
| Master Mastmaker | W. Shrubsole (1773–97); W. Banes (1797–8); H. Canham (1798–1801); E. Cheeseman (1801–22). |
| Master House Carpenter | J. King (1784–1814); T. Edgcombe (1814–22). |
| Master Joiner | J. Morse (1785–1811); T. Sole (1811–22). |
| Master Sailmaker | J. Clark (1768–97); W. Sole (1798–1830). |
| Master Smith | S. Coveney (1776–1800); W. Beal (1800–30). |
| Master Bricklayer | W. Holliday, snr (1779–1803); J. Bastard (1803–8); W. Holliday, jnr (1808–22). |
| Master Rigger (new post) | J. Kellock (1807–11); W. Burke (1812–19). |
| Master Measurer (new post) | J. Brooman (1810–20). |
| Surgeon | J. Thompson (1793–5); W. Murray (1796–9); J. J. White (1799–1803); T. T. Folds (1803–22). |

# 5 The officials

**Portsmouth yard**

| | |
|---|---|
| Master Shipwright | E. Tippett (1793–9); H. Peake (1799–1803); N. Diddams (1803–23). |
| Master Attendant | 1st J. Crane (1791–1810); J. Park (1810–23). 2nd C. Robb (1793–1803); J. Park (1803–10); T. Atkinson (1810–23). 3rd T. Moseley (1794–5); J. Park (1795–1803); J. Jackson (1803–4); W. Brown (1804–9); T. Atkinson (1809–10); W. Payne (1810–1816). |
| Clerk of the Cheque | J. Davies (1786–1800); T. Grant (1800–21). |
| Storekeeper | J. Clyde (1791–4); W. Gilbert (1794–1806); J. W. Nelson (1807); J. Allcot (1807–30). |
| Clerk of the Survey | T. Grant (1788–96); G. Smith (1796–1812); R. L. Mosse (1812–19). |
| 1st Assistant to Master Shipwright | H. Peake (1793–9); N. Diddams (1799–1801); H. Canham (1801–13); J. Peake (1813); T. Radcliffe (1813–34). |
| 2nd Assistant and, from 1801, Timber Master (new post) | R. J. Nelson (1793–8); N. Diddams (1798–9); D. Polhill (1799–1801); R. Moseberry (1801–24). |
| 3rd Assistant and Master Caulker (latter post lapsing in 1801) | D. Polhill (1790–9); J. Ancell (1799–1801); T. Strover (1801–2); S. Johns (1802–22) |
| Extra Assistants to Master Shipwright | J. Ancell (1797–9); J. Haynes (1801–4). |
| Master Boatbuilder | J. Bastard (1790–5); J. Ancell (1795–9); W. Maddock (1799–1801); B. Howell (1801–8); J. Bridges (1808–16). |
| Master Mastmaker | B. Griffiths (1793–1803); T. Radcliffe (1803–1813); J. Oakshott (1813–22). |
| Master House Carpenter | N. Vass (1777–1822). |
| Master Joiner | R. Pilgrem (1785–1802); S. Guyer (1803–22). |
| Master Sailmaker | R. Constable (1792–1821). |
| Master Smith | A. Brookes (1793–1809); B. Barber (1809–27). |
| Master Bricklayer | E. Brine (1780–1803); D. Haydon (1803–16). |

| | |
|---|---|
| Master Painter (new post) | W. Anderson (1804–30). |
| Master Rigger (new post) | J. Little (1807–9); T. Baikie (1809–11); G. Johnson (1811–23). |
| Master Measurer (new post) | R. Smith (1810–26). |
| Surgeon | D. R. Karr (1761–94); R. Mowbray (1794–5); J. Fidge (1795–1806); J. Walker (1806–22). |
| Engineer and Mechanist (new post) | S. Goodrich (1814–30). |
| Master of Wood Mills (new Post) | J. Burr (1814–28). |
| Master of Metal Mills (new post) | H. Vernon (1814–30). |
| Master of Millwrights (new post) | W. Kingston (1814–30). |

## Plymouth yard

| | |
|---|---|
| Master Shipwright | E. Sison (1793–5); J. Marshall (1795–1801); J. Tucker (1802–13); T. Roberts (1813–1815). |
| Master Attendant | 1st J. Smith (1790–1804); J. Jackson (1804–29); 2nd S. Hemmans (1790–9); J. Fraser (1799–1804); J. Douglas (1804–9); W. Brown (1809–23). |
| Clerk of the Cheque | J. Lloyd (1762–1801); B. Tucker (July–Nov. 1801); R. Pering (1801–22). |
| Storekeeper | G. Teait (1791–1801); J. N. Salt (1801–12); T. Hollinworth (1812–29). |
| Clerk of the Survey | J. Lugger (1791–1801); R. Kittoe (1801–3); T. Hollinworth (1803–12); P. Edgcumbe (1812–17). |
| 1st Assistant to Master Shipwright | J. Foott (1793–7); C. Kevern (1797–1801); J. Tucker (1801–2); W. Steer (1802–3); E. Churchill (1803–13); J. Peake (1813–15). |
| 2nd Assistant to Master Shipwright | C. Kevern (1793–97); J. Bastard (1797–1801); R. Seppings (1801–3); J. Jagoe (1803–10); M. Wellington (1810–11); J. Weekes (1811–13); O. Lang (1813–16). |

**Plymouth yard** (*contd*)

| | |
|---|---|
| 3rd Assistant and Master Caulker (latter post lapsing in 1801); and, from 1801. Timber Master (new post) | W. Collins (1779–1802); T. Strover (1802–13); J. Ancell (1814–15). |
| 4th Assistant (new post) | J. Ancell (1801–14); W. McCreight (1814–21). |
| Extra Assistant | T. Radcliffe (1808–9). |
| Master Boatbuilder | W. Tuson (1793–1803); J. Finsham (1803–17). |
| Master Mastmaker | T. Jenner (1785–1804); B. Crouch (1804–19). |
| Master House Carpenter | Justus Thompson (1774–94); John Thompson (1794–7); J. Pitts (1797–1820). |
| Master Joiner | W. Hayward (1785–1822). |
| Master Sailmaker | W. Soloman (1791–5); T. Tarraway (1795–1802); R. Frood (1802–5); R. Tarraway (1805–26). |
| Master Smith | W. Lemyn (1768–96); J. Pett (1796–1801); A. Moore (1801–19). |
| Master Bricklayer | J. Penkeville (1767–1803); R. May (1804–15). |
| Master Painter (new post) | W. Streek (April–Oct. 1804); T. Coulson (1804–25). |
| Master Rigger (new post) | W. Wilmot (1807–10); M. Sullivan (1810–18). |
| Master Measurer (new post) | J. Lee (1810–27). |
| Surgeon | R. Mowbray (1774–94); R. Sheppard (1794–1810); J. Bell (1810–24). |

*Table 27. The Navy Board and yard commissioners, 1793–1815*

**The Navy Board**

| | |
|---|---|
| Comptroller | H. Martin (1790–4); Sir A. S. Hamond (1794–1806); H. Nicholls (1806); Sir T. B. Thompson (1806–16). |
| Deputy Comptroller (new post 1793) | E. Le Cras (1793); Sir A. S. Hamond (1794); Sir S. Marshall (1794–5); C. Hope (1795–1801); H. Duncan (1801–6); Sir R. Barlow (1806–8); Sir F. J. Hartwell (1808–14); W. Shield (1814–16). |

| | |
|---|---|
| 1st Surveyor | Sir J. Henslow (1793–1806); Sir W. Rule (1806–13); Sir H. Peake (1813–22). |
| 2nd Surveyor | Sir W. Rule (1793–1806); H. Peake (1806–1813); J. Tucker (1813–22). |
| 3rd Surveyor (new post 1813) | Sir R. Seppings (1813–22). |
| Civil Commissioner, known until 1796 as Clerk of the Acts; thereafter a sea commissioner | G. Marsh (1773–1800); F. J. Hartwell (1801–8); R. G. Middleton (1808–29). |
| Civil Commissioner, known until 1796 as Comptroller of Victualling Accounts | W. Palmer (1773–1805); J. D. Thompson (1805–29). |
| Civil Commissioner, known until 1796 as Comptroller of Treasurer's Accounts | G. Rogers (1782–1801); B. Tucker (1801–4); Hon. H. Legge (1804–29). |
| Civil Commissioner, known until 1796 as Comptroller of Storekeepers' Accounts | Sir W. Bellingham (1790–1803); O. Markham (1803–5); Hon E. Bouverie (1805–24). |
| Sea Commissioner | Sir A. Hamond (1793–4); C. Hope (1794–5); S. Gambier (1796–1813); Hon E. R. Stewart (1813–29). |
| Sea Commissioner | S. Marshall (1793–4); H. Harmood (1795, 1796–1806); T. Hamilton (1806–13); P. Fraser (1813–23). |
| Sea Commissioner (post lapsed 1794) | S. Wallis (1787–94). |
| Civil Architect and Engineer (1808–12) | S. Bentham (1808–12). |
| Extra Commissioner for wage payments in London | I. Schomberg (1808–13); W. Shield (1813–14). |

### The yard commissioners

| | |
|---|---|
| Deptford and Woolwich (new post 1806) | C. Cunningham (1806–23). |
| Chatham | C. Proby (1771–99); F. J. Hartwell (1799–1801); C. Hope (1801–8); Sir R. Barlow (1808–23). |

---

**The yard commissioners** (*contd*)

| | |
|---|---|
| Sheerness | H. Harmood (1795–6); F. J. Hartwell (1796–9); H. Duncan (1800–1); I. Coffin (1801–5); Hon G. Grey (1805–6); W. Brown (1806–11); W. G. Lobb (1811–14); Hon C. Boyle (1814–22). |
| Portsmouth | Sir C. Saxton (1790–1806); Hon G. Grey (1806–28). |
| Plymouth | R. Fanshawe (1790–1816). |

---

# 6

# Yard management

Although each of the six major dockyards in England was a working unit complete in itself, all six were managed as complementary parts of one centralized organization. The Navy Board, located from 1787 at Somerset House in the Strand, was responsible for the whole of yard affairs, as it had been since the sixteenth century. Little had in fact changed since the establishment of the first dockyards. The system of management had of course been steadily adapted to the growth of the navy and in general it had stood the test of time. At the end of the eighteenth century, however, the principles upon which the system of management was based still remained those embodied in instructions laid down by the Duke of York in January 1662, and these principles were in many respects more suited to the social and political conditions of the mid-seventeenth century than to those of the late eighteenth century. With a new standard of public morality expected of civil servants, the administrative system within which these officials operated required adaptation. In addition, with a steadily increasing workload, new methods of performing business had to be devised, for by 1790 the traditional system was clearly as much a contributory cause of inefficiency as a means of preventing it.

The system had three chief features: centralization of control, three levels of management, and the checks that officials at each level were expected to place upon one another. Centralization was of course inevitable. The direction of the navy from the Admiralty required that the equipment and maintenance of the fleet should also be coordinated and controlled from London. Thus all accounts of work performed, earnings made, stores received and issued, and many of the day-to-day problems at each yard were referred to the Navy Office, where decisions were made by the Navy Board. The Board formed the key middle stage in the three-level hierarchy of management. Yet, as such, it was responsible to the Admiralty for yard affairs without always knowing exactly what was going on in the yards. Physically removed from both Admiralty and yards, it suffered particularly from problems of communication and control. At the Admiralty, the senior board was composed for the most part of politicians and sea officers who rarely had a complete understanding of the problems of civil administration. In the yards, the officers therefore had considerable independence and often contested points of procedure, while the yard commissioner, the Navy Board's representative, was in many situations virtually powerless.

The third feature of the system, the check of one official upon another, had originally been intended to enforce obedience to regulations. The commissioners at the Board had been directed in 1662 'to proceed by common council . . . endeavouring jointly to advance His Majesty's service without any private or indirect end', as a check upon which they were 'to trace' one another in their distinct and several duties and to sign the letters and orders of the board in triplicate.[1] In each yard, as a check upon the veracity of their contents, all letters to the Board about general matters were also to be signed by at least three of the principal officers. In addition, the officers from three departments were expected to sanction the receipt and issue of all stores and the measurement of all work performed by contract.

During the seventeenth century these three features had come to be considered indispensable to an organization that was geographically diffuse, subject to a monarchy of doubtful stability, and containing officials whose dedication to the interests of the public might be questionable. Yet under the stresses of the wars between 1793 and 1815, the weaknesses of the system were to challenge the ingenuity of reformers.

The immediate cause of difficulties was the growth in the workload imposed on the dockyards. To some extent the workload was related to the size of the navy. The yards were accustomed to wartime additions to the fleet as ships were hired or purchased into the navy during hostilities, and sold or taken to pieces at their termination. During the eighteenth century the alternation of war and peace had produced an almost cyclic effect in the pace and burden of dockyard work. The overall growth in the navy had, however, been relatively steady. In 1793 the navy was almost seven times the tonnage of the navy at the Restoration, the growth between 1756 and 1793 having been about 50 per cent.[2] After 1793, however, the rise in naval strength exceeded even the usual wartime growth. Between 1793 and 1802 the fleet almost doubled in size and almost tripled by 1809.[3] The effect was so to increase the burden of work imposed on yard officers, their clerks and the Navy Board that the perceivable increase in negligence, wastage, poor workmanship and fraud attained a scale that was to many minds intolerable.

The fundamental cause of this inefficiency was less obvious to contemporaries away from the dockyard scene. St Vincent, First Lord between 1801 and 1804, blamed the competence and attitude of the officials who headed the Navy Board and the departments in the yards. The truth was more simple. Most inefficiency stemmed from the inability of officials to attend to all the details of their work. Centralization exacerbated the problem: it concentrated business at the Navy Office and decisions at the Navy Board. The yard commissioners could have performed a more important role and might have reduced the pressure of work in London, but delegation of responsibility and authority to an individual commissioner was not reconcilable with either the traditional principle of collective management or the preservation of Board status, power and control. Within the yards the five principal officers – the Master Shipwright, Master Attendant, Clerk of the Cheque, Storekeeper and Clerk of the Survey – bore the brunt of the increased workload. Overburdened and short of assistance but required to operate a time-consuming check system, they had responsibility without adequate control, and they accordingly suffered the consequences when frauds or other signs of inefficiency were uncovered.

Of these five officers the Master Shipwright was regarded as the most important, since he directed those operations for which the dockyards primarily existed. He was consulted by the Navy Board more frequently than any other officer, had the most correspondence with the Board and possessed the most prestige. In addition he directed the largest proportion of men in each yard, including scavelmen and labourers as well as shipwrights and caulkers. Other departments such as those of the boatbuilders and mastmakers also fell under his influence, so that his personal organization and energy affected much of the yard. In 1662 he had been instructed 'to attend personally' the graving, caulking, docking, repairing and building of ships; he was responsible for the materials issued to his department and had to keep a record with the Storekeeper of these and all ships' carpenters' stores issued at his direction; and finally he was meant to ensure that all wages paid to men in his department had been properly earned. Beneath him were several assistants, two at Sheerness, three at most yards, but as many as five at Plymouth by 1808. Beneath them were a number of inferior officers, known as quartermen or leading men, ranging in 1810 from 14 at Sheerness to 38 at Chatham and 54 at Portsmouth and Plymouth.

The Master Attendant, the other principal 'operative' officer, supervised that part of yard operations not controlled by the Master Shipwright. He was responsible for piloting and surveying ships coming into harbour, for their docking and launching, graving or careening, and their subsequent mooring and movements in harbour. As he supervised their fitting and refitting he appropriated their equipment from the Storekeeper and had their sea stores delivered to their boatswains. For these purposes he controlled 'the Ordinary' – the shipkeepers who manned the ships in Ordinary – the 'extra men' who manned the yard boats, the riggers and riggers' labourers. Most of the major dockyards and many of the smaller ones had one Master Attendant, although by 1800 Chatham and Plymouth had two and Portsmouth three.

The clerical officer with the most influence was the Clerk of the Cheque, who dealt with the wages of all artificers, labourers and Ordinary. He kept a record of their date of entry, mustered them, checked accounts of their earnings, and made out the paybooks that were sent to the Navy Office. He was also responsible for mustering ships afloat but not in commission, including hired vessels, and for returning lists of absentees to London. Yard contingency expenses and seamen's pay allotments were paid from his office; and one of his clerks attended the receipt of ships' stores, checked contractors' deliveries and measured contractors', sawyers' and painters' work. The scale of these different duties varied according to the size of the yard, the area of the port, and the particular function of both. The offices at Deptford, Chatham, Portsmouth and Plymouth were always larger than those elsewhere: Deptford was the principal stores depot, while Chatham, Portsmouth and Plymouth were the yards from which clerks were sent as far as Blackstakes at the mouth of the Medway, the Needles and Torbay to muster ships.

The Storekeeper came next in prestige and importance. The materials for which he was responsible were not only crucial to national defence but had a very high market value: stores received and issued at Portsmouth in 1796 were worth over £½ million.[4] The Storekeeper was thus held personally accountable for all materials charged to his account. For this reason both he and the Navy Board were concerned to keep full accounts of all receipts and issues. These permitted the timely dispatch to the Navy Office of demands for deliveries of stores when the stock had fallen below an establishment level. The yards with the highest turnover were Portsmouth and Plymouth, the principal refitting yards, Deptford, from where materials were shipped to yards in Britain and abroad and to the fleet at sea, and Woolwich which dealt with the overflow from Deptford.

The fifth principal officer was the Clerk of the Survey, who surveyed all yard transactions. One of his clerks attended each transaction with every contractor whether it was a delivery of materials, a collection of old stores or the measurement of work performed by contract. He examined the amount of materials or work involved, the contract rate, and the total value of the transaction. When it complied with the terms of the contract the Clerk of the Survey issued a certificate for payment either at the office of the Clerk of the Cheque or at the Navy Office. For transactions within the yard the Clerk of the Survey made out warrants for the Storekeeper to issue stores to ships or materials for work in the yard. One of his clerks surveyed all boatswains' and carpenters' stores returned from ships, passed their related accounts and sent copies of the boatswains' accounts to the Navy Office so that they might receive their pay. The Clerk of the Survey kept accounts of all these transactions and made out quarterly and annual estimates of the expense of the navy for his particular yard under the headings of Wear and Tear, Extra and Ordinary. These permitted the Navy Board to produce the annual estimates for the navy that were submitted to Parliament.

The five principal officers clearly had their own distinct departmental responsibilities. Nevertheless, throughout their work the check system instituted in 1662 involved them in certain business together. The Clerk of the Survey was the most actively engaged in checking transactions, yet in the receipt and issue of materials, both within the yard and in dealings with contractors, three of the principal officers were always involved. The same applied to the measurement of and payment for work performed by contract. From 1810, with the appointment of Master Measurers, the measurement of work performed by yard artificers and the payment of their wages also involved three departments. Among those who worked in the yards, the system was taken for granted. Thus in 1801 St Vincent was informed that the 'grand principle of government in the dockyards' was the 'check officers bear on each other, the Clerk of the Cheque as to time, the Master Shipwright as to appropriation, the Clerk of the Survey as to receipt and returns, [and] the Storekeeper as to quantity, supply and expenditure'.[5] This was a simplified view. Other operative officers took the place of the Master Shipwright where work performed or materials received and issued were for their department. Also, the actual attendance at a check was usually left by the principal officers to one of their clerks. Nevertheless as a statement of principle the information St Vincent received was correct.

By the beginning of the Revolutionary War this check system was breaking down. The increasing workload of the principal officers gave rise to the neglect, or perfunctory performance, of checks by both the officers and their clerks. When up to three clerks, each from a separate office, attended a transaction of stores or measurement of contract work, it was easier for departments to co-operate than to check one another. This being the case, the officers even sanctioned the non-attendance of their clerks occasionally so that they could perform work of higher priority. In addition the officers themselves, though expected to sign letters relating to general yard business in triplicate, often signed them with little, if any, attempt to consider their contents. Samuel Bentham commented in 1808 that clerks who neglected their checks were 'able to compare and adjust their books previously to their being subject to superior inspection', while the officers had become 'very little scrupulous as to the opinions they sanction by their signature'.[6]

The failure of the check system to ensure that administrative business in each yard was performed as efficiently, and with as little cost to the public as possible, had become evident by 1790. In January of that year, Commissioner Fanshawe observed to the Comptroller, Charles Middleton, in connection with reports of 'repeated pilferings and embezzlements' at Plymouth, that there seemed to him 'to have long existed a general relaxation (though less in some than in other departments) from the system of regulation' which the Navy Board had wisely thought proper to establish, and that 'such relaxation seems to have produced all the irregularities naturally to be expected from it'.[7] The Board repeatedly issued orders requiring the officers or their clerks to maintain their checks but the mounting pressure of business in the yards militated against this. In 1797 the officers at Portsmouth warned the Board that 'according to the present system of conducting the general and established business' they themselves had never been able to attend the receipt of stores and timber. Similarly in 1796 two of these officers informed the Board, to exonerate themselves from any future blame, that they were signing bills to the value of over £1,400 annually without clerks from both of their offices attending to measure and record contract painters' work.[8]

Nonetheless, the weakness of the check system was not really impressed on the London boards until February 1802. Then, with evident alarm, the Navy Board reported to the Admiralty that it had discovered instances of 'glaring neglect of duty and disobedience of the Board's most positive orders', and that it was forced to conclude that 'the same relaxation in the cheques imposed by the board have pervaded each office and prevailed in most instances'. At the same time it reported that the yard officers 'pleaded in excuse' that they were unable 'to attend minutely to the several duties of their offices, so much increased during the late war', and that 'the number of clerks allowed . . . [was] by no means sufficient for the performance of the multifarious duties required of them'. In spite of the warnings it had received from the yards, the Navy Board was not inclined to defend the officers. Unless the great pressure of business during the last three or four years was admitted as some excuse, the Board observed, 'their conduct must be considered as highly culpable'.[9]

The yard officers were indeed responsible. Some in fact — the Master Shipwright, Master Attendant and Clerk of the Survey — had fewer duties to attend to after 1794 than formerly. Before this time they had been heavily involved in surveying transports for the navy: during the American War of Independence Middleton had complained that this had 'employed almost the whole of their time to the entire neglect of their own proper business'.[10] The re-establishment of the Transport Board in 1794 with its own agents and surveying staff thus significantly reduced their workload. The assistance afforded the officers had also increased: during the Revolutionary War the number of clerks in the yard offices grew steadily. Yet there was no criminal negligence. Additional clerks were not able to relieve the officers from all the growing pressure of work: clerks could undertake routine business but the more important details had to be inspected. Further clerical assistance would have helped, but was rarely granted when most needed. The greatest pressure of work occurred during bursts of intense activity to equip a squadron for a particular mission or to repair ships following a major battle. At these times the illness of clerks or extra calls of duty brought forth urgent appeals from officers for further assistance. Yet only occasionally did these bring the necessary help. Even when the Navy Board had been convinced that the situation in an office was desperate, the subordinate board then had to convince the Admiralty. Even then such requests were very reluctantly complied with, for the appointment of a temporary clerk was liable to form a precedent likely to lead to a permanent increase in the expense of the navy. In effect, this double administrative barrier served to keep the yard officers almost permanently short of adequate assistance. In consequence both the officers and their clerks were frequently under pressure to peform some of their duties either imperfectly or not at all.

This was the fundamental cause of the 'glaring neglect' that was brought to the notice of the Navy Board in February 1802. The yard check system had failed completely. Between 1799 and 1801 a foreman of the caulkers at Plymouth had obtained extra pay and allowances by making out notes claiming that he and his apprentices had often slept afloat. The Master Shipwright and Clerk of the Cheque were both required to countersign such notes but they had repeatedly passed them without discovering the fraud. The Master Shipwright explained that 'the multiplied and important duties of his situation would not admit of his investigating minutely every note of that description offered for his signature'; he had trusted to the integrity of the foreman, and when his notes were placed before him 'with a multiplicity of others' had simply signed them as part of his current business. The Clerk of the Cheque had also placed 'too great a degree of confidence' in a subordinate, his first clerk, who had been neither 'punctual in his duty' nor 'careful of the public expenditure'.[11]

An informer brought this fraud to the notice of the Navy Board, and while a committee of the Board was investigating it at Plymouth another failure of the check system was exposed. Clerks from the offices of the Storekeeper and Clerk of the Survey had failed to attend the measurement of contract painters' work and 'consequently no cheque whatever' had been observed over the Master Shipwright's clerks or measurers 'to detect their having placed to the contractor's account more work than had actually been performed'. The Clerk of the Survey explained that he had withdrawn his clerk from the duty 'in order to facilitate the more urgent business attending the storing and refitting of the fleet' and the pressure of business since that time had been such as to prevent his 'allowing a clerk wholly for that employment'.[12]

Had such instances of neglect been confined to Plymouth all might have been smoothed over. But six months later, in July 1802, another fraud was discovered at Woolwich. This, in conjunction with those at Plymouth, supplied the evidence St Vincent required to call for the Commission of Naval Enquiry. Yard officers at Woolwich discovered that a contractor for coopers' work had performed work at the yard on numerous occasions without either being sent for or being directed what to do. He had submitted notes for the performance of work that had been copied into a workmanship book at the Storekeeper's office, signed and returned without any survey being made of the work that was specified. At the end of each quarter the contractor had simply submitted an account for materials and labour with his signed notes; these had been compared with the workmanship book and a bill made out for payment of the account. As recently as 1797 the Navy Board had directed that three clerks, or at least two and one officer, should survey all work performed by contract and their measurements be entered in their respective office accounts, to which reference was to be made prior to the drafting of a bill. But the order had been completely ignored. In all, the contractor had submitted five accounts and his shortcoming was only discovered because of his own over-confidence: his last claim was for payment for over £1,000 for work and materials that in reality amounted to a mere £37.[13]

As a safeguard against frauds, oversights or simple mistakes the check system was clearly obsolete. Under the pressure of work it was as much a cause of negligence as a preventative. It acted as an additional burden on yard departments and, as three officers or clerks were usually involved, permitted them to rely too much on colleagues from other departments in work to which they should have devoted more of their own time. The system was nevertheless maintained and the yard officers made responsible for its failures. Under St Vincent seven heads of departments left the yards in disgrace and, to facilitate accountability, clerks were required to produce certificates of good conduct from their principals every time they received their pay. The Commission of Enquiry also forced officers to observe check regulations: in 1804 Lord Melville was told that the Commission gave rise to a 'system of terror'; informers were encouraged 'so that no officer had any confidence in those that were acting with them'.[14] The Commissioners of Revision made no alteration in the system but simply intended that 'every person entrusted with an office should be made strictly responsible for the regular execution of it'.[15] The system thus survived unchanged for the remainder of the Napoleonic War and was only modified in 1822 when the office of Clerk of the Survey was abolished.

If the officers' control of yard business was weak, the powers of the resident commissioner to improve it were even weaker. Theoretically members of the Navy Board, these commissioners were appointed to some refitting yards abroad as well as to the major ones in England. In 1793 there were five, stationed at Chatham, Portsmouth, Plymouth, Gibraltar and Halifax (Nova Scotia). By 1815 there were nine more: one was appointed to Sheerness in 1797 for the duration of the war; another was given the supervision of both Deptford and Woolwich in 1806; and the others were placed at Quebec,

Jamaica, Antigua, Malta, Cape of Good Hope, Madras and Bombay, as yards were established or the business of existing yards grew. They acted as the eyes and the voice of the Board, providing it with regular reports on yard operations and problems, passing on to the officers the directions of the Board, and making local contracts and arrangements affecting the smooth running of the yard. The difficulties of communication gave those commissioners abroad considerable independence, whereas those in England were closely supervised. All had the power to act when necessary without reference to the Board, but their decisions were subject to the approval of their London colleagues, who retained the right to make all permanent arrangements in the yards. Some commissioners reacted strongly against the checks placed on them by colleagues who were not immediately involved with the situation in the yards. These commissioners found their lack of authority irksome and disheartening. But the others, the majority, were content to refer their problems to the Board and appear to have enjoyed their relative freedom from responsibility.

Most commissioners were anyway sufficiently burdened with duties not to wish for further worries. Their general supervisory capacity required that each arrange the repair of vessels with the port admiral as specified in board warrants or as necessary in emergencies. He supplied the Navy Board with regular reports of all arrivals, dockings, sailings and other 'material occurrences' at the port; checked the attendance of officers and clerks, entered and discharged clerks, discharged incapable workmen, allotted apprentices to deserving men, and regulated the working hours of the yard. He also occasionally inspected yard stores, ensured that storeships were not detained when making deliveries, signed for such deliveries with the officers and, after June 1801, inspected the general store account of the yard. In addition he undertook all local contracts for work in the yard, for vessels for the navy, and for repairs to naval vessels in the merchant yards. Many of these duties were clearly formalities, performed as the yard officers required. Some were also sedentary. Nevertheless at least one commissioner found that, with a daily inspection of the yard and the ships under repair, his duties seemed 'to require more activity of body than of mind'.[16]

In common with those of the yard officers, the duties of the commissioners had also increased in weight. This was acknowledged in June 1801 when the resident commissioner was relieved during wartime of attendance at the payments of the yard and of ships in port. As a result, he should have had more time to attend to yard affairs, in particular to the supervision of his subordinates. The instructions issued to the commissioner in June 1801 gave him 'full authority over all persons whatsoever employed in the dockyard'. To keep people at their work he was expected to make himself 'perfect' in their duties, as laid down in the instructions issued by the Board, which, in common with officers' reports to the Board, were read and registered in his office. 'On manifest neglect of duty or proof of misconduct' by an officer or clerk, he was required to suspend him and report the circumstances to the Navy Board for the information of the Admiralty.[17]

Clear as his authority appeared, it rested on a very infirm foundation. At the principal yards business was already too extensive for the commissioner's knowledge of all instructions and details of procedure to be complete. Being incapable of ordering more than a suspension without application to London, his dependence on Board authority also weakened his local standing. Moreover the Board itself almost consciously undermined his authority by sending its orders to their actual executors, the yard officers, and by invariably insisting on the superiority of its own opinion over that of the commissioner's. The latter was in any case never very sure of his powers until late in 1801, when the Board issued him for the first time with a set of instructions. Hence, when he took a stand, the commissioner had no assurance that his decision would be supported. It was indeed more usually the case that he had to compromise with the policy of the Board or make concessions to the superior professional knowledge of the yard officers. Until 1801 the commissioner's position, as the relatively powerless representative of the Navy Board, was thus in fact an exceedingly difficult one, especially for an officer new to his post. Shortly after his appointment to Sheerness, Commissioner Coffin complained bitterly to the Board:

> When I came here you were directed by . . . the Admiralty to furnish me with instructions. How you have left me to wander in the dark is best known to yourselves. . . . If I am to receive any communication from an Admiral here and act on it independent of you the sooner it is made known to me the better. . . . I request not only to be furnished with my instructions without loss of time but that they may fully explain the relative situation of the Admiral commanding here and myself.[18]

In fact Coffin's relationship with the port admiral at Sheerness soon became the least of his worries. For Coffin, as for other commissioners, difficulties were more often encountered with naval officers using the yard to repair or refit and with the officers and men belonging to the yard.

With the former, and especially with officers who were more senior in the service, there was always the danger of serious disagreement when the commissioner was obliged to insist on the maintenance of Board regulations in the face of requests for stores or for the performance of work inconsistent with yard efficiency. Lord Keith informed the Select Committee on Finance in 1798 that he had 'too frequently known differences arise between Flag Officers and the Commissioners to the great detriment of the Service'.[19] Difficulties also arose with officers of equal or even of inferior rank. The military branch of the service being considered by some as higher in status than the civil, the arrogance or mere presumption of certain individuals was almost impossible to deal with. In 1805 Commissioner Grey at Sheerness was forced to complain to the Navy Board that a lieutenant had been in harbour four months and had 'invariably . . . applied for everything he has found out different in other brigs' from how they were in his own.[20] Similarly in 1810 Commissioner Shields, at Cape of Good Hope, was also forced to complain about a captain who had threatened him with a horse whip and whom the local commander-in-chief had refused to reprimand.[21] Such cases of 'disrespect' to the 'situation' of a commissioner were always referred to the Admiralty by the subordinate board, for even its authority did not stretch to commissioned naval officers.

Yet inevitably most of the commissioner's difficulties stemmed from his dealings with the men theoretically under his superintendence. The interests of the officers and of the workmen were invariably opposed to those of the commissioner and of the Navy Board. Thus an anonymous writer informed the Admiralty Board in July 1799 that it would find that

> every shipwright is against the Commissioner and for the Builder [the Master Shipwright] because the latter wishes to be popular and he gives the men all the Extra [pay for overtime or piecework] he possibly can and it often happens there is not work for them to do; the Builder and Commissioner is at variance and the men will resent it and you will find it will not end there; in the next place they will petition to have the Commissioner removed by anonymous letters; he is made acquainted with all their tricks but [is] not equal to all their proceedings.[22]

The commissioner's inability to get 'equal' with those who schemed to undermine further his position at the yard was seen by contemporaries to derive from a lack of patronage. Although he could suspend officers and discharge artificers, he was only capable of recommending the promotion of either, the appointment of the former being retained by the Admiralty and of the latter by the Navy Board. The Commissioners of Naval Enquiry noted this inability to enter, reward or promote artificers and observed that the resident commissioner 'appeared to have less influence over the workmen than any other officer'.[23]

This identification of his authority with the patronage available to him was expressed more forcibly by Lord Fortescue, Lord Lieutenant for Devon in April 1801, when workmen in Plymouth yard became involved *en masse* in food riots in the town. He wrote to the Duke of Portland:

> I must take the liberty to observe from the insight that I have already got it will be vain to expect any permanent result unless the Navy Board will make over to the Commissioner a great many powers which they now keep in their own hands and which would enable him to exercise a more summary authority over the workmen of all the different degrees in the yard.

And again two days later:

> . . . indeed if the Navy Board do not consent to part with more of the powers and of their patronage (which seems to be that part of which they are most retentive) than they as yet show any inclination to do, I am afraid it will be impossible to look to any reform which can hold out an appearance of remedy from day to day.[24]

Yet any delegation of powers to the resident commissioner would have meant a reduction in the standing of the Navy Board. Especially during times of social tension, when the Board stood in need of all its powers of control, such delegation was highly unlikely.

The effect of this relationship with the Board was to render the role of the resident commissioner rather less powerful in the business of yard management than his position as head of a dockyard implied. Most commissioners simply performed the role required by the Board without asserting themselves unduly to gain greater control than they were allowed. Not to have done so would have been unusual in naval officers accustomed to a hierarchy of command; it would also have entailed disputes with the Board and disagreements with the yard officers. Nevertheless at times a commissioner was appointed who was both conscious of the need for greater local control and was prepared to incur the opposition and rancour that would follow. Such an exception was Isaac Coffin who between 1801 and 1804 imposed himself on Sheerness dockyard with a determination that none of his colleagues at other yards revealed. But Coffin was placed in a situation that was itself unusual. He was the fourth commissioner at Sheerness since 1795, before which time it had been the responsibility of the commissioner at Chatham. The yard was an open thoroughfare and hulks that formed part of the breakwater were inhabited by artificers' families and widows. In effect, the yard officers were accustomed neither to receiving close supervision themselves nor to providing close regulation of the working area which many of the workmen regarded as a public right of way. Coffin enclosed the area of the dockyard and in no uncertain fashion demonstrated his determination for complete control by taking both the Board and the yard officers repeatedly to task whenever either failed to conform to his own administrative ideas.

Coffin's work at Sheerness revealed not only the value of an active resident commissioner but the malpractices which had developed in consequence of a lack of close supervision. Soon after his arrival he drew the attention of the Board to the officers who had allowed Extra to a Master Smith who had 'not done his duty for years' and had conducted work in the smiths' shop that exceeded the maximum value that could be undertaken without Board permission. He then informed the Board that if the officers had no right to act as they had done

> I do expect you will reprimand them for their neglect of duty for if my authority in this yard is not understood to be complete over every *officer* in it, it is useless my being sent here; and if you do not think proper to support me in correcting abuses and doing my duty I must beg leave to appeal . . . for an explanation of my office.[25]

Coffin followed this in January 1801 by bringing a series of inaccurate Extra notes to the notice of the Board. This subject 'escaped' the Board's attention during the pressure of business accompanying the equipment of the fleet for the Baltic and Coffin let it drop until the Admiralty visitation 18 months later. In May 1801 he refused on principle to allow the officers to have a private vessel repaired on a slip even though the Board gave permission. He maintained that it would 'have a very odd appearance' if 'such a custom' was permitted after he had refused the application and threatened to lay the matter before the Admiralty Board. The Navy Board continued to insist upon Coffin conforming to its ruling but eventually had to lay the matter before the senior board itself.[26] St Vincent sided with the commissioner and, confident of

Admiralty support, Coffin went on to investigate the conduct of each of the senior yard officers.

The check system within each yard made the connivance of other officers implicit in many misdemeanours committed by one of them. Coffin was thus led from the offences of one to those of another. Having discovered that numerous private vessels had been repaired at Sheerness without Board authority, Coffin first obtained the dismissal of the Master Shipwright. Then between August 1801 and September 1802 he accumulated charges against the Clerk of the Cheque, ranging from the payment of Extra to the absent Master Smith to entering under-sized and over-young boys as apprentices and setting off their earnings to officers as though they had been with up to six different gangs within 24 hours. Following the visitation of 1802 the Clerk of the Cheque was dismissed. In January 1803 the Storekeeper was suspended until cleared of conniving at embezzlement, and the Master Sailmaker was censured for having given away canvas to the value of £62 and for never having given an account of his men's earnings to the Clerk of the Cheque.

The nature of the punishment inflicted on the Master Sailmaker proved a further issue for dispute between Coffin and the Board. The officer's excuse for failing to submit accounts for the sailmakers' individual earnings was that 'he never knew it done in the time of his predecessor', an explanation consistent with the lack of revised standing orders relating to his department. At the Board the excuse was accepted and Coffin was directed to administer a reprimand. Coffin, however, could not stomach such lenience and rebuked the Board:

> you desire me to reprimand a man who confesses to have neglected his duty materially. . . . If I am not entirely ignorant of the powers confided to me by my Lords Commissioners of the Admiralty, fully expressed in the regulations of 21 May 1801, it is for me to reprimand any person under my direction who may deserve it without adverting to you and even suspend where I see good cause for so doing . . . why you should be induced to let off this Master Sailmaker so easy I cannot comprehend. . . Had I ordered this man before a magistrate he must have been convicted and might have been transported for fourteen years.

To Coffin the Board's failure to use properly the authority it withheld from him was in part responsible for the state of Sheerness dockyard. He continued:

> had reproofs any good effect very early indeed would it have been manifest for I began immediately on my arrival here to admonish and reprimand when the whole mass was corrupted and contaminated: officers and men alike, unprincipled rogues and robbers with very few exceptions – pillage, disobedience and idleness the order of the day – the superior officers having so far committed themselves by their frauds on the Government as to be unable to command their people. The principle once admitted that an officer holding a charge of any kind shall with impunity give away or embezzle the property of the Crown annihilates instantly all the force of divers acts of Parliament for the punishment of thieves.[27]

Neither the Board nor Coffin took this argument further. There was indeed little which the Board could retort in its own defence. Both were also probably influenced by the appointment of St Vincent's Commission of Naval Enquiry a month earlier.

In his campaign to obtain control at Sheerness, Coffin was fortunate in obtaining support at the Admiralty. St Vincent likewise desired to stamp out malpractices. He was 'persuaded that the more authority and responsibility' that was vested in the resident commissioner 'the more the internal arrangement and discipline' of each yard would be improved.[28] Thus when the practice was brought to his notice, he reproved the Navy Board for the occasions it had 'sent their orders into execution, not by sending them to the Commissioner whose duty it was to make the different officers of the yard comply with the regulation, but by directing it to the different officers and thereby . . . weakening the authority of the Commissioner who was expressly there as the head and soul of the yard'.[29] During his preparations for the Commission of Enquiry he employed the yard commissioners as Admiralty agents to secure the books and papers required for the investigation, which was regarded by many as directed against the Navy Board. In addition he ensured that they performed a more decisive role in yard operations, thereby reducing the occasions when reference was necessary to London. During the mobilization of 1803 the commissioners were directed to check and arrange all requisitions for stores for ships fitting for sea or receiving a rapid refit. Early in 1804, the port admirals were directed to communicate to the commissioner all orders which they received for the captains of ships requiring rapid dispatch, upon which the commissioner was 'to order the officers of the yard to comply therewith notwithstanding the usual instructions may not have been received' from the Navy Board.[30] Only the elderly Commissioner Saxton at Portsmouth expressed regret at this enhanced authority. He complained to the Navy Board in 1805 that he felt himself 'ill-placed' and his 'feelings hurt in being obliged to carry on the service in a mode so very novel'; he claimed he felt 'difficulty . . . in giving directions for the issue of stores upon every occasion to a very great extent without any authority' from either of the London boards.[31]

These developments under St Vincent were complemented by the adoption late in 1806 of revised instructions for the resident commissioner. These emphasized his place at the head of each dockyard and clearly defined his responsibilities. Henceforth relations between the Navy Board and the resident commissioner were less subject to interpretation according to the disposition of the individuals concerned and thus less likely to result in disputes and misunderstanding. Nevertheless, although they were aware that he should possess the 'chief influence' within each yard, the Commissioners of Revision pointed out that orders and instructions could not properly originate with him and that he could 'at all times report to the board every proof of meritorious service'.[32] Consequently the degree of control possessed by each resident commissioner continued to depend on the effort with which he wished to assert himself. No other First Lord interfered in yard management with the confidence and disregard for the Navy Board revealed by St Vincent. Relatively weak local control thus remained a major influence on dockyard efficiency for the rest of the Napoleonic War. Only in June 1822 was this weakness partly rectified. From this time correspondence to the yard was, by Admiralty order, addressed solely to the commissioner, who was required to issue all orders to the officers; conversely, all reports had to be made to the commissioner, who alone could 'correspond' with the Navy Board. In addition, after consultation with the officers, the commissioner had the direction of both management and operations within each yard.[33] The changes were slight but they marked a distinct break with traditional administrative arrangements.

Greater powers, more control and a larger clerical staff might have permitted the resident commissioner to relieve his colleagues at the Navy Board of more decisions and administrative duties. Yet centralization of control steadily increased the burden of work expected of the Board and its clerical workforce in the Navy Office. At the Board the usual response to wartime pressures was the appointment of additional commissioners. In late 1793 there were 11: the Comptroller, his deputy, two Surveyors, a Clerk of the Acts, three Comptrollers of Accounts and three extra commissioners. In 1794, when the Board was relieved of the transport business by the creation of the Transport Board, the extra commissioners were reduced to two. Two years later, in 1796, in line with the recommendations of the Commissioners on Fees, the offices of Clerk of the Acts, Comptroller of Treasurer's Accounts, Comptroller of Victualling Accounts and Comptroller of Storekeepers' Accounts were abolished, the three accounting officers becoming simply civil commissioners. The Board then remained at 10 until 1808, when the former Inspector General of Naval Works joined it with the title of Civil Architect and Engineer and a twelfth commissioner was added to supervise the payment of wages at the London Pay Office and at the two Thames yards. These offices were abolished in 1812 and 1814 respectively but a third Surveyor was appointed in 1813 to permit closer supervision of shipwright work. Thus in 1815, before the peace reduction, the Board again stood at 11.[34]

Perhaps the most important addition to the Board was the provision in 1793 for a Deputy Comptroller. In dealing with the First Lord of the Admiralty and in directing work in the Navy Office, the role of the Comptroller had become decisive. In 1662 the terms of his appointment had given him no more than equal standing among the other commissioners. But in 1796, as part of the reorganization recommended by the Commissioners on Fees, he was given 'a general superintending and directing power for the regular management of the business . . . in every branch of the Office'.[35] Sir Charles Middleton, Comptroller between 1778 and 1790, maintained that the office was 'of next consequence to the First Lord', believing that it was 'the mainspring belonging to everything that is naval . . . he must be in every part of . . . [the Navy Office] and know everything that is going on in and out of it'. He claimed that 'he should not only have consequence with the Board where he presides but carry respect into every part of the service'.[36] Both he and Sir Thomas Byam Martin, Comptroller between 1816 and 1831, wished the Comptroller to have a seat at the Board of Admiralty but neither achieved the aim.

At the Navy Board the Comptroller's principal duty was to ensure that the business before the Board was properly performed. This was no simple task. In 1662 the commissioners had been directed to meet twice a week but by July

1796 they were meeting six days a week and were even then unable to consider each item of business fully. In one day in July 1796 the Board drafted 63 letters; on others it drafted more than 40.[37] The management of much business by head clerks in the Navy Office relieved the Board of some pressure; but the lack of order in which the remainder was conducted was inimical to economy or efficiency. Middleton informed one of the Commissioners on Fees in 1787 that the Board had a correspondence with no less than 2,200 different people. Yet procedure at the Board remained the same as in 1662. It

> had its number of members doubled and its business increased an hundred fold and all continues to be transacted at one table with the same irregularity as matters come by chance before them. There is no division of business, no providing for dispatch. The consequences are hasty decisions, confusion, accounts passed without examination, a perplexing variety of opinion, professional matters submitted to landsmen and mere clerks, some members overloaded with business, others having little to do but to interrupt or confound the rest, while distraction and irresolution from this indigested heap is the portion of him who must bring things to some conclusion in the day, be it right or be it wrong. . . .[38]

The confusion at the Board inevitably affected the promptitude with which orders were directed to the yards and the relevance of those orders to circumstances in the yards. By 'introducing indiscriminately' all matters as they arose at the Board, the dictation of correspondence was 'continually interrupted', 'business of the utmost importance' was delayed and 'subjects of the greatest consequence permitted to pass often with little examination'.[39] In 1804 the Commissioners of Naval Enquiry attributed 'irregularities and abuses' in the system of Task and Job work to innovations in the method of employing and paying the workmen 'which have taken place within the last twenty years and principally during the late war: innovations adopted without due consideration . . . and pursued without that degree of attention which is particularly requisite in all new undertakings to prevent mistakes and correct such parts as experience may point out to be defective'. One of the Board's ill-considered orders was to double the pay of the contractors for horses at Plymouth at the same time as it doubled the maximum rates of pay the artificers could earn by Job.[40]

The Navy Board's burden of work was reduced in August 1794 by the formation of the Transport Board which relieved it of all transport business. The confusion was also reduced in August 1796 with the adoption of Middleton's recommendations for reorganization, embodied in the fifth report of the Commissioners on Fees. The business of the office was placed under the supervision of three committees, of correspondence, accounts and stores, each consisting of three commissioners. The Comptroller officially presided at each until 1808 when he was replaced by the senior commissioner at each committee. Differences of opinion which he could not settle, along with accounts and contracts, were referred to the full board. In 1813, with the appointment of the third Surveyor, a fourth committee was established to control improvements in shipbuilding and in yard facilities. These arrangements removed the greater part of the more routine business from the Board. After 1796 it settled into a pattern of three to four meetings a week during periods of mobilization and two meetings a week during periods of comparative calm. In addition meetings were relatively brief: in July 1801, a period of comparative calm, the average number of letters drafted by the board at five meetings was 11; in July 1803, a period of mobilization, the average for five of the longest meetings was still only 15.[41]

At the Navy Board order and stability were thus restored. Adjustments in procedure at the Board, at the committees and in the Navy Office itself naturally followed. In February 1799 the Comptroller, Sir Andrew Hamond, was still far from content with the reorganization: he did not think any benefit had resulted from it 'or that the business in general . . . [was] more expeditiously or better conducted than when it was carried on under the board at large'. He was particularly concerned that three chief clerks, who acted as secretaries to the committees, were overworked and their own office business falling into arrears; that in committee the signing of letters in triplicate was not always possible; that the reading of committee minutes at the Board took too long; and that the commissioners could no longer be fully acquainted with the work, ability and conduct of office clerks.[42] Flaws in the organization also had embarrassing consequences. In October 1802 the Navy Board's only explanation for the loss of Coffin's letter informing it of a fraud at Sheerness was 'the excessive hurry of business' in the spring of 1801 when a fleet was fitting for the Baltic: 'the fact we believe to be that when the . . . letter . . . was received and first read it was put by for consideration when there should be a fuller board and, the receipt of it having been acknowledged, it passed away into the office and was not thought of afterwards'.[43]

In time procedure was tightened up. The chief clerks were replaced by clerks as secretaries to the committees; readings of committee minutes at the Board were sometimes considered dispensable; and the commissioners were each given a share of office business to supervise. In January 1804 Hamond had no criticism of the reorganization to make to the Commissioners of Naval Enquiry; and in July 1806 the Commissioners of Naval Revision reported that the reorganization had fully answered expectations, though the Board required relief from the duty of passing accounts.

In the Navy Office the same process of expansion and subsequent reorganization took place as at the Board. In the Office the relationship between the growth of the navy and the increased workload was clearly expressed in a growth in the number of clerks. In 1782 there had been 84; by 1796 there were 101; by 1805, 155; and by 1813, including extra and temporary clerks, 204.[44] For one department, the Secretary's office, the period of most rapid growth in business was possibly that between 1798 and 1804: there the number of letters entered annually in the Secretary's letterbooks rose from 7,983 to 14,420.[45] Such increases in business, accompanied by a growth in the number of clerks, gradually enlarged all departments until some reached a size that was beyond the control of one chief clerk.

Until 1796 there were in all eight departments, some reflecting functions of the Navy Board not directly linked with the dockyards: the Secretary's office,

*Table 28. The responsibilities of individual Navy Board commissioners in 1803*

*Comptroller* To preside at the Board and at each Committee; to have a general superintending power over the business of the office in all its branches and to see that the whole be properly conducted.

### COMMITTEE FOR ACCOUNTS

*Civil Commissioner* To superintend the vouchers for bills made out in the office for Bills and Accounts, the examination of contingent Accounts for naval services and supplies, the making of the account of the Debt of the Navy, the claims for Extra Work from the yards and those for Travelling expenses, the collection of Ready Money and Ninety Day Bills and monthly accounts, the recovery of payments for supplies issued within and by navy departments, the examination of Certificates for stores (etc.) delivered at the dockyards, the money for the payment of the yards, outstanding debts to the Navy.

*Civil Commissioner* To superintend the examination of Cash Accounts of Clerks of the Cheque, Commanders in Chief (etc.), the comparison of Pay lists and progresses in the Foreign Accounts office, the accounts of persons employed in the purchase of stores on commission, the claims for and reports on naval services, the Bills of Exchange drawn on the Board.

*Sea Commissioner* To superintend the claims of civilians for naval sea services such as salvage and pilotage, the Contingent Account of the Receiver of Fees, the office for Seamen's wages, the examination of Gentlemen for Lieutenants, the journals delivered by Officers.

### COMMITTEE FOR CORRESPONDENCE

*Deputy Comptroller* To superintend the Ticket Office, irregularities in ships' books, the ships in Ordinary, improvements in rigging and sails, ships' establishments of men and guns, tenders (etc.).

*1st Surveyor* To superintend the draughts of ships to be built and to consider estimates for building, repairing and equipping them; to superintend the works in the yards and the state of repair of the yards, the establishment of the yards, the examination of Task and Job notes from the yards, the prices for piece work and the alterations in Extra work; alterations in ships; to observe works on ships and in the yards and to report irregularities.

*Civil Commissioner* To superintend contracts, the letters received and sent by the Committee of Correspondence, Ticket Office irregularities, stationery demands, Navy Board orders and business left undone, the allotment office.

### COMMITTEE FOR STORES

*2nd Surveyor* To superintend draughts of ships and committee business, the timber, masts, hemp and iron accounts and annual outlay, canvas sails, colours, cables, nails (etc.) in store and ordered, contract fulfilment, yard pay books, Task work and the establishment of the Rope yards, yard progresses.

*Sea Commissioner* To superintend the stores for foreign yards, beds, marine clothing and slops, naval transports and storeships.

*Sea or Civil Commissioner* To superintend the Store accounts of Captains and Storekeepers, the stores bought by and for foreign yards, the sales of old stores and warrant officers' accounts.

the offices for naval bills and accounts, for examining Treasurer's accounts and for examining Storekeepers' accounts, the Surveyors' department, the office for stores and slops, the office for calculating seamen's wages and that for making out tickets for seamen's pay. Subdivision of departments, though theoretically possible, had until 1796 been handicapped by the clerks' receipt of fees. Though their amount was officially laid down, their receipt made clerks susceptible to pecuniary influence and some, even on official fees, added considerably to their salaries. Those in particular who had reached positions to which the largest fees were attached naturally opposed reorganization. However, the way was cleared for it by the prohibition on the receipt of unofficial emoluments in the Navy Office in June 1796, the appointment of a Receiver of Fees and the establishment of a salary scale that provided similar earnings for clerks in each department according to their rank. By July 1803 three new departments had been created by dividing three existing ones. A contract office had been formed by removing two clerks from the Secretary's office; foreign accounts had become the work of a separate department from that for other bills and accounts; and stores and slops had become the business of two separate offices. In addition an allotment office had been formed to deal with the payment of seamen's wages allotted to dependents.

Centralization and the growth in business created a problem of control beyond the Navy Office as well as one within it. As the pace of yard operations became more heated, so too did the exchange of letters between the Board and the yard officials. At times when speed of work was essential, the physical problem of communication had a direct effect on yard performance. After surveying vessels requiring attention, yard officers invariably had to receive instructions from London before proceeding with refitting or repairs. The Navy Board had to secure Admiralty sanction to dock a ship, and this meant that officers could wait from two to five days according to their distance from London. The Navy Board had its own couriers who could reach Deptford in half an hour, Woolwich in less than an hour, Chatham in 4 hours, Sheerness in 6, Portsmouth in 8 and Plymouth in 24.[46] On occasions the Admiralty also sent messages to the yards by the chain of telegraphic stations established in 1795, though these occasions were rare.

The dependence of yard personnel on direction from London was matched by an equal dependence of the Navy Board on reports from the yard officers and commissioners. Inaccurate information from a yard completely handicapped both the subordinate board and the Admiralty. Removed from the scene of operations the Navy Board could neither see the progress in the works nor the alternatives available to improve yard performance. A gesture towards reducing this problem was made by the Board in 1804 when it had new printed views of the yards hung in its board room for use by the Commissioners. Nevertheless, on the occasions when the Board failed to consult yard officials about the purposes to which yard resources, facilities or vessels were allotted, it was still capable of committing gross administrative errors. For example, in 1796, when the Board selected the *Prince* (90) for an experiment in the technique of lengthening a vessel by cutting it in half and adding to it amidships, the choice of ship, the time and the location for the experiment were all criticized by Samuel Bentham. He claimed that the *Prince* had only been out of dock 'about a couple of months, was completely manned and stowed and ready for service' and sailed no worse than other ships of her size; that the experiment was ordered during a mobilization when the withdrawal of a 90-gun ship was a significant loss to the fleet; and that the Board directed the work to take place at Portsmouth where one dock was already occupied and the others urgently required to fit ships of the line for sea. A better choice for experiment, Bentham claimed, would have been another 90-gun ship, the *Duke*, that had been waiting to go into dock at Plymouth where she had been left in Ordinary on account of her reputation as the worst sailing ship in the fleet.[47]

Until 1806 the Navy Board's attempts to control administrative procedures in the yards was similarly inept. Throughout the eighteenth century the Board had issued standing orders to suit particular circumstances at each yard and as a result had authorized a variety of administrative procedures. The problem was compounded by the failure of the Board to revise the orders to create uniformity of procedure and in 1786 orders survived in the Navy Office, many of them contradictory or obsolete, dating back to 1658. In the yards at the end of the eighteenth century the problem continued to grow. Middleton observed in 1784: 'the necessity of framing orders to meet the changing circumstances of the service, to enforce former warrants and to check criminal neglect and abuses has multiplied our warrants to the yard officers to an incredible degree'. These orders had accumulated in the yards in the sequence in which they were issued and formed a barrier rather than an aid to those who wished to discover the orders relating to a particular operation or duty. Further orders simply added to the confusion. As their relevance to actual practice in the yards varied from yard to yard, officers had to interpret them according to their own mode of procedure and execute them as they saw fit. Middleton informed Pitt in 1786: 'such officers as were inclined to act properly had no fixed instructions to direct their conduct; those who had other views had so many holes to creep out at as put it out of the powers of office to detect'.[48] The Board had in fact lost control of administrative practice in the yards.

By the turn of the century the situation had become worse rather than better. The Board continued to issue a multitude of orders: the number rose progressively from just over 400 in 1801 to almost 850 in 1804.[49] Yet these efforts at control were often futile. In 1806 the Commissioners of Revision observed that 'the particular difference in the practice . . . in the execution of business in the several yards cannot be perfectly known at the Board and the orders given without that knowledge must still tend to add to the confusion'. As a result the yard officers continued to rely on experience rather than on standing orders to teach them their duties: those from different yards had 'formed very different conceptions of their duties. . . . An officer who had served half his life in one . . . yard, if removed to another, would find himself nearly as much at a loss to know his precise duty as if he had never been in the service'.[50]

By 1806, however, progress towards a solution of the problem was well advanced. As early as 1764 the Navy Board had been ordered to arrange and digest its standing orders, but the only digest to come from the Board was one produced by Middleton as a private pursuit during his years as Comptroller. In

1786 this only awaited 'a favourable opportunity' of being brought into use. It had, however, been virtually abandoned after the Admiralty under Chatham failed to show interest in it. Official work on a digest only began in the late 1790s: in 1798 Navy Office copies of orders were 'reviewed and arranged' and in 1801 the Clerks of the Cheque at each yard were directed to paste the orders they had received between 1780 and 1800 into ten guard books. By the end of 1801 the Board was able to issue a draft of their instructions to yard commissioners and in December 1804, a set of general instructions for inferior officers. By October 1805 the Board also had a selection and index of the orders considered to have been in force since 1792. This was used by the parliamentary Commissioners of Revision who were appointed in December 1804 specifically 'to revise the instructions and standing orders for the government of the departments of the navy' and 'to arrange and form a regular digest of the same'.[51] Led by Middleton, the Commissioners of Revision were able to complete what he had begun in the early 1780s. By December 1806 the yard commissioners and principal and inferior officers were all in possession of comprehensive instructions which remained the basis for yard management until the mid-nineteenth century.

It was the intention of the Commissioners of Revision to 'make each dockyard serve as a part only of one great machine'.[52] As they outlined the management of the yards in some detail, they undoubtedly contributed to greater uniformity of procedure. In that they also discussed many of the problems of management, their reports served too to inform succeeding Admiralty Boards of the nature of the business with which the Navy Board had to deal. To this extent their reports therefore contributed to the development of greater understanding between the naval boards.

The Commissioners' role in this respect was not without importance. The separation of the Admiralty and Navy Boards was as great a barrier to the unified control of yard business as the separation of the Navy Office from the yards. On the whole the naval officers and politicians who filled the senior board deferred to the superior experience in civil matters of the subordinate board. Political considerations dominated thinking at the Admiralty, however, where the First Lord was comfortably removed from the practical problems of management. Communicating on the whole by letter, the two boards sometimes failed to see eye to eye, usually when a First Lord considered he knew best and refused to discuss matters with the Comptroller. 'It may strike the Commissioners (on Fees)', Middleton wrote to Francis Baring in 1786, 'the frequent stress that is laid on the opposition and want of co-operation in the Admiralty Board for improving the service. It is not meant by this to accuse that board of any inattention or ill will to the public service. This disadvantage appears to arise entirely from the want of communication between the First Lord and the Comptroller'.[53]

Lack of effort on the part of one of these two officials to maintain good relations in spite of the occasional disagreement could have serious consequences. The disposition of the individuals concerned was a vital factor. Middleton lectured Howe in 1784: 'Allow me to observe, that as a proper degree of confidence placed in a person intrusted with the conduct of a most important department will give a favourable interpretation to even doubtful actions, so where there is a desire to find exceptions, the best conduct cannot expect to escape censure'.[54] A reluctance to place confidence in the Comptroller led also to the gradual breakdown of normal inter-board procedures and eventually to chaos. Middleton again to Chatham in 1788:

> It is not to be credited how much the increase or decrease of naval expences depend on a cordial communication between the First Lord of the Admiralty and the Comptroller of the Navy. If any want of confidence subsists here all kind of improvements must be at a stand. Attempts will be made to carry on the duty through the subordinate members of the Navy Board. Information will be sought for and received from persons not qualified to give it. Orders will be issued in ignorance. The discipline of office will be overturned, the proper control weakened and the subordinate branches left to themselves.[55]

These eventualities recurred with all their accompanying embarrassment and difficulties during one period between 1793 and 1815. St Vincent's reforming campaign between 1801 and 1804 produced a series of disagreements between the First Lord and the Comptroller, and unofficial relations were broken off in January 1803 over the issue of whether ships should be built by contract. 'To prevent any future misconception' the Comptroller was directed to make all his communications with the First Lord through the formal correspondence between the boards.[56] Had the Comptroller at that time, Sir Andrew Hamond, been as outspoken as Middleton, relations between the boards might have broken down altogether, resulting in the resignation of one or the other. But Hamond maintained the Navy Board's correspondence with the Admiralty with an obvious dignity and determination which only occasionally revealed complete loss of patience. Following the publication of the first report of St Vincent's Commission of Naval Enquiry, the Navy Board attempted to present a memorial to the House of Commons defending the measures which the report criticized. Characteristically, the First Lord refused to permit it.[57] However, St Vincent could not prevent Hamond stating in the Commons in June 1803 that since the First Lord entered the Admiralty 'there had been so strong a prejudice that it was impossible to go on as things now stood'.[58] St Vincent's policies eventually destroyed good relations with the timber and shipbuilding contractors as well as reducing morale in the naval departments. The Navy Board was nevertheless obliged to tolerate his administration until May 1804.

St Vincent was well-intentioned but over-enthusiastic and misguided. Even so, his efforts to obtain changes in the management of the affairs controlled by the subordinate board proved one point: that the Admiralty could have no lasting influence on the day-to-day conduct of dockyard business while the Navy Board existed. Yet sweeping constitutional changes in the structure of naval administration were out of the question until both king and public were ready to accept them. In the meantime the efforts of the First Lord to obtain reforms depended completely on the willingness of the Navy Board to effect them. If the Admiralty Board occasionally proved difficult in relations with the subordinate board, the situation was equally frustrating for reformers at the Admiralty. The Board system made for stability, but not for ease of communication, understanding or control.

# 7

# Politics and reformers

The dockyards attracted particular attention in the movement to curb wastage in public expenditure after 1780. During wartime, only expenditure on the army and military operations exceeded that of the naval departments and the greater part of naval expenditure went to meet the costs of materials and services provided in the dockyards. The succession of reports on dockyard management brought in their wake phases of improvement which together constituted a sustained period of reform unprecedented in the dockyards' history. Even though their performance was not markedly affected so far as the navy itself was concerned, the yards were far more economical in their use of resources by 1815. Of longer-term importance was the capacity for further change this period of reform engendered. The comprehensive standing orders provided by the Commissioners for Revising and Digesting the civil affairs of the navy gave the Navy Board for the first time the means of accurately controlling the activities of its subordinates. It could in consequence make changes in yard procedure with greater confidence that the changes would be uniformly adopted. Accompanying this new ability was a new attitude to administrative improvement. In the 1790s the Navy Board and Navy Office were the subjects of reform and the Board took a largely negative attitude to the experience. During the early 1800s the board was itself forced to implement changes, and the exercise was instructive. By the last years of the Napoleonic War, when the Board was faced with the recommendations of the Commissioners of Revision, it had both the knowledge and the will to propose and implement further changes of its own accord.

The degree to which the pace of change was quickening should not be exaggerated. The late Bernard Pool observed that 'throughout the life of the Navy Board there was a continuous process of refinement, with amendments designed to prevent for the future some difficulty . . . which hàd arisen . . . or to close a loophole which had allowed someone to avoid an obligation'.[1] Major innovations in yard management had occurred in the mid-eighteenth century, as the introduction of superannuation and piecework schemes demonstrate. Nevertheless the extent of change was limited and the pace relatively pedestrian. By the end of the century the process was both speeding up and affecting the whole system of naval administration. As the navy and the costs of maintaining it grew, so did the pressure for economy. It was then that reformers attracted attention and then, in the struggle to conserve or alter, that departmental politics intensified.

During the 1780s, when Charles Middleton was Comptroller, the Navy Board was on the whole a progressive body. Middleton ordered numerous improvements himself and also contributed to the recommendations of the Commissioners on Fees which he repeatedly urged on Pitt and Chatham, then First Lord. During the 1790s, however, Middleton's successors, especially Sir Andrew Hamond, were more conservative and the Navy Board tended in general to obstruct proposals for change. It had particular reason for resistance to the recommendations of the Commissioners on Fees; they entailed reductions in income at some levels in the Navy Office and dockyards which in time of war could only reduce morale and efficiency. As will be seen later, it also had strong reasons for objecting to the proposals of Samuel Bentham, appointed to the new Admiralty post of Inspector General of Naval Works in 1796.

The Navy Board was constitutionally suited for resistance to reform. Being responsible for the dockyards and in constant communication with the yard officers, it was more aware than the Admiralty of the problems that could arise in the adoption of ill-considered proposals for change. Administrative practice was relatively fragile. The Board was accordingly reluctant to allow alterations in procedure that had stood the test of time simply because interested parties had appealing ideas. Resistance of this sort was inherent in the position of the Navy Board and was an attribute of many other public boards. The Commissioners for examining the Public Accounts thus found elsewhere a propensity 'to disturb, to confound or to delay – when novelty of form is introduced and new principles applied to an old office'.[2] For individual members of the Navy Board, the tendency to act cautiously was ingrained by training and experience. Most had been brought up within the structure they were managing and were accustomed to its failings. Also, in any debate at the Board, the need for consensus tended to permit an ill-informed or conservatively-minded majority to overrule a better-informed or more open-minded minority. As junior commissioners 'could not help giving credit' to their seniors' greater experience, practices to which long-established commissioners were accustomed were usually maintained, however strong the arguments in favour of change.

The Admiralty had of course powers extending over the Navy Board. Although the latter was responsible for all ships out of commission, the Admiralty retained authority over every ship in the navy and provided the subordinate board with permission for work on each as it became necessary. Where the speed or the standard of work was considered inadequate, the Admiralty could and did demand explanations and occasionally punish or reward yard officers as appropriate. The Navy Board and yard officers were also susceptible to patronage. Although Board commissioners were appointed by letters patent under the Great Seal, the choice of their successors at death or retirement was a matter for the First Lord. The yard officers were more open to influence in that rising shipwright officers could expect to change yards every two or three years. Extraordinary expenditure in the Navy Office and yards was similarly a matter for the Admiralty: all estimates, whether for the repair of vessels or installation of new facilities, had to receive Admiralty sanction and no extra place could be created, even for a clerk, unless the senior board was 'satisfied of the necessity of the measure'.[3]

With such powers, one might assume that the Admiralty could ensure that the Navy Board managed the dockyards according to principles and methods of which the Admiralty approved. Yet this was not always the case, mainly because the Admiralty was in the first place ignorant of detailed procedure in the yards, and in the second, generally remained ignorant of the alternatives available to the Navy Board as change became possible. The subordinate board of course provided the Admiralty with all the reports it required from the yard officers. But these reports invariably conformed to the Navy Board's administrative views. After all, the subordinate board issued the orders with which the yard officers were expected to conform; and the officers' experience and opinions on methods of conducting business were accordingly shaped within the established framework of regulations. Given a period of peace the Board of Admiralty could undertake visitations of the dockyards for itself.[4] Even then, however, Admiralty commissioners rarely obtained the knowledge of yard business necessary to contest a point with the Navy Board. The political tenure of Admiralty places, and of the First Lord's place in particular, placed a time limit on the familiarity that could be obtained with the dockyards' internal affairs. Some commissioners were of course retained at the Admiralty under successive First Lords, while the appointment of sea officers to the Board provided it with an opinion on the naval effects of yard business. Nevertheless, by and large, Boards of Admiralty usually remained sufficiently ignorant of yard affairs to ensure that the authority of the Navy Board in this area was respected.

During the eighteenth century this limitation to the powers of the Admiralty was regarded as an advantage of the happy balance in the constitution of the naval departments. D. A. Baugh has observed that the average Englishman at that time 'preferred liberty to governmental efficiency'.[5] A relatively independent Navy Board with dockyards run according to principles and practices inherited from the seventeenth century was indeed undoubtedly of some benefit to tradesmen and contractors who dealt with the yards. Yet by the end of the century opinion in Parliament was gradually changing. Concern for economy increased the desire for governmental efficiency and this in turn called for closer, more stringent Admiralty control of the naval departments. The 1790s and early nineteenth century thus saw the Admiralty asserting itself in its supervisory capacity to a greater extent than it had for over a century. Knowledge of the naval departments was still at times evidently lacking, but this was a deficiency gradually made good by the series of reports produced by the Commissioners on Fees, of Naval Enquiry, of Naval Revision and the Select Committees on Finance. In fact, such was the pressure for governmental reform that the Admiralty could also avail itself of the constitutional powers of Crown and Parliament to impose its will on the Navy Board.

With the growth in opinion in favour of reform, the balance of power in the civil departments of navy thus shifted in favour of the Admiralty. Here power focussed on the First Lord. As the head of the Board of Admiralty, he was open to the influence of sea officers in service, who in the 1790s had few doubts that the dockyards were capable of improvement. As a Member of Parliament and of the government, the First Lord could not avoid the pressure for greater governmental efficiency and economy. His response to these pressures depended very much on his own inclinations and political experience. His personality and ability were both therefore primary factors in the process of reform.

The growth in pressure on the First Lord is reflected in the course of the recommendations of the Commissioners on Fees. During the 1780s few in government, and even fewer in the naval departments, were particularly concerned to see the traditional perquisites of office abolished. Charles Middleton found he had 'raised a nest of hornets' by simply contributing his own ideas to those of the Commissioners. However he remained optimistic, writing to Pitt in August 1786: 'I am aware of what I have to contend with both in and out of office; but I know at the same time that prudence, caution and firmness, with a single eye to the public good, under the countenance of an upright minister, is capable of bringing mighty matters to pass'. Yet when he resigned in March 1790 Middleton was completely disheartened. He complained to Pitt that the 'private ferment which has been raised against every kind of reform by those whose prejudice, whose ignorance or whose particular interest it was to oppose it, obtained all the attention'.[6] The naval reports of the Commissioners on Fees were eventually referred to the Admiralty in January 1792 and only adopted by order in council on 8 June 1796. Lord Spencer, then First Lord, was undoubtedly persuaded to adopt them by Middleton, who served as First Sea Lord in 1794–5. The recommendations for the dockyards, however, remained in abeyance for another five years and it required agitation from within as well as without the naval departments to obtain their adoption.

According to the Select Committee of Finance of 1797–8, the 'urgent pressure of public business' made it difficult for the naval boards to proceed with the 'detailed, laborious and calm investigation' which the subject required. Nevertheless the committee's chairman, Charles Abbot, made action, as soon as it became possible, almost unavoidable: 'Your committee think that the House and the public have reason to expect that on a return of peace many

*Table 29. First Lords of the Admiralty, 1793–1815*

| | |
|---|---|
| 2nd Earl of Chatham | 16 Jul. 1788–19 Dec. 1794 |
| 2nd Earl Spencer | 19 Dec. 1794–19 Feb. 1801 |
| 1st Earl of St Vincent | 19 Feb. 1801–15 May 1804 |
| 1st Viscount Melville | 15 May 1804–2 May 1805 |
| Sir Charles Middleton | |
| (created Lord Barham 1 May 1805) | 2 May 1805–10 Feb. 1806 |
| Hon. Charles Grey | |
| (styled Viscount Howick 11 April 1806) | 10 Feb. 1806–29 Sep. 1806 |
| Thomas Grenville | 29 Sept. 1806–6 Apr. 1807 |
| 3rd Lord Mulgrave | 6 Apr. 1807–4 May 1810 |
| Charles Yorke | 4 May 1810–25 Mar. 1812 |
| 2nd Viscount Melville | 25 Mar. 1812–2 May 1827 |

months will not be suffered to elapse without a steady determination being shown to examine into and report upon all the different departments to which the attention of the Admiralty Board was pointed so long agò as the 12th January 1792'.[7] In fact the Admiralty Board was to take action before the return of peace. From within the naval departments, Samuel Bentham, the new Inspector General of Naval Works, and Charles Abbot's stepbrother, agitated for Spencer to allow him to reorganize yard management according to the ideas he advocated.[8] Eventually Spencer gave way and permitted Bentham to co-operate with Evan Nepean, Secretary to the Board of Admiralty, in drawing up a scheme of reform based on the points recommended for change by the Commissioners on Fees. A major objection to the adoption of the whole range of these recommendations was the cost to the public of compensating yard artificers for the loss of their chips; this was estimated at £50,000 a year. The Comptroller at the Navy Board was also opposed to Bentham's administrative ideas and wished to 'stave it off' for another year.[9] Hamond in fact raised a series of objections to the Bentham–Nepean proposals but these appear to have been considered of little substance by Spencer. Indeed Bentham had his *Answers to the Comptroller's Objections* of July 1800 printed for general circulation. Spencer signed the Bentham–Nepean report in early 1801 and its proposals were effected by the order in council of 21 May 1801.

The changes subsequently effected in the dockyards, like those implemented in the Navy Office in 1796, in some respects marked the end of a period of 'traditional practice' and the beginning of one characterized by 'modern' methods of management. Chips and fees were both abolished, thereby reducing the expense to the public of materials and contracts. So also were premiums which formed a material barrier to the introduction of entry and promotion purely on merit. In addition, the changes in the dockyards 'pointed at other radical changes which would be proper in time of peace' – Bentham's schemes for the establishment of Timber Masters and a revision of the system of training apprentices. While the former marked the introduction to the yards of 'individual responsibility' as a considered administrative principle, the latter resulted in the introduction of theoretical education as well as practical training for some shipwright apprentices.

Spencer's resignation shortly after signing the Bentham–Nepean report made way for the appointment of St Vincent to the Admiralty. St Vincent's administration revealed most completely the powers and limitations of the Admiralty.[10] He himself was highly conscious of the desire in Parliament and in the navy for reform and was thus prepared to make full use of the power of public opinion. His readiness to overlook the traditional authority of the Navy Board created discord within the naval departments and contributed to the discrediting of his administration in Parliament. St Vincent nevertheless obtained legislation which the Navy Board was unable to resist; legislation which permitted a thorough scrutiny of every pocket of inefficiency and waste that was brought to his notice.

When he entered the Admiralty, St Vincent was already determined to restore the navy 'in all its branches to that vigour which can alone maintain our superiority at sea'. He had developed a particular interest in the dockyards, having spent the winter of 1798–9 at Gibraltar, where he had paid 'unremitted attention' to the means by which the yard there might be improved. He was, moreover, deeply concerned about the weight of debt with which the country was 'oppressed', believing that abuses in the naval departments not only added to the burden but if allowed to continue much longer 'must swallow up all the means of the country'.[11] St Vincent also brought with him to the Admiralty his own domineering personality and two equally overbearing colleagues. He himself had founded his naval reputation on 'strict discipline' and, 'accustomed to that promptitude which is the soul of military operations', had little hesitation in demanding 'a strict fulfilment of their duties' from civilians. Sir Thomas Troubridge and Captain Markham added to the military character of the Board, being two naval officers in comparison with whom St Vincent regarded himself as 'a mere lamb'. The strength of these three naval personalities at the Board resulted in the Admiralty Office being managed 'with the rigour of military discipline' and the Navy Board being treated at times as a junior and much inferior officer.[12]

St Vincent was fortunate in being favoured with the period of peace which his plans for reform required. The changes resulting from the recommendations of the Commissioners on Fees he saw as only a beginning. He wrote to Collingwood in March 1801: 'There is much to do and a late attempt of my great predecessor meets with every species of opposition and obloquy. I mean "a partial reform in our dockyards" and comparing small things with great (which must come or we are ruined) I shall have a very difficult task to perform if I preside at this board in time of peace'.[13] With the preliminaries to the Peace of Amiens signed on 1 October 1801, St Vincent wasted no time in preparing for a reforming campaign. By February 1802 he had decided that 'abuses and frauds' in the Extra work in the dockyards made 'a thorough retrospective enquiry' necessary and had 'in contemplation to recommend to His Majesty a Commission to enquire into it and other abuses'. In preparation he had the yard commissioners secure all the Extra notes issued since the beginning of the Revolutionary War; and to obtain further evidence, following the general election of July 1802, the Board of Admiralty itself undertook a yard visitation. From Plymouth on 29 August St Vincent informed Addington that they found 'abuses to such an extent as would require many months to go thoroughly into and the absolute necessity of a Commission of Enquiry to explore them appears to the Admiralty Board here in a much stronger light than ever'. The other yards confirmed the impression: 'Chatham dockyard appears ... a viler sink of corruption than any imagination ever formed. Portsmouth was bad enough but this beggars all description'.[14]

Addington was not convinced of the wisdom of a commission of inquiry but gave way before St Vincent. The Act appointing the new Commissioners (43 Geo. III, c. 16) received the royal assent on 29 December 1802. It empowered the Commissioners to inquire into all irregularities, frauds or abuses committed in the naval departments and prize agency and to report their observations for the prevention of such acts and for the better management of the business in future. St Vincent had intended that the Commission should have had the ability to examine witnesses under oath. But during the Commons debates on the bill there was considerable opposition to the creation of a 'new tribunal' with the power 'to endanger the freedom and security which the constitution intended every individual to enjoy'. Nevertheless, in the belief that 'not an hour should be lost in discovering and checking those frauds and corruptions which were generally admitted to exist', the bill passed without a division. However, in the Lords the Chancellor, Lord Eldon, inserted a clause permitting persons called upon by the Commission 'the right to refuse to answer when their answer was likely to incriminate them'. Among others, the king was relieved at the amendment, thereby obviating the evils 'which might easily have arisen from so delicate a business being framed by gentlemen of the navy instead of those conversant . . . in the nature of the laws of this kingdom'.[15]

In other respects the Commission largely reflected the wishes of St Vincent.

*Lord St Vincent, by Sir William Beechey*

He had the nomination of the Commissioners and they received selected papers relating to their inquiries from the Admiralty. As these papers dealt with frauds and oversights already revealed by the subordinate boards to the First Lord, the Commissioners' reports tended on the whole to consist of exhaustive descriptions of abuses already removed so far as the enforcement of regulations permitted. St Vincent and his Admiralty colleagues clearly intended much more from the Commission than this. But the Commissioners were completely handicapped by the Eldon clause. They themselves observed of the number of abuses, irregularities and defects to which they could make mention in their fourth report:

> If it should be thought that they are less numerous or less important than might be expected, it may be observed that it is an extremely difficult and invidious task to draw a discovery of incorrect or illegal transactions from parties interested or concerned in them, and that the statute from which our powers are derived discountenances enquiries which tend to make the parties examined criminate themselves or to expose them to pains or penalties.[16]

Had the Commissioners been able to examine witnesses under oath, they would undoubtedly have been able to obtain evidence for legal proceedings against many officials throughout the naval departments. Upon their resignations, not only would St Vincent then have been able to replace them with his own nominees but have been able to have reshaped the civil administration of the navy as he pleased. There is indeed evidence to suggest that St Vincent wanted either to force the members of the subordinate boards (and in particular the Navy Board) to resign or to abolish the boards altogether. William Marsden, Second Secretary at the Admiralty, recorded on 26 December 1802 that 'the Commission will in fact be a sort of protection to the inferior boards which have been in the situation of a toad under a harrow. To crush them was the object of the bill and the frauds in the dockyards (which we are daily detecting and punishing) are only a pretext.'[17] Certainly St Vincent's colleague, Markham, wished to see the subordinate boards abolished altogether. The idea was adopted by the Whig ministry of 1806 and was to be carried out after some of the same Whigs returned to office in 1830. At that time Lord Grey passed the idea on to Sir James Graham, then First Lord, who abolished the Victualling and Navy Boards in 1832.[18]

What in 1802 brought St Vincent to wish to rid himself of the Commissioners at the subordinate boards? In the first place, it is clear that he failed to appreciate the cumulative experience of the boards or the value of the methods by which they managed the business of their departments. In 1801 Middleton observed generally about naval officers, though clearly with St Vincent in mind:

> Sea officers are very seldom judges of the civil branches of the navy. They view it only in parts [and] are extremely ignorant of the principles on which the several cheques are founded. They imbibe prejudices against the civil boards and overturn in ignorance what has cost ages and long experience to establish.[19]

Secondly, in spite of his limited knowledge of the civil administration of the navy, St Vincent came to the conclusion during 1802 that the Navy Board had failed in its duty. Following the summer visitation, the Board was therefore censured for having permitted the public 'to be defrauded to a very considerable amount' and delinquencies to pass unpunished.[20] And thirdly, St Vincent was clearly frustrated by the fact that he could not dismiss the Commissioners at the subordinate boards because they were appointed by letters patent under the Great Seal. When they would not resign of their own accord, it became necessary to force them to do so.

The conflict between the Admiralty and Navy Boards during St Vincent's administration was accordingly a serious affair and was indeed recognized as such by contemporaries. Addington was conspicuously embarrassed by it. The introduction of the bill for the Commission of Enquiry contributed to the formation of a 'new opposition' group including Spencer, the former First Lord, and this group proceeded to attack St Vincent's administration in the *True Briton* and in 1803 in Parliament.[21] St Vincent, conscious as ever of the power of opinion in Parliament, was clearly aware that confidence in him would wane unless his aims and measures were vindicated. 'My public character', he wrote to Addington in June 1803, 'depends so much upon every part of the Admiralty being laid before the House of Commons.'[22] Yet his policies at the Admiralty were highly susceptible to attack, primarily due to his refusal to take the advice of the Navy Board. He pursued a policy of economy, which affected the pace at which the navy mobilized, even after the resumption of war in 1803. In the belief that by 'shoaling' artificers by ability he could improve the pace of new construction in the dockyards, he refrained from contracting with merchant builders for the construction of 74s; and in the hope that more large oak timber would then be available for the dockyards, he placed a check on the prices the Navy Board wished to pay the timber contractors. Eventually in 1804 he had to despatch Sir William Rule, the Surveyor, into the country to obtain timber. It was, however, his contempt for and treatment of subordinate naval administrators that was distasteful to those involved in government. His Commission of Naval Enquiry was an administrative inquisition. Sir Evan Nepean, Secretary to the Admiralty, though with little to fear himself, found its work aggravating and Marsden, the Second Secretary, anticipated an 'open quarrel' between Nepean and the Commission. A statement, attributed to Nepean, that his services were being 'thwarted' appeared in *The Times* in April 1803 and in January 1804 Nepean resigned. Marsden himself found his own position embarrassing. 'If I resign, I am afraid of its being said that I ran away from the new Commissioners. This is rather a curious dilemma; and though it looks like a joke it is serious enough.'[23]

As a major weakness in Addington's government, it was almost to be expected that St Vincent's administration should be attacked by Pitt in his first move in opposition to Addington. The latter himself later attributed the move to the fact that Pitt 'could not endure the conduct of Lord St Vincent and the Admiralty'. Having called for papers calculated to reveal the deficiencies in the First Lord's naval preparations, Pitt declared on 15 March 1804 that he was attempting to dispel 'that blind and false confidence which exposes the safety of our country' and that St Vincent was 'less brilliant and less able in a civil capacity than in that of a warlike one'.[24] Middleton, who had been following developments with interest, approved the attack. He commented to John Deas Thompson on 25 March:

> The King's recovery has put an end to the speculations of the day. Mr. Pitt has taken a dignified station, and if his late motion on the navy had succeeded, the Admiralty improvements would have been exposed. I don't know where he got his information; if I had, I could have put returns in his hands that would have been more to the purpose. I cannot however think they could have been granted at this moment. The neglect in building ships and supplying the yards with timber must be obvious to every intelligent observer. The defence of the country is a subject beyond the knowledge of people in general. It is very defective indeed. Our number of effective ships is very much below par and will be found so when ever the invasion is attempted.[25]

By this time naval officers like Collingwood had come to a similar conclusion. In naval as well as in administrative circles, St Vincent's resignation with Addington in May 1804 was consequently a cause of some relief. Controversy over the efficacy of St Vincent's three years at the Admiralty was prolonged by the publication of the reports of the Commission of Naval Enquiry, the impeachment of Melville and motions and pamphlets on the state of the navy. Public debate was, however, effectively terminated by a vote of thanks carried by the House of Commons in May 1806.

Whether St Vincent's administration was beneficial or detrimental to the navy remains a matter of contention. In the short term, as the conflict with the Navy Board suggests, it was undoubtedly detrimental. But in the long term the information about naval administration provided by the reports of the Commissioners of Naval Enquiry was certainly beneficial. St Vincent's importance in backing Samuel Bentham against the Navy Board will be noticed more fully later; yet it should be noted here that this too was advantageous in the long run. And if St Vincent's Admiralty is placed in the context of the general development of naval administration it is clear that it performed several necessary functions. There was much to put right in the conduct of the civil departments of the navy. There were abuses and mismanagement that required investigation. The prohibition on the taking of fees, chips, and other perquisites required an 'ogre' to ensure their total abolition; and their prohibition had to be accompanied by an obvious determination on the part of government to achieve greater probity and efficiency in the conduct of business. In these respects, St Vincent can now be seen to have filled a role of considerable importance for the future.

Even in the short term, however, there were some mitigating consequences. The Commission of Naval Enquiry led directly to two Acts, passed in July and August 1803, one to regulate the administration of the Chatham Chest and the other the distribution of prize money among seamen (43 Geo. III, c. 119, 160). Of more importance for the dockyards, two months after St Vincent's resignation the Navy Board issued 13 copies of the sixth report (on Plymouth and Woolwich yards) to each of the dockyard commissioners to be distributed among the officers with the simple recommendation 'to avoid in future the irregularities herein pointed out'.[26]

This report pointed in particular to 'the necessity of revising the instructions and digesting the immense mass of orders' which had been issued to the yard officers since the seventeenth century. To avoid renewing the Commission of Enquiry, but to further the process of reform, Pitt and Melville, St Vincent's successor, decided to replace it with a commission for revising the civil affairs of the navy. The Commission of Enquiry, though initially designed for an essentially negative purpose, thus eventually became a means of putting in train the more constructive work of administrative improvement and renewal.

It was at this stage that Middleton again appeared on the public scene. Since

*Lord Barham, by I. Downman*

1795 he had settled down to farming and domestic life at Teston in Kent. But he had, as he himself pointed out, 'more than a common share' of Melville's family blood in his veins (his mother having a Dundas for her mother and her father). Following Melville's succession to the Admiralty, he had therefore plied the new First Lord in a relatively disinterested, avuncular fashion with a succession of memoranda calculated to advise him on naval matters beyond his experience. However, the publication of the Commission of Enquiry's sixth report immediately changed the relationship. Middleton, who in the late 1780s had spent three years of his spare time personally revising the standing orders for the dockyards into several digest books, immediately brought the fact to Melville's notice. He pointed out that he still had the digests owing to the 'backwardness' with which his labours had been received in 1789, but that if Melville wished to complete them they contained the business 'ready done' to his hands. Moreover his own assistance would not be wanting and he would name other gentlemen 'qualified for the purpose'. 'The taking any other work of reformation in hand till this is completed', he claimed, was 'beginning at the wrong end.' Melville concurred in the necessity of revising the orders but did not commit himself. Middleton however pressed him. 'Now my dear Lord, as the distinction between peace and war is always brought forward by the sluggard in office for postponing business, I flatter myself you will not suffer it to stand in the way of these important branches of public improvement.'[27] Melville could not retract. By the end of the first week in September Middleton's friend, J. D. Thompson, the naval officer for Leith, was installed in the Navy Office with a clerk, concentrating into one list all the standing orders issued by the Navy Board since 1793 and then 'abstracting and arranging them into the book brought from Teston under the various heads therein mentioned'.[28] Melville visited Middleton at this time and the latter found him 'greatly disposed to carry proper regulations into execution and impatient to begin'. Middleton had therefore 'stimulated those acting under him' as far as he was able, believing 'not a moment should be lost while the power and disposition goes together'.[29]

Initially J. D. Thompson's work in the Navy Office was clearly an internal arrangement. The revision of the standing orders for one naval department led inevitably, however, to the revision of those of departments with which the first worked in concert. Middleton in mid-November had reached the stage at which he wished to have the Navy Board revise their instructions to sea as well as yard officers: these 'must go hand in hand and be made in perfect unison with one another'.[30] Pitt and Melville appreciated the point, and realized that a Commission able to undertake a comprehensive revision of the management of all the civil business of the navy was desirable. George Rose was approached for his opinion on Middleton as a possible member of such a Commission and replied in the superlative: 'really . . . beyond comparison the best man that could be found for one of them, probably the Chairman . . ., no man living stands higher in the public opinion for the faithful, able and diligent discharge of the duties of the situation he filled'.[31] The first draft of the Commission proposed the revision of standing orders on a relatively limited scale. Middleton acceded to it, nominating John Fordyce, the Surveyor General of Land Revenue, and J. D. Thompson for the other Commissioners. The second draft, however, altered the scale of the business, forced Middleton to enlarge his ideas and to propose further Commissioners: 'If the Commission had been simply confined to the arrangement of the dockyards as in the first draft, I should have been well satisfied with Mr. Fordyce and Mr. Thompson, but as soon as I discovered in the one that was sent me the introduction of accounts and other inferior offices, I saw clearly where the stress of the business would lay and on that account wished to provide for it.'[32]

The Commission of Naval Revision was consequently the product of several minds. Middleton clearly provided the inspiration and initial impetus, while Pitt and Melville enlarged its scope and took responsibility for its institution. In the event the Commission was established by letters patent under the Great Seal on 8 January 1805. Middleton was the chairman with two admirals – Sir Roger Curtis and William Domett – and two administrators – John Fordyce and Ambrose Serle, a Transport commissioner – to assist him. Thompson was not named but six months later obtained a place at the Navy Board. The Commission's brief was to revise the instructions for the government of all the civil departments of the navy, paying particular attention to 'the system and mode of accounting for the receipt and expenditure of monies and stores'. Its end product was to be a digest of instructions for each department, the instructions being adapted 'to the present very extensive scale' of the navy. In addition the Commission had to consider any matters referred to them by the Admiralty and the unadopted proposals of the Commissioners on Fees, of Naval Enquiry and Select Committee on Finance. In the case of proposals that appeared practicable, it was to consider and recommend the best means of carrying them into execution.[33]

To Middleton's mind, the Commission represented an attempt to salve naval administration from the misplaced efforts of reformers over the previous few years. Middleton naturally considered that if his recommendations to the Commissioners on Fees had been immediately adopted subsequent administrative problems would not have occurred. Politics, he felt, had prejudiced as well as delayed the implementation of these recommendations. The Bentham–Nepean revision of those for the dockyards had 'sadly garbled' them and altered them 'to the views of interested individuals'; 'whoever examines the whole . . . and will follow their progress . . . and what they ended in at last must see that the whole was a political job'. The sixth report of the Commissioners of Enquiry was 'of the same nature'. It possessed nothing new except for its study of Task work 'and can only be called an imperfect abstract of what had been so ably done to their hands by the first Commissioners [on Fees]'. If the latter's reports 'had been fairly dealt with they would have reached every abuse in course of time and without noise and opposition. . . . Politics mix with everything and therefore nothing is done as it ought to be.'[34]

Middleton's dislike of politics and its baneful influence on the process of administrative improvement was in marked contrast to St Vincent's willing entry into parliamentary politics with the object of obtaining the Commission of Naval Enquiry. Middleton acknowledged that St Vincent's inquiry had brought abuses to light and that the more they investigated, the easier it would be to devise checks for the future. But he believed the blame 'thrown on the Commissioners of the Navy' was 'illiberal and in many parts unjust for, notwithstanding the very great remissness of the dockyard officers and the abuses committed by themselves and instruments, it was out of the power of the Navy Board . . . to prevent them'. The Navy Board commissioners were 'overpowered' by work and unequal to their duties: 'the officers soon discovered the want of investigation and took advantage of it on every occasion.'[35] Middleton's attitudes clearly differed from St Vincent's; yet he was very soon to be placed in a position similar to that which St Vincent had held when he obtained the Commission of Enquiry. Early in May 1805 Melville was forced to resign from the Admiralty to face impeachment arising out of allegations made in the Commission of Enquiry's tenth report. As Treasurer of the Navy during the 1790s, Melville had been responsible for the failure of the Navy's Paymaster to observe Burke's 1782 Act requiring public money to be lodged in the Bank of England and kept separate from personal accounts. On Melville's resignation, Middleton was asked to replace him. In spite of his age, 79, and his dislike of politics, with the incentive of a peerage as Baron Barham, Middleton readily accepted the post.

With Middleton, now Lord Barham, First Lord of the Admiralty, the work of the Commission of Revision proceeded more slowly but in a fashion similar to that in which it had gone on before May 1805. The other Commissioners drafted reports which they submitted to Barham for additions and corrections. Barham himself concentrated on the dockyards, the Commission's first report on the duties of the yard commissioners and principal officers being approved by order in council in July. As might be expected from his administrative burden and his view of politics, he took little part even in Cabinet affairs. Charles Abbot noticed his absence from the Cabinet on 16 June and recorded that Barham had been there 'but once' since his appointment. 'He was wanted the other day between five and six but upon inquiry the Cabinet messenger brought for answer that he was gone to drink tea somewhere in the City.'[36] Although affairs at sea were clearly his main preoccupation, he did not lose interest in the Commission, writing to the king in September 1805 that 'the future welfare and perhaps existence' of the fleet might depend on its work.[37] As time wore on, however, and especially after Pitt died and he himself resigned from the Admiralty in February 1806, he steadily lost enthusiasm. A year earlier he had wished to extend the scope of the Commission further – 'as far as naval officers are concerned and even go into the Admiralty; for till that department is new arranged it is impossible to conduct its own [duties] with energy and still less those of the many departments under [it]'.[38] Yet following his resignation his letters to J. D. Thompson repeatedly expressed a despondency that reflected both his own fatigue and the indifference to the Commission of the various First Lords who succeeded him.

In March 1806 he was already frequently feeling 'a great reluctance in going on with the Board of revisal', being 'confident no good can arise from it with an adverse Admiralty and indifferent Ministry'. Proud of his authority on naval matters, he was not prepared to have his work turned to political use and was uncertain what the intentions of Grey, the new First Lord, were. All would soon be explained, he noted to Thompson at the end of March: 'If they are better acquainted with the subject without experience than we are with it, they must be inspired and all will go right; but if it is meant to take credit to themselves at our expence, it is a poor quibble. . . . At all events I am ready to take wing the moment hostilities begin. My credit is not concerned in continuing longer.'[39] By September, when Grenville replaced Grey at the Admiralty, the Commission's prospects looked brighter. The Admiralty had distributed to the yards the revised dockyard regulations, which seemed to indicate that the Navy Board had been able to find no objection to them and Fordyce felt relations between the Commission and the Admiralty were improving: 'If they get into that right train of concurring in whatever promotes the public service, we should show that there is no backwardness on our part to useful communication, though we don't step out of our proper road to court it while they keep off.'[40] Perhaps the most encouraging circumstance was the interest of the king. When Fordyce presented the sixth report to him in December 1806 'he continued his minute inquiries as to our proceedings and the progress we had in view respecting the introduction of the use of mechanical powers into the dockyards instead of manual labour'.[41]

By this time Barham had returned to Teston and Fordyce had assumed the Commission's leadership in London. 'We shall continue to send documents for your consideration and I shall never ask you to come to us except when there is something that really requires your attendance', Fordyce promised him in mid-December 1806. Barham appears to have been worn out, requiring at times Fordyce to organize him. Whether they were to revise the business of the Victualling Board had been in doubt, the Commission possibly being terminated at the end of the year, but in December this was settled. 'Now that we are to complete the business', Fordyce therefore wrote to Barham, 'I must beg of you to assist me in setting our colleagues to work in the execution of such parts as they can undertake. I mean that Serle must do what relates to the Transport Office and the two Admirals must do what relates to the Victualling and Sick and Hurt. Briggs [their clerical assistant] and I will make out a sort of table of contents for those reports so as to regulate the order in which the subjects are to be considered in them . . . and we must meet as a Board and distribute the business in that manner. We shall otherwise trifle away the time and nothing will be done.'[42]

Barham appears to have been perfectly content that Fordyce should now take the lead. For in addition to his long experience in government administration, after almost two years of investigating naval affairs, Fordyce had acquired a confidence in his knowledge of the civil departments of the navy that he had not possessed early in 1805. He had, too, come to share Barham's conviction that the future welfare of the country depended on carrying through many of the recommendations of the Commission of Revision. He explained his ideas to Barham in November 1806:

It seems probable now that Europe will soon be divided into three great Empires, Russia, France and England, while England can preserve the dominion of the sea; if she shall lose that dominion the whole may be under two or under one power. This country must therefore provide for a much greater navy than it ever had before – and we must keep that increase in view in our reports particularly in what relates to the proposed new dockyard which should be on a greater scale and on one that will admit of further increase. This country must not end the war without preserving the connection with S° America which affords the best chance of enabling us to afford the expense of such a navy and of providing a nursery of seamen superior to that of other nations. Our navy is to be considered as that on which our existence depends, more absolutely if possible than it ever did before; and too much care cannot be taken to guard against the effects of neglect, confusion from want of system and the ignorance which have been already explained in our reports, to insure the introduction of the great improvements from the use of mechanical powers instead of manual labour and to take all practical means of providing the timber and other necessary materials which we are to recommend in that [report] now under our consideration.

Fordyce was concerned that the Admiralty and Navy Boards could not properly attend to these 'great objects' and considered a superintending board should be formed for this purpose composed of great officers of state and chaired by the First Lord of the Admiralty.[43] Fordyce was still relatively idealistic at this stage. He was, however, soon to be forced to think in terms of strict practicalities.

A minor irritant at the end of 1806 was St Vincent's continuing interest in a new eastern dockyard. He was a close associate of Lord Howick and there was the possibility that he would take the credit for the Commission of Revision's recommendations in this respect. More important was the problem of having the Commission's reports accepted at the Admiralty. Most of the reports were completed in 1807, and in April Fordyce began a series of meetings with Mulgrave, Grenville's successor, aimed at finalizing the details of certain recommendations. The salary scales for the different departments proved a particularly sticky issue, the government being reluctant to print reports that might 'give extravagant expectations to the persons whose salaries we think should be increased'.[44] It also seemed necessary to convince Mulgrave of the military importance of the reports relating to the new dockyard and the supply of timber. By March 1808 Fordyce had had 'so many conversations' with Lord Mulgrave and others 'on the general object of improving and increasing our navy as the only means of supporting the rank of this country among nations' that he had no doubt that he had 'gone a little out of our civil line and wandered into the military one'.[45] The conversations were, however, an essential preliminary to the reports' adoption. For, as John Briggs observed, fear seemed 'to be a much more guiding principle with Lord Mulgrave than the spirit of amendment' and the reports seemed dependent on those around Mulgrave worrying him into acquiescence.[46]

Even after Fordyce had wound up the business of the Commission in March 1808, he still felt uncertain whether all their recommendations would be accepted. He made a point of advising Mulgrave that immediate steps were necessary to set in train the establishment of the new dockyard and the growth of a domestic supply of hemp. Yet he was sure nothing would be done, as was in fact to be the case. Nor was he 'sanguine as to any material reform being accomplished' within the naval departments. 'The Victualling Board goes on as it did before or rather worse [as do] those who are to preside in the committees into which the Navy Board is divided – the old system in short is a little broken in upon and the new one not introduced and there it is not unlikely for some time to remain.'[47]

Nevertheless, contrary to Fordyce's fears, during 1808 nine of the Commission's 13 unadopted reports were approved by order in council and two more in 1809. The secret reports on the timber situation and on the proposed new dockyard at Northfleet were never printed. Timber plantations were formed in accordance with the former but the Northfleet report was simply shelved. Yet approval of the reports by order in council was one thing; implementation of the recommendations was another. The third and eighth reports on the dockyards, ordered to be carried into effect by the Admiralty from 1 January 1810, posed too many problems for the Navy Board to solve immediately in addition to its ordinary workload. The eighth report indeed contained 'directions for such fundamental alterations' as nearly amounted 'to a total change of system in the dockyards'.[48] The recommendations contained in the reports consequently forced the Navy Board to consider both ways and means by which changes could be implemented without seriously impinging on the work of the Board or the running of the yards. The Board was accordingly forced into a process of regeneration which was itself highly self-instructive.

For the eighth report, which presented the greatest problems, the Navy Board initially adopted the strategy of making copies of those parts of the report necessary for the information of the yard commissioners and officers and asking them to return their observations and opinions on 'the best and readiest manner of carrying the same into execution'. By this method the Board hoped 'to obviate many difficulties which must be expected to arise in carrying into execution such a comprehensive system and to preserve consistency in giving our orders upon the variety of questions which will undoubtedly arise therefrom'. The yard commissioners and officers were given six to eight weeks for their consideration and response.[49] The eighth report recommended comprehensive alterations in the system of employing and paying the artificers by the piece and an entirely new establishment for the education of the 'superior class of shipwrights'. It was consequently easy to raise objections and 'numerous difficulties and obstructions' were accordingly started, especially by the officers at Plymouth. In May 1810, however, Charles Yorke succeeded Mulgrave and promptly ordered a committee of the Navy Board to visit the yards to investigate the problems.

It was at this point that John Payne came to the Navy Board's aid.[50] Although only 30, Payne was already renowned in the Navy Office for his industry and organizing ability. Little is known about his earlier life except that he had entered the office of the Clerk of the Acts in 1795 and risen to the place of chief clerk in the Secretary's office by the age of 27. Two years later, in 1809, realizing that the third and eighth reports of the Commissioners of Revision would lead to many different interpretations and subsequent confusion in the yards, he presented to the Navy Board a 59-page appraisal of the points where misconceptions were likely to arise and proposed a plan by which misunderstandings could be avoided. Some of his proposals were adopted during the first half of 1810. But it was during the visitation of the yards by the

Navy Board committee, which Payne accompanied as its secretary, that he really proved his worth. On its return the committee only presented to the Admiralty the minutes of its proceedings at the yards.[51] But during the first five months of 1811 it presented to the Admiralty four reports digesting and detailing all the irregularities that could be discovered to exist. Many had arisen on account of recommendations of the Commission of Revision that had already been sent to the yards and there given widely differing interpretations. The committee's reports were prepared by Payne and included the measures necessary to eradicate irregularities in the officers' observance of their own personal instructions, in the payment of officers and clerks, and in the system by which stores and timber were received and issued. It was in these reports that Payne revealed most clearly his ability to penetrate and amend the minute detail of regulations of considerable extent and complexity.

However, while Payne was preparing these post-visitation reports, the Admiralty had become impatient to adopt the third and eighth reports of the Commissioners of Revision. Yorke had quite clearly lost patience with the job, informing the Navy Board in December 1810 'that it is become absolutely requisite to put an immediate end to a repetition of the various frivolous representations which have been made during the course of carrying the king's recent orders in council into execution'. The Navy Board was directed to accompany any other 'statement of difficulties and the pointing out of real or supposed abuses' by the 'suggestion and recommendation of the means which may appear ... to be best calculated for remedying the same'.[52] The regulations contained in the Commissioners' third and eighth reports were simply ordered to take effect from 1 January 1811. However, at the end of the first quarter of that year, it was found that the system by which accounts of work performed by the piece were returned to the Clerk of the Cheque was attended with considerable delays and demanded a considerable addition to the number of clerks available, while the accounts themselves required greater uniformity of execution. The yards could not be paid for the Lady Quarter at the appointed time and there was reason to fear that 'the greatest confusion and disorder would ensue'.

The Navy Board immediately turned to Payne, who was willing to go to the yards immediately to remove the difficulties. On 18 May he was able to recommend several temporary expedients which on trial proved effective; and on 12 August he recommended regulations necessary for a permanent system. According to Payne, the measurement and accounting of all piecework could then 'be carried on upon an uniform, efficient and economical system beneficial at once to the fair claims of the workmen and to the interests of the public'. The Admiralty immediately adopted the proposals, ordering on 14 August the regulations to be carried into effect from 1 October 1811. 'As in matters of this extensive and complicated nature it could not be expected that any written instructions could be sufficiently explicit to convey an exact and uniform understanding of new regulations to be acted upon at six different dockyards', Payne was ordered to the yards himself. At five of the yards he remained a matter of days and at most two weeks; but at Plymouth he met with 'impediments' that obliged him to remain at the yard two months. His regulations were nevertheless successful and were confirmed as such by most yard officers. Payne acknowledged that the plan was not all of his own making and that he had simply amended what already existed or had been proposed by the Commissioners of Revision. Nevertheless many of the minor procedural details and the arrangement of them into a unified and operable whole were indisputably his work. Payne calculated that the new method of managing Task and Job work made a saving of £5,000 a year over the system previously in force, and a saving of £15,000 over the system proposed by the Commissioners of Revision.[53]

Payne's work on the measurement and accounting of work by the piece led him in 1811 to devise a volume of tables to expedite the costing of men's earnings. During the course of the year, Payne also began to consider the scheme of prices devised by committees of dockyard officers and paid since 1 January. Like the prices before them, these rendered some earnings too high and some too low, and in October were ordered to be further revised. In April 1812 Payne visited Sheerness to investigate the grounds of some particularly high earnings and was able by the end of June 1812 to devise a method of discovering, even as works proceeded, those works that had been overpriced and those underpriced during the formation of the schemes. With tables that permitted the immediate calculation of men's earnings and a system of adjusting piecework prices, and thus of controlling the wages bill, Payne was able to suggest the payment of all earnings weekly, as subsistence money then was. As weekly payments permitted the abolition of the quarterly pay day holidays, this proposal entailed both the saving of four extra days' wages, paid as compensation for a loss of working time, and the employment of the artificers four extra days each year.

It was to introduce these further schemes of improvement that at the end of June 1812 the Navy Board proposed to the Admiralty that Payne should receive a special appointment. The Board had found that Payne's proposals of 1810–11 for the receipt and issue of stores and timber had worked well on a trial at Woolwich and Plymouth, and it wanted Payne to supervise the extension of this system to the other yards as well. Yet both projects involved 'great delicacy and difficulty', an investigation of the accounts of each yard department, and the request for information from the heads of those departments as well as others; so the Board feared obstruction in the yards. Earlier Payne had 'encountered great obstacles from his official situation not being superior to that of persons in whose departments he had to prosecute his inquiries' and the Board was 'fearful of still greater impediments to a more enlarged plan of investigation'. The Board acknowledged that its own commissioners ought really to be undertaking the work but pointed out that all were fully occupied with 'the current business that daily occurs'. The measures put forward, moreover, were not of a kind that occurred in the common course of business:

They are, on the contrary, intended to effect very essential alterations and we may confidently add improvements in the present system of things: great care and circumspection will therefore be necessary in the adjustment of all the minute parts of the intended arrangements to give the altered system its full effect. Small circumstances may in practice embarrass a plan generally beneficial and perhaps fewer allowances would be made in the case of altering an old system whose operation was understood than in constructing a new one, should unforeseen embarrassments arise. On this general ground alone it is desirable that the execution of any new measure of magnitude should be superintended, if possible, by the person who proposed it.[54]

The 2nd Viscount Melville, Yorke's successor as First Lord, concurred in the 'propriety' of a special appointment for Payne and said he would obtain government sanction for it.[55] Meanwhile Payne continued his work in the Navy Office, turning his attention in his spare time to the 'state of the navy', to which public attention had been drawn by the extraordinarily rapid decay of the *Queen Charlotte* (100). By mid-October, however, Melville was 'wavering' and told the Comptroller that 'there were great difficulties in the way of making a new appointment'. Payne, thought Melville, might be sent to the yards as the assistant to a Navy Board commissioner. Indeed, later that month Liverpool, First Lord of the Treasury and prime minister, met the Comptroller personally and told him that the appointment should not take place. It was nevertheless agreed that Payne should be despatched 'with all the powers' that the Admiralty and Navy Boards could give him and that Melville 'would himself take measures to prevent obstruction at Plymouth'. Payne was pleased at the decision but uncertain about the future:

After what has passed I certainly did not expect this conclusion – but at the same time I am ready to admit that Ministers cannot at all times do what they could wish, though they have no other motive than the good of the service – but what I think I have more reason to complain of is that at present I am without any positive assurance that I shall be noticed hereafter. I can scarcely doubt Lord M's disposition to do what is right but his present intentions, if they are favourable to me, will not influence his successors.[56]

Payne had good reason to be concerned about the future. Six weeks later he fell ill. On 30 December 1812 he died. He was 32 and left a wife and three sons all under four years of age. A post mortem suggested that the cause of death was meningitis and his wife petitioned for a pension on the grounds that 'his life was sacrificed to over-exertions in the publick service'. The Navy Board strongly supported the petition, explicitly attributing 'the origin of that disorder which proved fatal' to Payne's application, labour and 'severe anxiety of mind'. The Board accompanied the petition with a detailed account of Payne's extra service which concluded with the statement that his improvements upon the recommendations of the Commissioners of Revision saved the public almost £72,000 a year. Nevertheless there was no instance of a widow's pension on the ordinary estimate of the navy 'during the whole of the late century or since' that could be employed 'as a precedent favourable to the suit of Mrs. Payne'. Her request for a pension was therefore turned down.[57]

The civil departments of the navy lost a particularly able administrator in the death of John Payne. Yet the support he received from the Navy Board was as important for the future of dockyard management as the work which was terminated by his premature death. For it reflected the fact that by 1812 the Board clearly appreciated the difficulties of introducing new ideas and the necessity for a man in whom it had confidence to devise and introduce new regulations as the board's representative. The employment of Payne was in this sense a new technique for making improvements and denoted a greater readiness on the part of the board to alter long-established methods of managing the yards. In a similar situation a decade earlier, faced with the recommendations of the Commissioners on Fees, the Navy Board had revealed no such willingness to implement new procedures. The Admiralty had in the end to employ Nepean and Bentham to consider the Fees report and to impose their revision of the recommendations on the Navy Board.

The attitude of the Navy Board to change was thus itself changing. Yet in

*Samuel Bentham, by Henry Edridge*

applying the recommendations of the Commissioners of Naval Revision the Navy Board was in fact reinforcing a traditional system of management and ignoring a modern principle which was already being aired. Barham's administrative ideas had been formed in the eighteenth century when collective forms of management were the vogue, and in the early nineteenth century he was still wedded to them. The first report of the Commissioners of Revision accordingly declared the Commissioners' intention not to depart from the principles adopted by the Duke of York and Mr Pepys and laid down for the civil departments of the navy in 1662: 'they have stood the test of time and have been found by long trial to be well adapted to great objects of their institution'.[58] The Commissioners' recommendations thus perpetuated a traditional system well into the nineteenth century. Yet since 1796 Samuel Bentham had been sowing the seeds of an alternative administrative theory which was only to be fully accepted in the 1820s. It has been generally assumed that Jeremy Bentham was the first to advocate individual responsibility, expressed in the term 'single-seated functionaries';[59] but his brother Samuel was acting on the idea from the time of his appointment to the office of Inspector General of Naval Works until his retirement from the naval departments at the end of 1812. He acted on it, moreover, in spite of being forced into a countervailing system in 1808, when his department was transferred from the Admiralty to the Navy Office. The consequence was that he obtained for it from the Navy Board a degree of tolerance which marked the first stages of a departure from traditional ideas.

Bentham was of course appointed in 1796 to make improvements in the physical facilities and equipment of the navy.[60] He was, however, deeply aware that improvements of the nature he was expected to make were completely dependent on the administrative context in which the decisions affecting them were made. He thus attributed the apparent failure of the Navy Board to make significant progress in the design of ships and nature of yard facilities partly to the Board Commissioners' lack of knowledge and partly to their lack of time. They had little knowledge 'of the great variety of arts and manufactures which, though they contribute to the efficiency of the naval departments, are not carried on in the dockyards or other naval establishments'. They authorized trials of suggested improvements but their lack of scientific knowledge prevented them appreciating suggestions based on theory rather than on practice.[61] Preoccupation with the immediate business of the Board, moreover, prevented them from interesting themselves fully in improvements: they 'have been confined to and their time fully occupied by the charge of carrying on the several businesses in the beaten track in which they have hitherto been carried on, whereby they have in general neither leisure to attend to nor indeed adequate information to judge of anything that may be offered in the way of improvements'.[62] Yet Bentham believed that lack of knowledge and lack of time, important as they were, were simply subsidiary effects of a system of collective management which by its nature stifled interest, initiative and enterprise.

After 1796 Navy Board commissioners spent some of their time sitting on one of three committees. Even so, throughout the wars, the Board continued to operate according to the principle laid down in 1662, proceeding 'by common council and argument of most voices, endeavouring jointly to advance His Majesty's service without private or indirect end'. The system was justified in the seventeenth century when a sense of responsibility to the public was virtually non-existent. Then indeed, to make sure that commissioners served only the Crown, they were to be able 'to trace' one another in their distinct and several duties, and at least three members were to sign Board letters and orders. Yet by the late eighteenth century the system prevented the board dealing with a great and increasing mass of business speedily and efficiently. Particular items rarely received the attention they often deserved. According to Bentham, proposals for improvements suffered in particular. They were subject to the will of the majority: 'no one member can do anything against the opinion of the rest nor without the concurrence of a majority of them'.[63] When new ideas were adopted, the responsibility for seeing them carried out was diffused vaguely among the commissioners; individually they felt a comparatively slight sense of responsibility. An individual introducing an idea had no need for concern over his mistakes should it prove a failure – the Board would screen him. Conversely, if the idea was a success, the individual was given little incentive to bring forward further ideas, as the credit for them was diffused among the Board.[64]

Bentham thought the traditional system of corporate responsibility also promoted negligence and stifled originality in the dockyards. Again, according to the 1662 regulations, letters to the Navy Board relating to the conduct of general yard business had to be signed in triplicate as a check upon the veracity of their contents. Within the yards, departments were so organized that even in the routine issue and receipt of stores, measurement of contract work and calculation of wages, the business was checked and signed for by at least two officers or clerks, each from a different department. Bentham believed that such divided responsibility led to laxity. Yard officers became 'very little scrupulous as to the opinions they sanction by their signature'; they proceeded with a want of thought that was 'the natural result of a system under which the conduct of the thoughtful is not distinguished or distinguishable from that of the thoughtless'.[65]

Holding such views, Bentham naturally organized his office on the principle of individual responsibility. Though provided with assistants, as Inspector General he alone was responsible for every aspect of the office's business. Bentham thought that such accountability would ensure that justice was done to every proposed improvement: 'the investigation of every proposal referred to or proceeding from an officer so circumstanced may be expected to be pursued to the utmost of his abilities'. He assumed, moreover, that his office was 'considered by all parties as an experiment'. He accordingly took it upon himself 'to prove how far it might be advantageous to commit any branch of the civil department of the navy to that kind of individual management which, having been adopted universally in private undertakings however extensive, has contributed greatly to the increase of the wealth of the country and which . . . in the military branch of the naval department has effected those services which constitute the security of the country'.[66] Bentham's proof consisted of showing that his office was more efficient than the Navy Board, that he was right more often than the Board. Yet the Navy Board was an unwilling party to this experiment and Bentham naturally incurred its opposition. He was repeatedly having the Board's improvement plans referred to him by the Admiralty; or investigating existing arrangements in the dockyards, and making highly critical reports upon them so as to forward his own ideas. The Navy Board soon grew weary with him. It complained in July 1802, for example, of Bentham's report on the distribution of timber to the yards: 'we are sensible . . . that some unavoidable errors and oversights will occur which in retracing our steps may be as obvious to us as to any person and the discovery of them by that means be attended with at least as much advantage for the public service as if permitted by their Lordships to be pointed out to us by General Bentham with a charge of extravagance [and] improvidence . . . with which his letters are so replete'.[67]

The conflict of ideas between the Inspector General and the Navy Board placed Bentham constantly on the offensive, the Board on the defensive. Harmonious relations were virtually out of the question. And there was another even deeper source of antagonism that reinforced the ideological opposition and made conflict inevitable. This was the constitutional rivalry arising from their mutual interest in the dockyards, yet separate responsibility to the Admiralty. No works in the yards were placed permanently under the Inspector General's control. But being authorized by the Admiralty to investigate any aspect of dockyard management that he wished, and at various times having to supervise civil building and other works of improvement in the yards, Bentham clearly appeared both to the Navy Board and the yard officers as a rival power. His activities often interfered in the smooth running of the yards. The machinery he introduced did not conform to yard routine and regulations: the steam engines and furnaces for the wood and metal mills had to be attended at night, and the dredging vessel required riggers and scavelmen who were not normally employed in yard craft. Yet Bentham's activities represented more than a disruptive influence of this sort. In 1804, for example, he was allowed three or four officers to instruct in superintending the fitting of carronades on his non-recoil principle and the Navy Board was forced to complain:

> he does not confine himself to the selection of three or four subordinate officers . . . but he requests that seven of the most efficient subordinate officers may be put under his exclusive direction – viz. one from each of the yards and a seventh to be employed at any of the yards as he may think proper. The loss which the public service will sustain by taking this number of officers (and men who will be required to act under them) from the general duties of the yards is a consideration tho' material in itself, yet of a secondary nature when compared with the consequences that must ensue from the introduction of an executive Authority in *each* of the dockyards independent of the principal officers and of the jurisdiction of this board.[68]

For the Navy Board, the situation was exacerbated by the attachment of Bentham's office to the Admiralty. Being administratively closer to the First Lord, Bentham could easily be regarded as enjoying more influence than the Navy Board, an observation which was not lost on the yard officers. Before

1805 the Admiralty did nothing to dispel the impression by occasionally asking Bentham for recommendations for promotion from among the officers with whom he was acquainted. His recommendations did the Admiralty a service by widening the choice in its selection of officers;[69] but for the Navy Board, which had always recommended the inferior officers who would be considered for promotion, the extension of consultations to Bentham was galling. It was more than a matter of involuntarily sharing traditional patronage; its loss of influence meant less control. As it explained to the Commissioners of Revision in 1805:

> the support he [Bentham] has had has given so great an influence among the superior and inferior officers of the dockyards as to lessen the deference and respect which had heretofore been paid to the Navy Board and consequently to diminish their authority. This end has been attained by evincing to the officers that the road to promotion lies in conciliating the good opinion and favour of the Inspector General so that we have no doubt there are now many officers in the dockyards who have attached themselves to the Inspector General and who are consequently indifferent as to the sentiments the Navy Board may entertain of them.[70]

Relations between the subordinate board and Bentham were controlled to a large extent by the First Lord. Spencer was fairly neutral, but St Vincent clearly favoured Bentham against the Board. St Vincent's support enabled Bentham to make his 'radical changes' in the system of apprenticeship and to introduce Timber Masters with instructions based on the idea of individual responsibility. The innovations gave the Navy Board cause to despair of ever introducing 'regularity of system' into yard management,[71] but St Vincent adopted the idea of individual responsibility with alacrity. The third report of the Commissioners of Naval Enquiry recommended that the Navy Board commissioners be allotted a proportionate and proper part of Navy Office business to be placed under their immediate superintendence and responsibility. The report was printed in June 1803 and St Vincent acted on it two months later.[72] On the other hand Melville and Barham, St Vincent's successors, were sympathetic to the difficulties of the Board, while the Commissioners of Revision were receptive to its views on the office of the Inspector General. The latter were informed that Bentham's investigations and criticisms of Navy Board management were more of a handicap than an aid, and simply wasted Board time: 'We have no hesitation in saying that by this constant and unnecessary occupation and waste of time we have been prevented from directing our attention to subjects of greater moment.' The service in consequence had suffered 'frequent delays'.[73] In a private capacity, Barham had already received an account from at least one Navy Board commissioner on Bentham's activities and had decided views of his own as to Bentham's knowledge of dockyard affairs.[74] As chairman of the Commissioners of Revision, it is therefore unlikely that he had any reservations about recommending the office of the Inspector General be abolished.

This occurred by order in council of 28 October 1807. Bentham, however, was absent at the time. In the summer of 1805 he went to Russia to oversee the building of ships for the Royal Navy and only returned shortly after the order in council. Bentham believed that he had been sent to Russia 'to keep him out of the way', and a consideration of this sort probably did contribute to the decision to send the Inspector rather than a shipwright officer from the dockyards. The mission was nonetheless a considerable diplomatic and strategic venture. At a time when the supply of oak for shipbuilding had become seriously depleted in England, the Tzar was believed to be favourably disposed to the construction of British warships at Archangel. A scheme in which Bentham would superintend the construction of two 74s and two 36-gun frigates was accordingly proposed by Lord Melville in January 1805 and was accepted by the government by June, when Bentham received his instructions. It was arranged that the Mechanist in the Inspector General's office, Simon Goodrich, should deputize for Bentham while he took metal fittings, tools, assistants and family to Russia to finalize the negotiations and carry out the work. In the event, the mission was a failure. The Tzar's favourable disposition was merely the interpretation placed on a civil diplomatic reply to the British application to build ships in Russia. Bentham therefore returned home in December 1807.[75] On finding his office abolished and most of its establishment, including himself, transferred to the Navy Office, he protested at length. But Lord Mulgrave, at that time First Lord, was influenced neither by his arguments for retaining an officer with individual responsibility nor by a eulogistic account of his achievements. In December 1808 Bentham and his assistants duly became the department of the Civil Architect and Engineer at the Navy Office. In spite of further indignant protests, Bentham had to take a junior place at the Navy Board and even become a member of the committee of correspondence.[76]

The transfer to the Navy Office resolved the conflict which had marred relations between the Navy Board and Bentham. As a single voice at the Board, he could no longer impose his views on it as he had done from the Admiralty. Yet, personally humiliated, with his belief in individual responsibility discredited, he did not willingly take part in a system of corporate management against which he felt committed. Not surprisingly, he achieved little in his four years as Architect and Engineer. He was consulted on yard improvements but remained on the periphery of major works. The plans he proposed for Sheerness yard and the Plymouth Breakwater were both dismissed, the former for being 'of vast expense and dubious expediency'.[77] Most of the time, he appears to have absented himself from both the Navy Board and the committee of correspondence. Early in November 1812 John Payne observed that Bentham's face had not been seen in the Navy Office 'for a good while'.[78] No doubt on that account, it was later that month that Bentham's second office was abolished and Bentham himself pensioned off with a regular sum of £1,000 and extra allowances amounting to £500, a total amount that was twice the salary he had received as Inspector General.

Bentham's appointment as Architect and Engineer was a failure. While at the Navy Board, however, he did succeed in making individual responsibility an issue once again. For on occasions the Navy Board preferred to submit his proposals to the Admiralty as coming from an individual rather than from the Board as a whole. In August 1811 this was the case with his paper on the proposed breakwater at Plymouth. The Board of Admiralty returned it, according to the Admiralty Secretary, because

> their Lordships . . . do not conceive that a minute drawn up by an individual member of your board could be intended by you to be transmitted as an official document to be submitted for their consideration, more especially such a minute as the one in question, which their Lordships direct me to observe is couched in terms so extraordinary, indecorous and unofficial as to excite considerable surprize that it was not immediately returned by you to the member whose name it bears.

The Admiralty required that all future proposals be made by the Board 'in the usual manner'.[79] The Navy Board replied that it was their 'usual practice' to forward reports or minutes from individual 'professional members' or committees of the Board, and 'in conformity with this practice' forwarded two more papers on the breakwater written by Bentham. At the Admiralty an investigation immediately took place into 'instances of minutes of individuals so transmitted'. A search was made by the Admiralty 'keeper of records' through all the Navy Board correspondence in the ten years prior to Bentham's appointment to the Navy Board. Not one precedent was found. The reports of the Surveyors or of visiting committees had indeed always been transmitted in that way, but the only other instances had occurred since Bentham's appointment. The Board of Admiralty consequently returned Bentham's two latest papers, referring the Navy Board to its earlier letter.[80]

The incident is trivial in itself. It nonetheless reflects more than Bentham's persistence in adhering to his particular belief. His determination had forced the Navy Board to accept the idea that a specialist at the Board should have his views put forward, even if they were unacceptable to his colleagues. One could argue that the Board had been weak in failing to suppress Bentham, or that the Board was attempting to expose and discredit him. Indeed it was ironic that the Navy Board should have been put in the position of having to defend the principle that had moved Bentham in his criticism of the Board before 1808. Yet, set alongside the Board's clear comprehension of the difficulties of administrative innovation, as reflected in its support for Payne, the incident also suggests a flexibility on the part of the Board which is consistent with its growing administrative awareness. In comparison with the Admiralty's strict adherence to the traditional rule – that only recommendations should be put forward which had full Board approval – the attitude of the Navy Board appears refreshingly reasonable. With new members, most of whom did not recall the years of Bentham's opposition to the Navy Board a decade earlier, there was no reason for the Board to feel vindictive. Bentham was undoubtedly a difficult colleague and his retirement in 1812 was quite certainly welcomed. Even so, in the meantime, the Navy Board successfully accommodated him – and in the process increased the extent to which it represented to the senior board the opinions of its individual members.

Unlike the Navy Board, in 1811 the Admiralty refused to compromise with the new administrative theory. Nevertheless, with time and the pressure for post-war economies, the concept of individual responsibility was also to be adopted at the Admiralty. In 1822 economies resulted in the abolition in the yards of the post of Clerk of the Survey, one of the cross-checking principal officers; and in 1832 Sir James Graham abolished the Navy and Victualling Boards in order to give each Admiralty commissioner individual responsibility for a naval department. At the same time the posts of dockyard commissioner and port admiral were combined to form the single post of yard superintendent. As in other government departments, though somewhat earlier than elsewhere, policy in the naval departments was thus to favour Bentham's idea rather than the traditional labour-intensive concept of corporate or divided responsibility. Yet in 1811 Bentham was still the radical with controversial notions; while the Board of Admiralty, like the Commissioners of Revision, accepted, and thus maintained, conventional practice. As he had been since 1796, Bentham was therefore still at odds with the system. It was, though, a system that was gradually becoming more pliant as reforms, new ideas and experience created in naval administrators an 'enlightenment' they had not possessed 20 years earlier.

# Conclusion

The developments in the management of the royal dockyards between 1793 and 1815 were in many ways similar to those that were made in the construction of ships during the last half of the Napoleonic War. In the eighteenth century both the scale of yard business and the size of ships had increased steadily. Consequently by 1793 the systems by which the yards were managed and ships were built were supporting burdens far greater than those for which they had initially been conceived. Both still worked tolerably well; neither was on the point of collapse. But both revealed signs of weakness and stress, to which their familiars had become accustomed. The frames of large ships worked, sometimes alarmingly, and often needed reinforcement. Yard management too was loose and not always reliable in performance: the yard officers were incapable of performing their regulation checks upon one another, no one person — even the resident commissioner — had any real control over yard affairs, and the Navy Board was overwhelmed by business with which it dealt without order or priority.

Yard management and ship construction therefore both attracted reformers, their efforts producing in time systems that operated more effectively. By the end of the wars ships were being built upon Seppings's system of diagonal bracing, while the yards had benefitted from the adoption of the recommendations of a succession of parliamentary commissions as well as the more individual efforts of Samuel Bentham, St Vincent, Barham and the less known John Payne. As a result ships and yards were probably able to perform slightly more swiftly — although not noticeably so. The main benefit in each case was that the 'mechanics' were improved. Through a thorough examination and revision of the systems upon which they operated, the internal arrangement of ships and yards were alike adapted to the burdens they had to bear and made more economical in their use of resources.

The similarities between developments in shipbuilding and those in the dockyards were of course superficial. The analogy nevertheless has the value of emphasizing the structural nature of yard improvements during the wars. The yards were composed of many different parts — physical and administrative — each part influencing to a small degree the manner in which the whole operated. The physical components had the most direct effect on performance. But the actual technology employed to conduct yard operations altered very little; the semaphore between the Admiralty and the main ports was not usually used to transmit messages relating to yard business; and the only additions to docking facilities, Bentham's deep docks at Portsmouth, made no significant impression on the average speed with which ships of the line were returned to sea. The next major addition to docking facilities was only made when the Sheerness extension was completed after the Napoleonic War. To be sure, steam power, mass-production block manufacture and the latest metal recycling methods made their appearance; but their impression on the speed with which ships could refit and repair was limited. The refitting of frigates continued to take about two months, 74s four months, while the length of time of repairs simply depended on the thoroughness with which they were performed.

Change on a much wider front occurred in the administrative components: in the regulations governing informal payments and in the managerial procedures which affected every official and artificer. These developments were not the result of naval officers demanding particular improvements in dockyard service, but were a product of that drive for greater economy and efficiency running throughout government at the time. The effects were nonetheless beneficial to the sea-going service. Through numerous minor changes, yard management became more systematic and dependable and its servants more professional.

Until relatively recently, naval and political historians regarded the creation and reports of St Vincent's Commission of Naval Enquiry as sure evidence of the inefficiency of the machinery of civil administration and of the corruption of its human parts. There was indeed much to put right, but the deficiencies should not be overstated. The Navy Board, and no doubt the other civil boards beneath the Admiralty, had always attempted to remove problems where it could. At the end of the eighteenth century, moreover, the Navy Board and yard officers had not been immune from rising public expectations of greater efficiency and probity in the conduct of public affairs. Consequently, by the end of the Revolutionary War, changes in attitude and in the pace of procedural change had already taken place. St Vincent and his Commission simply added to the momentum. In so doing, the reports of the commission revealed much that blackened the name of the Navy Board for ever. But the Navy Board was at that time still inexperienced in the process and techniques of reform and was clearly preoccupied with the needs of a navy of unprecedented size. However, probably to the relief of the Board, the Commissioners of Naval Enquiry made the efficiency of the civil administration such an issue that the task of considering necessary reforms was temporarily taken from it and placed with the Commission of Naval Revision. This Commission pointed the way ahead, its reports recommending the reforms still needed and suggesting the means by which they might be accomplished. For the Navy Board the process of reform was simplified; its readiness to make changes doubled. Consequently from 1810 until about 1813 the process of detailed amendment was intensified, only gradually slackening towards the end of the war.

Administrative change during the Revolutionary and Napoleonic Wars was thus a continuation of an earlier and more gradual process. Nevertheless the areas of yard management it affected were so various, and the alterations in places so complete, that the period can justly be described as one of revolution.

Traditional practice, and the theory by which it was maintained, was everywhere questioned and considered against alternatives. Change did not of course stop with the conclusion of hostilities; it continued under the pressure for post-war economies. However, the war years were the formative ones, with new ideas being voiced and many being tried.

Perhaps the most important of these ideas, Samuel Bentham's concept of individual responsibility, was applied in time to the greater part of public administration. Yet initially it was, as Bentham saw it, a panacea for the confusing dispersal of responsibility among cross-checking dockyard officers and the corporation of Navy Board commissioners. The principle was applied with the utmost conviction between 1801 and 1804 by St Vincent, who discharged seven negligent or otherwise incapable yard officers and demanded that Board commissioners each be given areas of Navy Office business for their individual superintendence. Only in 1832, with the abolition of the Navy Board and concentration of control on individually responsible Admiralty Lords, was the idea carried significantly further in naval administration. But by then, through the writings of Samuel's brother Jeremy, it was more generally accepted.

In 1832 the concentration of control at the Admiralty was a logical step. During the eighteenth century the dockyard officers had a high degree of independence. This was gradually reduced during the war years, control from the Navy Board steadily being tightened, partly through the standardization of accounts and accounting procedures, but mainly through the issue of new standing orders, first by the Navy Board and then by the Commissioners of Revision. Thereafter dockyard officials had far less freedom of manoeuvre and could be pinned to a precise definition of their duties. Control from within the Navy Office was also improved by the more systematic distribution of business. Sections of the office were subdivided to promote the specialization of each department, and the commissioners were divided into three committees – of correspondence, accounts and stores – to dispose of routine business for which a full board was unnecessary. The arrangement permitted the commissioners to interest themselves in those areas of office business for which they were responsible, and reserved matters of fundamental importance for meetings of the Board.

In the yards control was not concentrated on a single official until 1822 when the yard commissioner became the only person who could 'correspond' with the Navy Board. However, the main thrust of alterations in yard procedure was towards greater economy. Developments in some areas of course tended towards *both* efficiency in work performance and less profusion in public expenditure. The improvements in Task and Job work were a prime example. These wars were the first in which shipwright work at all six yards was performed by the piece and the prices set on work required repeated adjustment. Payment for piecework that was equitable to the men and the public encouraged the artificers to perform as much work as possible, for they knew that they received a fair reward. Accordingly more work was performed – yet without extravagant payments being made for work that was overpriced. John Payne's production of tables for the rapid calculation of piecework earnings had similar dual benefits. Artificers could be paid weekly, giving them a prompt return and immediate incentive for sustained labour. At the same time quarterly pay day holidays became unnecessary, creating another day of work and obviating the need to compensate the men with a day's pay for time lost while being paid.

These advantages stemmed primarily from improvements in accountancy. Accounts had, it is true, been a natural part of naval administration since its earliest existence. In the dockyards at the end of the eighteenth century, however, the methods by which accounts were compiled differed from yard to yard, as did their presentation and the amount of detail they contained. Yard efficiency demanded that greater system be introduced, especially in the Storekeepers' accounts which gave control of stocks of materials and equipment. But it was the threat of parliamentary charges of wastage of public funds that forced the Navy Board to improve the keeping and use of accounts relating to wages. The Commissioners of Naval Enquiry demonstrated in their sixth report that the Board's own accounts could be used against it; to show in one case, for example, that the sums paid out in wages for the repair of seven ships in 1800 and 1801 exceeded the value put on the work by over 20 per cent. Its own security necessitated that the Board use accounts to the full to check and control expenditure. Attempts on the part of yard officers to perfect their methods were therefore accompanied by efforts on the part of the Navy Board to standardize the best methods throughout the yards. This was eventually achieved after the adoption of a multitude of pro-formas proposed by the Commissioners of Revision and through the work of John Payne. By the end of the Napoleonic Wars accountancy for both stores and wages was clearly felt by the Navy Board to have attained a level commensurate to the standard expected by the public for the control of government expenditure.

The drive towards more economical management in the dockyards was assisted by an increasing public respect for civil servants – initially partly resulting from greater knowledge of the amount and nature of their informal earnings, later from knowledge that such earnings were curtailed. Greater trust was accompanied by an appreciation of the apparent paradox that higher expenditure was sometimes the only way to achieve long-term savings. Thus economies were achieved, though indirectly, after 1797 when the rate at which supplies were granted to the navy was increased from £4–£7 a man per lunar month. More funds reduced the naval debt and permitted the more regular payment of navy bills, a reduction of the period before they became payable, and a consequent reduction in the interest payable upon them. In addition, the solvency of the navy not only permitted artificers to be paid on time but facilitated the reduction in the interval between pay days from a quarter to a week. This in turn reduced the artificers' tendency to run into debt and the amount of interest to which they became liable.

While the availability of greater funds reduced wastage in public expenditure, so too did the enlargement of the number of officers in the dockyards. The business of converting measured work into earnings by the piece was so specialized and intricate that it demanded a professional officer, independent of other operative and clerical officers. The cost of the office establishments required by the Master Measurers must have been offset by the savings made through accuracy in the pricing of work and calculation of wages. The Timber

Masters must too have reduced wastage through their attention to the quality of the wood received and the propriety with which timbers were selected for conversion. The Inspector of Canvas undoubtedly had a similar influence on the amount of canvas wasted. Together these new officers certainly made for greater savings than the more direct means adopted to check losses from theft: the employment of outside inspectors to look for stolen goods, the strengthening of the law against receiving, and the great enlargement of the nightly armed guard.

One major change which was initially adopted to achieve a reduction in the wages bill, but which gave rise in time to greater learning in the shipwright trade, was the reform of apprenticeship. Although the Portsmouth School of Naval Architecture catered only for a young élite, the establishment of the school in 1811 was official acknowledgment that shipbuilding, with a growing body of theory atached to it, was no longer an art but a science. A decade earlier, the abolition of premiums and the binding of all apprentices to the principal officer in each department had reduced the importance of connection to promotion, especially the link forged by the apprenticeship of a boy to a rising officer. Further provisions for the training of apprentices were necessary later in the nineteenth century to ensure that the ground for the selection of officers was merit alone. Nevertheless the Napoleonic War saw the first steps in that direction.

The fostering of greater professionalism on the part of yard and Navy Office officials was probably the single most important development during this period. In part it was the effect of that search for efficiency through the appointment of principal officers and clerks on merit. It had also to do with the abolition of fees, premiums and other informal payments. Having become completely dependent on government for their one certain source of income, officials had no other loyalties to consider. The clerks, it is true, suffered from their loss of fees and their salary scales had to be altered several times to suit their particular circumstances. But their image as public servants, and on reflection their self-esteem, was undoubtedly improved, reinforced as it was by the wartime successes of the navy and the ultimate victory.

New and heavier managerial demands generated professionalism too. Greater specialization and delegation were necessary. At the level of the Navy Board, the division of the commissioners into committees and their superintendence of areas of office business have been mentioned. However, it was accompanied by a new dependence on outside professionals for the supervision of projects for which the commissioners had neither the time nor the knowledge. As Inspector General, Samuel Bentham supervised the construction of the Portsmouth docks and deepened basin himself, but left the organization of the block mill to Brunel and the copper mill to an experienced manager from private industry. Later the Navy Board followed the latter course. Great confidence was placed in John Rennie, his plans being adopted for both the Sheerness extension and Plymouth Breakwater, and his expertise employed to forward the work. The Board dealt similarly with the difficulties of making detailed administrative changes – by the delegation of particular tasks to John Payne. In the yards, the very task of maintaining in commission 600–700 vessels involved not only an enlargement in the scale of the officers' responsibilities but taxed and extended their professional knowledge. The great number of ships required at sea necessitated periodically that old vessels be doubled or braced or both, while the timber crisis involved adaptation to the use of new or unconventional combinations of materials. Seppings's system of diagonal bracing was the principal spin-off; but the main achievement was that the yard officers coped – through resourcefulness and application in their specialist areas.

By the end of the Napoleonic War the Navy Office and dockyard official was in many ways a different public servant from his predecessor of the 1790s. By 1815 there was a new generation of officials who had only youthful memories of practices in the late eighteenth century. Their attitudes were formed by the experience of the wars. New emphases in promotion, payment and responsibility were undoubtedly connected in their minds, and accordingly sanctified, by naval achievements in the wars. Underlying all these formative influences, moreover, was a new discipline. In the 1790s management in the Navy Office and dockyards had been relatively lax. Out-moded administrative practice, combined with an unprecedented burden of business, made it so. St Vincent recognized it as such, even though he did not fully understand its causes. St Vincent's subsequent attempt to instil discipline – his discharge of the seven yard officers and campaign to rid himself of the sitting Navy Board commissioners – did little to remove the basic causes of laxity. His administration nonetheless rooted itself in the memory of every official; it became part of naval tradition. In this sense it provided an object lesson in the need for self-discipline in the control and management of public affairs. Thereafter self-discipline seems to have been recognized as a primary condition of office. It complemented the demand for probity on the part of all public officials, permitted that growing appreciation of Samuel Bentham's concept of individual responsibility, and was implicit in the tightening grip of the centre upon the subordinate naval departments.

Between 1793 and 1815 there were thus three major developments in the dockyards: tendencies towards greater efficiency in management, economy in the use of resources and professionalism on the part of officials. In general it is clear that, though the standards of officials rose as public expectations rose, changes in administrative procedures making for greater economy and efficiency lagged behind. Even so, by 1815, expectations, standards and the efficiency of procedures seem to have been approaching a balance. There were more changes to come – in 1822, 1832 and later; but the most hectic period of radical, detailed change on a wide front appears to have been over. In spite of the strains, though faults were found with the work of a few individuals, most officials acquitted themselves with credit. The artificers too cannot be left from the reckoning. Even during the crisis with the workforce of 1801, the regularity of ships fitting, refitting and repairing did not seriously falter. By the end of the wars confidence in the yards and the civil administration of the navy had never been higher – complementing and contributing to that confidence in Britain's command at sea. It was faith well placed. By 1815 each dockyard had come to serve 'as a part only of one great machine' – a machine, moreover, of immense power and capacity.

# Abbreviations

*Note* Places of publication are given only for works published outside the United Kingdom. In abbreviating titles of periodicals, the commonly accepted usage of, e.g., *J.* for *Journal*, *Mag.* for *Magazine* etc., has been adopted. Other abbreviations are listed below.

BL      British Library
CR      Commons Reports
DRO     Devon Record Office
*MM*     *Mariner's Mirror*
NMM     National Maritime Museum
NRS     Navy Records Society
PP      Parliamentary Papers
PRO     Public Record Office
*QR*     *Quarterly Review*
SRO     Scottish Record Office

# Notes

## Introduction

1 M. Oppenheim, *A History of the Administration of the Royal Navy and of Merchant Shipping in relation to the Navy, 1509–1660* (1896), 34, 39–40.
2 *Ibid.*, 71.
3 E. F. S. Fisher (retired Deputy Director of Stores at the Admiralty), 'List of Officers who have held local charge of naval stores, 1514–1965' (c. 1965), 2.
4 Oppenheim, *op. cit.*, 36, 69, 365; see also NMM, REC/2 (99a).
5 D. A. Baugh, *British Naval Administration in the Age of Walpole* (Princeton, 1965), 272.
6 Oppenheim, *op. cit.*, 69–70, 209, 296; Baugh, *op. cit.*, 267.
7 Oppenheim, 150, 210, 363–4; Baugh, 268.
8 *Ibid.*, 269–72.
9 J. Ehrman, *The Navy in the War of William III, 1689–1697* (1953), 416–8; Baugh, *op. cit.* 273–5.
10 For the early history of the Ordnance Office see H. C. Tomlinson, *Guns and Government, The Ordnance Office under the later Stuarts* (1979), 1–10.
11 J. M. Collinge, *Navy Board Officials, 1660–1832* ('Officice-holders in Modern Britain', VII, 1978), 22. A sixth Commissioner was officially a member of the Board but rarely attended as he resided at Chatham.
12 For brief histories of these departments see R. J. B. Knight (ed.) *Guide to the Manuscripts in the National Maritime Museum* (2 vols, 1978, 1980), II, 9–11.
13 Collinge, *op. cit.*, 8, 18, 23–4.
14 NMM, ADM. DP/201B, account dated 25 Apr. 1821.
15 NMM, ADM. BP/13, 12 April 1793; ADM. BP/34A, 2 Apr. 1814.
16 Brief histories of the minor yards are given in Fisher, *op. cit.*, 8–46.
17 R. A. Wadia, *The Bombay Dockyard and the Wadia Master Builders* (Bombay, 1955), 192, 194.
18 The establishment of the yards abroad at the end of 1814 were as follows: Gibraltar 5 officers/170 artificers and labourers; Malta 5/378; Jamaica 5/309; Antigua 5/327; Barbados 2/126; Bermuda 4/47; Halifax 5/241; Bombay 4/100; Madras 4/516; Cape of Good Hope 5/92; Rio de Janeiro 11 labourers. NMM, ADM. BP/34B, 14 Dec. 1814.
19 N. Baker, 'Changing attitudes towards government in eighteenth century Britain', in *Statesmen, Scholars and Merchants*, ed. A. Whiteman, J. S. Bromley and P. G. M. Dickson, (1973), 202–19.
20 Collinge, *op. cit.*, 8.
21 For the increase in knowledge about public finance see the comment of George Rose in 1806 in J. E. D. Binney, *British Public Finance and Administration, 1774–92* (1958), 254.

22  NMM, POR/G/5, 15 June 1822.
23  See D. Bonner Smith, 'The abolition of the Navy Board', *MM*, xxxi (1945), 154–9.
24  For the influence of the reports on Sir James Graham in 1832, see his proposals for reform entitled 'Consolidation of the Navy Board and Victualling Board', 6 Dec. 1831: microfilm of Graham MSS in Cambridge University Library.

## 1  Yard operations

1  R. Glover, *Britain at Bay. Defense against Bonaparte, 1803–14* (1973), 19; 'The French fleet, 1807–1814; Britain's problem and Madison's opportunity., *J. Modern History*, xxxix (1967), 233–52; C. J. Reynolds, *Command of the Sea. The History and Strategy of Maritime Empires* (New York, 1974), 310.
2  *The Letters and Papers of Sir Thomas Byam Martin*, ed. Sir R. Vesey Hamilton (NRS., 3 vols., 1898–1902). III, 388.
3  These and later figures relating to the size of British naval forces are based on the appendices in W. James, *Naval History of Great Britain, 1793–1837* (6 vols., 1847).
4  NMM, Middleton MSS, MID/10/3/20–24; notes at NMM made by C. J. Pitcairn-Jones from List Books (PRO, ADM. 8/).
5  J. Fincham, *A History of Marine Architecture* (1851), 116, 156; *Naval Papers respecting Copenhagen, Portugal and the Dardanelles presented to Parliament in 1808* (1809), 5; NMM, MID/1/67/45.
6  For observations on the earlier history of the blockade system see *The Letters and Papers of Charles, Lord Barham, 1758–1813*, ed. Sir J. Knox Laughton (3 vols., NRS, 1907–11), II, 386–7.
7  NMM, MID/10/3/20–24; *QR*, viii (1812), 57.
8  NMM, MID/10/4/3, 'Sir H. Popham on blockade', 28 July 1805.
9  NMM, MID/10/3/7–8.
10  NMM, ADM. BP/15B, 18 Aug. 1795.
11  NMM, Abstract of Progresses (original at PRO). The following pages contain a number of statements based on an examination of the 74s in existence between 1801 and 1805.
12  In November 1812, for example, the Admiralty could simply request to know when the ships of the line building would be launched, the number of ships of the line that would be brought forward from the Ordinary and the total size of the force that would be available for service in each of the following three years: NMM, ADM. BP/32C, 26 Nov. 1812.
13  NMM, ADM. A/2962, 10 March 1803.
14  PRO, ADM. 106/1917, 10 June 1803; ADM. 106/2232, 5 Nov. 1803.
15  C. Derrick, *Memoirs of the Rise and Progress of the Royal Navy* (1806), 249; NMM, MID/1/141/1.
16  NMM, MID/1/107/35.
17  NMM, MID/2/13/6, 'Naval matters, the substance sent to Lord Melville', draft memorandum, 22 June 1804.
18  Fincham, *op. cit.*, 143.
19  NMM, ADM/7/6, see weekly accounts of ships fitting, 29 Jan–26 Mar. 1807; ADM. A/3069, 1 Feb. 1812.
20  *Observations and Instruction for the use of . . . officers of the Royal Navy on all the material points of professional duty* (1804), 12.
21  *Ibid.*, 13.
22  DRO, Sidmouth MSS, c. 1803/ON3; *Letters of Lord Barham*, III, 83.

23  J. S. Tucker, *Memoirs of Admiral the Right Honourable Earl of St Vincent* (2 vols., 1844), II, 80; PRO, ADM. 106/1918, 4, 13, 22 May 1805; ADM. 106/1820, 1, 12, 15, 26 Jan. 1806.
24  Ships of the line had all their shingle ballast removed; those of 74 guns or more had their iron ballast removed too; those that were smaller sometimes retained their iron. NMM, ADM. Q/3320, 4 Aug. 1795.
25  See also C. Pengelly, *The First Bellorophon* (1966), 229.
26  *Observations and Instructions*, 23–7.
27  S. Bentham, *Services Rendered in the Civil Department of the Navy* (1813), 50–2.
28  NMM, ADM. A/2941, 15 June 1801; ADM. B/213, 4 Jan. 1804.
29  James, *op. cit.*, III, 185. For Nelson's complaints about his ships see *The Dispatches and Letters of Vice Admiral Lord Viscount Nelson*, ed. Sir N. H. Nicholas (7 vols., 1844–6), V, 299, 306–7, 319, 334, 354. For comments of other officers see G. Cornwallis-West, *The Life and letters of Admiral Cornwallis* (1927), 398, 409; G. L. Newnham Collingwood, *A Selection from the Correspondence of Vice Admiral Lord Collingwood* (1929), 95, 98.
30  *The Letters of Lord St Vincent, 1801–4*, ed. D. Bonner Smith (NRS, 2 vols., 1921, 1926). III, 320.
31  Sir J. Borlase Warren, *A View of the Naval Force of Great Britain* (1791), 17.
32  R. Pering, *A Brief Inquiry into the Causes of the Premature Decay in our Wooden Bulwarks* (1812); *QR*, VIII (1812), 32.
33  NMM, ADM./Y/4, 30 April 1806; ADM. BP/28, 10 Feb. 1808; ADM. BP/32B, 6 June 1812.
34  *QR*, VIII (1812), 32, 36.
35  NMM, ADM. BP/32B, 6 June 1812.
36  NMM, ADM. BP/33C, 24 July 1813, 9–10.
37  *3rd Report of the Commissioners for Revising and Digesting the Civil Affairs of His Majesty's Navy*, CR 1806 (312), V, 451; NMM, ADM. Y/5, 4 July 1806.
38  NMM, CHA/K/19, 10 Apr. 1811; CHA. B/17, 13 June 1811.
39  NMM, ADM. BP/32C, 20 July 1812.
40  Average excludes arrived-docked periods during Peace of Amiens when ships were sometimes placed in Ordinary as part of the peace reduction before being docked for repair.
41  PRO, ADM. 106/1844, 10, 12, 15 May, 14 June 1801; ADM. 106/2234, 27 July 1804.
42  NMM, ADM. BP/34B, 1 June 1813.
43  *11th Report of the Commissioners appointed to inquire into the state and condition of the Woods, Forests and Land Revenues of the Crown*, CJ, XLVII, 363; Fincham, *op. cit.*, 112–13; *QR*, VIII (1812), 53.
44  PRO, ADM. 106/2513, 1 Nov. 1802; ADM. 106/1937, 21 Apr. 1804; SRO, Melville MSS. GD 51/2/390.
45  PRO, ADM. 106/1937, 26 Nov. 1804.
46  Derrick, *op. cit.*, 208; *Naval Chronicle*, VI (1801), 341; PRO ADM. 106/2231, 26 Jan. 1803; ADM. 106/1845, 16 Feb. 1804.
47  PRO, ADM. 106/1937, 20 May 1805; SRO, GD 51/2/338, 339 (parts 1 and 2).
48  James, *op. cit.*, IV, 183, 366; NMM, BGY/P/3.
49  PRO, ADM. 106/1870, 22 Feb. 1805.
50  NMM, ADM. Y/5, 25 July 1806.
51  *Ibid.*, 12 Dec. 1806.
52  NMM, ADM. BP/32C, 26 Nov. 1812; ADM. BP/33C, 24 July 1813, 13–14.
53  PRO, ADM. 106/2230, 25 Aug. 1802.
54  NMM, ADM. BP/30B, 23 July 1810.
55  NMM, ADM. A/2990, 24 July 1805; PRO, ADM. 106/2237, 17 Aug. 1805.

56  NMM, Abstract of Progresses.
57  *QR*, xi (1814), 215–52.
58  PP 1805 (192), VIII, 277.
59  SRO, GD 51/2/137; PRO, ADM. 106/2234, 22 May 1804.
60  DRO., Sidmouth MSS, c. 1804/ON; Tucker, *op. cit.*, II, 223.
61  PRO, ADM. 106/2229, 24 June 1802.
62  SRO, GD 51/217.
63  PRO, ADM. 106/2236, 27 Mar. 1805; ADM. 106/2237, 17 Aug. 1805.
64  NMM, ADM. BP/34B, 27 June 1814.
65  NMM, ADM. BP/32C, 26 Nov. 1812.
66  R. A. Wadia, *The Bombay Dockyard and the Wadia Master Builders* (Bombay, 1955), 188.
67  NMM, ADM. BP/33C, 24 July 1813.
68  *QR*, viii (1812), 30.
69  PRO, ADM. 106/2234, 25 Apr. 1804.
70  *Ibid.*, 27 July 1804.
71  NMM, ADM. BP/17B, 24 June 1797; ADM. BP/35A, 27 June 1815.
72  James *op. cit.*, III, 375; Fincham, *op. cit.*, 200, 205.
73  *11th Report of the Commissioners on Land Revenue*, 280, 362–3; G. Snodgrass, *A Letter . . . to the Right Honourable Henry Dundas on the Mode of improving the Navy of Great Britain* (1797); Fincham, *op. cit.*, 113–14; PRO, ADM. 106/2230, 7 Oct. 1802; ADM. 106/2234, 16 June 1804; ADM. 106/2516, 1 July 1805.
74  NMM, ADM. 7/5, 9 Sept. 1806. I am grateful to Mr Brian Lavery for referring me to this letter.
75  D. K. Brown, 'The structural improvements to wooden ships instigated by Robert Seppings', *Naval Architect*, no. 3 (1979), 103–4.
76  NMM, CHA. B/9, 19 May 1805, 97–8.
77  NMM, CHA. K/17, 26 Mar. 1810; ADM. A/3047, 30 Apr. 1810.
78  NMM, CHA. K/22, 12 Sept. 1812; CHA. B/18, 9 Oct. 1812.
79  See for example R. F. S. Blake, *Descriptions of Various Plans for the Improvement of Naval Architecture* (1833). The proposed improvements, for which Blake claimed credit, dated back to 1796 and included the round stern adopted by Seppings in 1817.
80  *An Autobiographical Memoir of Sir John Barrow* (1847), 311–12; NMM, YORKE MSS, YOR/16a.
81  NMM, YOR/18.
82  NMM, ADM. B/207, 17 June 1803; ADM. Y/4, 4 Nov. 1806.
83  *QR*, viii (1812), 53.

## 2 The facilities

1  Report of John Rennie, civil engineer, to the Commissioners of Revision on the reference to his consideration of the state of the present royal dockyards, 14 May 1805: BL, Add. MSS 27, 884.
2  *Selections from the Correspondence of Admiral J. Markham during 1801–04 and 1806–07*, ed. Sir Clements Markham (NRS, 1904), 331.
3  PRO, ADM. 106/1918, 18 Sept. 1805.
4  *Correspondence of Admiral Markham*, 331–2.
5  PRO, ADM. 106/2228, 26 Jan. 1802; ADM. 106/1869, 5 July 1804.
6  PRO, ADM. 106/1844, 14 Oct. 1801; ADM. 106/1845, 11 Jan., 10 Mar. 23 Nov. 1803; NMM, ADM. B/206, 3 Dec. 1803.
7  SRO, GD51/2/377.

8  C. Dupin, *Two Excursions to the Ports of England, Scotland and Ireland in 1816, 1817 and 1818* (1819), 101.

9  R. J. B. Knight, 'The royal dockyards in England at the time of the American War of Independence' (PhD. Thesis, University of London, 1972), 323–4.

10  NMM, MID/14/13; 'Observations on the Estimates given into Parliament by the Navy Board', 21 Mar. 1786; J. Coad, 'Historic architecture of H.M. Naval Base Portsmouth, 1700–1850', *MM*, LXVII (1981), 18.

11  *The Letters and Papers of Charles, Lord Barham 1758–1813*, ed. Sir J. Knox Laughton (3 vols., NRS, 1907–11), II, 246–7; NMM, MID/8/4/8.

12  *11th Report of the Commissioners on Land Revenue*, 362.

13  See, for example, Sir J. Borlase Warren, *A View of the Naval Force of Great Britain* (1791); *17th Report of the Select Committee on Finance* (1797), Appendix G5, Reports of Committees of the House of Commons, 1797–1803, XII, 342.

14  *The Private Papers of George, Second Earl Spencer, 1794–1801*, ed. J. S. Corbett, H. W. Richmond (4 vols., NRS, 1913–24), I, 48.

15  J. Fincham, *A History of Marine Architecture* (1851), 126; M. S. Bentham, *The Life of the Brigadier-General Sir Samuel Bentham, K.S.G.* (1862), 99.

16  *Correspondence of Admiral Markham*, 342.

17  *Papers of Earl Spencer*, I, 46.

18  *The Diary and Correspondence of Charles Abbot, Lord Colchester*, ed. C. Abbot (3 vols., 1861), I, 40.

19  *17th Report of the Select Committee on Finance* (1797), Appendix G5, 342.

20  PRO, ADM. 106/2233, 18 Feb. 1804; ADM. 106/2516, 27 May, 7 Sept. 1805; ADM. 1/3527, 29 Jan. 1806.

21  NMM, ADM. BP/18A, 13 March 1798; PRO, ADM. 1/3526, 13 May 1801; ADM. 106/2235, 27 Sept. 1804.

22  PRO, ADM. 1/3526, 19 Apr. 1800; ADM. 106/1844, 25 Nov. 1800; ADM. 106/1853, 12 Mar. 1801.

23  PRO, ADM. 1/3526, 27 Sept. 1801; ADM. 106/1883, 12 Feb. 1805.

24  NMM, ADM. Q/3320, 8 Apr. 1797.

25  NMM, ADM. BP/15A, 13 June 1795; ADM. Q.3320, 29 May 1795. PRO, ADM. 1/3525, 5 Apr, 1798.

26  NMM, ADM. Q/3320, 4 Aug. 1795.

27  NMM, ADM. Q/3320, 21 Dec. 1797, 19 Apr. 1798, 17 Feb. 1800; PRO, ADM. 1/3527, 24 Sept. 1805; Fincham, *op. cit.*, 128–9; Dupin, *op. cit.*, 101.

28  NMM, ADM. Q/3320, 21 Dec. 1797.

29  *Ibid.*, 15 Sept. 1801.

30  NMM, Grey MSS, GRE/8, f.57.

31  PRO, ADM. 106/2232, 30 Dec. 1803.

32  PRO, ADM. 106/2236, 16 Apr. 1805.

33  NMM, ADM. A/3022, 30 Mar. 1808.

34  PRO, ADM. 1/3526, 31 May 1803.

35  PRO, ADM. 1/3527, 13 Nov. 1804.

36  R. Sutherland Horne, *The Blockmills in H.M. Dockyard Portsmouth* (1968), 4. For scale drawings of the machines see A. Rees, *Naval Architecture* (1819–20), 165–83.

37  PRO, ADM. 106/2232, 18 July 1803; K. R. Gilbert, *The Portsmouth Blockmaking Machinery* (Science Museum Monograph, 1965), 5.

38  PRO, ADM. 106/2514, 13 July, 12 Oct., 12 Nov. 1803; ADM. 106/1883, 8 Nov. 1803, 18 Jan. 1804; ADM. 106/2233, 29 Mar. 1803; ADM. 106/2515, 25 Apr 1804; NMM, ADM. B/216, 27 July 1804.

39  NMM, ADM. B/212, 7 Dec. 1803.

40  PRO, ADM. 106/2233, 21 Jan. 1804; ADM. 106/1883, 8 Oct. 1804; ADM. 1/3527, 5 May 1806; NMM, ADM. B/216, 27 July 1804.

41 PRO, ADM. 106/1883, 23 May 1805; Gilbert, *op. cit.*, 1. The number of blocks required to fit a 74-gun ship was 922.
42 NMM, LBK/54, f.167, 7 June 1808.
43 NMM, ADM. BP/25A, 24 Nov. 1804.
44 PRO, ADM. 106/2232, 1 Oct. 1803; ADM. 106/2516, 24 Sept. 1805; NMM, ADM. BP/24B, c. 5 May 1804.
45 PRO, ADM. 106/2232, 2 Aug. 1803.
46 NMM, ADM. BP/24A, 5 May 1804; ADM. B/217, 16 Feb. 1805; PRO, ADM. 106/2236, 5 Jan. 1805.
47 NMM, ADM. BP/29B, 26 Aug. 1809.
48 PRO, ADM. 106/2237, 20 Aug. 1805; NMM, ADM. 7/5, 22 July 1806.
49 PRO, ADM. 1/3526, 19 Apr. 1800; BL Add. MSS 27,884.
50 Ibid., fos.11, 13.
51 Appendix at NMM, CAD/A/10. For Rennie's plan for the yard see NMM, CMP/35.
52 NMM, MID/1/18/3.
53 A. W. Skempton, *A History of the Steam Dredger, 1797–1830* (1975), 2–7; PRO, ADM. 106/2232, 9 July 1803.
54 PRO, ADM. 106/1883, 11 May 1805.
55 PRO, ADM. 106/2275, 28 Sept. 1805; NMM, ADM. BP/29B, 16 Oct. 1809; ADM., BP/30B, 27 Oct. 1810; ADM., BP/33C, 24 July 1813.
56 NMM, MID/1/67/45; S. Smiles, *Lives of the Engineers* (3 vols., 1862), II, 244.
57 NMM, ADM. BP/35B, 25 July 1815.
58 *8th Report from the Select Committee on Finance* (1818), CR 1818 (97), III, 155–6.
59 PRO, ADM. 106/2228, 30 Oct. 1801; PP 1805 (193), VIII, 487.
60 *8th Report from the Select Committee on Finance* (1818), 154–5.
61 *6th Report from the Select Committee on Finance* (1817), CR 1817 (410), IV, 223.
62 *8th Report from the Select Committee on Finance* (1818), 153–4; PP 1826 (164), XX, 505–11.
63 PRO, ADM. 106/2231, 16 Feb. 1803; NMM, ADM. BP/30B, 20 Dec. 1810; BL Add. MSS 27,884, f. 3.
64 NMM, ADM. BP/35B, 13 July 1815.
65 L. H. Merrett, 'A most important undertaking: the building of the Plymouth Breakwater', *Transport History*, v (1977), 153–64.
66 PP 1812 (44, 65) X, 177–85.
67 NMM, ADM. BP/31A, 21 Jan. 1811; ADM. BP/31B, 26 Oct. 1811.
68 The official completion date was not until 1841, by which time $3\frac{1}{2}$ million tons of stone had been used. The pier extending from Andurn Point was never built. See Merrett, *op. cit.*; also Smiles, *op. cit.*, II, 252–63.
69 Dupin, *op. cit.*, 5, 15, 19.
70 NMM, ADM. BP/33C, 24 July 1813.
71 PRO, ADM. 106/2539, 28 Apr. 1806.
72 Dupin, *op. cit.*, 14, 19; W. Wildash, *The History and Antiquities of Rochester and its Environs* (1817), 328–9.
73 Dupin, *op. cit.*, 12.
74 NMM, ADM. BP/31B, 4 Dec. 1811.
75 NMM, ADM. BP/35B, 7 July 1815.
76 NMM, POR. D/27, 11 May 1797.
77 NMM, ADM. BP/32C, 14 Dec. 1812.

## 3 The materials

1 NMM, MID/6/4/19.
2 NMM, CAD/A/10, Appendices to unprinted 15th Report of the Commissioners of Naval Revision, Appendix 152.
3 *Ibid.*, Appendix 147.
4 *Ibid.*, Appendix 152.
5 NMM, ADM. BP/13, 18 Jan. 1793.
6 R. G. Albion, *Forests and Sea Power, The Timber Problem and the Royal Navy 1652–1862* (Cambridge, Mass., 1926), 337; A. W. Crosby, *America, Russia, Hemp and Napoleon: American Trade with Russia and the Baltic, 1783–1812* (Ohio, 1965), 110, 144, 195, 230.
7 *The Saumarez Papers*, Selections from the Baltic Correspondence of Vice Admiral Sir James Saumarez, 1808–1812, ed. A. N. Ryan (NRS, 1968), XX–XXI; Crosby, *op. cit.*, 117.
8 *QR*, VIII (1812), 45–51.
9 Albion, *op. cit.*, 355–7.
10 NMM, ADM. BP/27, 15 Dec. 1807; ADM. BP/28, 2 Jan., 31 May 1808; ADM. BP/29B, 15 Sept., 5, 16 Oct., 13 Nov. 1809.
11 NMM, ADM. BP/28, n.d.; ADM. BP/32B, 12 May 1812.
12 PRO, ADM. 106/2234, 6 Apr. 1804.
13 NMM, ADM. B/211, 20 Oct. 1803; PRO., ADM. 106/2234, 6 Apr, 1804.
14 PRO, ADM. 49/36; see also B. Pool, *Navy Board Contracts 1660–1832* (1966), 120–6.
15 *3rd Report of the Commissioners appointed to inquire into Irregularities, Frauds and Abuses practised in the Naval Departments and in the business of the Prize Agency*, CR 1802–2 (109), IV, 175–187; *6th Report of the Commissioners of Naval Enquiry*, CR 1803–4 (83), III, 96–108.
16 PRO, ADM. 106/2236, 31 Jan. 1805; ADM. 106/1937, 11 June 1805; See also N. Baker, *Government and Contractors: The Treasury and War Supplies, 1775–1783* (1971), 138–9, 146.
17 J. E. D. Binney, *British Public Finance and Administration, 1774–92* (1958), 141–2.
18 *Ibid.*, 143.
19 PRO, ADM. 7/567, n.d.; ADM. 49/39, n.d.; DRO, Sidmouth MSS c. 1801/ON. 23.
20 PRO, ADM. 106/2230, 16 Dec. 1802; P. Crimmin, 'Admiralty administration, 1783–1806' (M.Phil. thesis, University of London, 1968), 183–5.
21 Albion, *op. cit.*, 316.
22 PRO, ADM. 106/2231, 10 Feb. 1803; ADM. 106/2234, 2 Apr. 1804; ADM. 106/2515, 8, 26 June 1804; ADM. 106/2236, 2 Mar. 1805; ADM. 106/2516, 6 Mar. 1805.
23 Binney, *op. cit.*, 77–8, 82–3.
24 NMM, ADM. BP/27, 23 Feb., 7 Mar. 11807; ADM. BP/32C, 31 Aug. 1812.
25 For comments on the timber shortage in the 1780s see B. Slade to C. Middleton, 24 Mar. 1786, NMM, MID/1/169.
26 PRO, ADM. 106/1883, 8 May 1804.
27 NMM, ADM. BP/26, 16 Apr. 1806.
28 PRO, ADM. 106/2231, 2, 22 Feb. 1803; ADM. 106/2514, 19 Apr, 1803.
29 PRO, ADM. 106/2230, 8 Feb. 1803.
30 PRO, ADM. 106/2233, 24 Mar. 1804; NMM, ADM. A/2974, 27 Mar. 1804; PP 1805 (205), VIII, 613–14.
31 *Ibid.*, PRO, ADM. 106/2233, 29 Mar. 1804; NMM, ADM. BP/24A, 17 Apr. 1804.

32  J. Fincham, *A History of Marine Architecture* (1851), 217–19; Albion, *op. cit.*, 325–33, 361–9; '14th Report of the Commissioners of Naval Revision' (unprinted copy at PRO, ADM. 106/3110); *1st Report from the Select Committee on the Woods, Forests and Land Revenues of the Crown*, CR 1849 (513), XX, 488–9.
33  PRO, ADM. 106/2516, 22 Feb., 11 May, 21, 22 Nov., 27 Dec. 1805; ADM. 106/1937, 21 May 1805.
34  PRO, ADM. 106/2514, 18 Nov. 1803.
35  *Ibid.*
36  NMM, MID/1/43/1.
37  *9th Report of the Commissioners of Naval Enquiry*, CR 1805 (1), II, 6.
38  PRO, ADM. 106/2515, 13 March 1804.
39  NMM, ADM. BP/32B, 27 June 1812.
40  NMM, ADM. BP/35B, 19 July 1815.
41  C. Derrick, *Memoirs of the Rise and Progress of the Royal Navy* (1806), 216.
42  PRO, ADM. 1/5126, 14 Mar. 1801.
43  PP 1806 (2), XI, 665.
44  *6th Report of the Commissioners of Naval Enquiry*, Appendix 116, p. 402.
45  PP 1805 (193), VIII, 506.
46  *Further proceedings of the Lords Commissioners of the Admiralty respecting the matters stated in the Reports of the Committee of Finance, as far as they relate to the Naval Departments*, Reports of Committees of the House of Commons 1797–1803, XIII, 835.
47  PRO, ADM. 106/2513, 15 Oct. 1801.
48  PRO, ADM. 106/1820, 27 Apr. 1804; ADM. 106/1883, 8 May 1804.
49  PRO, ADM. 106/2232, 21 Oct. 1803.
50  NMM, ADM. BP/29B, 14 Oct. 1809.
51  For an account of stores set apart in berths at Chatham, Portsmouth and Plymouth see NMM, ADM. BP/15B, 22 Oct. 1795.
52  PRO, ADM. 1/3525, 5 Apr. 1798.
53  PRO, ADM. 106/2237, 10 July 1805.
54  *31st Report from the Select Committee on Finance* (1798), Appendix D5b Reports of Committees of the House of Commons 1797–1803, XIII, 494–5.
55  PRO, ADM. 106/1810, 27 May 1805.
56  PRO, ADM. 106/1937, 25 Feb., 1 Mar., 9 May, 15 Oct. 1804; NMM, ADM. BP/33A, 25, 27 Mar, 1813.
57  PRO, ADM, 106/2513, 8, 28 Dec. 1802.
58  PRO, ADM. 106/1883, 2 Nov. 1805.
59  PRO, ADM. 106/2516, 23 Jan. 1805.
60  PRO, ADM. 106/1845, 14 Sept. 1803.
61  PRO, ADM. 106/2514, 31 Dec. 1804.
62  For embezzlement in the late eighteenth century see R. J. B. Knight, 'Pilfering and theft from the dockyards at the time of the American War of Independece', *MM*, LXI (1975), 215–25.
63  R. Vesey Hamilton, *Naval Administration* (1896), 14.
64  Cobbett's *Parliamentary History*, XXXVI, 1143.
65  P. Colquhoun, *A Treatise on the Police of the Metropolis* (1796), 70.
66  PRO, ADM. 1/5126, 14 Mar. 1801.
67  PRO, ADM. 106/1869, 16, 18 Dec. 1803.
68  PRO, ADM. 106/1809, 7 June 1801; *A Collection of Statutes relating to the Admiralty, Navy etc.* (1810), 602–16.
69  *6th Report of the Commissioners of Naval Enquiry*, Appendix 116, 402.
70  PRO, ADM. 106/1807, 31 Jan. 1803.
71  PRO, ADM. 106/1869, 16 Dec. 1803, 6 Oct. 1805.

72 PRO, ADM. 106/2227, 8 Apr, 1801.
73 *Ibid.*, 26 May, 11 July 1801; ADM. 106/2230, 17 Nov. 1802; ADM. 106/2231, 31 Jan. 1803; ADM. 106/2515, 22 Dec. 1804.
74 NMM, ADM. BP/33A, 25 Mar. 1813.

## 4 The workforce

1 See Portsmouth register of entries and discharges, 1793–1801, NMM, POR/J/4.
2 *11th Report of the Commissioners appointed to inquire into the . . . Land Revenues of the Crown*, 364.
3 Cobbett's *Parliamentary Debates*, I, 891; PP 1805 (193), VIII, 485.
4 PRO, ADM. 106/2237, 17 Aug. 1805.
5 NMM, ADM. BP/32A, 9 Mar. 1812.
6 NNM, ADM. BP/15B, 4 Sept. 1795.
7 *Memoir of the Life of William Marsden* (1838), 102–3.
8 PP 1806 (2), XI, 665.
9 PRO, ADM. 7/344, 6 Oct. 1802; ADM. 106/2514, 2 Mar. 1803; *6th Report of the Commissioners of Naval Enquiry*, Appendix 4, 196.
10 PP 1805 (193), VIII, 545.
11 NMM, ADM. B/201, 7 Apr. 1801.
12 PP 1805 (193), VIII, 509.
13 PRO, ADM. 1/5198, 20 Jan. 1804.
14 *6th Report of the Commissioners of Naval Enquiry*, 23–4.
15 J. M. Haas, 'The introduction of Taskwork into the royal dockyards, 1775', *J. British Studies*, VIII (1969), 44–68.
16 *6th Report of the Commissioners of Naval Enquiry*, 39–40, 46; PRO, ADM. 106/1883, 5 Mar, 1804; ADM. 106/2236, 27 Mar, 1805; ADM. 106/2237, 17 Aug. 1805.
17 NMM, ADM. BP/32A, 9 Mar. 1812.
18 I. J. Prothero, *Artisans and Politics in Early Nineteenth-Century London, John Gast and his Times* (1979), 41; *8th Report of the Commissioners of Naval Revision* (not printed as a parliamentary report; dockyard copy at NMM), 11.
19 PRO, ADM. 106/1869, 3 May 1805; ADM. 106/2513, 29 June 1804; *Naval Chronicle*, XIV (1805), 284, 341.
20 PRO, ADM. 106/1810, 14 Apr. 29 Nov. 1805; ADM. 106/2516, 27 Aug. 1805; ADM. 106/2237, 19 Sept. 1805.
21 NMM, ADM. BP/32B, 27 June 1812.
22 *31st Report of the Select Committee on Finance* (1798), Appendix D.10, p. 498; PRO, ADM. 106/2227, 17 Jan. 1801; ADM. 106/2513, 29 June 1801.
23 *6th Report of the Commissioners of Naval Enquiry*, Appendix 120, 408–11; *3rd Report of the Commissioners of Naval Revision*, 424; PRO, ADM. 106/2513, 29 June 1801.
24 PRO, ADM. 106/2513, 1 Sept. 1802; ADM. 106/2231, 15 Mar, 1803; ADM. 106/2232, 6 Oct. 1803; ADM. 106/2234, 19 June 1804; ADM. 106/2237, 10 Aug. 1805; NMM, ADM. B/208, 21 Mar. 1803.
25 NMM, ADM. BP/33C, 24 July, 20 Aug. 1813; ADM. BP/34B, 31 May 1814.
26 PRO, ADM. 106/2236, 5, 15 Mar. 1805; NMM, ADM. BP/24B, 31 Dec. 1814.
27 NMM, ADM. BP/29B, 18 Dec. 1809.
28 PRO, ADM. 106/2231, 23 Mar. 1803; ADM. 106/1809, 16 June 1803; ADM. 106/2232, 25 Oct., 7 Dec. 1803; ADM. 106/2235, 6 Nov. 1804; ADM. 106/1938, 12 Mar. 1806.
29 PRO, ADM. 106/2229, 5 May 1802.

30  PRO, ADM. 106/2231, 26 Jan., 22, 25, 29 Mar. 1803; ADM. 106/2514, 16 Mar., 10 May, 16 Nov., 24 Dec. 1803; ADM. 106/2234, 6, 16, 24 July 1804; ADM. 106/2516, 28 Jan., 27 Mar., 20 May, 1 Aug., 20 Dec. 1805; ADM. 106/1884, 7 Jan. 1806.

31  PRO, ADM. 106/2513, 10 Aug. 1802.

32  *Ibid.*, 5 Nov. 1802.

33  PRO, ADM. 106/2230, 6 Dec. 1802.

34  PP 1805 (193), VIII, 463.

35  PRO, ADM. 1/3526, 22 Nov. 1802.

36  PRO, ADM. 106/2513, 29 June 1801, 7 Dec. 1802.

37  NMM, ADM. B/208, 9, 15 Mar. 1803.

38  NMM, ADM. A/2945, account of 19 Dec. 1814 filed at 30 Oct. 1801; ADM. BP/24A, 27 Feb. 1804.

39  PRO, ADM. 106/2234, 24 April 1804; ADM. 106/2515, 27 Apr. 1804; ADM. 106/2237, 13 Dec. 1804; *3rd Report of the Commissioners of Naval Revision*, 424.

40  For the amounts paid to officers see NMM, ADM. B/207, 12 June 1803.

41  *3rd Report of the Commissioners of Naval Revision*, 423–5.

42  PRO, ADM. 1/3527, paper 3, 84–9; *Ibid.*, 6 June 1808; M. S. Bentham, *The Life of the Brigadier-General Sir Samuel Bentham, K.S.G.* (1862), 8.

43  NMM, ADM. B/214, 7 April 1804; PRO, ADM. 106/1937, 20, 21 Apr, 1804; ADM. 106/2236, 25 Feb. 1805.

44  *3rd Report of the Commissioners of Naval Revision*, 425–34; NMM, ADM. BP/30A, 12 Mar. 1810.

45  NMM, ADM. BP/33C, 31 Dec. 1813.

46  NMM, ADM. BP/30B, 16 Nov. 1810.

47  S. Pollard, 'Laissez-faire and shipbuilding', *Economic History R.*, 2nd ser., V (1953), 98–115.

48  NMM, ADM. BP/21B, 2 Jan. 1800; PRO, ADM. 106/2230, 1 Oct. 1802; *6th Report of the Commissioners of Naval Enquiry*, 16, 498–9.

49  *Ibid.*, 342.

50  NMM, WYN/105, 8 Oct. 1803.

51  *The Letters and Papers of Charles, Lord Barham, 1758–1813*, ed. Sir J. Knox Laughton (3 vols., NRS, 1907–11), III, 72; SRO, GD 51/2/271/16.

52  NMM, MID. 13/1/63.

53  NMM, ADM. BP/28, 7 Sept. 1808; ADM. BP/29B, 10 Oct. 1809; ADM. BP/30A, 12 March 1810; J. M. Haas, 'Methods of wage payment in the royal dockyards, 1775–1865', *Maritime History*, v (1977), 99–115.

54  NMM, ADM. BP/21B, 20 Oct. 1800.

55  PRO, ADM. 106/1810, 2 May 1805; ADM. 106/2516, 4 May 1805.

56  *6th Report of the Commissioners of Naval Enquiry*, 19.

57  PRO, ADM. 106/1937, 28 July 1804.

58  NMM, ADM. BP/31B, 1 Oct, 1811; ADM. BP/33A, 25 Mar. 1813; *6th Report from the Select Committee on Finance* (1817), 234, 236.

59  *6th Report of the Commissioners of Naval Enquiry*, 28–35.

60  PRO, ADM. 106/2515, 8 Mar, 1804; ADM. 106/1937, 5 Mar., 11 May 1804; NMM, ADM. B/214, 9, 13, 21 Apr. 1804.

61  NMM, ADM. BP/30B, 19 Dec. 1810; ADM. BP/33A, 25 Mar. 1813; PRO, ADM. 106/2536, pp. 28, 30, 8 Dec. 1810, 17 Dec. 1813.

62  NMM, ADM. BP/33A, 25 Mar. 1813.

63  NMM, ADM. BP/31B, 12 Aug. 1811.

64  PRO, ADM. 106/1936, 3 Nov. 1813.

65  PRO, ADM. 106/2232, 7 Dec. 1803.

66  NMM, ADM. B/214, 7 Apr. 1804.

67 PRO, ADM. 106/1937, 20 Apr. 1804.
68 PRO, ADM. 106/2233, 5, 31 Mar. 1804.
69 *3rd Report of the Commissioners of Naval Revision*, 448–9; NMM, ADM. BP/30A, 12 Mar. 1810; ADM. BP/30B, 21 Dec. 1810.
70 PRO. ADM. 106/1937, 26 Nov. 1804.
71 NMM, MID. 8/6/13.
72 DRO, Sidmouth MSS c. 1797, ON. 3.
73 NMM, ADM. BP/15B, 25 Sept. 1795.
74 NMM, ADM. BP/17A, 11 Jan. 1797; PRO., ADM. 1/5126, 20 Jan. 1800.
75 See W. Shrubsole, *A Plea in Favour of the Shipwrights Belonging to Royal Dockyards* (1770).
76 NMM, ADM. BP/15A, 6 Apr. 1795; ADM. BP/16A, 9 Jan. 1796; ADM. BP/17A, 17 Jan. 1797; PRO. ADM. 106/2513, 20 May 1801; ADM. 106/2236, 16 Apr. 1805.
77 For John Gast's experience of the process by which the artificers chose their leaders see Prothero, *op. cit.*, 17.
78 For a more detailed account of events see R. A. Morriss, 'Labour relations in the royal dockyards, 1801–1805', *MM*, LXII (1976), 337–46.
79 PRO, HO. 42/61, f. 391.
80 *Ibid.*, f. 593; NMM, ADM. A/2939, 4 Apr. 1801.
81 PRO, ADM. 106/1844, 13 Apr. 1801.
82 *The Letters of Lord St Vincent, 1801–4*, ed. D. Bonner Smith (NRS, 2 vols, 1921, 1926), II, 168; PRO, ADM. 106/3244, 11 May 1801.
83 PRO, HO. 28/27, 13 Apr. 1801; NMM, ADM. BP/21A, 27 May 1801.
84 PRO, HO. 42/61, f. 614; ADM. 106/2227, 17 June 1801.
85 NMM. ADM. BP/21A, 27 May 1801; PRO, HO. 42/61, f. 593; HO. 42/62, f. 324.
86 PRO, ADM. 106/3244, 26 Apr., 18 May 1801.
87 PRO, ADM. 7/305, 14 Apr. 1801.
88 PRO, ADM. 106/3244, 13 May 1801.
89 Morriss, 'Labour relations', 343.
90 *3rd Report of the Commissioners of Naval Revision*, 456.

## 5 The officials

1 *The Letters and Papers of Charles, Lord Barham, 1758–1813*, ed. Sir J. Knox Laughton (3 vols., NRS, 1907–11), II, 177.
2 PRO, ADM. 106/2513, 28 Aug., 1 Sept. 1801; ADM. 106/2514, 12 Mar. 1803.
3 NMM, ADM. BP/13, 18 Apr, 1793; J. M. Collinge, *Navy Board Officials, 1660–1832* (Office-holders in Modern Britain', VII, 1978), 10.
4 *4th Report of the Commissioners of Naval Revision*, CR 1809 (120), VI, 45; see also pp. 80–3 in volume containing appendices at NMM.
5 *5th Report of the Commissioners appointed to inquire into Fees, Gratuities, Perquisites and Emoluments which are, or have been lately, received in the several Public Offices*, 1786, Appendices 113, 115, C.R. 1806 (309), vii, 260–75; *6th Report of the Commissioners on Fees*, Appendices 32, 66, 109, 133, 186, 235, 237, CR 1806 (309), VIII, 340, 360, 390, 406, 442, 476, 482–505; *17th Report of the Select Committee on Finance* (1797), Appendix D3, 336; PRO, ADM. 49/36; R. J. B. Knight, 'The royal dockyards in England at the time of the American War of Independence' (Ph.D. thesis, University of London, 1972), 234.
6 *Letters of Lord Barham*, II, 245–6; *17th Report of the Select Committee on Finance* (1797), Appendix B1, 331–3; NMM, ADM. B/204, 18 Mar. 1802.

7 NMM, ADM. BP/20, 2 June 1800.
8 NMM, ADM. BP/27, 6 Mar, 1807.
9 SRO, GD51/2/206.
10 NMM, ADM. BP/28, 28 Mar. 1808.
11 NMM, ADM. BP/23B, 15 July 1803.
12 PRO, ADM. 1/5126, 26 Feb. 1801.
13 PRO, ADM. 1/5127, June 1805.
14 PRO, ADM. 106/2234, 18 July 1804.
15 PRO, ADM. 1/5126, 28 Feb. 1801; NMM, ADM. BP/22B, 13, 19 Nov. 1802.
16 NMM, ADM. BP/20B, 18 July 1800.
17 NMM, ADM. BP/21A, 26 Mar, 1801; ADM. BP/26, 14 Nov. 1806.
18 PRO, ADM. 106/1869, 18 Aug. 1803.
19 PRO, ADM. 1/5126, Mar, 1801; ADM. 1/5127, 13 May 1808.
20 PRO, ADM. 106/2237, 5 Oct, 1805.
21 Collinge, op. cit., 14.
22 NMM, ADM. BP/31B, 15 Nov. 1811.
23 NMM, ADM. BP/35B, 5 July 1815.
24 Collinge, op. cit., 15.
25 PRO, ADM. 106/2229, 21 May, 4, 5 June 1802.
26 NMM, ADM. BP/33A, 20 Feb. 1813.
27 NMM, ADM. BP/35B, 26 Sept. 1815.
28 NMM, MID/13/5/1; ADM. BP/32B, 20 May 1812.
29 Collinge, op. cit., 8.
30 Ibid., 14.
31 PRO, ADM. 106/1918, 23 Oct. 1805.
32 NMM, ADM. A/2943, 31 Aug. 1801; ADM. BP/27, 22 Aug. 1807; PRO, ADM. 1/3527, 18 May 1805.
33 PRO, ADM. 106/1917, 11 June 1803.
34 31st Report of the Select Committee on Finance (1797), Appendix D. 11, p. 499.
35 NMM, ADM. BP/17A, 5 May 1797; PRO, ADM. 106/2227, 16 July 1801. For the shipwrights' side to this affair see I. J. Prothero, Artisans and Politics in Early Nineteenth Century London, John Gast and his Times (1979), 17.
36 PRO, ADM. 42/247; 6th Report of the Commissioners of Naval Enquiry, 122.
37 Ibid., 31.
38 Ibid., 121–4.
39 PRO, ADM. 106/2534, 706–7.
40 PRO, ADM. 106/2235, 15 Sept. 1804; ADM. 42/251.
41 PRO, ADM. 106/1845, 24 Feb. 1805.
42 PRO, ADM. 106/2236, 29 Apr. 1805.
43 PRO, ADM. 106/1937, 26 Oct. 1805.
44 NMM, ADM. BP/28, 28 Mar. 1808.
45 NMM, ADM. A/2945, account of 14 Dec. 1814 filed at 30 Oct. 1801.
46 NMM, ADM. B/207, 12 Jan. 1803.
47 PP, 1805 (193), VIII, 463; PRO, ADM. 106/1883, 29 Apr. 1803.
48 6th Report of the Commissioners of Naval Enquiry, Appendix 4, 196; PRO, ADM. 106/2229, 15 May 1802.
49 PP, 1805 (193), VIII, 463.
50 NMM, ADM. BP/33C, 20 Sept. 1813.
51 NMM, Lists of yard officers. Two officers, Edward Tippett in 1800 and Henry Peake in 1803, in fact moved from Portsmouth to Deptford. This suggests that Deptford still had a slightly higher status than the two larger yards.
52 NMM, ADM. BP/35C, 23 Nov. 1815.
53 Letters of Lord Barham, III, 295.

54 *The Letters of Lord St Vincent, 1801–4*, ed. D. Bonner Smith (NRS, 2 vols., 1921, 1926), I, 302, 304; II, 207.
55 *Letters of Lord Barham*, III, 34.
56 *Ibid.*, II, 219.
57 *Letters of Lord St Vincent*, II, 167, 176–7.
58 NMM, MID/8/6–11.
59 R. J. B. Knight, 'Sandwich, Middleton and dockyard appointments', *MM*, LVII (1971), 175–92.
60 NMM, ADM. BP/31B, 18 Oct. 1811.
61 NMM, ADM. BP/29B, 27 Oct. 1809.
62 NMM, ADM. BP/28, 28Mar. 1808.
63 NMM, ADM. BP/19B, 21 Oct. 1799; PRO, ADM. 106/2227, 26 May 1801.
64 *Further Proceedings of the Admiralty* on the reports of the 1797 Select Committee on Finance, 826.
65 PRO., ADM. 106/2664, 17 July 1801; NMM, ADM. BP/25A, 17, 27 Apr. 1805; ADM. BP/35A, 1 Feb. 1815.
66 NMM, ADM. BP/28, 28 Mar. 1808.
67 PRO, ADM. 106/2227, 1, 11, 13 July 1801.
68 NMM, ADM. BP/22B, 29 Nov. 1802; *Letters of Lord St Vincent*, II, 167.
69 SRO, GD.51/2/940.
70 PRO, ADM. 106/2227, 2 June 1801.
71 NMM, MID/2/1/1.
72 *The Letters and Papers of Sir Thomas Byam Martin*, ed. Sir R. Vesey Hamilton (NRS, 3 vols., 1898–1902), III, 274.
73 *Memoir of the Life of William Marsden* (1838), 103–4.
74 PP, 1807 (119), IV, 113
75 NMM, ADM. BP/30B, 14 Sept. 1810.
76 NMM, ADM. BP/27, 6 Mar. 1807; *6th Report from the Select Committee on Finance* (1817), 228,
77 NMM, ADM. BP/30B, 7 Aug. 1810.
78 PRO, ADM. 106/1869, 30 Apr. 1805; ADM. 106/1810, 12 May 1805; ADM. 106/2237, 10 June 1805.
79 *6th Report from the Select Committee on Finance* (1817), 228.
80 *Letters of Lord Barham*, II, 330.
81 NMM, MID/8/6–11.
82 *6th Report of the Commissioners of Naval Enquiry*, Appendix 12, p. 261.
83 *Selections from the Correspondence of Admiral J. Markham during 1801–4 and 1806–7*, ed. Sir Clements Markham (NRS, 1904), 26; B. Pool, *Navy Board Contracts 1660–1832* (1966), 118.
84 PP, 1805 (203), VIII, 242.

## 6 Yard management

1 *Economy of H.M. Navy Office* (1717), 20–1.
2 C. Derrick, *Memoirs of the Rise and Progress of the Royal Navy* (1806), 83, 145, 204.
3 W. James, *Naval History of Great Britain, 1793–1837* (6 vols., 1847), I, 445; III, 504; IV, 480; VI, 398.
4 PRO, ADM. 1/5126, 14 Mar. 1801.
5 *Ibid.*, 10 Mar. 1801.

6 PRO, ADM. 1/3527, 'Observations on the abolishing altogether the office of Inspector General of Naval Works considered as an appendage to the Admiralty office', 13.

7 *The Letters and Papers of Charles, Lord Barham 1758–1813*, ed. Sir J. Knox Laughton (3 vols., NRS 1907–11), II, 333–4.

8 NMM, POR. D/27, 28 Sept, 1796, 26 Sept. 1797.

9 *6th Report of the Commissioners of Naval Enquiry*, Appendix 114, pp. 397–400; PRO, ADM. 106/2229, 17 Feb. 1802.

10 *Letters of Lord Barham*, I, 248–9.

11 *6th Report of the Commissioners of Naval Enquiry*, Appendix 115, p. 400; PRO, ADM. 106/2229, 17 Feb. 1802.

12 *6th Report of the Commissioners of Naval Enquiry*, Appendix 114, 117, pp. 397, 403.

13 PRO, ADM. 106/2230, 17 July 1802.

14 SRO, GD.51/2/940.

15 *1st Report of the Commissioners for Revising and Digesting the Civil Affairs of His Majesty's Navy*, CR 1806 (8), V, 95.

16 PRO, ADM. 106/1869, 30 Apr. 1805.

17 PRO, ADM. 106/2227, 30 June 1801.

18 PRO, ADM. 106/1844, 22 Aug. 1801.

19 *31st Report from the Select Committee on Finance* (1798), Appendix D.3, pp. 494.

20 PRO, ADM. 106/1845, 11 Dec. 1805.

21 NMM, ADM. BP/30A, 20 Feb. 1810.

22 NMM, ADM. BP/18A, July 1799.

23 *6th Report of the Commissioners of Naval Enquiry*, p. 3.

24 PRO, HO. 42/61, fos. 735, 741, 28, 30 Apr. 1801.

25 NMM, ADM. BP/21B, 26 Oct. 1800.

26 PRO, ADM. 106/1844, 10, 12, 16 May 1801; ADM. 106/2227, 19 May 1801.

27 PRO, ADM. 106/1845, 10 Jan. 1803.

28 *The Letters of Lord St Vincent, 1801–4*, ed. D. Bonner Smith (NRS, 2 vols., 1921, 1926), II, 173.

29 PP, 1805(193), VIII, 463.

30 PRO, ADM. 106/2515, 28 Feb. 1804.

31 PRO, ADM. 106/1869, 24 Apr. 26 July 1805.

32 *1st Report of the Commissioners of Naval Revision*, 17–18.

33 NMM, POR. G/5, 15 June 1822. I am grateful to Mr R. Stewart for this reference.

34 Collinge, *Navy Board Officials, 1660–1832*; ('Office-holders in Modern Britain', VII, 1978), 19; *Navy List*.

35 Collinge, *op. cit.*, 19.

36 *Letters of Lord Barham*, III, 33, 36–7.

37 PRO, ADM. 106/2659, 1 July 1796, 48 Letters; 14 July, 63 letters, 16 July, 46 letters.

38 NMM, MID/2/1/1, encl., 'Loose observations and hints on the proposed reformation of the Navy Board'.

39 *Letters of Lord Barham*, II, 226.

40 *6th Report of the Commissioners of Naval Enquiry*, 96–108, 124.

41 PRO, ADM. 106/2664, 3, 14, 17, 24, 28 July 1801; ADM. 106/2666, 1, 12, 15, 22, 26 July 1803.

42 NMM, ADM. BP/19A, 13 Feb. 1799.

43 PRO, ADM. 106/2230, 1 Oct. 1802.

44 *17th Report from the Select Committee on Finance* (1797), Appendix D.3, pp. 336–7; PRO ADM. 106/2237, 4 Dec. 1805; NMM ADM. BP/35B, 5 July 1815; ADM. DP/201B, account of 25 Apr. 1821.

45 NMM, ADM. BP/27, 6 Mar. 1807.
46 C. Dupin, *Two Excursions to the Ports of England, Scotland and Ireland in 1816, 1817 and 1818* (1819), 9.
47 PRO, ADM. 1/3527, 'Observations' on abolishing the office of the IGNW, 42–6.
48 *Letters of Lord Barham*, II, 188, 225–6, 299.
49 PRO, ADM. 106/2513 and 2514.
50 *2nd Report of the Commissioners of Naval Revision*, CR 1806(92), V, 248.
51 PRO, ADM. 106/2534.
52 *2nd Report of the Commissioners of Naval Revision*, p. 4.
53 NMM, MID/2/1/1.
54 NMM, MID/2/24/4.
55 NMM, MID/2/39/1, 'Observations on the Estimates given into Parliament by the Navy Board, 21 March 1786'.
56 *Letters of Lord St Vincent*, II, 203.
57 PRO, ADM. 106/2236, 5 Apr. 1805.
58 *Letters of Lord St Vincent*, II, 39.

## 7 Politics and reformers

1 B. Pool, *Navy Board Contracts 1660–1832* (1966), 65.
2 Quoted in J. Ehrman, *The Younger Pitt: The Years of Acclaim* (1969), 320.
3 PRO, ADM. 106/2231, 14 Apr. 1803; *17th Report of the Select Committee on Finance* 1797, Appendix B1, 331.
4 J. M. Haas, 'The royal dockyards: the earliest visitations and reforms, 1749–1778', *Historical J.*, XIII (1970), 191–215.
5 D. A. Baugh, *British Naval Administration in the Age of Walpole* (Princeton, 1965), 504.
6 *The Letters and Paper of Charles, Lord Barham, 1758–1813*, ed. Sir John Knox Laughton (3 vols., NRS, 1907–11), II, 30, 218, 350.
7 *31st Report of the Select Committee on Finance* (1798), 486.
8 Both Samuel and Jeremy Bentham co-operated closely with Charles Abbot: BL Add. MSS 33,543, fos. 111, 325, 334, 427, 433, 435, 550. See also L. J. Hume, 'Bentham's Panopticon: an administrative history', *Historical Studies* (of Australia and New Zealand), XV (1973), 703–21.
9 BL Add. MSS 33,543, f. 334; *The Diary and Correspondence of Charles Abbot, Lord Colchester*, ed. C. Abbot (3 vols., 1861), I, 221.
10 For the politics of St Vincent's administration see J. R. Breihan, 'The Addington party and the navy in British politics 1801–1806', in *New Aspects of Naval History*, ed. C. L. Symonds (Annapolis, 1981), 163–89.
11 *Letters of Lord St Vincent 1801–4*, ed. D. Bonner Smith (NRS, 2 vols., 1921, 1926), I, 378–80; DRO, Sidmouth MSS, 1797/ON3; G. J. Marcus, *A Naval History of England: The Age of Nelson* (1971), 142.
12 *The Private Correspondence of Admiral Lord Collingwood* ed. E. Hughes (NRS, 1957), 147, 155; *The Letters and Papers of Sir Thomas Byam Martin*, ed. Sir R. Vesey Hamilton (NRS, 3 vols., 1898–1902), III, 500.
13 *Letters of Lord St Vincent*, I, 379–80.
14 *Ibid.*, II, 141, 181, 193–4.
15 *Memoir of the Life of William Marsden* (1838), 103–4; H. Twiss, *The Public and Private Life of Lord Chancellor Eldon* (2 vols., 1846), I, 280.

16 *4th Report of the Commissioners of Naval Enquiry*, CR 1802–3 (160), IV, 266.
17 *Memoir of the Life of William Marsden*, 103–4.
18 *Selections from the Correspondence of Admiral J. Markham during 1801–4 and 1806–7*, ed. Sir Clements Markham (NRS, 1904), xv; *Letters of Sir Thomas Byam Martin*, III, 384; *An Autobiographical Memoir of Sir John Barrow* (1847), 405; J. T. Ward, *Sir James Graham* (1967), 128.
19 NMM, AGC/M/11.
20 PP 1805 (203), VIII, 239.
21 *Letters of Lord St Vincent*, II, 19, 31.
22 *Ibid.*, II, 216.
23 *Ibid.*, II, 40, 49; *Memoir of the Life of William Marsden*, 103–4.
24 *Letters of Sir Thomas Byam Martin*, III, 195; Cobbett's *Parlimentary Debates*, I, 874–927.
25 NMM, MID/13/1/49.
26 PRO, ADM. 106/2515, 23 July 1804.
27 NMM, MID/2/13/7; SRO, GD51/2/220/2, 3.
28 NMM, MID/1/186/8.
29 NMM, MID/13/1/52.
30 SRO, GD51/2/266/2.
31 SRO, GD51/271/6.
32 SRO, GD 1/2/271/16.
33 NMM, MID/6/11/7.
34 *Letters of Lord Barham*, III, 32, 55–6.
35 SRO, GD51/2/220/3, 275/1.
36 *Diary and Correspondence of Lord Colchester*, II, 11.
37 *Letters of Lord Barham*, III, 101.
38 *Ibid.*, III, 71–2.
39 NMM, MID/13/1/93; MID/13/1/91.
40 NMM, MID/1/67/16.
41 NMM, MID/1/67/20.
42 *Ibid.*
43 NMM, MID/1/67/19.
44 NMM, MID/1/67/34.
45 NMM, MID/1/67/44.
46 NMM, MID/1/18/3.
47 NMM, MID/1/67/51.
48 NMM, ADM. BP/30A, 12 Mar. 1810.
49 *Ibid.*, 12 Mar. 1810.
50 A complete account of Payne's activities between 1810 and 1812 is given in NMM, ADM. BP/33A, 25 Mar. 1813.
51 NMM, ADM. BP/30B, 17 Nov. 1810.
52 *Ibid.*, 19 Dec. 1810, encl.
53 NMM, ADM. BP/32B, 27 May 1812.
54 *Ibid.*, 27 June 1812.
55 NMM, ADM. BP/32C, 15 Aug. 1812.
56 NMM, MID/1/141/2.
57 NMM, ADM. BP/33A, 25 Mar. 1813 encl.
58 *1st Report of the Commissioners of Naval Revision*, 9.
59 Jeremy Bentham's first use of the idea of individual responsibility appears to have been in August 1808 in his strictures on the Audit Board: University College London, Bentham MSS Box 122, f. 254. See also B. B. Schaffer, 'The idea of the Ministerial Department: Bentham, Mill and Bagehot', *Australian J. of Politics and History*, III (1957–8), 60.

60 For a more complete account of Samuel Bentham's years as Inspector General see R. A. Morriss, 'Samuel Bentham and the management of the royal dockyards, 1796–1807', *Bull. Inst. Historical Research*, LIV(1981), 226–40.

61 PRO, ADM. 1/3527, 'Observations' on abolishing the office of the IGNW, 6.

62 PRO, ADM. 1/3525, 29 Feb. 1796.

63 *Ibid.*, 29 Feb. 1796.

64 PRO, ADM. 1/3527, 'Observations' on abolishing the office of the IGNW, 77–8.

65 *Ibid.*, 14, 52.

66 *Ibid.*, 10; ADM. 1/3527, 6 June 1808.

67 NMM, ADM. BP/22B, 26 July 1802.

68 PRO, ADM. 106/2235, 22 Oct. 1804.

69 PRO, ADM. 1/3527, 'Observations' on abolishing the office of the IGNW, 92–6.

70 *4th Report of the Commissioners of Naval Revision*, Appendix 61, 205; see volume containing appendices at NMM.

71 *Ibid.*, 205.

72 *3rd Report of the Commissioners of Naval Enquiry*, 188; PRO ADM. 106/2232, 20 Oct. 1803.

73 *4th Report of the Commissioners of Naval Revision*, Appendix 61, 205.

74 NMM, MID/1/70/2; MID/13/1/31.

75 Pool, *op. cit.*, 129; M.S. Bentham, *The Life of the Brigadier-General Sir Samuel Bentham, K.S.G.* (1862), 236; *Diary and Correspondence of Lord Colchester*, II, 13; PRO, ADM. 106/2539, 29 July 1805.

76 PRO, ADM. 1/3527, 9 Mar., 10 June, 17 Dec. 1808.

77 NMM, ADM. BP/32A, 7 Mar, 1812, encl.

78 NMM, MID/1/141/2.

79 NMM, ADM. BP/31B, 22 Aug. 1811.

80 *Ibid.*, 23 Oct. 1811.

# Sources of tables
# and plans

## Tables

1–3  W. James, *Naval History of Great Britain 1793–1837* (6 vols., 1847), tables 1–25.
 4  SRO, Melville MSS GD51/2/847.
 5  James, *op. cit.*, tables 1–25.
 6  NMM, CAD/A/10, Appendix 32.
 7  D. A. Baugh, *British Naval Administration in the Age of Walpole* (Princeton, 1965), 263–75; BL Add. MSS 27,884; PRO, ADM. 140/555, parts 14, 18.
 8  PRO, ADM. 106/2237, 17 Aug. 1805.
 9  NMM, MID/8/5/4.
10  SRO, GD51/2/786/2; PP 1805 (152), VIII, 306; NMM, ADM. BP/14, 13 Mar. 1794; ADM. BP/26, 31 Jan. 1806; ADM. BP/27, 31 Jan. 1807.
11  NMM, ADM. BP/31A, 6 Jan. 1811, encl.
12  NMM, ADM. BP/34B, 20 May 1814.
13  SRO, Melville MSS GD/51/2/786/2; PP 1805 (152), VIII, 306.
14  NMM, CAD/A/10, Appendices 71, 72.
15  *6th Report of the Commissioners of Naval Enquiry*, 16–121.
16  PP 1823 (417), XIII, 188–9.
17  Most of the figures used for this graph were derived from the regular twice-yearly accounts in NMM, ADM. BP/13–35C.
18  NMM, ADM. BP/34A, 2 Apr. 1814.
19  NMM, ADM. DP/201B, account dated 25 Apr. 1821.
20  PP 1814–15 (206), IX, 125–31.
21  *5th Report of the Commissioners on Fees*, Appendix 113, pp. 262–3; NMM, ADM. BP/15B, 21 Aug. 1795; ADM. BP/26, 14 Nov. 1806; ADM. BP/27, at 1 Feb. 1807; ADM. BP/33A, 20 Feb. 1813; ADM. BP/35B, 26 Sept. 1815.
22  *6th Report of the Commissioners on Fees*, 390–1; PRO, ADM. 42/92, 99; NMM, ADM. BP/33A, 20 Feb. 1813.
23  NMM, ADM. A/2945, account dated 14 Dec. 1814 filed at 30 Oct. 1801; ADM. BP/31A, 30 Jan. 1811; NMM, Lists of yard officers.
24  *6th Report of the Commissioners on Fees*, 390–1; PRO, ADM. 42/92, 99.
25  *17th Report of the Select Committee on Finance* (1797), Appendix D3, 336–7; J. M. Collinge, *Navy Board Officials, 1660–1832* ('Office holders in modern Britain', VII, 1978).
26  NMM, Lists of yard officers.
27  Collinge, *op. cit.; Royal Kalender; Navy List*.
28  NMM, ADM. BP/23B, 20 Oct. 1803.
29  J. C. Sainty, *Admiralty Officials 1660–1870* (1975).

**Plans**

Plymouth yard in 1808: NMM, ADM/Y/PD/4.
Portsmouth yard in 1810: PRO, ADM. 140/555/18.
Chatham yard in 1811: PRO, ADM. 140/16.
Deptford yard in 1810: NMM, ADM/Y/D/6.
Sheerness yard in 1794: PRO, ADM. 140/666.
Woolwich yard in 1814: PRO, ADM. 140/1139.

# Note on principal sources

A relatively complete list of the primary and secondary sources used for this book will be found in the thesis for which my work on the dockyards was initially undertaken. This is entitled 'The administration of the royal dockyards during the Revolutionary and Napoleonic Wars, with special reference to the period 1801–5' (University of London, 1978). Reference should also be made to the thesis of Dr R. J. B. Knight, 'The royal dockyards in England at the time of the American War of Independence' (University of London, 1972), which was my own particular starting point and an invaluable guide to dockyard affairs for the slightly earlier period.

The system of yard management and its gradual amendment during the late eighteenth and early nineteenth centuries was reconstructed from the series of reports from parliamentary commissions and committees on finance. Of these, the most informative were the *5th* and *6th Reports of the Commissioners appointed to inquire into fees, gratuities, perquisites and emoluments*; the *17th* and *31st Reports of the Select Committee on Finance*, 1797, combined with the subsequent *Further proceedings of the Lords Commissioners of the Admiralty respecting the matters stated in the Reports of the Committee of Finance as far as they relate to the Naval Departments*; the *6th Report of the Commissioners appointed to inquire into Irregularities, Frauds and Abuses practiced in the Naval Department and in the business of the Prize Agency*, 1804, and the *1st, 2nd, 3rd, 4th, 8th* and *14th Reports of the Commissioners for Revising and Digesting the Civil Affairs of His Majesty's Navy*, 1806–9. The 8th report of the Commissioners of Naval Revision is not printed among the parliamentary reports but the copy as distributed to the yards is in the library of the National Maritime Museum; the 14th report is also unprinted but exists in manuscript in the Public Record Office.

The actual operation of the administrative system is documented in the records of the Admiralty, Navy Board and yard officials which exist in great quantity in the Public Record Office and National Maritime Museum. The most useful of the Admiralty papers at the Public Record Office (ADM. 1/) were the letters received from the Inspector General of Naval Works and the petitions from yard and Navy Office employees. Among the Navy Board's records (ADM. 106/), the most informative were the copy-books of letters to the Admiralty Board and of standing orders to the yards, and the letters received by the Board from the commissioners and officers at Chatham, Sheerness, Portsmouth and Plymouth. The National Maritime Museum has the actual letters sent to the Admiralty from the Navy Board with their respective enclosures (ADM. B/, ADM. BP/ and ADM. Y/). There too are the Admiralty's letters and orders to the Navy Board (ADM. A/), including those relating to works proposed by the Inspector General (ADM. Q/). Among the Museum's 'local records of the Royal navy' are also several series of letters and orders from the Navy Board to the Chatham and Portsmouth commissioners and officers and copy-books of their letters in reply.

Private opinions on administrative questions were gained from the private papers of senior officials and from the numerous pamphlets on naval affairs. At the National Maritime Museum, the papers of Charles Middleton, Lord Barham (MID/), Charles Yorke (YOR), and the Hon. Sir George Grey (GRE/) all proved useful, as did those of Henry Dundas, Viscount Melville, in the British Library (Add. MSS 41,079) and Scottish Record Office, Edinburgh (GD/52/). The Sidmouth MSS in the Devon Record Office and Bentham papers in the British Library and in University College London were also consulted. Selections from the letters and papers of Lord Barham, Sir Thomas Byam Martin, Admiral J. Markham, Sir James Saumarez, the Second Earl Spencer and Lord St Vincent, printed for the Navy Records Society, supplemented the manuscript collections.

A considerable number of pamphlets relate to the civil affairs of the navy in this period. The majority pertain to four main themes: the problem of decay in ships of war and that of supplying the navy with timber; the question of a new naval arsenal and the controversy over the conduct of St Vincent at the Admiralty. All are a source of interesting comment. But those relating to St Vincent's administration in particular are conspicuous for their political bias and have been used with caution.

Two other sources were of particular use as an introduction to the progress of technological innovation in the yards. These were Samuel Bentham's own account of his achievements as Inspector General of Naval Works and as Civil Architect and Engineer, *Services Rendered in the Civil Department of the Navy* (1813), and his wife's biography of him, *The Life of the Brigadier-General Sir Samuel Bentham K.S.G.* (1862). These sources were, however, best used in conjunction with corroborating administrative papers. Bentham's view and understanding of yard affairs was invariably partial and he sometimes claimed more for himself than that with which others would have credited him. His wife's *Life*, a eulogistic tribute to Bentham, usefully summarizes his career and views, but is too loyal to his memory and written too long after events to be wholly reliable.

# Glossary

**ballast**  A quantity of iron, stone or gravel placed in a ship's hold to increase her draught, to improve her stability and to regulate the trim.

**beakhead**  A small platform immediately above the bows of large ships, at the level of the upper deck, occasionally for the use of a gun but chiefly for the convenience of the men working the ship.

**bilge**  That full part of a ship's bottom, on either side of the keel, having a more or less horizontal inclination and on which the ship would rest if allowed to ground.

**bowsprit**  The spar projecting ahead of a ship above the bows.

**braces**  Pieces of iron or timber used to strengthen a ship's hull. Also the term for part of the hinge upon which the rudder turns (*see* pintles), and for the ropes used to swing the sails.

**careening**  The operation of heaving a ship over on one side to reveal the other side of her bottom and permit it to be cleaned, repaired or caulked.

**caulking**  The driving of a quantity of oakum (or strands of old ropes, untwisted, pulled apart and made up into threads) into the seams of the planks in a ship's decks or sides to prevent the entrance of water.

**ceiling**  The plank lining on the inner side of a ship's hull.

**charter party**  Legal agreement between a ship-owner and a merchant for the hire of a ship and delivery of a cargo.

**coak**  The metal bearing at the centre of the rotating pulley within a block.

**cofferdams**  Watertight cases used in constructing the foundations for bridges, wharves or sea-walls.

**colours**  Flags.

**compass timber**  Timber that is curved in shape through natural growth.

**coppering**  The casing or sheathing of a ship's bottom with copper sheets, a practice adopted to prevent hull timbers being bored by the worm, *toredo navalis*, and to reduce the rate of accumulation of weeds and mollusca.

**deadwood**  Blocks of timber attached to the keel at its two ends to fill the angles between the keel, stem- and stern-posts, and to provide a foundation for the erection of other bow and stern timbers.

**draught**  The depth of a body of water necessary for a ship to float.

**'extra'**  Piecework or overtime, for which the rates of payment were above the standard daily rates.

**extra men**  Men employed under the Masters Attendant to crew yard boats.

**futtocks**  Parts of a ship's frame timbers, situated between the keel and the top-timbers and giving strength to the sides. Those next to the keel were called the ground or first futtocks, the rest the second, third, fourth and, in large vessels, the fifth futtocks.

**grain cut**  The shaping of timber that does not naturally conform to a required pattern by cutting across the grain.

**graving**   The cleaning of ship's bottom when she is deliberately laid aground for the recess of a tide.

**gunwale**   The upper edge of a boat's side.

**hawser house**   Storehouse for hawsers – large ropes, or small cables, consisting of three or four strands.

**'horsed'**   Forcibly carried, probably seated on a length of wood, by a group of men.

**Job work**   The system of piecework designed for the repair of ships.

**keel**   The lowest longitudinal timber in a ship's structure; it supports and unites the whole framework.

**kersey**   Coarse cloth woven from long wool.

**knees**   Curved pieces of timber used to support the deck beams of a ship and to connect them to her frame timbers. Timber knees were gradually superseded by iron knees.

**lignum vitae**   A very hard, dark-coloured and close-grained wood that grows in tropical America, the name literally meaning 'wood of life'.

**magazine**   A room built into the forward or after part of a ship's hold to store gunpowder.

**mizzen rigging**   The rigging supporting the mast nearest the stern of a ship.

**neap tides**   The tides at the beginning of the moon's second and fourth quarters.

**'night'**   A period of overtime lasting five hours.

**Ordinary**   The ships laid up at the dockyards. The term is also applied to the establishment of men employed to live aboard and maintain those ships.

**penstock**   Sluice or flood-gate for controlling the level of a body of water.

**pigs**   Oblong masses of metal cast from a smelting furnace.

**pintles**   Pins or hooks fastened to the back of a rudder with their points downwards for the purpose of hanging the rudder from braces attached to the stern-post.

**riders**   Additional interior ribs bolted to existing timbers for the purpose of strengthening a ship's frame.

**scarphing**   The joining of two pieces of timber, their ends being tapered and overlapped, coaked and bolted together.

**scavelmen**   Men employed primarily to clear docks and slips of mud and rubbish.

**shackle**   A ring bolted to timber for the purpose of securing ropes.

**sheave**   The pulley inside a block which rotates around a pin.

**shelfing**   Timbers attached horizontally to the inner sides of ships to support beams and knees.

**slops**   Ready-made clothing and bedding supplied to naval vessels for the outfit of seamen.

**spring tides**   High tides occurring shortly after the new and full moon in each month.

**standards**   Inverted knees placed on a deck instead of beneath it and used to support timbers above.

**stem-post**   The timber erected and attached to the keel at the bow of a ship. The two sides of the ship are joined to it and the upper end supports the bowsprit.

**stern-post**   A long straight piece of timber erected on the end of the keel to form the rear end of a ship and to support the rudder.

**Task work**   The system of piecework designed for new ship construction.

**'tide'**   A period of overtime lasting $1\frac{1}{2}$ hours.

**topping house**   Workshop in which the fibrous ends of the hemp plant are combed with a hatchel in the process of rope-making.

**tree nails**   Long cylindrical pins of oak from 1 inch to $1\frac{1}{2}$ inches in diameter, and from 1 foot to $3\frac{1}{2}$ feet in length; used to fasten the inner and outer planks of a ship to the frame timbers.

**trenail mooters**   Artificers who shaped the tree nails to size.

**triennial trimmings**  The regular refitting received by ships in the eighteenth century about every three years.

**trusses**  Reinforcing timbers used to strengthen the frames of old ships.

**tumbling home**  The inward inclination of a ship's sides above the broadest part of its hull.

**twice-laid stuff**  Rope made from worn rope that had been taken apart and relaid.

**waterways**  Long pieces of thick timber bolted horizontally to a ship's sides so as to connect the sides to the decks, while also forming channels along which water could drain from the cambered decks to the scuppers – holes cut through the waterways.

# Index

NORWAY

SWEDEN

St Petersburg

RUSSIA

Baltic

Riga

Memel

BRITAIN

Danzig

London

GERMANY

FRANCE

Corsica

Toulon

Leghorn

SPAIN

ITALY

Minorca

Gibraltar

Malta

MEDITERRANEAN

Alexandria

EGYPT

Calcutta

INDIA

Bombay

Madras

Malabar Coast

Trincomalee

Pena

Ceylon

INDIAN OCEAN

Mauritius

Cape of Good Hope